Mysticism and Cognition

Studies in Religion · 1

Edited by Per Bilde, Armin W. Geertz,
Lars Kruse-Blinkenberg, Ole Riis and
Erik Reenberg Sand

Birgitta Mark

Mysticism and Cognition
The Cognitive Development of
John of the Cross as Revealed in
his Works

AARHUS UNIVERSITY PRESS

Copyright: Aarhus University Press, 2000
Cover: *Juan de Avila* (oil on canvas, c. 1746) by Pierre Subleyras (1699-1749)
Birmingham Museums and Art Gallery/Bridgeman Art Library
Printed in the UK by the Alden Press, Oxford
ISBN 87 7288 782 6

Published with financial support from the Danish Research
Council for the Humanities and Aarhus University Research
Foundation

AARHUS UNIVERSITY PRESS
Langelandsgade 177
DK-8200 Aarhus N
Fax (+ 45) 8942 5380

73 Lime Walk
Headington, Oxford OX3 7AD
Fax (+ 44) 1865 750 079

Box 511
Oakville, Conn. 06779
Fax (+ 1) 860 945 9468

ANSI/NISO
Z39.48-1992

Preface

The work on this book was initiated as a Ph.D. project with the intention of contributing to a more profound understanding of mystical experience. I wished in other words to engage in the attempt to explain mystical experience. This evidently necessitated that the investigation of John of the Cross' works was founded on theories that could help explain some of the particiular aspects of mystical experience as displayed in the works of John of the Cross. However, none of the existing theories of mysticism appeared to suit the task of explaining the mystical experience of John of the Cross very well. The theories of mysticism could neither explain his mystical states of consciousness, his mystical development nor the relation of these two aspects and his mystical ideas. In short, I found myself in the position of needing to look for general theories of the human mind as a basis for explaining mystical experience. Among the more general theories of psychology, neurology and communication, I ended up selecting those specific, cognitive theories that seemed most relevant for the explanation of the diverse aspects of mystical experience. Indeed it seems to me that cognitive theories have much to contribute not only to the understanding of mystical experience, but of religious experience in general.

Fortunately, I have not been completely alone on my journey into the field of cognitive psychology. I have been guided very competently by E. Thomas Lawson whom I wish to thank not only for his more general guidance and advice, but especially for innumerable discussions that have contributed to the clarification of my theoretical understanding in general and of mystical experience in particular. I furthermore wish to thank him for taking the time and the trouble to read and criticize this work — also at some of its more unfinished stages, just as he has been willing to discuss general as well as specific subjects of this book over and over again.

I also wish to thank the Danish Research Council for the Humanities and Aarhus University Research Foundation for their economic support in the publication of this book.

Aarhus, January 2000   *Birgitta Mark*

Contents

Introduction

Initiating a study of mystical experience, it seems pertinent first to delimit the concept. I will suggest that the concept of mystical experience covers three aspects of a person's general experience, that is to say, mystical ideas, mystical states of consciousness, and mystical development. It is a precondition for having mystical experience that one has mystical ideas. The point of departure for mystical experience is the person's conception that it is possible to have mystical experience. The continuation of mystical experience is the coincident recurrence of mystical states of consciousness (which can be fostered in various ways) and the gradually progressing mystical development. In accord with John of the Cross, it seems that some degree of mystical development is a prerequisite for the realization of mystical states, implying that the former anticipates the latter. At some point, a person can furthermore be expected to begin to reconsider his/her mystical states and mystical development or, in the terminology of cognitive psychology, to redescribe the representations of the knowledge sustaining the mystical states and the related development. This representational redescription will presumably both promote further mystical development and yield conceptual development in the form of changing conceptualizations of the accumulated mystical experience at any point in time.

It is furthermore relevant to manifest my general presumptions about mystical experience. As a starting point for the investigation of this field of study, I assume that mystical experience, like all other kinds of human experience, is constrained by the cognitive equipment of the human mind and that the mind is naturally equipped for mystical experience.[1] On the basis of this, it can be expected that mystical states of consciousness and the related mystical development are the outcome of the extraordinary capitalization on ordinary, cognitive resources. This further implies that the capacity for mystical experience is not restricted to selected individuals but may be shared by everyone. Accordingly, it should be possible to apply theories and methods that have proven to be valuable and expedient in the study of other aspects of human experience.

---

1. This is in agreement with and in extension of P. Boyer's theory of the naturalness of religious ideas (1994 and 1995a).

Finally, it is relevant to outline how the diverse aspects of mystical experience can be expected to appear in the general experience of a person. Along with that I shall briefly present the more general hypotheses sustaining the explanations of John of the Cross' mystical experience offered in the present work. The essence of mystical experience is the idea that it is possible to go beyond the natural and human way of experiencing. Yet, the specific kind of experience potentially springing from these ideas is mainly brought out during certain states of consciousness that can be classified as mystical

Before delineating how the diverse aspects of mystical experience are related to one another, chronologically and causally, it should be underscored that, in general, they are mutually interdependent and multicausal. There is, nonetheless, some degree of chronological sequence in each of the aspects of mystical experience. Thus, there is no doubt that mystical ideas are primary. Without them, there will be no mystical experience at all. On the basis of such mystical ideas, a person may develop a strategy that will serve to initiate the process of mystical development which, in turn, will facilitate the realization of mystical states of consciousness. On the basis of John of the Cross' writings, it seems that a useful method for the initiation of mystical development is to internalize and intensify attention to mystical conceptions. The process of internalizing and intensifying attention can furthermore be fostered by the reduction of sensory stimulation. The implementation of a method designed for mystical development may indeed initiate the process of developing mystically. At some point, mystical development will be so relatively advanced that actual mystical states can be attained. My general understanding of mystical states of consciousness is first of all based upon a synthesis of S.A. Greenfield's theory of consciousness and A.R. Damasio's theory of emotions. Mystical consciousness can be defined as the internalized consciousness of mystical content in such quantity that there is unawareness of the external world. In the case of John of the Cross, the contents of mystical consciousness can be identified as conceptions of the love between God and his soul, coupled with the responding emotions of that love. Every mystical consciousness will, in itself, yield some minor degree of mystical development. The mystical development resulting from mystical consciousness will, in turn, improve the cognitive conditions of subsequent mystical states. Mystical development will gradually permit mystical states to grow deeper, more extended, and more lasting. The quality of mystical consciousness may similarly change as a result of mystical development but this will be contingent on the more specific mystical ideas sustaining the content of mystical consciousness. In general, it seems that the main cause of mystical development is the recurrence of mystical states of consciousness.

Mystical experience additionally encompasses a more purely conceptual aspect which is the mystic's potential development of his/her conceptualization of mystical states and mystical development. For an explanation of this aspect of mystical experience, I shall take my point of departure in A. Karmiloff-Smith's theory that the recurrent redescription of cognitive representations of information promotes development beyond the mastery of a particular behaviour. In extension of this theory, I will suggest that the process of redescribing cognitive representations is promoted and accelerated considerably by the process of describing the mystical experience in written form and subsequently interpreting the written. To put it differently, the joint processes of redescribing the cognitive representations of the knowledge sustaining the general mystical experience, describing this, and interpreting the described, will yield a developmental product that differs qualitatively from that of mystical development. However, it is not unlikely that these processes additionally foster mystical development itself. Thus, the primary products of the processes of redescription, description, and interpretation are the changing conceptualizations of mystical experience. A secondary product of these processes may be the further improvement of the ability for mystical consciousness.

In John of the Cross' case, the one work that particularly documents his conceptual development through the display of the process of interpretation is his *Spiritual Canticle*. The reason for this is that the work has been modified repeatedly during a period of several years. In my view, the major changes have been motivated by changes in his way of understanding his mystical states and mystical development. Hence, the incongruities of parts of the work provide exceptional evidence for John of the Cross' conceptual development.

The present theory of mystical experience is based on and takes its point of departure in John of the Cross' works. As pointed out above, John of the Cross' mystical experience started out with his mystical ideas, continued with mystical development, and, from some particular point onwards, with the realization of mystical states. At some unidentifiable point, John of the Cross has furthermore begun to redescribe his mystical experience representationally and later on to describe it in his works, thus initiating the process of interpretation.

Yet, the evidence of the part of his mystical experience pertaining to his mystical states and mystical development is filtered through his changing interpretations of his writings, motivated (I assume) by changes in his conceptualizations of the described. Accordingly, his works primarily reveal the products of interpretation and the process of interpreting his own works. For that reason, I have deemed it expedient to violate the predicted order of the progression of mystical experience and initiate my explanation of John of the

Cross' mystical experience with that of his conceptual development based upon his *Spiritual Canticle*.

I. Delimiting the field of study

Defining the concept of mystical experience

A comment on definitions

The generally accepted scientific concept of definitions seems to be inherited from positivism and presupposes the possibility of resolving a concrete problem conclusively. It presumes that it is possible to catch the true reality in a definition. In accord with this notion, a definition of a scientific concept should (1) correlate empirical reality *correctly* and (2) pertain to all aspects of evidence (if not, specialists will be ready with evidence challenging the definition). Consequently, we have unending controversies over definitions of scientific concepts. In fact, nothing (least of all the history of science) really indicates that the positivist project of defining concepts correctly is realizable. Thus, in order to elude the numerous pitholes inherent in the project of defining, many scholars have either chosen to do without definitions or to suggest exceedingly broad and inclusive definitions. But really, the fact that infeasible and insurmountable criteria have been set up for definitions should not be held against them.

The pretended segregation of definitions from the theories from which they spring is truly preposterous. In the words of E.T. Lawson and R.N. McCauley, 'definitions are driven by and grounded in explanatory theories' wherefore they are 'only as good as the theories that inspire them. Correspondingly, those theories are only as good as the problem solving power, explanatory suggestiveness, generality, and empirical testability of their principles.' (1993, 217). Consequently, a definition is nothing but a compression of a theory.

Reflections on the terminology of mysticism

Mysticism is originally a concept introduced by Christian mystics themselves. It is thus a Christian theological concept that has been adopted by scholars of mysticism to refer to a certain aspect of human experience. In general, the concept of mystical experience has (rather indistinctly) been used primarily as a reference to a specific kind of states of consciousness (mystical experience*s*) and secondarily to stages of a certain kind of development (stages of mystical experience). In my view, mystical experience refers to the specific part of a person's general experience that relates to mystical states, mystical develop-

ment, and mystical ideas. The common use of the concept of mystical experience as alternatingly referring to general mystical development and actual
mystical states is much too diffuse and vague to be useful in a scientific
context, not to mention the exclusion of the ideas sustaining the mystical states
and mystical development.

During the last couple of decades, concepts like mysticism, shamanism,
and the like have been criticized for being too limited. The criticism has been
motivated by a focus on the similarities of diverse kinds of religious states of
consciousness (e.g., shamanist, possession, mystical, etc.) at the expense of the
dissimilarities. Instead, many of these scholars have attempted to do without
the more excluding concepts, like mysticism, and have chosen to replace them
with more inclusive concepts, like ecstasy or altered states of consciousness.
In my view, this is no solution to the problem. The criticism aimed at the
conventional concepts can easily be inverted and pointed at the new concepts.
Concepts like ecstasy and altered states of consciousness are much too
inclusive and general to do the job on their own. Moreover, the substitution
of old concepts with new ones does not in itself contribute to solving the
problem of defining the concepts.

A minor point related to the concept of altered states of consciousness is
that it is focused on the *alteration* of a state (of consciousness). Logically, the
concept of altered states of consciousness does not refer to a certain kind of
conscious state but rather to a process producing a change. Accordingly, a
wakeful state of consciousness is, in principle, an altered state in relation to
a dream state or a mystical state and the other way round.

With respect to the concept of ecstasy, it seems likely that some of the
problems embedded in some of the scientific definitions have derived from the
conventional uses of it, inasmuch as it is a commonly used notion from the
Christian tradition in which it typically refers to the more advanced, mystical
states. This use is motivated by a theological discrimination between the less
divine states of an undeveloped mystic and the more divine states of a highly
developed one. That being so, the Christian use of the concept is — along with
all of the problems — adopted by R. Fischer for whom ecstasy denotes the
most non-ordinary states of the specific kind achievable by 'Western travellers'. It should be emphasized that, in his view, the most non-ordinary states
of 'Western travellers' have more in common with equally non-ordinary states
of 'Eastern travellers' than with more ordinary states of either kind.[1] In E.J.
Collins' use (definition would be an exaggeration), on the other hand, ecstasy
rather indistinctly refers to various types of the most non-ordinary states.

---

1. Fischer does not seem to consider a sharp distinction of religious and non-religious
   states of consciousness relevant.

In both cases, ecstasy only refers to the more extreme degrees of the various types of non-ordinary states. Hence, both Fischer and Collins elevate some selected similarities (by *degree* of extraordinariness) at the expense of the *kind* of extraordinariness. I doubt that this is a scientifically justifiable preference. Such definitions ultimately presuppose the relevance of likening the extraordinary states of a fully developed shamanist with those of a fully developed mystic at the expense of likening earlier and later states of the shamanist and the mystic respectively.

On the whole, I do not see the point in selecting the more general concept *at the expense* of the more concrete concepts (or the other way round for that sake). In my view, a general concept should be added to the concrete concepts (both of which need to be defined according to a theory). Ultimately, I do not think that the main point is whether one prefers one concept or another but rather how one defines the concepts. Accordingly, various concepts may do. In my view, there is no need to substitute old concepts just because they are embedded with problems of convention (otherwise, science would have to change concepts constantly instead of just redefining them). Yet, when it comes to the construction of new scientific concepts (which may take decades), I would suggest that one picks and chooses until finding one that is suitable. Accordingly, I will suggest that with respect to the diverse types of non-ordinary states, there are good reasons to hold on to the traditional concepts of the history of religions, inasmuch as they (apparently) demarcate various fields of study that are relevant to keep apart. At the more general level, I will suggest that the fairly vague concept of extraordinary states (of consciousness) (implying that there are varying degrees and kinds of extraordinariness) is best fit for the task of delimiting this very comprehensive aspect of human experience.

Consciousness

The point of departure for a definition of mystical experience should be an understanding of mystical consciousness which has to be based on an understanding of consciousness. A general understanding of consciousness is prerequisite for an understanding of the specific mystical consciousness. The question of consciousness — and the diverse subquestions following in the wake of it — has, for decades, been a matter of major concern for researchers from a number of fields, like psychology, neurology, and philosophy. With respect to consciousness in general, I shall rely on the neurologist S.A. Greenfield's theory of consciousness (1995). Greenfield aims to explain consciousness both at the neurological and the cognitive levels of analysis.

The fundament of the theory is the hypothesis that shifting groups of neurons of varying size procure consciousness at different times. The point of departure for the theory is the more general observation that although the brain does not function as one homogenous mass of neurons, different groups of neurons often can do the same job. In more general terms, this means that there is some degree of specialization among the various brain regions, at the same time as there is considerable redundancy of neuronal groups (Greenfield 1995, 34 and 40). The importance of this for a theory of consciousness is that consciousness is not an event occurring in one particular region of the brain and is not generated by one particular group of neurons specialized in consciousness. An indefinite number of neuronal groups in various brain regions will contribute to consciousness at different times. Yet, only one group of neurons generate consciousness at one time. Shifting groups of neurons will thus be temporarily specialized in the generation of consciousness. In short, there is only one predominant consciousness at a time and consciousness can be generated in various parts of the brain (Greenfield 1995, 88). Another important aspect of Greenfield's theory is that the prevailing consciousness at one particular time is focused on an epicenter. The notion of an epicenter serves to connect the neurological and the cognitive level of analysis. In neurological terms, it implies that a small group of neurons works as an epicenter recruiting a larger group of neurons around it. The strength of the epicenter is determined by the number of neurons and the number and strengths of the synaptic connections of the group of neurons constituting the epicenter (jointly delimiting the maximum amount of electricity of the group of neurons) (Greenfield 1995, 155). At the cognitive level of description, an epicenter is the central focus of that which one is conscious of at any one time, and the strength of it is dependent on the cognitive value of the epicenter and the number of associations related to the epicenter (Greenfield 1995, 78, 93, 96, and 155).

The depth of consciousness is graded, implying that there can be *more* or *less* consciousness. The quantity of consciousness at any one time depends on the size of the particular group of neurons — the gestalt in Greenfield's terminology. The larger the gestalt, the more consciousness. Whether a particular epicenter actually assembles a small or a large group of neurons at a given time depends on several factors. The size of the gestalt developing around a center of focus of consciousness is dependent on (1) the level of arousal, (2) the weights of the synapses constraining the potential level of activity, (3) the ongoing level of activity (as already active neurons are more sensitive than inactive neurons), and finally (4) the strength of the epicenter, because a strong group of neurons (a large one with a great amount of intrinsic eletricity) is more apt to recruit a large gestalt than a weak group of neurons (Greenfield 1995, 123 and 155).

Arousal is clearly the more complex of these four factors and is described as an energizing power that permeates both body and brain through the activation of neurons. In general, the level of arousal is regulated by the interrelation of a number of chemicals (termed either neurotransmitters or neuromodulators) affecting the general degree of activation in the brain. When the level of arousal is high gestalts are easily formed but this simultaneously implies that there will be considerable competition among gestalts which results in rapid shifts of the predominant gestalts. Hence, gestalts will not grow very large and consciousness not very deep as it will shift from one thing to another. With moderate or low levels of arousal, relatively stronger epicenters are required for the formation of gestalts. Evidently, this also reduces competition among gestalts so that once a gestalt is formed it will have much more time to increase in size. With a low level of arousal, very strong epicenters are required for the formation of larger gestalts. Dreaming states set this off as they are characterized with a low level of arousal and multiple competing neuronal groups unrestrained by sensory inputs. For a gestalt to grow large and produce a deep consciousness of something during dreaming, an epicenter would have to be very strong and this is typically not the case with cognitively derived epicenters (Greenfield 1995, 101-3). In short, the best conditions for the formation of large gestalts are a moderate level of arousal and the existence of strong epicenters.

In extension of the issue of gestalt size and the quantity of consciousness there is that of the maintenance of a prevailing gestalt and the durability of the consciousness of something. This is mainly a matter of competition among potential gestalts. When arousal is low, so is competition and when arousal is high, so is competition. Yet, there will always be some degree of competition among potential gestalts in a conscious state. Greenfield suggests that the reason why only one gestalt can be formed at any one time (which is the reason why consciousness is unified) is that the size of a group of neurons large enough to generate consciousness precludes the formation of an equally large group of neurons at the same time (Greenfield 1995, 89). In general, it can be said that the stronger the epicenter of a predominant group of neurons is *in relation* to the epicenters of other competing neuronal groups, the longer the neuronal gestalt generating a particular consciousness is prone to last.

The question of what it is that gives a particular consciousness its specific quality as distinct from that of other consciousnesses can now be put. Neurologically, the quality of consciousness is conditioned by the very specific composition of neurons making up the gestalt generating consciousness at any one time (Greenfield 1995, 96). At this level of explanation, a particular consciousness is what it is because of what is going on in and between the communicating synapses within the group of neurons concerned. To put it somewhat squarely, every little change in neuronal cooperation is apt to produce a change in the quality of consciousness. Translating this into cognitive terms, the quality of the particular consciousness of something is determined by that something and the associations it is capable of producing. The consciousness of one thing is not the same as the consciousness of another thing (irrespective of whether this is from within — or outside of — the mind). Similarly, the consciousness of something triggering certain associations at one time is not identical with the consciousness of the same something triggering other associations at a different time.

The theory really has far-reaching implications for the understanding of learning and development, because the potential quality and quantity of consciousness is constrained by the accumulated experience of a subject. The point is that, if consciousness emerges in relation to the complexity of neuronal interaction and the degree of complexity increases with experience, then the variability of consciousness in quality and quantity is directly proportional with the developmental state of a person at any point in time. Consciousness can be expected to expand both in depth and in the range of possible contents as a person matures in response to experience.

In the real world, consciousness is in constant change implying that ultimately it is infeasible to identify or analyze consciousness except at points in time. A particular consciousness only exists for a more or less extended period of time. In the concrete, it may be more relevant to speak of states of consciousness where the notion of a state of consciousness (synonymous with that of a train of consciousness) refers to a period of time during which consciousness shifts smoothly among closely connected contents (presumably giving the subject an impression of a single consciousness). Hence, a state of consciousness comprises several associated consciousnesses (cf. Greenfield 1995, 89). When the quality of consciousness shifts fundamentally there is similarly a shift in the state of consciousness. For an understanding of consciousness one similarly needs to consider how one state of consciousness changes into another state and how dissimilar states of consciousness are related. Greenfield's hypothesis is that consciousness is continuously variable in the sense that there are no abrupt or discontinuous shifts from one state to another. States of consciousness are distributed along a continuum stretching from various states of wakefulness to a state of unconscious sleep.

Mystical consciousness

Greenfield's theory has numerous and varied implications for an understanding of mystical experience. First of all the intricate matter of what a mystical state of consciousness really is stands out. Thereupon, there is the issue of mystical development and what this implies for the potential quality, depth, and duration of mystical states. In the light of an understanding of mystical states of consciousness and how these are affected by mystical development, it should be possible to answer the highly pressing question of what it is that makes mystical states so special.

Addressing the first point, it should be clear that if Greenfield's theory is correct, then a state of consciousness — including a mystical one — is what it is because of the specific combination of the quantity and quality of consciousness (where the quality is dependent on the particular focus of consciousness and the associations it triggers). A mystical state of consciousness springs from the knowledge base (understood in a very broad sense as comprising all kinds of stored representations, including those of emotions) of the mystic's mind. The possibility of having mystical states of consciousness is thus inextricably bound to the religious — or more specifically, the mystical — ideas constituting the source of such states. In this way, the mystical ideas coupled with the general knowledge present in the mind of a mystic at any point in time stipulate the possible range of experiential contents of mystical states as well as it delimits their depth, extension, and duration.

This leads to the issue of mystical development, because the cognitive representations related to both mystical ideas and general knowledge are bound to change in various ways as a result of mystical (and other kinds of) development. The reason why mystical states can be expected to change as development proceeds is that more and more cognitive representations related to mystical emotions and mystical conceptions are stored in the mind of the mystic as mystical experience gradually builds up through the recurrence of mystical states and, to a lesser extent, as a result of the representational redescription of them. The more that a person is conscious of various cognitive representations related to mystical emotions and conceptions (where the amount is calculated as the total sum of frequency, depth, and duration of the consciousness of a particular mystical focus) the more associations can be triggered — and the more easily are they triggered — by some mystical focus of consciousness. At the micro-level of describing the parts of the system, the point is that the more neurons that are activated (in number of neurons and duration of time) in the generation of mystical emotions and conceptions, the more representations related to such emotions and conceptions will be added to the representational knowledge reserve.

Turning to the point about what it is that makes mystical states so very special, it is rather certain that the core of the matter with respect to the *quality* of mystical states lies in the personal history of a mystic with a strong stress on the *religious*, conceptual background. It is the accumulated experience of a person that constrains the potential representational content of a mystical state. At the cognitive level, an explanation of what is special to the quality of mystical states therefore needs to take the combined ordinary and mystical developmental background of the mystic into account. Theorists of mysticism have generally looked upon the content of mystical states as a matter of which there is very little to say because the texts reporting the states are so obscure in this respect. Truly, mystical texts are often rather ambiguous and open to interpretation. This does not mean, though, that they are more or less meaningless and that just about anything can be read into them. If, for instance, the works of John of the Cross are estimated as a whole where every part should be read in the context of the other parts and, if this whole further is positioned in the metaphorical, theological, and mystical context of his time as well as the relevant aspects of his personal history, then this body of texts is no more ambiguous than other such bodies of texts. A great deal of the ambiguity really stems from the intricacy and seeming incongruity of the numerous related parts of works that are written over a long period of time, often combined with some degree of ideological, linguistic, and experiential alienness to the theorist. Hence, mystical texts, like the works of John of the Cross, do indeed impart something important about the quality of mystical states.

Basically it can be stated that according to John of the Cross, mystical states may involve either one or two of two dissimilar elements, namely conceptual and emotional representations respectively. The first concerns cognitive representations typically related to various religious conceptions. In the teachings of John of the Cross, those cognitive representations that are of more conceptual and specific character are almost entirely regarded as a negative element that should be disposed of the sooner the better. Consequently, it is also an element that in itself is given very little attention. John of the Cross mainly concerns himself with how to get rid of such representations — during mystical states in the course of development — and less with their particular content. The second element pertains to emotions and feelings somehow related to mystical ideas. It seems that in John of the Cross' view, the realization of these feelings in mystical states (and eventually in the supposed post-mystical stage) is the main goal of mystical development. As could be expected, he has therefore also devoted great efforts to portray those feelings. Apparently, all mystical feelings are variations on the theme of love. Just as in the case of ordinary love, mystical feelings of love cover a whole range of emotions related to the loving relationship between two persons, namely the mystic and an imagined other (God in the case of John of the Cross). With the poetic celebration of love in his *Spiritual Canticle* as the source, love at a minimum comprises feelings of longing for the other, frustration from insufficient intimacy with the other, uneasiness or worry about losing the other, extreme excitement and culminating joy over finally being with or winning the other, as well as pleasure and peacefulness because of simply being with the other.

At the neurological level, the theory proposed by A. Damasio in Descartes' Error contributes to throw quite a bit more light on the issue of the quality of mystical consciousness and especially that of the more advanced parts of mystical development. In Damasio's theory of emotions and feelings, the former are the continuosly changing body structure and body state (where body includes heart, lung, viscera, and muscles and is distinguished analytically from nervous tissue) and the latter are the cognitive representations (experience) of emotions juxtaposed with those cognitive representations that initiated the emotional changes. The body state representations are qualifiers of the other more conceptual representations (of ideas, external objects, events etc.). This means that emotional representations give quality of pleasure or pain (goodness or badness) to other representations (Damasio 1987, introduction, 139, 145, and 159). The juxtaposition of emotional representations and the more conceptual representations triggering the emotions requires the involvement of three neuronal events. The first is a representation of the causative entity (the more conceptual representation in my terminology), the second is a representation of the current body state (that is, of the emotion), and the third is a representation of the correlation of the two (Damasio 1987, 162).

A brief digression is appropriate at this point. R. Llinás and U. Ribary have provided evidence of a magnetic scanning activity in the brain that, in my view, combines very well with Damasio's theory that cognitive representations triggering emotions are correlated with representations of those emotions. I will suggest that it is this scanning activity that takes care of the correlation of the body state representations and the more conceptual representations. It seems pertinent to refer this evidence here as it may prove to be productive for the construction of a theory of mystical states. The evidence shows that the neural system possesses a capacity to combine separated information about activities at a level superior to that of inter-subsystemic communication. A continuous scanning of large areas of the brain secures correlation of information. During wakeful states this scanning process is repeatedly reset whenever sensory inputs are received. The scanning activity arises out of a coherent magnetic activity oscillating between specific and non-specific loops in the neural system. Llinás and Ribary suggest that the specific loops provide the content from sense perception whereas the non-specific loops secure a temporal binding of isolated but related events. In this way, otherwise separated information about events is combined into a single cognitive representation.[2]

The evidence from the work of Llinás and Ribary further demonstrates a difference between dream states and wakeful states. As opposed to wakeful states, the scanning activity is completely unaffected by sensory inputs during dream states. This is particularly interesting in the context of mystical states as they, like dream states, apparently do not involve sensory activities. Since the oscillatory activity is not continually being reset during dream states, it is also better organized than during wakefulness. Llinás and Ribary suggest that, unlike wakeful states, the special characteristic of dream states is an increased attentiveness to the intrinsic state in which the system generating conscious experience is unaddressable by sensory inputs (Llinás and Ribary 1993).

In extension of the point made by Llinás and Ribary, I will suggest that the internalization of attention in mystical states enables an exceptional attentiveness to emotional representations. In the more advanced mystical states during which consciousness grows extremely deep at the same time, as it is focused more and more on the emotional representations, the consciousness of mystical emotions of love grows extraordinarily deep giving rise to mystical states of purely emotional content (or at least, mystical states, which seem that way to the subject).

Before proceeding to connect Damasio's theory with the evidence in the works of John of the Cross, it seems pertinent first to offer a definition of my invented notion of mystical emotions of love. I use this notion as a metaphor for a variety of emotions generated in response to mystical conceptions of love insofar as these are considered to be mystical love by John of the Cross.

If Damasio's definition of feelings and emotions is adopted and coupled with the evidence in the works of John of the Cross that the more advanced mystical states are free of the more conceptual representations, then the inevitable conclusion must be that proficiency in mystical love means that only mystical *emotions* of love are represented while mystical *feelings* of love are eluded. To put it differently, it means that only various body states, encompassed by the notion of emotions of mystical love, are generated and represented during such mystical states. The more conceptual representations of mystical love — and obviously the juxtaposition of the two kinds of representations — are, on the contrary, absent. The mystical emotions of love

---

2. Llinás and Ribary suggest that this evidence explains consciousness at the neurobiological level. Accordingly, the evidence is interpreted to mean that consciousness is a surveying 'instance' or property combining related (and unrelated?) information about physically scattered, cognitive processes (for a general critique of this interpretation of the evidence, see Greenfield 1995, 131-33).

are doubtlessly triggered by the more conceptual representations of mystical love. Following this reasoning, it would thus be the more conceptual representations that initiate a mystical state even though those representations discontinue shortly after the shift to the consciousness of mystical emotions of love. Going into a little more detail with this, I will suggest a slightly diverging alternative explanation of the matter. It seems likely that mystical consciousness generally involves representations of both conceptions and emotions of mystical love, although in varying proportions. In the more advanced mystical states it is not necessarily the case that the more conceptual representations are eliminated but that they are relegated to the periphery of consciousness thereby reducing (or maybe even eliminating) the awareness of them. In accordance with John of the Cross, it seems that consciousness in the more advanced mystical states is predominated completely by representations of emotions of mystical love.

Turning to the quantity of mystical consciousness, it seems pertinent to initiate the point with a discussion of the evidence in the works of John of the Cross and evidence of other non-ordinary states of consciousness in relation to Greenfield's theory of consciousness. Some of those non-ordinary states that may contribute to an understanding of the quantity of mystical consciousness are various psychopathological states and some drug induced states. Apparently, depressive and schizophrenic states are two opposites in the continuum of the quantity of consciousness. Depressive states are characterized with a very deep consciousness, reduced sensitivity to the environment, little physical movement, a smooth transition from the consciousness of one thing to another, and enhanced experience of pain. All this can be explained with the existence of very large neuronal gestalts and the connectedness of the epicenters recruiting the shifting neuronal gestalts. Schizophrenic states, on the contrary, are characterized with rapidly shifting consciousnesses between dissociated foci, restlessness and incessant movement, inordinate attentiveness to the external environment, and little awareness of pain. This can be explained with the rapid shift between small and disconnected neuronal gestalts. The effects of hallucinogenic drugs are typically very similar to that of schizophrenia, that is to say, rapid shifts of consciousness and disconnectedness of consciousnesses. Still, Greenfield points out that in some cases such drugs have the opposite effect so that the subject becomes obsessed with a single object or thought producing a state more similar to a depressive state (Greenfield 1995, 90, 174, and 183).

Concerning the depth and connectedness of consciousness, mystical states will supposedly change drastically in the course of mystical development. Following John of the Cross, it seems nevertheless that mystical states in general are characterized with consciousness of considerable depth and, in particular, with smooth shifts from one focus of consciousness to another closely associated focus. Similarly, it is clear that there is little or no sensitivity to the external world in mystical states, just as there seems to be a heightened awareness of pain (although this latter point changes with development). Hence, it appears that mystical states have much in common with depressive states and with the less common drug-induced states regarding the quantity of consciousness. Accordingly, it seems most likely that consciousness in mystical states is generated from large neuronal gestalts (presumably getting larger as the developmental process advances) where the epicenters taking over from one another are closely associated.

With respect to the quantity of mystical consciousness, the pre-mystic personal and religious background of a mystic constitute only minor factors for the explanation of what it is that makes a mystical state of consciousness dissimilar to ordinary states. Mystical development, on the contrary, holds an important key to open up an investigation of the point. The point is that the mystic's intense and repeated attention to the various foci of potential mystical consciousnesses and the gradually increasing frequency and depth of actual mystical states jointly produce an extraordinary capacity for the *quantity* and connectedness of the mystical consciousnesses forming a mystical state. It seems to be the gradual build-up of relatively few mystically related epicenters rather than (or maybe even at the expense of) other epicenters that little by little reduces the degree of competition among neuronal gestalts generating consciousness thereby simultaneously favouring mystical consciousness at the expense of ordinary consciousness, certain mystical consciousnesses at the expense of others, and deeper and more connected mystical consciousnesses.

This is not yet the whole story about what it is that makes mystical states differ fundamentally from ordinary states of consciousness, though. With respect to the more advanced mystical states, it appears that consciousness during such states is very homogeneous and coherent. This apparent homogeneity of a mystical state could, in principle, either be the result of a single consciousness generated by a gestalt assembled around a single epicenter or it could stem from the sequence of gestalts formed around very closely associated epicenters. In the latter case, the one strong epicenter would be able to recruit another associated epicenter to take over. It seems more likely that it is the connectedness of a sequence of associated mystical consciousnesses that produces a harmonious and homogeneous mystical state. The combination of consciousness unrestrained by sensory inputs combined with extended temporal perseverance of each consciousness and connectedness and coherence of the sequence of consciousness is not characteristic of any ordinary states. Dreaming states are the only ordinary states of consciousness that are as imperceptible to inputs from the external world as are mystical states. Though, as opposed to mystical states, dreaming is characterized by rapidly shifting and highly disconnected consciousnesses (Greenfield 1995, 100-101). Those ordinary states that come closest to mystical states in quantity of consciousness and internalization of attention are daydreaming states which presumably are characterized with large neuronal gestalts formed around strong epicenters and where there is a very high degree of unreceptiveness to sensory inputs (cf. Greenfield 1995, 170). In comparation with mystical states (at least the more advanced ones) it appears that consciousness in day-dreaming states is much more easily distracted. The combination of a large quantity of consciousness, a very smooth shift between consciousnesses of closely connected contents, unreceptiveness to sensory inputs, and the specific quality of consciousness of mystical conceptions and/or emotions seems to be special to mystical states occurring from some point in the developmental process and on. This corresponds with the evidence provided by Llinás and Ribary that the magnetic scanning of the brain is better organized when it is unrestrained by sensory input. It furthermore supports the point they make that it is the increased attention to the intrinsic state and the unawareness of the external world that is characteristic of and special to dream states.

Extraordinary states of consciousness

I shall initiate this section asking some few questions and then turn to a discussion of how (if at all) they can be answered. Is it possible to identify an interface of all kinds of extraordinary states of consciousness and thus all kinds of extraordinary experience? Is there a common difference between various extraordinary states of consciousness and various ordinary states? Or, to put it differently, do dissimilar extraordinary states all share some attributes that are shared by no ordinary states of consciousness? In the light of Greenfield's theory of consciousness, a distinction of the similarities and dissimilarities of the diverse kinds of conscious states should be based on the two fundamental aspects of consciousness, namely the quality and the quantity of consciousness. A possible intersection of conscious states with respect to the quality (the specific content) of consciousness will be contingent on the knowledge reserve supplying the content of consciousness. Similarities of the quantity (the depth and extension) of conscious states will be conditioned by several factors. The depth, extension, and connnectedness of the consciousnesses of a particular state is restrained by the level of arousal and the strength of the epicenter around which the neuronal gestalt generating the consciousness is assembled. In reality, the factors conditioning the quality and the quantity of consciousness are mutually interdependent, because it is the very specific neuronal activities that give consciousness its specific quality.

Both the content and the depth, extension, and duration of consciousness will be constrained by the knowledge reserve of the person concerned.

A general classification of types of conscious states will therefore need to take both of the two aspects of consciousness into account, implying that classification may either produce a very broad and highly incoherent group of conscious states or it may produce a number of more narrow subgroups of conscious states. Consequently, it may be advantageous to classify differently when different aspects (at a minimum those of the quality and quantity) of states of consciousness are given priority. In general, the potential quantities of extraordinary consciousness may be classified along a continuum stretching from the very large neuronal gestalts generating the consciousness of a depressed person or a mystic to the small neuronal gestalts generating the consciousness of a schizophrene or drug-induced (or maybe possessed) person. With Greenfield's theory as the point of departure, it should be possible to make a rough catalogue of the diversity of the quantities of consciousness. With such a catalogue, the task of classifying the diverse types of religious, extraordinary states of consciousness according to the respective similarities and dissimilarities, other than those of the conceptual systems, would be facilitated very much. A classification of the potential qualities of consciousness will have to be based upon the more general cultures and conceptual systems delimiting the predictable range of kinds of extraordinary states of consciousness. Yet, it should be underscored that an actual classification (based on either the aspect of the quantity or the quality of consciousness) has to be founded on comparative studies of the diverse kinds of extraordinary states. And this is beyond the scope of this study.

In my view, neither the quantity nor the quality of consciousness can be used to define a *coherent* category of either extraordinary states in general, or a more exclusive category entailing religious, extraordinary states only. With respect to the quantity of dissimilar kinds of extraordinary states, one might simply point to the diversity of pathological states of consciousness (depression and schizophrenia have been mentioned). Similarly, the contrast between the extreme motor activities of a possessed person and the complete immobility of a subject during a mystical state are indications of equally fundamental differences in quantity of the diverse kinds of religious, extraordinary states. Turning to the possibility of a qualitative intersection of extraordinary states, one fundamental difference is that some states are religious and others not. Among the religious states, some will be conceived of as positive and others as negative by the subject. Moreover, some religious states will be construed on the basis of a religious system defining the bounds of extraordinary encounters with the superhuman powers of the religion concerned, while other states will not be part of such a well defined religious tradition.

There is no actual intersection of all extraordinary states with respect to either the quantity or the quality of consciousness. Yet, in relation to wakeful states, extraordinary states seemingly do have something in common — and that is consciousness in extreme quantities. Either the consciousnesses of an extraordinary state are very enduring (due to the very large groups of neurons generating them) or they are very short-lived (due to the very small groups of neurons generating them). Still, if the extremity of the quantity of consciousness is used as the criterion for a category of extraordinary states of consciousness, then, dream states should apparently also be deemed extraordinary, and that would hardly contribute to an understanding and a classification of extraordinary states. Hence, I would suggest that there is really not very much holding a general category of extraordinary states together, no matter whether it is the more inclusive or the more exclusive one. Yet, the common feeling that there are some kinds of conscious states that should be deemed extraordinary in one way or another suggests, even if it is little, that there is nonetheless a point in classifying dissimilar kinds of extraordinary states into one or more categories. With respect to the very general category, I would suggest that this category is simply held together by the mutual property of such states, which is that they are not part of the common experience of the major part of humanity. Truly, this is not much, but it is in fact possible to approximate the essence of the category a little further by attempting to explain *why* it is not part of the experience common to all people. In accord with my general understanding of mystical experience, I would suggest that the reason why some kinds of experience — and the conscious states during which they are first manifested — are common to *all* people, while other kinds of experience and conscious states are common only to *some* people, is because the first arises out of the predisposed development mainly realized during childhood, whereas the second kind arises out of individualized development, realized at any point in the life of a person in response to some kind of non-ordinary stimulation of the cognitive system (possibly in combination with some non-ordinary genetic disposition). The full display of extraordinary states of consciousness thus requires a certain kind of development specifically related to the kind of state in question (just as ordinary states of consciousness will be affected by ordinary kinds of development).

The developmental aspect of extraordinary kinds of experience further implies that the category of extraordinary states of consciousness will be graded and have fuzzy boundaries (for a discussion of these types of categories, see Lakoff 1987, e.g., 45).

The same holds good for a category of mystical states. I shall illustrate the matter using mystical states as an example. Concerning the graded character of the mystical states in a more general category of extraordinary states, the point is that the mystical states of an undeveloped mystic will be less central to the category than those of a fully developed mystic. The fuzziness of the category boundary similarly pertains to degrees of development of the mystic having a mystical state. As an example, the mystical state of an undeveloped mystic may be very close to an ordinary state with internalized attention to mystical conceptions like a daydreaming state with consciousness of the love between God and the soul.

A definition of mystical experience

In my view, mystical experience simply refers to the part of a person's experience that includes conceptions or feelings of mystical content typically displayed in mystical states and (possibly) resulting in mystical development. A definition of mystical experience should therefore entail subdefinitions of each of these aspects. Taking the points one by one, mystical conceptions constitute the part of a person's (or a group of persons') religious ideas that delineate the possibilities of direct human encounter with superhuman agents in the course of a person's life. Mystical feelings emerge from emotions triggered in response to mystical conceptions. Still, the essence of the concept of mystical experience is the part of a person's experience that is either displayed in, or resulting from, mystical states of consciousness. It is during the mystical states that mystical conceptions and, in particular, mystical feelings are fully brought out. And, first of all, it is the recurrence of mystical states (often promoted by certain kinds of behaviour and sensory deprivation) that produces mystical development. If a definition of mystical conceptions constitutes the foundation of a definition of the more general concept of mystical experience (in the sense that mystical conceptions inevitably will be the most primitive origin of all other aspects of mystical experience) then a definition of mystical states of consciousness will constitute the construction (or the building) of the definition of mystical experience. It is therefore mystical states that need to be defined in the first place and therefore demand the major concern. The concept of mystical states can be defined as referring to the consciousness focused on mystical matters in such quantity that there is unawareness of the external environment. The quantity of consciousness delimits the depth and extension of consciousness required for a state to be mystical. The quality of consciousness, on the other hand, delimits the possible contents of mystical consciousness and is supplied by the knowledge reserve sustaining the mystical conceptions and mystical feelings.

The above implies that a person must deem it possible to have a mystical state in order to have a mystical state. Ultimately, this further implies that a person who considers it feasible to have direct contact with superhuman powers should be considered a mystic. Yet, a person who has not yet had any mystical states will evidently be a highly unexperienced and consequently undeveloped mystic. The core of the matter is that a person may be more or less of a mystic depending on the degree of mystical development (which, in turn, is contingent on the amount of mystical experience) of the person. There will indeed be indefinite degrees of mystical experienc distributed along a continuum of mystical development starting with the inception of a person's first mystical conception and terminating, eventually, on the death of a fully developed mystic.

II.   The state of theory of mysticism

Theories of mysticism

A general outline

Among historians of religion there is a more or less connected tradition of approaching the study of mysticism.[1] To a great extent the scholars of a period have attended to the questions asked by their predecessors, although the problems often have been presented from an inverted perspective, just as new questions occasionally have been added to the old. The diverse scholarly tendencies cannot be specified chronologically, though. The differences tend to be displayed through diverging preferences for certain questions (and answers) at the expense of others. In spite of this, all scholars of mysticism have wrestled with one particular problem. In the whole history of the study of mysticism, the relation of similarities and dissimilarities between mystical states reported from different religious traditions has been of principal concern.

Introducing theories of mysticism, it seems relevant to outline the opposing positions rather schematically in order to give the reader an overview of the various approaches to the field of study. The principal dispute pertains to the view of the relative similarity or dissimilarity of mystical states (experiences) within diverse religious traditions. The question asked is whether mystical states are formed by the cultural tradition of the mystic or not. At the one extreme, there is the viewpoint that the character of a mystical state is unconditionally contingent on the religious and cultural background of the mystic[2] (a cultural reductionist stance). At the other extreme, is the proposition

---

1. Apparently, historians of religion have, for some reason, often failed to correlate their results with those from other disciplines, even when they were investigating the same subject.
2. For some reason, the more specific personal background of a mystic as a potential element of influence is rarely stressed by scholars of mysticism. In my view, this is a problem, since personal history is not simply made up of cultural and religious tradition. Several factors may influence the make-up of an individual. In the very last instance, one should therefore expect singularity and distinctiveness of the particular mystical experience of a person. In fact, I do not see why the relation of mystical experience and the background of a person should differ in any significant way from that of other kinds of experience and personal background.

that a mystical state acquires its specific character from a source that is *independent* of the context of the mystic. In extension of this, scholars disagree on the issue of the degree of singularity or identity of distinct mystical states. Actually, the debate does not so much concern the similarity of particular mystical states as whether mystical states within one religious tradition are/can be identical with those of another tradition. To support the argument that mystical experience transcends cultural and religious tradition, it has been maintained that this aspect of human experience is, in particular, ineffable. Hence, diverging descriptions can be discarded as matters of expressive and not of experiential diversity. Consequently, mystical experience is, according to this view, ultimately inexplorable.

Mysticism is exceptional

A general trait of various approaches to the study of mysticism is the presumption that it is a very special, religious phenomenon. Mystical experiences of diverse religious traditions have more in common with each other than with the traditions to which the mystics belong. W. James, for instance, considered the resemblances between mystical states to be far the most salient, whereas he deemed the differences less important (James 1902, lec. 16-17; Almond 1982, ch. 7). Similarly, E. Underhill has proposed that all mystical states are alike, although the descriptions of them differ considerably. Basically, N. Smart agrees with this view (Smart 1986; Almond 1982, ch. 3 and 7). Others, like R.C. Zaehner and R. Otto, have attempted to account for both similarities and dissimilarities by proposing that there is a limited number of types of mystical states (Almond 1982, ch. 1, 4-5 and 7).[3]

Scholars suggesting that there is a (small) number of types of mystical states similarly consider the reported content to be of major significance for an understanding of mysticism. Thus, the classifications of types of mystical states is based on their reported content. Zaehner distinguishes three such classes. The first is defined as panenhenic and is an experience of oneness with the external world (providing the insight that unity underlies multiplicity). The second is monistic and is an interior experience of being separated from anything that is not oneself. Both of these lead to a feeling of indistinction between subject and object, but, while the first includes the external world, the second excludes it. The third is theistic and is an interior experience like the

---

3. In his *Mystical Experience and Religious Doctrine* (1982), P. Almond competently presents the more important theories of mysticism until more recent times wherefore there is no point in going into any detail about these here. He treats the more influential, recent theories in part I and briefly reviews some additional theories in part II.

monistic. The difference is that the theistic experience, contrary to the monistic, retains the (normal) subject-object polarity where God is felt to be distinct from the subject. (Almond 1982, ch. 2). Otto, on the other hand, identifies two classes of mystical experience. The one is introspective (looking into the depths of Self) leading to an undifferentiated unity where the ordinary polarity of subject and object is transcended. The other is unifying (looking out upon the world) perceiving unity where multiplicity prevails (Almond 1982, ch. 5). W.T. Stace falls somewhere in between the two groups, inasmuch as he suggests that there are introvertive and extrovertive mystical states but that they ultimately are contentless and therefore alike (see Almond 1982, 73). Common to these studies is an ambition to clarify the content (less-ness) or the essence of mystical states.

Along with the emphasis on similarities typically goes the conception of mystical states as contentless. The basic argument is that the reason why mystical states are alike is not that they all are equipped with identical content but that they are free of content.[4] Therefore they are also beyond influence from the religious tradition of the mystic to whom they occur. Mystical experience is completely different from, and out of the reach of, ordinary experience. The proponents of the view that mystical states are similar, generally distinguish the actual mystical state sharply from the subsequent conceptualization of it (interpretation in the general terminology of theories of mysticism). Several of these scholars have followed James in pointing to the incommunicability of mystical states of consciousness as an explanation for the dissimilarities in the accounts of the states in spite of their argued identity. N. Smart is an exception to this. His explanation of the discordance between mystical 'experiences' and 'interpretations' is that the latter, which he defines as 'ramifications', may enter into the former. In his view, ramification and experience should still be investigated separately since the 'interpretation' *adds* to the 'experience' rather than it *affects* it. Hence, it is not necessarily the mystical 'experience' that is communicated, it could just as well be the 'interpretation' of it (see Smart 1986; Almond 1982, ch. 3; Moore 1973).

The idea of contentless mystical states ('experiences'), which is the foundation of the argument of the identity of distinct mystical states, truly deserves a comment. The conviction about the contentlessness of mystical states really stands and falls with the claim of ineffability, inasmuch as both the identity and the contentlessness of mystical states actually is contradicted

---

4. Those that are claimed to have a specifiable content (say, visions and the like) may be considered religious but not mystical. Smart, for instance, proposes such a distinction. In his terminology, only the empty states are mystical while all others are numinous (see Smart 1983).

by evidence.[5] Descriptions of mystical states vary depending on the religious traditions and on the particular mystic. This fact is, of course, easily discarded as unimportant by the proponents of the hypothesis and explained as resulting from the incommunicability of such states wherefore the variations only pertain to the level of expression. The contentlessness and the ineffability of mystical states constitute two reciprocally supportive aspects of the diverse more or less coincident theories. In other words, the theory of contentlessness leans to a great extent on the supposition that mystical states are incommunicable. And this is a point of view that scholars unreservedly have adopted from the mystics themselves.[6] Together, the postulates of the contentlessness and ineffability of mystical states really make up a waterproof and self-reliant hypothesis. In particular, the supposition that mystical states are indescribable anyway, really has tripped up theoretical advancement, even if it has been a great advantage for speculation. It is not easy to get anywhere with a theory, if evidence of the subject is completely unreliable anyway.

Mediated experience

During the last thirty years, the discussion has shifted somewhat towards a focus on the dissimilarities of mystical states typical of each of the diverse religious traditions and, furthermore, to an emphasis on the mystic's own conceptualization of the states. The theoretical incentive for this shift has been a conviction that each of the various renditions of mysticism has much in common with the particular religious tradition in which they arise. I shall dedicate somewhat more attention to this perspective on mysticism than I did to the previous one. I do not intend to go through a whole number of theories meticulously, though, but will select the main points from those scholars who pin down the major issues of the debate.

If I were to point out any single scholar who has stirred up the debate, it would have to be S.T. Katz. In *Mysticism and Philosophical Analysis*, a book edited by Katz himself, he advances a theory that emphatically opposes the hypothesis that mystical states ('experiences' in his terminology) are un-

---

5. Admittedly, many mystics *claim* that their (more advanced) mystical states are free of form and content. John of the Cross is one of those mystics. He nonetheless provides his readers with descriptions of his most advanced mystical states that strongly indicate that even these have not been free of content, although the content may not be easily specified.

6. John of the Cross can be taken as a spokesman of ineffability and provides superior nourishment for the theory of it (Juan de la Cruz 1988, Subida 2.26:1 and Noche 2. 17:3). Yet, he actually indicates that divine inspiration makes description possible (Juan de la Cruz 1988, Cántico prologo 1).

influenced by culture. He emphasizes the socio-cultural element in mystical experience. In his view, it is unthinkable that mystical states are not affected in any way by the cultural background of the mystic. Disputing several theories of mysticism, contemporary as well as earlier, he argues that there is no pure and unmediated experience, mystical or otherwise. His proposition is that the socio-religious environment over-determines the mystical state. Mystical experience within one religious tradition is therefore barely identical with, or even similar to, that of another. The traditional images, faith, symbols, and expectations actually define what is experienced. It is this that structures a mystical state and gives it a certain form. In this way, culturally shaped beliefs form the mystical state, although the state may in turn contribute to form the beliefs. In addition to this, Katz defends the view that it is not only cultural tradition that determines the make-up of a mystical state. It is likewise conditioned by cognitive factors (1978) although he does not specify these any further.

In extension of his theory of culture-bound mystical experience, he further considers other aspects of mysticism in relation to external factors, like the mystic's conservatism and the importance of spiritual guides and role models. This part of his theory primarily concerns the role played by mysticism in the development of religion in general. Katz points out that since the background of a mystic defines the bounds of what can be experienced as well as it constrains the expression of it, mysticism is, to a great extent, conservative. His motivation for taking up the problem of the (relative) conservatism of mysticism seems partially to be a reaction against a tendency to view mysticism as an innovative, original, and radical form of religiousness. He nonetheless acknowledges that mysticism may also be radical. In reality, it oscillates between originality and traditionality[7] (1983, intro. and ch. 1). Thus, the potentials of mystical states and the descriptions of them are already outlined by tradition at the same time, as it is constrained by the cognitive equipment of a mystic.

---

7. With respect to the relative conservatism of mystics pointed out by Katz, I would like to make some few remarks. It is important that Katz has drawn attention to the conjunction of radicality and conservatism in mysticism. In my understanding, it is not only mysticism that is at once radical and conservative, though. It holds for all aspects of religion. And for culture. In some cases (of religion, mysticism, politics, etc.) and/or periods, conservatism may predominate while innovativeness and radicality may prevail in other cases and/or other periods. The extent to which the one or the other predominates depends on the more general historical context. Whether an individual, an institution, or a whole society ends up being more or less conservative or radical is contingent on innumerable factors. Similarly, it is incidental and unpredictable which factors will have minor and which will have major influence.

There seems to be reasonable consensus among recent scholars of mysticism that Katz has brought out some of the major problems involved in theories of the subject. He has pointed out that the decontextualization of mystical states (justified by the premise of their contentlessness) is unacceptable (if not preposterous). In his own words 'The notion of unmediated experience seems, if not self-contradictory, at best empty.' (1978, 26). In spite of the relative agreement that it is compelling to (re)install mysticism in religious traditions, there is some disagreement regarding the degree of relevance of the argument. The main question is whether all mystical states are influenced by tradition to the same degree, and — in particular — if there are exceptions to the rule. Is it possible for some mystical states to escape cultural influence?

P. Almond suggests a hypothesis that mediates the positions of the argument of contentlessness and tradition independency versus that of tradition dependency of mystical states. Almond agrees with Katz that the religious tradition of a mystic no doubt will affect his/her mysticism. At the same time, he is not convinced that there was nothing at all to the claim of contentlessness and hence (in his view) the transcendence of tradition. His argument is that in some mystical traditions (he mentions the Theravadin as an example) mystical progress achieved through meditative techniques leads to continuously less content-filled states of mystical experience until at last contentless states are obtained. Almond further suggests that it is only the mystical states ('experiences') of the earlier stages that are influenced by tradition whereas the contentless states of the ultimate stage are identical and transcend the cultural context (1982, 176 and 178).

Almond's hypothesis may in fact be construed as just another version of the theory of contentlessness and culture-independency of mystical experience. The disagreement seems primarily to concern that which is actually going on in the so-called content-filled and contentless mystical states. The debate basically seems to revolve around the question of the generation of cognitive representations. If my interpretation of the debate is correct, mystical development would, in accord with Almond, lead to a gradual reduction in the generation of cognitive representations during mystical states, eventually eliminating them. Katz, who does not consider the issue explicitly, concludes that whatever goes on in mystical states is given form by the cultural background of the mystic. He does not state whether this form is representational or imagelike but he emphasizes that mystical states have form and that this form is their essence and identity. 'Without it they would be nothing but a set of nerve impulses', he says (1983, 62).[8] Consequently, the dispute really is centred around evidence of a certain kind of mystical states. Katz simply seems to dismiss this body of evidence as either irrelevant or non-existent. Almond, on the other hand, interprets such evidence in strict accordance with the theories going back to James (an understanding that reproduces the mystics' own).[9]

The problem of 'interpretation'

First of all, it seems relevant to draw attention to the widespread distrust in evidence of mystical experience. Almond, for instance, acknowledges the possibility of an actual gap between mystical experience and expression (1982, 149). In my view, there is reason to question the purpose of this. Basically, there is no way of determining the relative discord between experience and expression, neither in the case of mysticism nor in other cases. So far, I concede to Almond's suggestion. Hence, it is not unlikely that the relation is best described as a gap in many cases. Such cases would provide little evidence of the experience of course but may comprise important documents of the relation.[10]

In a more general perspective, the notion of 'interpretation' has been considered and elaborated most thoroughly by P.G. Moore. In Moore's use of the notion, interpretation refers to a particular mystic's conceptualization of

8. A few comments are pertinent in this context. It should be underscored that there will be no cognition without neuronal activity implying that there will be no mystical states without nerve impulses. Cognitive representations of mystical content emerge from neuronal activities. There is no way of separating the cognitive product from the neuronal processes. It can furthermore be expected that the neuronal activities themselves have been conditioned by the general experience of a person.

9. Yet, it is relevant to point out that Almond actually seems to exaggerate Katz' argument (although it may be nothing but a matter of terminology). While Katz speaks of mystical experience being *over-determined* by the cultural milieu (1978, 46) Almond considers the possibility that mystical experiences are not necessarily *determined* by the context (1982, 167). I do not think that Katz has meant to argue that mystical states are determined by the cultural background of a mystic. Over-determination is a term generally used to signify that the over-determining factors have some degree of influence on that which is over-determined. As an example, the (French) structural-marxists have used the concept to signify that the social, political, and ideological 'superstructure' influences the economical 'infrastructure' claimed to be determinant of the structure of society by Marx. A similar signification seems to be intended by Katz, that is to say, that the religious and social environment has *some degree* of influence on the actual mystical state.

10. In fact, this aspect of Almond's view relates specifically to his explicit and particular mistrust in expressions of 'panenhenic or extrovertive' mystical states (see e.g. 1982, 141). Hereby he suggests, as far as I can see, an unjustified preference for some testimonies at the expense of others (that can be dismissed as invalidated by the gap between experience and expression).

his/her mystical experience with a primary focus on mystical states ('experiences'). In his view, interpretation of mystical experience involves several facets that ought to be discriminated theoretically. He suggests that four types of interpretation can be distinguished, namely; 1) retrospective, 2) reflexive, 3) incorporated, and 4) raw experience.

1) Retrospective interpretation continues over a very long period implying that it really does not refer to one particular but to several mystical states.

2) Reflexive interpretation is formulated during a particular mystical state or immediately afterwards.

3) Incorporated interpretation concerns elements in a mystical state that derive from or are conditioned by prior beliefs, expectations, and intentions. He further differentiates between two such types, namely ideas and images formed into hallucinations (reflected interpretation) and features of the state that parallel beliefs or doctrine (assimilated interpretation).

4) Raw experience relates to features in a mystical state that are unaffected by prior beliefs etc. (1978, 108-11).

In general, the diverse aspects of interpretation are related to different points in time, namely before, during, and after a mystical state.

Moore's analytical distinction of the various interpretational aspects or levels has drawn attention to some fundamental problems concerning the relation of cultural background, mystical state, and the expression of this. But there are also a number of problems involved in his theory. Inasmuch as the discrimination of the first three types of interpretation, retrospective, reflexive, and incorporated, has become rather generally accepted among scholars of mysticism, I shall discuss them in some detail. The fourth type of interpretation, raw experience, has been debated throughout the history of the study of mysticism and equally deserves some remarks. I shall begin with a consideration of the relation of the four types of interpretation and then continue with a discussion of each of them.

Moore's attempt to discriminate types of interpretation that are undertaken at various points in time in relation to a particular mystical state is very important but his concrete classification of types of interpretation is far from unproblematic. Incorporated interpretation really antecedes a mystical state whereas retrospective interpretation succeeds it. Reflexive interpretation and raw experience are both actualized during the particular mystical state. Hence, the discrimination of the latter two is not founded on the *time* of producing the interpretation but on the *identification of a difference in kind* or, more specifically, of their *source*. Thus, the classification of the types involves an inconsistency concerning the justification of the distinction of the discrete classes. This is fully displayed, though, in the labelling of the types where retrospective interpretation is labelled according to the time of production, while the other three are named after their mode of production (incorporating or reflecting something or nothing).

Concerning the distinction between reflexive interpretation and raw experience it would be very difficult to discern aspects of interpretation influenced by the cultural tradition as opposed to aspects that were purely inspired by the actual mystical state. Of course, it would seem plausible that the generation of a vision of the Virgin Mary in a mystical state had been under considerable influence from the Christian tradition. But what about the generation of some indefinite feeling of something that seems like love? Is it a 'raw' product of the mystical state? Or is it (partially) a product of the Christian tradition of divine love? Or some other tradition of love? Or could it be a product of having felt love for one's mother? Etc. It would not be easy to say what it is that has formed such a feeling. And the distinction of reflexive interpretation and raw experience would be very similar to this example, even if it is a little burlesque. It is a presumption that it should be possible to discriminate such elements. The identification of them would simply have to be inferred. I doubt that this will be very useful for the study of mysticism.

The distinction between incorporated, reflexive, and even retrospective interpretation is pervaded with similar problems. How can one tell whether some specific 'interpretational' product has been carried out during the mystical state, if it is a derivative of elements from the tradition that have conditioned the mystical state, or finally, if it has been applied after the mystical state? There is no way of carrying out such discriminations in empirical cases. This has to do with the nature of evidence of the matter. Such evidence almost exclusively stems from mystics' own testimonies, written or otherwise.[11] Such testimonies are normally produced after the mystical states. Evidence produced during a mystical state (if it exists)[12] might document reflexive interpretation as distinct from retrospective but not as distinct from incorporated interpretation.

---

11. Actually, observance of a person in a mystical (or other extraordinary) state might provide other kinds of evidence, just as electrical recording of the brain has proven to do. Such data are still very scarce, though. Moreover, such material is hardly going to revolutionize existing data.
12. This kind of evidence might be provided from possession or shamanist states where a change in behaviour in the medium or shamanist is observable, just as the subjects might express aspects of their conscious state.

So far, I have pointed out that the various types of interpretation (conceptualization, in my terminology) distinguished by Moore cannot be applied in the more concrete study of mysticism. Though, as a more philosophical contribution to theories of mysticism they might still be relevant. It might advance theoretical insight into the nature of the mystics' own way of understanding their mystical states and it might furthermore be useful to keep the analytical distinction in mind in the concrete study. Whether this is the case depends on the relevance and coherence of the discrete types of interpretation in Moore's theory. I shall now turn to a discussion of this issue.

The first type to be considered is 'incorporated interpretation'. I do not see how this can be classified as *interpretation* (in the meaning of conceptualization). Incorporated interpretation refers to the fact that various states of consciousness (including mystical) are affected by the innumerable components of the everyday life of a person. In my opinion, the relation of these components and mystical experience is that the former are part of a whole complex of constituent factors contributing to form both particular mystical states and the unfolding of development. But the relation is itself contingent on development. The way that the specific background of an individual contributes to form a mystical state is through development. The reason why ideas, images, etc. are capable of modifying a particular mystical state is that the content of consciousness draws upon representations already stored in the cognitive system. Stated a little more generally, the cognitive system needs to employ whatever material is available. And since the channel of information from the external environment (typically?) is cut off (or at least impinged on) during mystical states, the material has to be within the system. In extension of this, I would like to stress that all aspects of the developmental background of a mystic may potentially affect a particular mystical state and the ensuing mystical development. Only the more specific influence from images and the like are easily identifiable, though.

In my view, the reason why the religious and other background is capable of influencing particular mystical states is that it already has conditioned the development of the person. If ideas, images, beliefs etc. *enter into* (Katz) or *condition* (Moore) a mystical state, it is because they already have entered into and conditioned the mind of the person having the mystical state. In extension of this understanding, incorporated interpretation may simply be subsumed under the notion of developmental background. With respect to both mystical and ordinary experience, it appears that the relation of particular states of consciousness and development is dialectical and reciprocally influential.[13]

---

13. As opposed to the general definition of the concept of interpretation as it is used by most scholars of mysticism (referring to the subject's own understanding of particular

The second type of interpretation identified by Moore is reflexive and is carried out during a particular, mystical state. Moore and other scholars with him seem to view reflexive interpretation as the more specific representations generated during a mystical state, typically images and the like produced in hallucinatory states. In my opinion, this aspect of mystical states is far better conceived of as cognitive representations purely and simply. It is not impossible, though (in principle, at least) that cognitive representations are redescribed coincidentally with their generation in which case the outcome of the redescription would correspond to Moore's reflexive interpretation. For all I know, there is no evidence of such simultaneous representational generation and redescription. Indeed, the concept of reflexive interpretation does involve a major problem for the study of it, as it cannot be documented.

Since both reflexive interpretation and raw experience are brought out during a mystical state, it seems appropriate to consider the latter in extension of the former. For rather obvious reasons, the idea of this third type of interpretation, raw experience, is not equally incorporable into all theories. Katz' idea that mystical experience, unstructured by the images and ideas provided by tradition, is nothing but a set of nerve impulses is a conspicuous example of a theory that is incompatible with this idea (1983, 62; but see also Geels 1982, 51). The notion of raw experience implies that this part of interpretation is derived from something in the mystical state itself unaffected by the developmental background of the mystic. With the notion of raw experience, Moore adopts the problem (hunting theorists of mysticism) of explaining where the content of a mystical state comes from. There are, after all, only two theoretical possibilities, namely the superhuman powers or the mind of the mystic (processing both cognitive and external events, objects etc.). Consciousness is not in itself capable of generating anything as it emerges from the activities of the brain and derives its content from the cognitive knowledge reserve or the coincident perception of the external environment. Mystical consciousness, which is completely (or partially?) un-affected by sensory inputs, gets its content from the mind of the mystic and this has inescapably been affected by the person's accumulated experience, both mystical and ordinary.

Yet, I would like to point out that the dispute (pervading all theories of mysticism without exception) may be a little blown up by the specific way that the background of a person has been considered as entering into a particular mystical state. The point is that the prevalent talk of beliefs,

states of consciousness) I will suggest a definition of interpretation that excludes the conceptualization of internal states and includes only that of objects, events, and the like that are external to the person.

expectations, images, and the like being incorporated into a particular state is particularly relevant in connection with more hallucinatory states. It is a fact that little is known about the way that the cultural background of a person affects a particular mystical state, since evidence of the matter is not available for scientific investigation. That which is documented has already been subject to retrospective reflection by the mystic. Certainly, evidence indicates that some mystical states have been formed in very direct correspondence with the more specific ideas and beliefs of the mystic concerned. The mystic may report to have seen certain images, doubtlessly inspired by beliefs or images of the religious tradition. In these cases it is reasonable to assume that the images etc. have been incorporated into the particular mystical state and have given it this particular form. But in the numerous other cases where no such representations or mental images are specified in the reports, we know next to nothing about the way that the cognitive representations in a mystical state have been affected by the background of the mystic. A theory of whether they have been affected or not has to be deduced. There is no point in trying to line up evidence of this from within the field of mysticism as it does not exist. Either one has to make do without evidence, which is what most scholars of mysticism have done, or one needs to look for evidence from other fields (the nature of the human mind, for instance). The latter is what I will suggest. In the light of such evidence it does not seem particularly plausible that mystical states and the way they are represented cognitively can be unaffected by the background of a person. Yet, such evidence does not give any idea at all of *how* mystical states can be affected by tradition etc. Hence, I am back where I started: there is no such evidence. Since this is the case, I would suggest showing some degree of unobtrusiveness when theorizing about the way that 'tradition' *enters* into mystical states. A consequence of this could be the consent to vagueness. And it is exactly the opposite that is displayed in the suggestions of images, beliefs etc. entering into mystical states. It is not unlikely that the disagreement between some of the authors endorsing the possibility of raw experience and others opposing it would be much less outspoken, if the 'incorporated interpretation' were less specified. The problem seems to be that the notion that all mystical states are under influence from tradition does not leave room for many of the reports of mystical states that are claimed to be form- and imageless (borrowing the the terminology of John of the Cross).

The fourth and final type of interpretation distinguished by Moore is the retrospective. Retrospective interpretation is, as the notion suggests, carried out after the aspect of mystical experience that it relates. As Moore emphasizes, retrospective interpretation normally unfolds over a very long period and further relates to several mystical states. To complicate the matter even more, the character of the mystical states interpreted retrospectively, supposedly changes with time (1978, 111).[14] For that reason, mystics' state-ments about their mystical experience give only indirect evidence of it. The retrospective interpretation is the only one of Moore's four types of interpretation of which there is any evidence. And even in this case there will only be any evidence of retrospective interpretation if the mystic concerned has chosen to report his thoughts in a form that is available to scholarly analysis. In most cases such form will be written.

In this place, it seems pertinent to point out that, in my definition, the mystic's own interpretation of his/her mystical experience refers only to the reflections on his/her own written (or otherwise) testimonies of (some aspect of) his/her experience. Interpretation is, in this definition, a process involving the conscious reconsideration of something that is external to the mind of the mystic (although this something is a product of the mystic's mind aided by the exploitation of the part of the environment providing the tool for the testimony, often pen and paper). Accordingly, mystical experience may be redescribed representationally, or it may be written or talked about, whereas only the explicit products of these processes can be interpreted. With such a definition of interpretation, the only aspect of Moore's types of interpretation included in the category is the more explicit part of the retrospective interpretation. In my understanding of the matter, reflexive interpretation refers to mystical consciousness itself, the more implicit part of retrospective interpretation refers to representational redescriptions, and incorporated interpretation is an aspect of development.

Summary

Historians of religion viewing mysticism as an exceptional aspect of human experience have typically focused on actual mystical states. For most of these scholars (with the exception of Smart, Zaehner, and Otto), a complete dismissal of the significance of the various religious traditions of mystics have gone along with the focus on the real mystical experience (realized in mystical states). Other scholars have reacted strongly against the view that mystical experience should/could be self-reliant and independent of other experience. As a constructive alternative, many of them have chosen to focus on the

---

14. In this context, it seems appropriate to mention that Geels criticizes that Moore, in his 1978 article, does not take the time-factor into consideration as a cause of changes occurring in the period between particular states and later interpretation (1982, 51 and 54). This seems an unjustified criticism to me as Moore explicitly mentions this aspect. That aside, I agree with Geels that the time factor and the nature of memory are of major importance.

relation of mystical states and the socio-religious background. This new perspective has contributed importantly to the study of mysticism. Not only is it advantageous for the general explanation of mysticism as dependent on other aspects of religious life but it also contributes to the understanding of textual and other evidence of mystical experience.

The limitations of recent theories of mysticism

I would like to indicate some significant aspects of mysticism which, to my knowledge, have not as yet been attended to. In my view, there are at least two elements of mysticism that have been undervalued, namely the cognitive constraints on mystical experience and the complexity of the background. Although some scholars of mysticism have reacted against the tendential disregard of the significance of the context, they have not necessarily renounced other aspects of the theories in question. In spite of the criticism, the criticizers have adopted the tradition of stressing the study of mystical states (experiences) at the expense of mystical development (which would be mystical experience in their terms, even if it is attended to rarely).[15] In my opinion, the tendency to view the two aspects of mysticism in isolation is a fundamental mistake. It completely disregards the constraints that the cognitive system imposes on human experience. Actually, Katz has drawn attention to this aspect already in his 1978 article (26) but no scholars (including himself) have taken any further consequences of it, neither in theoretical advances nor in the more concrete studies of mysticism. The consequence of Katz' unspecified suggestion would be that the study of mysticism takes the nature of the human mind into consideration. This implies that just as the external surroundings of a mystic affect the mystical states, so does both the cognitive make-up and the individual (developmental) background of the mystic affect mystical experience as an interrelated complex of mystical states and general development. Little has been done to understand the problems involved in mystical development and the relation of these three components.

Katz' installment of mysticism in the world has eliminated the isolation of mystical states from the surroundings of the mystic. His outline of a new conception of mysticism has been accepted by several scholars in this field. Recent studies of mysticism rarely ignore the importance of the background of the mystic. Still, there has been a tendency to overlook Katz' stress on the significance of the *socio*-religious environment in favour of a focus on the

---

15. G.M. Jantzen is an exception as she reverses the attention to focus on the stages of mystical experience at the expense of mystical states (1989, 189).

general religious tradition of a mystic (this criticism includes Katz himself). The issue of the background has often been viewed as a matter of whether a mystic belongs to the Hindu, Buddhist, Sufi, Christian, etc. tradition.

I suggest that numerous aspects of the background may influence mystical experience in general. Evidently, the religious tradition will have the most fundamental influence on the mystical experience of an individual (in fact, this may be subject to change, now that the character of religiousness changes and seems to become more synthesized). No other single factors can compete with effects exerted by this aspect of tradition.[16] Yet, two points should be added to this. The first is that the religious tradition does not rule out influence from other aspects of a person's life. The second, and main point, is that the more specific religious background of a person is not necessarily easily identified.[17] The point is that the factors influencing the development of an individual can be expected to be both accidental and multifarious. They are not easily gathered from the end product. Hence, the (immediate) identification of the more general religious tradition is only part of the job of recognizing the background of a particular mystic. Moreover, the relevance of the nature of the mind is dismissed completely.

Interdisciplinary approaches to extraordinary states

Introduction

Lately there have been numerous attempts to approach various kinds of extraordinary states from unconventional angles. Many scholars have focused on the remarkable similarities between different types of extraordinary states and some have come up with hypotheses of the relation of the diverse types. Some degree of interdisciplinary fusion is characteristic of this kind of approach. Especially, the more theoretical endeavours have made use of evidence and theories from more than one discipline. I am aware that I include scholars and theories of considerable diversity in this section. My

---

16. The influence of religious traditions is further enhanced inasmuch as it is (or has been) rather common for mystics to live a life within religious communities separated from the non-religious life.
17. The literature on John of the Cross clearly presents the problem. Numerous scholars have made an attempt to identify the aspects of the religious tradition in 16th century Spain that have contributed to form his theology and mystical teachings. The picture is altogether multifarious (see e.g. Vilnet 1949; Crisógono 1975; Wilhelmsen 1980). If one were further to specify what had affected his particular mystical states, the task would be even more hopeless.

motivation for this grouping is that the scholars in question share a dissatisfaction with more traditional explanations. In addition, they all intend to contribute to a generalization of the field of study either by constructing general theories or by uncovering evidence of similarities of different types of extraordinary states. I do not intent to discuss the theories in depth and I shall further limit my concern to a few selected approaches.

It is suitable first to outline the variance in the theoretical and evidential focus. Theoretically, some studies have focused on the extraordinariness of some kinds of conscious states while ignoring the more conceptual level, thereby avoiding the distinction of religious and non-religious conceptualizations. Other studies have concentrated on extraordinary states in religious contexts. With respect to the evidence, some scholars base their theories on evidence deriving from either psychological or neurological experiments. Others aim to supplement religious evidence with psychological or neurological data as a foundation for theorizing.

I definitely sympathize with these endeavours, both the interdisciplinariness of the approaches and the attempt to construct a general theory of distinct types of extraordinary states. But in close connection to this approval, I would like to emphasize that it is a field of study that has been explored very poorly. Research into all of the subfields is deficient, inasmuch as neither of the various types of extraordinary states have been adequately studied. And this holds true for all disciplines without exception. In psychology, data primarily derive from drug-induced states (often with a focus on the changes in state of consciousness related to them). In the study of religion, two major weaknesses stand out, namely the lack of comparative studies and the insufficiency of the theoretical explanations. In neurology, the study of extraordinary states is still new and the basis of evidence of the various types and their interrelationship is still very weak. Furthermore, the data in many cases still remain unexplained at the neurological level of analysis. Another point is that such evidence is far from being ready to support other fields of evidence and theory. In fact, theories and documentation are often so flimsy that generalizations based on such data alone are prone to lead to quite lofty hypotheses.

Inasmuch as not only theories but also evidence are inadequate, scholarly progress is not just a matter of assembling a whole bulk of fragmented evidence and coming up with a coherent theory of it. A great deal of work has to be done from the ground. Theoretical generalizations require comparable evidence (comparative studies would be expedient). Similarly, some degree of reliability of existent data in one discipline would be convenient before the findings are transferred to other disciplines as support of very general theories. The lack of evidence is a very good reason to be cautious with generalizations.

Now that I have pointed out my scruples, I shall turn to consider the advantages of this kind of approach to extraordinary states. Traditionally, there has been a tendency to investigate classes of extraordinary states separately. It is not actually the case that scholars have concentrated on the dissimilarities between the various types of states. It is more as if they have ignored the potential similarities of the types. Contrary to this, many recent approaches to extraordinary states take the apparent similarities of classes of states as a starting point. There is, of course, a vast divergence in both the problems and the advantages of the specific studies. Some scholars have focused on more or less salient characteristics common to all of the distinct classes of states. Others investigate a particular subject or aspect of it.

All in all, I think that the theoretical and interdisciplinary approach to various types of extraordinary states is of pivotal import and bearing. The intentions of many studies settling with the approaches and theories of their predecessors are both requisite and approvable. But it is also pervaded with difficulties. Some scholars seem to regard the vagueness and scarcity of data as a legitimization to make do without evidence at all. It really is a problem that some authors uncritically have incorporated evidence from other disciplines although much of the data concerned were very scarce and still unexplained. Such evidence (unexplained and uncertain) is easily employed as support for highflying hypotheses or even postulates since there is no conflicting evidence to challenge them. I think that it is judicious to take the consequence of the extensive uncertainty of available evidence of extraordinary states and take evidence of ordinary states and development into account.

The critique of conventional theories

I shall initiate this section with a discussion of one of the early scholars exploring and relating various types of states of consciousness. Twenty-five years ago (in 1975), C. Tart published a book where he presented his version of a theory of states of consciousness including altered states of consciousness (ASC). Tart is a psychologist and has approached the subject from a psychological perspective. His research has included psychological experiments on various kinds of states (including drug induced states, sleep states, hypnosis, and the like). His theory is to a great extent supported with evidence from such experiments. It is further relevant to point out that his professed theoretical point of departure is systems theory.

Tart distinguishes the conservative and the radical view of mind. As could be expected, he counts himself among the radicals. He points out that it is almost universally accepted among Western scientists that awareness and consciousness are products of brain functioning implying that the former two cannot do without the latter. This is where Tart embraces the radical view that awareness can be partially outside (or beyond) brain functioning. Parapsychological phenomena are instances of awareness independent of brain functioning. In his view, evidence of various kinds of ASC's supports the prospects of such immaterial autonomy of awareness (1975, ch. 3).[18] For my own part, I must confess that I am a conservative. Tart seems to place himself right between the traditional religious views and more recent (and conservative) psychology. Parapsychological phenomena are psychological to the extent that they are human products but they are parapsychological to the extent that they are self-reliant. He seems to acknowledge that the psychological is bound to the physical but just as there, in his view, is some extraphysical reality, so is there an extra- (or para)psychological reality. His main encouragement for the espousal of this radical view of mind is to allow belief systems to affect physical reality directly. In fact, it is beyond my comprehension why he sees a need for making such a detour around some extraphysical and extra-psychological reality. The presumption that cognition emerges from neuronal activities does not in any way rule out the possibility that cognition similarly affects those neuronal activities.[19]

A new paradigm explanation

J.E. Collins represents a theoretical school of thought that in many ways picks up the thread from Tart. Collins proposes a theory of mysticism that primarily is based on (or generated from the analysis of, as he says) 'mystical data' (1991, 185), that is to say, textual reports of mystical experience. As opposed to Tart who keeps to psychological theory and evidence, Collins supplies and corroborates his theory with both neurological and psychological theory and evidence. Collins agrees with Tart's dissatisfaction with earlier theories which he classifies as 'old paradigm' and 'orthodox' contrary to the 'new paradigm' and 'heterodox' adopted by himself.

In his choice of supportive theories he consistently picks the more

---

18. A. Hardy champions an equally radical view when he proposes that the human mind has a purely mental (or spiritual) dimension detached from the chemico-physical (1979, 44). Hardy's suggestions are nothing but religious explanations in (attempted) scientific disguise, though.

19. Possibly, he actually disputes a view that the relation of neuronal events and cognitive behaviour is causal and one-directional, implying that neuronal activities cause cognitive behaviour which in turn has no influence whatever on the neuronal activities.

'heterodox' theories while avoiding the more 'orthodox' ones. He justifies the relevance of this selectiveness by arguing that they fit the mystics' own accounts better. Collins' purpose is to locate a scientific theory in agreement with reports of mystical experience in order to provide the accounts with a scientific explanation and foundation. In extension of this, he further aims to verify the validity of evidence furnished by individual introspection (say, mystical) for scientific purposes. He aims to demonstrate that the mystics' own conceptualizations to a great extent correspond with some mystically experienced reality.[20] The reason why the mystics' own understandings of their experience parallel reality is, in his view, that a non-material reality truly exists (1991, 185-86 and 219).[21] Collins seems to be at great pains to assure his readers of the scientificness of his approach and ensuing theory. Apparently, he is a little worried that the 'heterodoxity' of the supportive theories should seem unscientific in the eyes of his readers (and thus lose in persuasive power). Apparently, he tries to make up for this obstacle by certifying the fame and prominence of the authors of the 'heterodox' theories, in spite of their discredit in 'orthodox' scientific circles (cf. his references to Pribram, Bohm, and Tart, see Collins 1991, 207, 209, and 224).

More specifically, Collins intends to furnish two particular aspects of mysticism with an explanation. On the one hand his ambition is to pin down what is actually experienced during mystical (and other extraordinary) states. On the other hand he argues that the potential of experiencing such non-material reality is founded on the neural make-up of the brain (and not only that of the human brain, it seems, 1991, 191). Hence, he discusses neurological evidence of the physiological foundation of mystical and like states. Collins' apologetic purpose of providing mystics' own interpretations with a scientific make-up is in itself unscientific. His point of departure is the premise that the mystics are right in their claims. He believes that there is a non-material, causal reality. His encouragement for supporting the mystics' conceptuali-

20. Wilhelmsen joins Collins defense of the truth that mystical reality underlies mystical experience when she argues for the rationality of mystical experience. Wilhelmsen wishes, on the one hand, to secure the divine source of mystical experience and, on the other hand, to certify the rationality of this (mystical experience and, seemingly, its source) (1980, 314).

21. Actually, Collins expresses his ambitions very clearly when he imparts that 'The reasons why a heterodox scientific theory is more useful to a discussion of mysticism than an orthodox scientific theory arise out of the nature of our particular problem. For we are looking for a scientific interpretation of mysticism which agrees with mystics in acknowledging that non-material reality exists and is available for interaction with human consciousness by the use of certain introspective techniques.' (1991, 219).

zations with scientific explanations seems to be that he wishes to render them cogent and persuasive. A missionary task, it seems.

Provision of data at the neurological level

In the seventies, neurological research in non-ordinary states seems to have been of main concern, especially among american scientists. Evidence of the subject was collected from various experiments, especially on zen and yoga meditation but also with photic and sonic stimulation. It was found that certain changes in the neural system go along with changes in state of consciousness. I shall briefly present some of these findings.

For one thing, various kinds of meditation have been shown to alter the functioning of the autonomous nervous system (ANS) comprising the sympathetic and the parasympathetic system. Stimulation of the sympathetic system engender ergotropic excitation which is associated with heightened activity and emotional responsivity, whereas stimulation of the parasympathetic system engenders trophotropic excitation which is associated with drowsiness and sleep. In ordinary, wakeful states there is an oscillating balance between the two kinds of excitation whereas extraordinary states induced by meditation are characterized by the dominance of either ergotropic or trophotropic excitation (in the latter case combined with some degree of ergotropic excitation, it seems, which may be the reason why sleep is not induced). It seems that exceeding stimulation of the one system eventually affects the other system (because excess neuronal discharges overflow to the opposite system) (Gellhorn and Kiely 1972; but see also Lex 1979; Laughlin and d'Aquili 1979; Turner 1985).

It has further been found that the changes in frequency of neuronal firings recorded in electroencephalograms (EEGs), are related to changes in cognitive states. According to E. Gellhorn and W.F. Kiely, an extraordinary state achieved by yoga meditative technique shows an EEG very similar to that characteristic of dream states (and to some extent of some psychotic states) (1972, 401). Still, S. Knox, who specifically has studied the relationship between neuronal frequencies and cognitive states, reaches the conclusion that, although certain neuronal rythms typically coincide with specific cognitive states, there is no causal relation of the two. Her point is that identical EEGs are reported to have been perceived very differently. She further points out that it is improbable that the rather few identified rythms (alfa, beta, and theta) map all of the changes in neuronal frequency. According to her, evidence indicates that neuronal rythms are far more nuanced (1981).

Already in the early sixties, A. Neher supplied neurological evidence that neuronal firing rythms can be affected in various ways. His research documented that the neural system responds to rythmic sound stimulation and to certain behaviour (responsiveness to light stimuli had been known for decades). As could be expected, the sound rythms and the types of behaviour in question are typical of some rituals during which it is common to have extraordinary states. Neher's explanation of these findings, is that the frequencies of neuronal firings (in various areas of the brain) adapt to the various rythms of the sound. Moreover, Neher's research documented that the neuronal firing rate furthermore is reinforced by light stimulation of similar frequency (1962).

In the middle of the seventies neurobiologists discovered that neural systems are capable of producing several morphine-like substances endogeneously, now generally classified as *endorphins* or *enkephalins* (Saffran 1982; Prince 1982; Changeux 1985, 89 and 106). This certainly was a breakthrough for neurology. It was additionally found that the release of enkephalins followed from specific activities and was fostered by specific conditions of the external environment which were both part of many religious rituals. Certain behaviour and conditions are known to increase the level of enkephalins. Diverse kinds of psychological and physical stress can be mentioned. Hectic motor activity like dancing, trembling, and shaking are typical of many religious rituals which, at some point, will cause a heightened level of enkephalins. But also exposure to extreme temperatures, starvation, dehydration, and the like seem to liberate enkephalins (Prince 1982a; Prince 1982b; Jilek 1982). With this supplementary finding, enkephalins became a subject of interest for researchers from several disciplines. One reason why goal-directed behaviour is apt to elicit the release of enkephalins is that various activites and conditions more or less directly stimulate specific centers in the brain where the enkephalins are stored.

Enkephalins work in several areas of the neural system and have diverse (and for a great deal unknown) effects depending on the functions of the specific subsystem affected. It is therefore likely that the specific activities and conditions that will stimulate some part of the system or other relate to the functions of the diverse neural subsystems. One such relation is known to exist between pain and the release of enkephalins (Changeux 1985, 103-7). Yet, it seems that an increase in the level of enkephalins in one part of the system are often followed by a similar increase in other parts. (Changeux 1985, 113). Thus, it is possible that enkephalins initially are released in one part of the neural system but that this either leads to an increase in other parts or that other parts are stimulated more indirectly.

Until now the effects of enkephalins are far from having been investigated exhaustively, but they are known to have other effects than analgesia. As mentioned, enkephalins influence several areas in the neural system. It is therefore not surprising that enkephalins relieve psychological pain in addition to physical. In general, the functions of enkephalins seem to be directed at nocuous events or conditions in the internal environment. In this way, the release of enkephalins in the neural system supposedly causes a feeling of pleasure by eliminating tension and stress (for a more technical treatment of the workings of enkephalins, see Henry 1982; cf. also Saffran 1982). However, antinociception is not necessarily the whole story, as sexual stimulation similarly leads to a very high level of the content of enkephalins both in the blood and in the central nervous system. The evidence of such endogenous methods of generating pleasure and cutting off the awareness of harmful incidents is very important for the study of extraordinary states. It is not unlikely that enkephalins are responsible for some of the cognitive changes characteristic of various kinds of extraordinary states.

Application of neurological evidence

Some theorists of extraordinary states believe that neurological data provide explanations of the causes of the alterations of states of consciousness. I shall briefly review some of the hypotheses representing such a view.

The identification of a cause...

R. Fischer bases a theory of various kinds of extraordinary states on the evidence of changes in the relation of the ergotropic and trophotropic systems in the ANS. Fischer emphasizes that he wishes to include all aspects of states of consciousness, both the physiological and the psychological aspects. He considers conscious experience to emanate from cognitive 'interpretation' of subcortical arousal. He suggests that changes in states of consciousness are caused by either trophotropic or ergotropic excitation, ultimately resulting in overflow to the opposite system. The first leads to what he calls hypoarousal while the second leads to hyperarousal (typically? involving hallucinations). He depicts the difference as a 'voyage' from bottom to top along the contour of a circle but in converse directions. In his view, ergotropic excitation leads to the kind of extraordinary states typical of 'Western travellers'. In this classification he includes as diverse states: dream states (slight arousal), some psychotic states (hyperarousal), and mystical rapture (ecstasy) where only the last seems to result in overflow to the trophotropic system. As opposed to this, trophotropic excitation leads to extraordinary states reported by 'Eastern travellers' all achieved by meditative techniques and described as either tranquil relaxation or hypoarousal (1986).[22] Fischer seems to presume that: (1)

behaviour stimulating either of the two systems in the ANS causes change in its way of functioning; (2a) these changes in turn alter the state of consciousness of an individual and (2b) it is these changes that are 'interpreted' cognitively thus resulting in various kinds of extraordinary, conscious experience.

While (1) seems to be well documented by various studies (especially Neher 1962), I find the assumption (2a), and thus also (2b), very problematic. For all I know, there is no evidence and not even any indications that the changes in the functioning of the ANS are the sole *cause* of the change in state of consciousness. It may be one of many interrelated causes. Or it may be a cause at one stage in the process. Or it may be an effect of other changes. Concerning (2) b. it is therefore also very uncertain that it is these particular neuronal processes that are 'interpreted' cognitively and generate conscious experience, as he expresses it. I doubt that the relation of neuronal activities and state of consciousness is one of simple causes and effects, as implied in Fischer's theory.

Furthermore, Fischer's classification of two contrasting ways of achieving two fundamentally dissimilar kinds of states that *in their most extreme form are similar*, deserves some critical comment.

First, Fischer does not discuss why various kinds of more or less extraordinary states of the 'Western' and 'Eastern' kind respectively are nonetheless reported very differently. The distinction of only two classes, each including a great diversity of conscious states, involves the problem of explaining the differences within each of the classes, if only one cause of the changes in state of consciousness is identified.[23]

Second, the view that the more extreme forms of the two kinds of extraordinary states are similar, implies that the content of consciousness depends simply on the activities in the ANS, that is, the simultaneous excitation of both the subsystems. I do not intend to deny that this may contribute to or be part of the content of consciousness (it may, for instance, condition the emotional response to something). But in agreement with John of the Cross' works it is rather certain that the content of mystical consciousness in his case (and presumably that of many other Christian mystics)

22. It is not quite clear what the means of achieving 'mystical rapture' are, if they do not include meditative techniques.
23. Besides, the elevation of the distinction between a 'Western' and an 'Eastern' style of states of consciousness seems highly prejudiced and preconceived.

has mainly been emotional, an emotional content that more specifically can be described as emotions of love. And the changes in the ANS are not responsible for the generation of emotions (see Damasio 1987 for a thorough presentation of evidence and a theory of emotions). Third, Fischer's complete disregard for the possibility that a person's beliefs and views influence the range of possible states of consciousness of the person seems absolutely preposterous to me. Altogether, his argument that a very short chain of single causes and effects produce the fundamental change of conscious state, combined with his complete inattention to the importance of the more specific cultural differences, produce a theory that simplify the issue of extraordinary states (religious and irreligious) to such an extent that the diversity of conscious states is reduced to a matter of degrees of two varieties.

...and of a primary and a secondary cause

Fischer is not the only author who has focused on the changes of the functioning in the ANS as a main cause of the specific consciousness in extraordinary states. These particular neural changes similarly constitute the starting point for the theories proposed by B. Lex on the one hand and E.G. d'Aquili and C.D. Laughlin, Jr. on the other hand. Although similarly based on evidence of changes in the ANS, these theories diverge somewhat from Fischer's. The authors point out that the specific changes in question are characteristic both of extraordinary states of consciousness, like those generated in ritual contexts (possession, for instance) and of sleep, orgasm, and psychotic states. The changes concern the relation of the two subsystems in the ANS, namely the parasympathetic (related to trophotropic excitation) and the sympathetic (related to ergotropic excitation). As mentioned above, there is a constant alternation in the subsystemic level of activation in wakeful states. As opposed to this, extraordinary states are characterized with an escalation towards an equal and simultaneous activation of both subsystems and, consequently, their neuronal discharges (apparently through the continuous stimulation of one of the systems). Ultimately, this results in coincident ergotropic and trophotropic excitation which may cause a temporary, optimum and simultaneous stimulation of both the sympathetic and the parasympathetic system (Lex 1979; d'Aquili and Laughlin 1979, 156-78).

Like Fischer, they suggest that it is these changes that cause the alteration of a state of consciousness. Yet, according to both Lex and d'Aquili and Laughlin it is not the changes in the ANS themselves that are perceived consciously. The changes in the ANS cause a change in the relation of the cerebral hemispheres resulting in right-hemispheric dominance in extraordinary states (as opposed to the ordinary state)[24] and this is supposed to alter the mode of experiencing.[25] It is thus the right hemispheric dominance that produces 'oceanic' feelings, ineffability, hallucinations (Lex 1979, 128) or a feeling of unity (between oneself and other participants in a ritual) (d'Aquili and Laughlin 1979, 157).[26]

I would like to attach some few critical comments to this explanation. Apparently, these scholars believe that the neural changes in the ANS are the main cause inducing extraordinary states. They further seem to believe that these particular changes, namely the change in the relation of the subsystems and the effect this has on hemispheric dominance, explain states of consciousness. In other words, they suggest that there is a fairly simple causal relationship between one kind of changes and the alteration of a state of consciousness. The issue of why the changes in the neural system sometimes induce orgasm, sometimes some kind of ecstasy, and other times psychotic states is not really considered. Their answer might be that this depends on the *way* that the changes concerned are achieved (as suggested by Fischer 1986) implying that the ritually controlled stimulation would account for the induction of ecstasy and not some other state. However, if this is the case, then it is not really the changes in the ANS and the hemispheric relationship that cause an extraordinary state of consciousness. In other words, the explanation remains circular: Either the changes in the neural system are causally related to the changes in cognitive state (in which case the variation of the latter remains unexplained), or the variations in cognitive state are explained by the different cognitive behaviour, and then there is no causal relationship between the neural changes and the changes in state of consciousness.

Moreover, Lex does not present any evidence for her hypothesis that right hemispheric dominance should account for 'oceanic' feelings, hallucinations,

---

24. Actually, left-hemispheric dominance is only tendential. Changeux suggests that there is some degree of genetic predisposition for dominance of either hemisphere, usually the left, while epigenetic development determines the end product (1985, 239-42). Thus, individual exceptions are not uncommon (in some cases of lefthandedness, for instance) just as cultural variations are predictable.
25. When it comes to explaining how the change in hemispheric dominance should come about, the two hypotheses diverge slightly. Lex does not specify why and how the changes in the ANS result in changes in hemispheric dominance (1979, 128-30). Laughlin and d'Aquili suggest that, on the one hand, there is some unidentified connection between the non-dominant (right?) hemisphere and the trophotropic system and, on the other hand, there is a corresponding connection between the dominant (left?) hemisphere and the ergotropic system (1979, 175).
26. Cf. Lex (1979); d'Aquili and Laughlin (1979, 156-59 and 174-77); Turner (1985, 260) who refers (and embraces) the hypothesis proposed by d'Aquili and Laughlin.

and ineffability. Indeed, she supports it with a reference to Ornstein's pos-
tulate that most hallucinations result from lack of left hemispheric functioning
caused by sleep deprivation, hunger, and extreme bodily temperatures (Lex
1979, 127). I doubt that there is any evidence for this (for a presentation of
evidence of hallucinations, see Changeux 1985, 146 and 151). I suspect that the
assumed coupling of right hemispheric dominance and hallucinations simply
is based on evidence of the characteristics of the right hemisphere (see Sperry
1982 for a description of these) of which especially its synthetical and non-
sequential processing of input and its tolerance towards inconsistencies of
diverse inputs, nicely fit some of the various reports of extraordinary states.
However, the cultural variation in hemispheric dominance strongly indicates
that dominance of either hemisphere is developed over a long period and it
is unlikely that such development could be modified instantaneously as would
be the case, if it were to result from temporary changes in a particular neural
system. Thus, if hemispheric dominance accounts for the extraordinary state
of consciousness (which is not impossible, of course) a change in the
relationship would presumably have to be developed over a long period. With
respect to the supposition that simultaneous discharges from the sympathetic
and parasympathetic systems should cause right hemispheric dominance, it is
barely known how the changes identifiable at the neurological level of analysis
affect cognitive functioning.[27]

With respect to the hypothesis of right-hemispheric dominance, there does
indeed seem to be some connection between the cerebral hemispheres and the
ANS. The point is that attention and concentration are known to stimulate the
ergotropic system and non-concentration to stimulate the trophotropic (this is
supposedly exploited in the diverse meditative methods, just as it presumably
is the reason why specific behaviour affects the ANS). Yet, most kinds of
concentration involve both hemispheres to some extent (although it typically
is focused in either of the two hemispheres, depending on the task) (Changeux
1985, 163; Sperry 1982) wheras non-concentration occupies neither hemisphere
specifically.

Some comments on the search for specific causes

Now that I have drawn attention to some problems involved in the presented
hypotheses it seems fitting to proceed with some more general comments. In
the light of Damasio's theory, it seems plausible that the changes in the ANS

---

27. Lex hypothesizes about the relation (1979, 128) whereas d'Aquili and Laughlin seem
    to take it for granted (1979, 157) without presenting the research indicating this. All in
    all, their hypotheses are rather insufficiently documented.

are generated in response to some cognitive behaviour. The change in the functioning of the ANS is thus itself an effect of cognitive functions. This is also implied in Fischer's theory (as he distinguishes two basically dissimilar ways of affecting the ANS) and may or may not be an assumption underlying the theories of Lex and d'Aquili and Laughlin respectively (but if it is, it is not considered very important). Yet, the fact that the changes in the ANS characterize highly dissimilar kinds of conscious states (including both ordinary and extraordinary states) suggests that they are generated as a non-specific response to a great variety of conscious states. I further concede that these changes may be represented cognitively. This is in fact the core of the theories in question. The representations of the subsystemic, neural changes constitute the content of consciousness in various kinds of more or less extraordinary states and the degree of the changes accounts for the degree of the extraordinariness of the resulting state of consciousness. This explanation entails one insurmountable obstacle, though. And this is, that it does not answer the question why a great variety of conscious states emerge from a single change in the neural system. I will argue that although specific behaviour intended to induce a certain extraordinary state of consciousness may affect the ANS in the described way, this does not necessarily mean that these changes are special to extraordinary states. In extension of this, it is most unlikely that these changes alone (or mediated by a secondary effect as in the theories of Lex and d'Aquili and Laughlin) account for the extraordinariness of various states of consciousness. Presumably the changes *are* represented cognitively and thus may *contribute* to the content of consciousness, but it is most unlikely that they constitute the dominant, not to mention the only, content of dissimilar kinds of extraordinary consciousness. The problem with the theories in question is that they suggest no explanation of the variation in extraordinary states recognizable both at the cultural and the individual level.

In my opinion, it is hardly the case that cognitive states are contingent on a few factors, implying that it is unlikely that single causes can be identified as support for adequate explanations. Explaining states of consciousness is barely a matter of linking specific causes with specific effects. It seems more plausible that consciousness arises out of an indefinite number of reciprocally influential processes generated in a highly complex web of inter- and intra-connected neurons. In accordance with such a conception of the mind, changes in one part of the system will presumably (sooner or later) be followed by one or more changes in other parts. And from these changes others will supposedly ensue. With such an understanding, it is further explainable that fundamental changes in behaviour (say, hectic dancing or various kinds of meditation), external stimuli (music, extreme temperatures, exposure to pain) will affect processes in the system. Some changes are known to result in the release of enkephalins and others to affect the ANS. But all such changes (which, according to this view, are both causes and effects) are prone to induce other changes, identifiable either at the neurological or the cognitive level of description. Hence, it is predictable that numerous processes in various parts of the system are altered in the period from the initiation of stimulation (say, the change of behaviour or whatever) and the noticeable changes in state of consciousness.

III. Development in a general perspective

Levels of analysis and description

Levels of analyzing mysticism

Introducing neurological and cognitive theories, it seems pertinent to distinguish the more predominant concepts of the mind/brain. At a very general level, two contrasting views can be discriminated, namely the dualist and the materialist. The principal divergence of the two views is whether cognitive processes really are segregated from physical processes (the dualist view) or the two aspects are inseparable in reality (the materialist view). In fact, most contemporary scholars are materialists, though, wherefore these are of main interest here. Materialist stances can be divided into two major groupings, namely the reductionist and the functionalist respectively, depending on the theoretical level of analysis. The point is that the cognitive system can be described and analyzed either at the level of neurons (the parts of the system) or at the level of the cognitive functions implemented by the neurons in cooperation. The reductionists investigate a particular aspect of the mind/brain at the neurological level of analysis, that is to say, at the level of the specific parts of the system. The functionalists, on the other hand, simply presuppose the neurological level while limiting their analyses to the cognitive level of functions. Hence, the connection of the physical and the cognitive is explained by the notion of implementation.

Mystical experience at once refers to actual mystical states of consciousness and some more constant changes in the subject, either resulting from the actual states or otherwise, that can be subsumed under the notion of mystical development. Mystical experience additionally involves a more purely conceptual aspect consisting in the continuous redescription of cognitive representations related to mystical states and mystical development. The process of representational redescription gradually results in more sophisticated and generalized conceptualizations of the redescribed cognitive representations.

Like other kinds of human experience, mystical experience emerges from the interaction of processes that can be described and analyzed at various levels, say, the neurological, the cognitive, and the cultural. The most basic level of analysis is the neurological where various aspects of mystical experience are related to particular processes (and products) in various parts of the neural system. At this level, the concern is the neuronal processes generating mystical consciousness and mystical development. Evidently, one needs to rely on evidence and theories of general aspects of neurology for the investigation of the mystical experience of John of the Cross. At the cognitive level of explanation, the components of mystical experience are related to various cognitive events like the consciousness of mystical conceptions or the related feelings and the developmental products of recurrent mystical states. These internal processes do not exist in isolation since a person must interact with the external environment. The more specific external environment of a person will therefore influence the the way that the life of that person forms. The mystical experience of an individual can be analyzed and described at the neurological, the cognitive, and the cultural level, but in the concrete life of a person, the three levels are intermingled and the respective internal processes and external events affect one another mutually. Mystical experience emerges from the interaction of activities in the internal system and the external environment.

Regarding the relation of the three levels of analysis and description, it is not a matter of reducing the one to the others or of determining one as the cause of the others. Each level affects and is affected by the others in a mutually interdependent relation of multiple causes and effects.[1] Accordingly, the concrete, mystical experience of a person is the total and very complex outcome of several interrelated and interdependent factors and processes. In order to clarify the matter somewhat, I shall propose a schematical outline of the relative abstractness and observability of processes and products at the diverse levels of description and analysis (see fig. 1).

From a theoretical perspective the development of the mind is extremely complex. Moreover, it is not possible to inquire into the actual processes causing development wherefore only the products comprise evidence for theorizing. Theoretical certainty at this extremely high level of abstraction is unrealizable. Still, the acknowledgement that only partial understanding with only some degree of certainty is attainable in this field of study should not keep scholars from exploring it. The elaboration of more and more nuanced and advanced theories of the mind and the development of it does contribute to an understanding of both. In spite of the relative uncertainty of cognitive theories — the degree of certainty depending on the level of abstraction and the evidence currently available — this field is so fundamental that it is related to and relevant for all humanist studies without exception. Considering the diversity of the relevant approaches, a simplified delineation and some exam-

---

1. See also Changeux and Dehaene (1993, 364 and 366).

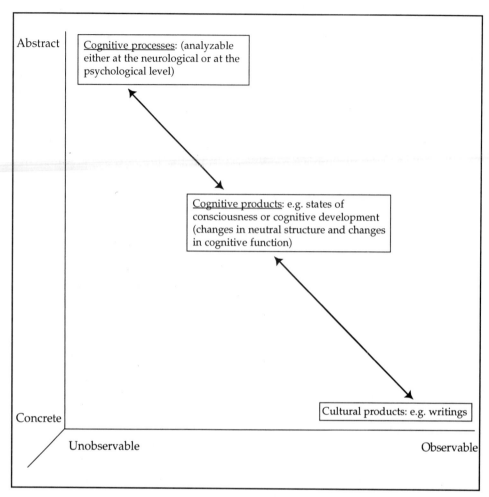

Fig. 1. Schematical presentation of the relation of processes and products at the diverse levels of analysis

ples of the interrelation of evidence and theories at the various levels of analysis may be illustrative (see fig. 2).

Most studies of development concern the normal, ordinary development of children from infancy to adolescence. This is no wonder, of course, since this is the period where the fundamental part of development normally is brought out. So, for good reasons few scholars have addressed the issue of adult development. Likewise, few scholars have addressed the topic of kinds of non-pathological development that exceed or deviate from the ordinary and

Levels	Examples of aspects of theories	Examples of evidence
Neurological	Changeux: Development is triggered and affected by experience	Measurable changes in neurological structure
Cognitive	Thelen and Smith: Development is triggered and affected by experience but motivated by desire. Karmiloff-Smith: Development is caused by spontaneous redescription of cognitive representations	Changes in performance and behaviour
Cultural	This author: The process of writing and interpretation accelerates the process of representational redescription and these two processes jointly cause conceptual development	The interpretational levels and layers in John of the Cross' Spiritual Canticle

Fig. 2. Delineation and examples of selected aspects of theories and evidence at the diverse levels of analysis

which often do not start before the ordinary has been, or almost has been, fulfilled. Various kinds of such non- or extraordinary development, that in most cases commence well after or during adolescence, can be mentioned. In the present context, a particular kind of extraordinary development, that is to say, mystical, is of primary concern. From the perspective of developmental theory, it is a new point on the agenda that grown-ups may *initiate* development of a particular kind that is not pathological. Even though it is certainly not the case that the majority of people unexpectedly start to develop a basically new ability or conceptual understanding in the middle of life, it is certainly not so uncommon as to have been predominantly ignored by scholars exploring human development (studies of pathological development aside). It is therefore time that we begin to address this important issue. And it is essential that the evidence is analyzed from a theoretical perspective in order to understand particular kinds of adult development, not only in isolation but also in relation to the development of children and in relation to other kinds of such adult development.[2]

The relation of the neurological and the cognitive level

It seems pertinent to initiate this section with a brief discussion of the relevance of neurological theories for the study of mysticism. It may indeed appear unnecessary to pick on neurological theories for an explanation of mysticism. Indeed, there are no grounds *of principle* for this. It is possible to make do with cognitive explanations alone. On the other hand, there are important theoretical reasons for it. Neurological evidence and theories may contribute to the understanding of cognitive abilities (like mystical abilities) because neuronal capacity delimits the ultimate possibilities of, and constraints on, cognitive abilities. Whether cognitive abilities are innate (but awaiting maturation), predisposed (and needing to be developed), or only potential, they presuppose (directly or indirectly corresponding) neuronal potentials. The neurological theories that I consider relevant for the study of mysticism explain general aspects of the cognitive system at the level of its parts, that is, they explain the neuronal processes and products out of which cognition emerges. Hence, the neurological level of description does, in principle, constitute the fundament of all other levels of description of cognition. Consequently, neurological theories are very flexible with respect to both transfer to other domains (like that of mysticism) and combination with other theories. And this is an inestimable advantage for the understanding of mysticism which is a highly underexplained field.

Cognition emerges out of neuronal actitivites. The analytical distinction of cognitive and neuronal processes and products does not imply that the two levels are separated in reality. The two levels do not function isolated, as cognitive functions emerge from, cause, and influence neuronal activity, just as neuronal activity generally results in cognitive functions. In practice, the neuronal is indistinguishable from the cognitive (or the physical from the psychological), yet it is most advantageous for scientific research to distinguish the two levels analytically.

One of the problems involved in the relation of the neurological and the cognitive levels of description and analysis is to explain how specific cognitive domains relate to neuronal structures. The principal question is, if specific abilities are directly related to equally specific neuronal structures. I shall not attempt to answer this here but only present two opposing views. J.-P.

---

2. The latter should be based on comparative studies and will not be of major concern in the following, even though it is an extremely important issue.

Changeux and S. Dehaene suggest (as a working hypothesis) that there is in fact a 'type-to-type physical identity' between levels of organization in the brain and cognitive processes. They stress that their attempt is to reconstruct cognitive functions from their neuronal components from a neurobiological perspective. It is not an attempt to reduce the one to the other (1993, 364). A. Gopnik and H.M. Wellman, on the contrary, hold that it is unlikely 'that all interesting cognitive domains will be the result of distinct neurological structures' (1994, 287-88). This may be interpreted to mean either that there is not a one-to-one (causal) relation of the neuronal and the cognitive levels, or that there is more to the cognitive than the neural (that is to say, that something extra, which does not involve neuronal processes, may arise from cognitive processes themselves). They develop their somewhat ambiguous statement, firstly, by referring to evidence furnished by connectionist models of the mind indicating that single, neural structures are the source of the performance of various, distinct tasks on the basis of which they conclude that cognitive domains will not reduce to neural domains and secondly, by stating that psychology will not neatly reduce to neurology. I take these declarations to mean that there is not a one-to-one causal relationship between the two levels and that they are not suggesting that something purely cognitive arises from cognition itself (a rather preposterous stance indeed).

I agree with Gopnik and Wellman that there is not necessarily a one-to-one relation of cognitive domains or functions and particular neural structures. And it is surely not a one directional causal relationship where the one simply causes the other (as neurological evidence shows). I also agree that psychology cannot be reduced to neurology. On the other hand, it would not make more sense to argue that cognitive states are the cause of neural states (reducing neurology to psychology) as this really does not catch the complexity of the relation. The relationship is much more nuanced and complicated than that and cannot be explained by causality. Cognition arises out of neuronal activity (anything else is pure idealism). But cognitive abilities cannot be explained by explaining neuronal or other physical processes and their interaction with the environment alone (Hornsby 1986, 115). Cognitive states need (and deserve) to be explained as cognitive. Cognitive states are based on and cannot do without neurological states but the former are not identical with the latter (Hornsby 1986, 96).

Theories of development

Predetermination and maturation or predisposition and development

Disagreeing cognitive theories first of all collide on one point which is the question of how the human neonate is equipped to handle the environment. This issue basically involves two closely connected elements, namely the degree of innate properties or predisposition and the character of the process of maturation or development.[3]

I shall now turn to a more specific discussion of evidence and theories of factors influencing cognitive development. The fundamental theoretical question concerns the extent to which (if at all) the mind is predetermined or predisposed to develop particular properties. Most scholars assume that humans are born either with some basic properties or the predisposition for developing them.[4] Numerous psychological experiments with babies have provided evidence of this. The trouble is whether the various results of such experiments should be interpreted as evidence of innate properties or predisposition for development. The problem is not only that experimentation with babies is difficult and yields rather uncertain and ambiguous (sometimes even opposing) results, leaving much to interpretation, but also that cognitive theorizing in general is impeded by the difficulty of studying the mind in any direct way. The ongoing processes in the mind are the concern of cognitive theories. Obviously, these cannot be investigated directly. Only the products of cognitive processes (ideas, concepts, images, and the like) can be explored empirically, more or less directly. But even these cognitive products set limits for scientific inquiries, inasmuch as they rarely present themselves unambiguously for direct study.

Cognitive psychologists continuously construct and carry out more and more advanced experiments especially with babies and young children in order to investigate early, cognitive development. Such experiments have shown that babies very early and prior to any instruction possess characteristic abilities for different kinds of categorization. Still, unless the experiments have been made with neonates, it is almost impossible to determine whether the properties are innate (in an immature form) or already at such early stages

3. Following A. Bates and J.L. Elman, the concept of maturation, as it is used by psychologists, 'refers to the timely appearance or unfolding of behaviours that are predestined, in their structure and their sequence, by a well-defined genetic program.' In the same place, they refer a definition of development suggesting that it is a process leading to an increase in the number of parts of the system and an increase in the organization of the parts (1993, 624). In my view, it is not necessarily the case that the developmental product of an extended process at any point involves both an increase in the number and organization of the parts, even if that may be the result at the end of the process.

4. The influential neuroscientist, Edelman is one of the few (even if he is somewhat ambiguous on the point) maintaining a view that the mind of a human neonate is like a tabula rasa (for a review see Plotkin 1991, especially 488-89).

have been developed in more or less individual ways on the basis of pre-disposition, since even a few hours of exposure to particular stimuli may initiate predisposed development. A tabula rasa theorist would further argue for the possibility that the properties have been developed individually from the ground in response to experience, in which case the resulting similarities would be due to an invariant environment. Aiming to inquire into the possible innate properties of the mind, it is necessary to attend to the abilities of babies born within very few hours. As such evidence is scarce, so is our knowledge of the matter. I shall only discuss the question of innate or predisposed properties briefly, though, as it is not a matter of primary concern for the understanding of adult development.

Many experiments have been devoted to the aim of showing that the minds of babies are far from being blank slates. According to many cognitive psychologists, even neonates have some initial knowledge about the world and its inhabitants. The argument is that infants possess knowledge in the form of 'core principles' that are specific for the various domains of the mind and which enable the infant to generalize about the environment. For example, even young babies have the basic knowledge about action that objects move according to principles of cohesion, contact, and contiguity. Based on this fundamental knowledge about action, babies know that an inanimate object cannot start moving by itself but needs the aid of an agent (Carey and Spelke 1994, 175). Likewise, psychological experiments attempting to investigate postnatal processing of auditory input have shown that 12-hour-old infants are able to discriminate linguistic sounds from other sounds. Furthermore, it has been shown that 4-day-old (but *not* 12-hour-old) infants are sensitive to dif-ferences between languages (for a detailed summary of these experiments, see Karmiloff-Smith 1992, 36-37).

In general, the theoretical arguments for and against strong nativism concern the limits of individual and cultural variation. More concretely, the debate converges on whether the concepts of basic knowledge are subject to change or not. Is the domain of specific 'core principles' changeable or not? Evidence is increasing of the ability of very young children to generalize and categorize (construct 'theories') for specific domains. But evidence helping to solve the problem about exactly when and how a particular kind of knowledge comes into an infant's head is still very deficient. One of the real problems facing cognitive theories of development is that all evidence can be interpreted as supporting opposite theories. The ambiguity of interpretation is, of course, a general obstacle for theorizing but for cognitive theories the problem is specifically linked to two factors, namely; 1) the above mentioned gap between the object of study (cognitive processes) and evidence (cognitive products), and 2) the instability of cognitive products, that is, the dynamic and changing character of percepts, concepts, and images.

The evidence of an infant's ability to discriminate language, illustrates the problem of interpretation very well. As support of a strong nativist position, it can be argued that there is an innate language module in the mind enabling the neonate to identify language and the slightly matured infant to discriminate between languages. Yet, the evidence could also be interpreted to support a theory of development affected by experience. Here two possibilites should be acknowledged. Either, the evidence could be an indication that the ability to identify linguistic sounds is innate but combines with a rapid development for which the infant is predisposed and which makes it possible for the baby to distinguish one language from another.[5] Or, the evidence may be interpreted to indicate that humans do not possess innate properties for language processing but that they are predisposed for the development of a specific language domain. Considering the rapid (3½ days) improvement in auditory input processing, it would not be surprising if development had similarly taken place during the first 12 hours after birth (assuming that the infant actually hears people talking) not to mention a possible pre-natal developmental change.[6]

Naturally, it is not possible to generalize from the scarce evidence of one single, cognitive domain. Still, the evidence that even very young infants have some ability for language discrimination strongly indicates that humans either are born with some fundamental properties of specific domains or that the development of these properties is strongly predisposed. The evidence of extremely rapid improvements in infants' abilities further indicate that if some properties actually are innate then these are only very fundamental and effectively supported and complemented with development that is facilitated by predisposition. In general, I think that evidence is much too weak to determine whether the more fundamental properties are innate or pre-disposed. Contrary to this, the evidence against the more extreme positions, namely strong nativism and tabula rasa theories, is very convincing.

Whether developmental processes are described in terms of maturation or development depends on the theoretical stance regarding the mind's postnatal condition. Scholars adopting a strong nativist stance tend to understand postnatal processes as maturation or enrichment of innate properties that are

5. This hypothesis is supported by M.H. Johnson's research on face recognition (see e.g., Johnson 1993, 703-18).
6. Thus, as Karmiloff-Smith points out, why were nine months of exposure to a native language not sufficient to enable the neonate to discriminate it from other languages? (1992, 37). Actually, six months might be more to the point as the embryo is incapable of hearing the first couple of months.

specific for the various domains of the mind. The way that maturation will unfold is already predetermined, so, even though it is initiated (or 'triggered') by experience, the specific outcome of maturation is not determined or even influenced by experience (Bates and Elman 1993, 624). Researchers additionally disagree on the issue of which specific domains that are equipped with a basic knowledge at birth and which are not, as well as on the question of how well they are equipped.[7] Opposing the stronger nativist theories are a wide and varied range of theories that are bound by the point of view that the human mind at birth not only awaits maturation but a highly unpredictable developmental process. In accordance with such theories, development will be affected by the concrete experience that an individual is exposed to. The extent to which experience is assumed to influence development depends on the theory in question.

Without making too strong a point out of it, it should also be mentioned that diverging definitions of the term *learning* are related respectively to the maturational versus the developmental views of postnatal processes. S. Carey and E. Spelke, for instance, view learning as enrichment of innate knowledge or 'core principles' in their terms (1994, 169, and 179). Here Carey and Spelke use learning synonymously with maturation (as it is defined by Bates and Elman) seemingly preferring the term learning for that of maturation. Contrary to this view, Bates and Elman sum up three typical definitions of learning as (1) systematic, behavioural change due to experience, (2) acquisition of knowledge, or (3) a shaping of behaviour resulting from experience (1993, 624). In my view, the first is not a defintion of learning but of development. The third, on the other hand, is much too weak a definition (as also noticed by Bates and Elman) to be useful in a scientific context. In fact it is almost indistinguishable from the 'folk theoretical' notion of 'bringing up' a child.[8] In concordance with both A. Clark and Changeux, I take learning to be storage of information synonymous with acquisition of knowledge (Clark 1991; Changeux 1985). Learning is not an arbitrary process, though, as it is not all information that is stored in memory. Hence, the process of learning is highly selective (Changeux 1985, 139).[9]

7. A very good overview of the diversities of nativist positions is given in *Mapping the Mind*, which is a collection of papers from a symposium on cognitive psychology (Hirschfeld and Gelman 1994).
8. 'Folk theory' is a commonly used concept in cognitive theories and does *not* refer to theories used by the 'folk'. It refers to the everyday 'theories' used by all human beings. Hence, the distinction of 'folk' and 'scientific' theories is a distinction in kind. For example, see Clark 1991, ch. 3, for a discussion of 'folk' theories.
9. As opposed to this view, G. Edelman considers learning to be instructional whereas he regards memory as selective. Probably, this disagreement arises from Edelman's rather

A further disagreement between strong nativist and developmentalist theories concerns the relation of specific domains. Nativists hold that the domains are informationally encapsulated modules implying that there is no communication between them at all. Contrary to that, Karmiloff-Smith, for instance, argues that domains become specified (and supposedly not modularized) through development (see Karmiloff-Smith 1992 for a full discussion). The controversy between nativists and non-nativists is particularly relevant for an understanding of human development since informational encapsulation would be a hindrance for conceptual change. Contrary to that, continuous communication between specific domains would allow and facilitate conceptual changes.

Domain specific development

Most cognitive theories of development agree that the human mind incorporates a number of specific domains related to dissimilar domains of knowledge and behaviour.[10] Cognitive theories disagree, on the other hand, with respect to the degree of specialization of the domains of neonates and the degree of interdomain communication. Roughly, the divergence of the theoretical positions may be delineated as implying either a high degree of initial specialization with very little or no communication among cognitive

---

    problematic definition of learning as necessarily involving a teacher (see Plotkin 1991, 495).

10. Due to the very varied uses of the concept 'behaviour' a brief discussion of it is germane. J. Hornsby criticizes the more extreme definitions of it and suggests one that does not totally disregard common sense knowledge (that is to say, 'folk psychology'). At the one extreme, she criticizes the use of the concept according to which behaviour refers to both physical and mental outputs or, as she puts it, 'both a brain's output and a person's output' (1986, 96). In my view, the problem with this concept primarily ensues from the considerable breadth of it. With this concept, all internal human processes and their products can be included in the concept of behaviour. The concept is undifferentiated, inclusive, and imprecise. At the other extreme, Hornsby criticizes the (functionalist) concept of behaviour defining it as referring to bodily movements but not actions (as these generally are intentional and presuppose beliefs and desires). Accordingly, behaviour does not denote action, but only effects of actions (1986, 99 and onwards). Truly, this concept is stringent, easy-to-handle, and easy-to-define. Yet, instead of proposing an equally stringent definition of behaviour, Hornsby advices cognitive theorists to stick more closely to the less definite everyday use of the concept denoting actions, or more precisely, that which an agent does (Hornsby 1986; Clark 1991, ch. 3; Barsalou 1992, introduction). With this concept of behaviour, the object that the concept covers is easily delimited, that is to say, action. But action is itself somewhat less definite than, say, bodily movements as it does not isolate the purely physical aspects to the absolute exclusion of the intentional.

domains or a lower degree of initial specialization and a higher degree of communication among domains. As opposed to this basic disagreement, though, most theorists agree on a number of other fundamental points. It is thus rather generally assumed that the communicative connections with other domains vary considerably from domain to domain. Similarly, it is a general assumption that the diverse cognitive domains are developed separately.

In the following, I shall present the cognitive theory of domain specific development suggested by the psychologist A. Karmiloff-Smith. She suggests that the degree of predisposition or predetermination for specialization varies considerably among, and even within, the diverse domains. The more specific developmental processes will therefore also vary from one cognitive domain to another. Several aspects of developmental processes are similar for all cognitive domains, though. This means that it is possible to describe and explain these aspects of the progression of the development of the human mind in general. In *Beyond Modularity*, Karmiloff-Smith (1992) proposes to describe and explain the processes resulting in the cognitive development of children.

Before turning to a presentation of Karmiloff-Smith's theory it is worthwhile first to consider the more fundamental aspects of the concept of a cognitive domain and the development of it. The theory implies that a cognitive domain initially needs to undergo some basic development for the processing of information for which it is predisposed or predetermined. As development proceeds, the domain becomes gradually more specialized for the processing of the specific information. Along with this development, the domain gradually builds up the sets of representations of information that will constitute the developed domain. At some point, this part of the developmental process results in the mastery of the behaviour sustained by the specific, cognitive domain.

Behavioural mastery is the point of departure for the developmental processes of major concern in Karmiloff-Smith's theory. The notion of behavioural mastery is therefore essential to the theory. In her definition, the notion implies that a particular behaviour is mastered (implying that it can be performed automatically but without flexibility) and the sustaining domain stabilized (implying that the representations have attained some degree of stability). More specifically, she illustrates her points with the example of learning to play the piano. The mastery of playing a piece on the piano is reached when the whole piece can be played automatically from beginning to end. Although, at that point, the person is not yet able to play only part of the piece, play variations of a theme, or mix it with other pieces. There is still no flexibility of the behaviour (1992, 16).

For most cognitive theorists the mastery of some behaviour is the final product of the development of a domain. Yet, for Karmiloff-Smith it is the starting point of a developmental process that differs qualitatively from that of knowledge acquisition and the specialization of a domain. The essence of the developmental process leading to behavioural mastery is the acquisition of new knowledge in the form of cognitive representations. The developmental process going beyond behavioural mastery involves the recurrent redescriptions of the acquired representations. The theory aims at describing and explaining the cognitive processes of representational redescription. According to Karmiloff-Smith, a cognitive domain is composed of several micro-domains. During the process of representational redescription, the sets of representations constituting the various micro-domains are repeatedly redescribed in asynchronous phases. The products of the process are increasingly more compressed and less detailed re-representations of the information. Through redescription, the representations are changed into more abstract formats permitting greater cognitive flexibility due to the increasing accessibility of information to other parts of the cognitive system than the part storing the representations. The processes of representational redescription are domain general implying that the processes operate in the same way in all of the cognitive domains. Yet, the process is implemented in the diverse domains at different times and is constrained by the content and the format of the representations of the specific domains and micro-domains.

More specifically, Karmiloff-Smith suggests that development involves at least three phases of processing the same information. The first phase is that of knowledge acquisition and leads to behavioural mastery. During this phase, focus is directed at information obtained from one's own environment, and new representations are added to the existing representations without changing these. The developmental processes leading to behavioural change are (typically) promoted by conflict which means that negative feedback about own errors promotes further development. The second phase initiates the redescription of representations and renders representations more abstract but, at the same time, it often results in behavioural regress as well. During this phase, focus is directed at internal representations that are redescribed into a new form. As opposed to the processes resulting in behavioural change, the processes of representational redescription are typically fostered by positive feedback about own successes.

The third phase is the continuation of representational redescription and results in increasing consciousness and accessibility of knowledge and the regain of behavioural perfection. During this phase, internal representations are combined with information from the external environment.

With respect to the products of representational redescription, Karmiloff-

Smith stresses the point that each new representational format is added to the existing format(s). For instance, the more abstract representations do not supersede the more detailed, perceptual representations. Karmiloff-Smith suggests that knowledge is represented in at least four formats. In the terminology of the theory, the first level is the *Implicit* corresponding to the developmental point of behavioural mastery. At this level, the representations are detailed and perceptual and there are no connections permitting intra- or interdomain communication. The second level is termed *Explicit-1*. At this level, the representations of the *Implicit* level are compressed into a new and simplified format. There are potential intra- and interdomain links but as yet there is not any conscious access to representations and they are not formed into language. The third level is termed *Explicit-2*. The representations of this level are redescriptions of the representations at level *Explicit-1*. There is now conscious access to representations but they are not yet formed into language. The final level is termed *Explicit-3* and is the level where the redescribed representations of the previous level are consciously accessible and in linguistic form (Karmiloff-Smith 1992, ch.1).

Karmiloff-Smith underscores the point that the developmental processes until the point of behavioural mastery and the processes of representational redescription yield two kinds of developmental products. The initial processes of knowledge acquisition result in behavioural change, whereas representational redescription results in representational change (see Karmiloff-Smith 1992, 19 where the relation of the two dissimilar developmental processes are represented graphically).

I would suggest that the two qualitatively dissimilar developmental processes be termed 'behavioural' and 'conceptual' development, respectively, yielding either change in behaviour or concepts.[11]

Cognitive plasticity explained at the level of neurons

Having acknowledged the importance of investigating the degrees of disposition and possible innate properties for an understanding of development in general, I shall now turn to theories of development focusing on the question about what it is that permits the cognitive system to respond to experience. This ability is generally termed plasticity and can be studied either

---

11. For the purpose of studying the developmental changes involved in mystical experience on the basis of religious texts, the more general term 'concept' is more suitable as reference to actual changes identifiable through the analysis of works like those of John of the Cross, than the more psychologically precise term 'representation'.

at the neurological or the cognitive level of analysis. In the following, I shall present selected aspects of neurological theories and evidence that are relevant for the understanding of mystical experience. Very little is known about the neuronal processes from which mystical states and mystical development emerge, and obviously nothing is known about this with regard to John of the Cross in particular. In this chapter, selected neurological theories of development are addressed to the extent relevant for a construction of a theory on John of the Cross' mystical experience, insofar as this can be reconstructed from his own testimony. Accordingly, the concern is not neurological theories and evidence of mysticism, but general aspects of the brain's processes.

Initially, I shall consider some of the more general, theoretical questions about the plasticity enabling cognitive development. The reason why these very general matters are relevant for the study of John of the Cross (and the other way round) is that mystical development drops right into the heart of the debate about the degrees of brain plasticity and innate cognitive equipment. In my opinion, the possibility of diverse kinds of extraordinary (say, mystical) abilities initiated in adulthood is in itself an important argument for some degree of plasticity in the adult brain. And this in turn is an argument for some degree of preceding plasticity of the brain of newborn and older children. If there was no plasticity in the brain of a neonate, it would be unlikely that plasticity should suddenly emerge in an adult brain. Hence, some degree of plasticity in the brains of neonates is a precondition for the preservation of plasticity throughout life. And the preservation of some degree of plasticity is a precondition for unpredictable development initiated in adulthood. On the other hand, plasticity in the brains of newborns is no guarantee of any degree of plasticity in the brains of adults. In my view, the concrete study of John of the Cross' mystical development may contribute to an understanding of lifelong development as a complex and multicausal process where innate predisposition and experience-related factors combine.

With respect to the fundamental conditions of human life, like normal development and the cohesion of social groups, there are conspicuous developmental advantages in both predisposition and plasticity. On the one hand, innate predisposition (or even better, but also involving more problems, predetermination) fosters the development of an individual and makes him/her more efficient. Furthermore, it guarantees some degree of common properties among individuals. The more innate predisposition or predetermination, the broader the shared knowledge of the species. Some shared knowledge is essential for social life, communication, and maintenance of stability within the various groups of a species. On the other hand, neuronal plasticity enables experience-dependent development, generally termed 'epigenesis' in neuro-logical literature, which facilitates both individual and group adaptation to changes in the external environment. Adaptability is the *sine qua non* for survival, both at the level of the individual and at the level of the group. However, epigenetic development is simultaneously the fundament of exten-sive variability which hardly enhances group cohesion and maintenance of social stability. Thus, there are advantages and disadvantages with both innateness and plasticity. The advantages of innate predisposition and epi-genesis are complementary and non-overlapping, inasmuch as the goals of the two types of processes are different. The innate predisposition for the deve-lopment of certain properties and not others constrains development and thus inhibits plasticity and reduces variability. The more specific the predisposition is, the less plasticity there will be — and the other way round. The variations in the environment comprise a third factor regulating variations within and between human groups. If most individuals are exposed to a relatively un-varied environment, then epigenetic processes will barely result in drastic vari-ations. Thus, epigenesis may in many situations contribute to non-variation and shared knowledge (just like predisposition or predetermination). Differen-ces in the environment of groups and individuals therefore comprise a major factor in the complex determination of the degree of variation as opposed to common properties. Very often the environment is highly similar for indivi-duals within a group, whereas — generally — it differs considerably more between groups. Presumably, the degree of common knowledge and abilities would only be very basic, if it were not the case that the invariance of the environment contributed to this goal. As mentioned, it is a precondition for the individual development of mystical abilities in adulthood that some minimum degree of brain plasticity is maintained long after puberty. And for this to be possible some plasticity must exist from the beginning. At the neurological level, several questions can be asked about plasticity:

1) In which way is the neural system plastic? This is a very general problem and the one that most of the existing theories are concerned with.
2) Does plasticity persevere? And, if so —
3) How does the neural system preserve plasticity?

The latter two aspects of plasticity are very important for later development, and thus for the capacity to develop mystical abilities in adulthood. Evidently, a discussion of them must take its point of departure in some basic under-standing of what there is to preserve, wherefore a presentation of theories attempting to answer the first question seems germane.

Neuronal competition — the foundation of plasticity

The first question is *how* the neural system is capable of responding to experience. Which neuronal processes permit the brain to be plastic? A coherent and very convincing general theory of neural plasticity has been proposed by Changeux (1985; Changeux and Dehaene, 1993).[12] A general premise for the theory is the notion that the cognitive and the neural aspects of internal processes are inherently intertwined and mutually interdependent (see e.g. Changeux and Dehaene 1993, 379).

The theory is that the human brain develops through epigenetic processes of selection determined by experience. The point of departure of the neural system is what he terms the 'genetic envelope' which determines which neuronal processes will be brought out, and in which way, as well as it controls the unfolding of the processes. The synaptic connections of neurons (the junctions where the information 'paths' leading to and from neurons meet) are the focus of early, neural development as they comprise the centre of neuronal communication. In the words of Changeux, 'The final tuning of the adult neural network takes place at the ultimate communication channel between neurons — the synapse' (1985, 223). Changeux explains that in early development, the neural system is characterized by extensive redundancy and diversity (and hence disorder) among synaptic connections in the neural network. This redundancy is caused by an over-production of synapses in early development. During this period in which the degree of redundancy is very high, the system is not stable yet. Redundancy is rapidly reduced, though, through the selection of synaptic survivors and losers in the network. As development proceeds, the synapses gradually reduce in number and settle in an ordered pattern (Greenough et al. 1993, 295-96). In this way, through selective processes, order and stability emerge from disorder and instability.

According to the theory, selection is regulated by neuronal activities arising from interneuronal communication. Those neurons firing most actively in response to input are selected whereas inactive or less active neurons are eliminated. The activities of the neurons may be spontaneous as neural systems constantly are active, but generally neuronal activities are evoked and regulated by interaction with the environment. In this way, neurons modify spontaneous firing as a function of input (Changeux and Dehaene 1993, 366

12. Basically, Changeux's theory is in agreement with Edelman's theory of neural plasticity, although the two theories diverge on major points, for example concerning the condition of the brain at birth (see Changeux 1993, 374; Plotkin 1991, 488-89).

and Changeux 1985, 83 and 134). Through these *epigenetic* processes, the 'development of neuronal singularities are controlled by the activity of the developing network' as Changeux puts it (1985, 229).

Selective and stabilizing processes unfold in phases successively moving across the diverse regions of the neural system. These phases presumably correspond in some way or other (but not necessarily directly) to some of the sensitive periods of learning and the various phases of cognitive development. The developmental phases of childhood are related to various abilities and performances and together comprise one long sensitive period. The duration of the periods during which stabilization takes place is itself influenced by experience. Stimulation and experience influence not only the quality of the product resulting from development but also the efficiency of the developmental process. Thus, deprivation from relevant sensory stimulation seems to prolong the sensitive period of the development of a particular ability (Greenough et al. 1993, 298).[13]

The fundament of the theory of epigenesis is that it is the experience of an individual in combination with innate predisposition that determine the adult phenotypic, neural structure. It is the epigenetic processes in the neural system that result in plasticity and thus in variability. The variability from which individual variations emerge is thereby intrinsic as the epigenetic processes themselves are inscribed in the genetic envelope.

It should be emphasized that the variability of neuronal organization apparently enhances as a result of evolution. This means that variability increases in parallel with the increasing complexity of neural systems (Changeux 1985, 212 and 227). P.R. Huttenlocher attempts to explain this based on evidence of the development of *more simple* versus *more complex* brains, respectively. In simple neural systems, *programmed* neuron death is a major factor of development, contrary to the development of complex systems, where it is synaptic elimination *based on experience* (as proposed by Changeux) that is important for development. Huttenlocher further suggests that the reason why programmed neuron death is unnecessary for the development of complex brains is that it is presumably easier for developing neurons to find a target of innervation (and thus a means of survival) in a system of great diversity and complexity than in a simple system (1993, 120).

Furthermore, it should be pointed out that variability only describes possibility, not necessity. Variability makes individual differences possible, thereby permitting cultural diversion at another level, but it does not pre-

---

13. This is also supported by evidence from P. Marler's research on the development of birds' ability to sing which shows that deprivation from stimulation of conspecific song seriously prolongs the sensitive period (1993, 475).

determine a certain, not even a minimum, amount of actual variation. Almost inescapably, some diversion will result from the variability inscribed in the process but whether the products (individuals, cultures, or specific aspects of the latter) will differ to a greater or lesser extent depends on the context and is therefore arbitrary (to the extent that genetic predisposition and variability permits). In connection with this, it should further be emphasized that variations at one level (neuronal organization, for instance) are not necessarily related to corresponding variations at another level (say, behavioural and performative abilities). Accordingly, different inputs may cause distinct neural systems (organization and function in particular), but similar behavioural capacities. In this way, the dissimilar experiences of individuals may lead to similar performative abilities, although based on dissimilar neural structures (Changeux 1985, 247). Hence, considerable differences in the concrete internal organization of particular brains do not necessarily result in differences between the outputs that the individuals concerned are capable of producing.

Moreover, it seems that the way that experience influences the neural system of an individual varies considerably. So, different inputs are apt to cause differences in neural structure at the same time as *identical* inputs may cause differences in neural structure. However rudimentary the existing organization of a developing neural system is, it structures the input that it receives and imposes a certain order on it (Greenough, et al. 1993). Greenough, et al. give an example of how the condition of existing neural structures may affect the way that stimulation influences their further development. Salient differences in the neural structure of areas processing auditory information result from the processing of similar input in sighted and visually deprived individuals, respectively (as experiments with animals show) (1993, 299). Inquiring into the potentials of human development, it is important to understand how much the development of neural systems and the products of such development are contingent on the particular experiential background of the individual in question. Stressing this involves the risk of giving the impression that this is (nearly) all there is to development. And this is hardly the case as the evidence of innate properties and/or predispositions clearly shows.

In general, human development presumably arises out of an extremely complex web of interacting neuronal processes relating in highly unpredictable ways to cognitive functions. In extension of this, it should once again be emphasized that some specific behavioural output not necessarily correlates, let alone reflects, specific aspects of the internal organization of a particular brain.

The preservation of plasticity

With respect to the development of mystical abilities, the main concern is the issue of the preservation of neuronal plasticity. An attempt to clarify the question about how long plasticity is preserved in the neural system necessitates a discussion of evidence indicating that plasticity is not restricted to childhood and that some degree of plasticity really is retained throughout life. Still, it should be pointed out that the actual development of mystical abilities inititated in adulthood[14] in itself comprises striking evidence for the existence of some kind of neuronal plasticity in human adults.

A very remarkable body of neurological evidence of the preservation of plasticity derives from studies of the capacity of adult primates' to learn fundamentally new kinds of behaviour. A team of researchers, M.M. Merzenich, W.M. Jenkins, G. Recanzone, and colleagues, have carried out various experiments exposing monkeys to new and unusual stimulations and demands, followed by electrophysiological 'mappings' of changes in neural structure. The experiments have focused on changes in cortical areas related to altered use of the hands arising from (1) amputation of a digit, (2) fusion (suturing) of two digits, (3) reseparation of the fused digits, and finally, (4) training in diverse tasks of tactile discrimination. All of the experiments document that the neocortex has a remarkable capacity to respond to functional changes in the use of the hands. Merzenich et al. express these changes in terms of reorganization of cortical representations in areas (specific somatosensory fields) in the neural system resulting from altered inputs due to the diverse changes in the conditions of the use of the hands.

Merzenich et al. propose a very general hypothesis that neuronal plasticity is inherent and results from normal, lifelong, neocortical processes of mammalian brains. The results from the training of monkeys in very specific tasks constitute the most important evidence for this general aspect of the theory. The evidence from experiments inflicting injuries on the animals only show that changes occur as a consequence of physical, pathological disturbances. The evidence from the specific training, on the contrary, strongly support the hypothesis that neuronal plasticity is perfectly normal (Merzenich et al. 1990, 873, Jenkins et al. 1990 (a), 574, and (b), 82). They conclude that experience alters the neural structure (the cortical maps, in their terms) in general, at least in the neocortex (subcortical structures have proven to be less plastic). In short, the evidence indicates that cortical structures at any point

---

14. I admit that it can be discussed whether mystical development really is *initiated* in adulthood as all evidence is open to interpretation. In my view, though, there is no doubt that John of the Cross started developing his mystical abilities as a grown man. I would suggest that probably it is not only mystical development that typically is initiated in adolescence or adulthood but also the development of other kinds of extraordinary abilities like that of shamanism, possession etc.

reflect (or represent) the life lived by the individual concerned.

The evidence from the experiments carried out by Merzenich and his colleagues not only supports the more general theory but also contributes to an understanding of more specific aspects of neuronal plasticity. Especially, the experiments involving no injuries reveal important aspects of learning and individual variability. As could be expected, the intense training during the experiments has (generally) led to improvement in performance of the tasks concerned. The analysis of the cause of this improvement is particularly elucidating. According to the researchers, the initial stage of the improvement results from the learning of an efficient strategy and the generalization of behaviour. The second stage of improvement is, on the contrary, caused by changes in neural structure.[15] Concerning these stages, it is important to point out that the cognitive learning of a strategy results in a very rapid improvement whereas the subsequent neuronal changes engender a more gradual performative improvement (Recanzone et al. 1992, 1022 and 1027). The point that the two aspects of learning, the changes in cognitive ability and neural structure, respectively, complement and succeed one another in stages, yields important insights into the potential elements of development. Moreover, it suggests at least one reason why development unfolds in stages and substages. But it also complicates this (already complicated) topic further, even if coincidentally throwing new light on it.

Another aspect of the performative improvement resulting from the specific training is that the learned behaviour is 'forgotten' after some time if stimulation is discontinued (Recanzone et al. 1992, 1022). This indicates that learning is temporary and that the knowledge enabling a certain kind of behaviour needs to be reacquired more or less frequently. This reservation apart, the forgetting of learned behaviour is most probably related to a reduction (or disappearance) of the changes in neural structure once the specific stimulation is discontinued. The changes in neural structure resulting from new ways of behaviour have indeed proven to either reduce or totally disappear after some time (Jenkins et al. 1990 (b), 98-99). Accordingly, it appears that learning only affects neural structure as long as the learned abilities are in use, which is consistent with the theory that it is the neuronal activities that affect neural structures.

The above presented research further clarifies the issue of the degree of plasticity. It shows that it is the very concrete experience of an individual that influences the neural structure. The experiments give evidence of significant

---

15. The evidence indicates that part of the improvement in performance directly correlates changes in (that is to say, enlargement of) the cortical area (of representation) in question (Recanzone et al. 1992, 1040).

individual variabilities in neural structure (Recanzone et al. 1992, 1039). Furthermore, the research has documented considerable, if not extreme, variations in learning *periods* (Recanzone et al. 1992, 1028). Still, it should be repeated that variability not necessarily causes variation and that variations in neuronal structure need not result in behavioural variations.

Plasticity changes with age

All in all, there is strong evidence that mammalian brains are plastic and that some plasticity is maintained throughout life. The problem is to explain how human brains remain plastic. W.T. Greenough et al. have put forward an hypothesis that experience may influence neural phenotype in two different ways. It is a challenging theory of how neuronal plasticity probably *changes* with age. The first kind of plasticity is termed *experience-expectant* and secures that the anatomy of (mammalian) brains of all members of a species are influenced by experience in very much the same way because this kind of plasticity is strongly constrained by predisposed expectations. Experience-expectant plasticity primarily characterizes early development as it unfolds in young children. At the neurological level, experience-expectant plasticity can be explained with the theory of epigenetic processes which are enabled by an over-production of synaptic connections followed by a selection of those synapses that are most fit for survival, leaving the lesser fit to die. Experience-expectant, neuronal processes are oriented towards types of information in the environment to which all individuals are normally exposed (light and darkness, for instance).

The second kind of plasticity is termed *experience-dependent*. This is far less constrained by genetic predispositions than the experience-expectant and permits experience to influence the neural structure of an individual in unique ways. This kind of neuronal plasticity is particularly important for the understanding of adult development (like mystical) because it is developed on the basis of individual experience. Experience-dependent neuronal processes are oriented towards information in the environment that is relevant for the individual, in particular, and it is contingent upon very concrete conditions. The hypothesis is that experience-dependent plasticity is enabled through the generation of new synaptic connections and primarily (if not only) relies on the generation of new synapses in response to particular stimulation demanding new reactions from the system (as opposed to the automatic over-production of synapses in early development). It is possible that a minor over-production of synapses is involved also in this type of plasticity but, if this is the case, then the system needs to secure such over-production constantly as it cannot predict when more synapses will be needed for selection (Greenough et al. 1993). The theory provides an explanation of highly individualized kinds of adult development.[16] One problem with much of the neurological evidence, though, is that it is not necessarily based on studies of human, neural systems.[17] Huttenlocher's research in the development of human brains based on morphometric studies[18] is therefore of major interest. Greenough et al. have provided evidence that neural systems (even if more simple than those of humans) are capable of generating new synaptic connections throughout life in ways that change with age. In addition to this, Huttenlocher presents evidence that adult humans have a capacity for elongating the neuronal pathways (the dendrites) bringing messages from one neuron to another. He suggests that this capacity works to compensate for the inescapable loss of neurons in old age (1993, 119). Altogether it seems to be the ability to expand the web of inter-neuronal communication that persists (and maybe even improves?) throughout life.

Summing up the point, it is fairly certain that plasticity is preserved throughout life in some way or other, at least in parts of the brain. As mentioned earlier, Greenough, et al., suggest that it is the experience-dependent plasticity that makes adult development possible. They further suggest that not all neural regions are capable of developing in adulthood. In

16. The experience-dependent plasticity forms a basis for the capacity for neural development also far beyond the period of the normal development of children. But the ability to generate new synapses is not in itself sufficient for such development as the system also needs to be capable of continuously supplying the synapses with blood. Concerning this issue, Greenough, et al., have shown that the ability to support an increasing amount of synapses with blood does not necessarily fit the ability to generate the synapses. Normally, the blood supply is adapted to the number of synapses but if an adult (a rat in the experimental case) is exposed to a *major* change from a non-stimulating to a highly stimulating and demanding environment, then the neural system is incapable of keeping up the support of blood for the increasing amount of synapses. On the basis of their research, Greenough, et al., conclude that the capacity for supporting new synapses declines with age (1993, 319-21).

17. Presumably, there is no risk in assuming that what holds good for more simple brains lower on the evolutionary scale also holds good for more complex brains higher (and highest) on the scale. But since neuronal complexity is the fundament of adaptability (made possible by the capacity to learn from experience) it is likely that human brains possess kinds of neuronal plasticity that more simple brains do not possess (Cf. Clark 1991, ch. 4). The average duration of life of a species may also affect the relative plasticity or rigidity of the neural system in old age just as it may affect the actual complexity of the system. Huttenlocher discusses these and other problems involved in the transfer of evidence from lower to higher animal brains (1993, 120). According to him, we should expect plasticity to be retained to a far greater extent in complex than in simple neural systems.

18. Confer Huttenlocher for a discussion of the problems implied in this method which does not give a dynamic picture of neural systems (1993, 119-20).

correspondence with their theory, the generation of new synaptic connections is very localized (as opposed to the automatic over-production of synapses in childhood) and occurs in direct response to neuronal activities related to information processing (1993). A consequence of the theory is that any kind of cognitive development in adults is only potential and that the actual unfolding of it depends on the particular experience of an individual. If the theory is correct, it explains why the development of some kind of extraordinary ability is (1) in general rather uncommon, and (2) much more common in some cultures and some historical periods than in others, inasmuch as particular cultures may emphasize this element in various ways.

IV. Conditions affecting the credibility of evidence of mystical experience

As I have emphasized before, John of the Cross' mystical experience involves recurrent mystical states and mystical development. Presumably, he has redescribed both of these aspects of his experience representationally over an extended period and only then communicated the product of the process of redescription. In the present context, the concern is not so much the actual redescriptive and communicative processes or the resulting products, but the cognitive constraints on those processes. The reason why this issue needs to be taken into accout is that the cognitive constraints have set the bounds of the potential processes of redescription and communication and therefore also of the products of these which make up the existing evidence of John of the Cross' mystical experience.

Cognitive constraints on communication

Communication of mystical experience does not differ from that of other experience.[1] It follows the rules and constraints of all human communication.[2] It also works by the same means as other interpersonal communication.[3] Communication is contingent on various factors wherefore it needs to be adapted to various conditions in order to be successful. Firstly, the respective backgrounds of the sender and the receiver, and their relationship, are significant. This aspect of communication may be evident but should nonetheless be pointed out. It is particularly important for the communication of mystical and other extraordinary experience because it is extraordinary and thus shared

1. This needs to be emphasized because several scholars of John of the Cross (in agreement with James' ineffability criterion) have defended the specificity of communicating mystical experience (e.g. Baruzi 1942; Orozco 1959, 176; López-Baralt 1978, 19, 20 and 28; Wilhelmsen 1980, 315).
2. For a treatment of such rules, see Shannon and Weaver (1963); Sperber and Wilson (1988).
3. For a theory of those means, see Johnson (1987) and Lakoff (1987). For a presentation of a hypothesis of the processes underlying the generation of meaning, see Clark (1991, ch. 6). And for a discussion of the importance of the context of meaning, see Lawson and McCauley (1990, ch. 6).

by only a number of individuals.[4] The lack of commonality of experience imposes extra demands on communication. Thus, both the sender and the receiver will need to invest an additional effort in the process of communication. The greater the certainty of coincident and mutual experience, the less complicated communication will be, and vice versa. In cases of common experience (expected or real) the sender may leave much to be inferred by the receiver. The sender may therefore choose a very open form of expression for the purpose or simply leave a part of the message out (this aspect of communication is discussed in detail by D. Sperber and D. Wilson 1988).[5] In cases where the experience exclusively is on the part of the sender a considerably higher degree of redundancy is requisite.

Secondly, the means of communication is equally important as the sender may select from a number of options. Having decided to formulate a message in written language there are other choices to make. For instance, the sender may choose to express him/herself in more or less open or closed texts. In my use of the notion, an open text leaves much to inference, as opposed to a closed text which is more definite and unambiguous.[6] Expressive openness can be achieved either by indefinite expression (typically involving references to common experience)[7] or lack of redundancy. Closedness, on the contrary, is obtainable either through definite expression (mathematical language is an extreme case) or excessive redundancy.[8]

Using John of the Cross' writings as an example, his poetic works are characterized with a considerable openness. The expression is condensed (little redundancy) and highly metaphorical (with references to all kinds of biologically or culturally shared experience). In his prose works, he makes an effort to close the expression somewhat. His general procedure is, in the first place, to add considerable redundancy to the descriptions. He states similar

4. Wilhelmsen sees this as an insurmountable hindrance of communicating mystical experience to inexperienced persons (1980, 294, 379, and 382).
5. This actually explains the often mystified expressions, like mana, numen etc. of many religions which C. Lévi-Strauss has termed 'signifiant flottant' (1950) by which he means to indicate that the term is capable of filling out a hole that an undefinable content (signifié) otherwise would leave, if the term (the signifiant) had been more rigid. As I see it, it is not so much because this information, *in particular*, cannot be formed into language but because it is not considered necessary to take the (admittedly, considerable) trouble to do it. Experience of it is supposed to be common for all receivers of the message.
6. It seems appropriate to emphasize that U. Eco's definition of the notion of open and closed texts is the exact opposite of the one I suggest here (e.g. 1979, introduction).
7. As in the use of metaphors, for instance (see Johnson 1987; Lakoff 1987).
8. To give an idea of the average redundancy in spoken language, Weaver notes that it is 50% in everyday English (1963, 104).

points of view in several diverging ways. Thereupon, he tries to reduce the ambiguity of the metaphors. This he does partly by referring to tradition (theology, philosophy, contemporary spirituality, etc.) and partly by elaborating and extending the metaphors meticulously (the metaphor of the night is a conspicuous example). In this way, he attempts to help his readers squeeze out all possible meanings of the poetry[9] (a task that would otherwise have been entrusted to every reader). In fact, John of the Cross partially succeeds in the task of closing his open expressions. He does not succeed though in actually constructing closed texts, but that was hardly his intention. There is no doubt that he himself considered his poetry to be more true to his intended message than his commentaries on the poems.

Finally, it is also conceivable that not all kinds of information is equally easy to communicate. Some types of information may be more indefinite and indeterminate than others. Events might be more difficult to describe than tangible objects, and cognitive events might put greater demands on communication than events in the external world, etc. Hence, it is not surprising that feelings, e.g., like those generated in mystical states, are not easily communicated. This aspect of communicating the diverse aspects of mystical experience is also stressed by Moore who similarly points out that the facility of expression varies considerably depending on that which is to be described (1978, 104).

The general point about all this is that for the success of communication it is convenient that the means and the level of redundancy are fitted to the conditions of communication and that which is to be communicated. The effectiveness of communication, or the communicative success, at once relies on the appropriateness of the expressive means and the abilities for and the efforts invested in expression and comprehension by the sender and the receiver, respectively. It is not unlikely that the attempt to communicate mystical experience will be met with obstacles, both because of the expectable inexperience of potential receivers and because of the difficulties involved in the expression of personal ideas and feelings. Yet, there is no reason to believe though that the hindrances will actually block communication, as it may be quite successful if only the means and the efforts are fitted to the concrete conditions (cf. Moore 1978, 105).

Similarly, it is no surprise that various forms of more ambiguous and evocative language often are favoured by mystics. In the words of Moore, 'The power of such language to evoke or communicate experience is clearly very

---

9. This is particularly evident in his Spiritual Canticle and less so in the Ascent of Mount Carmel and the Dark Night of the Soul.

great in non-mystical contexts, and there is no reason to suppose that mystics do not use it equally effectively.' (1978, 105). The core of the matter is that mystical experience as a complex of mystical states and mystical development like all other aspects of human experience, is subject to certain constraints imposed on communication.

Still, it is also predictable that there will be a considerable distance between mystical experience and the expression of it. And, this doesn't only apply to mysticism. It holds good for the communication of all human experience, although in varying degrees. In this context, I wish to stress that there is no justification for the skepticism and mistrust so typical of many theories of mysticism towards the mystics' own accounts of their experience. C.A. Keller, for instance, demonstrates such an attitude to rather an extreme extent when he argues that the scholarly study of mysticism should limit itself to the study of mystical language. In his own words 'The study of mysticism is primarily, if not exclusively, a philological and an exegetical enterprise' (1978, 95). This would really be a loss for the study of religion.

The memory of mystical experience

The major part of the available evidence of John of the Cross' mystical experience has supposedly already been redescribed representationally several times and is thus the outcome of a long process of redescription. Consequently, there is a considerable distance in both time and content between a particular aspect of mystical experience and the writings providing evidence for it. The process of representational redescription may, in principle, be initiated simultaneously with the events or circumstances redescribed. If this has been the case in the mystical experience of John of the Cross, there is no evidence for it, though. For that reason there are no direct testimonies of his mystical experience in general. Therefore, the problems that this involves for the interpretation of the evidence will be far more significant concerning some elements of mystical experience than others, which further means that the evidence of the various elements is not equally reliable. The constraints on memory will supposedly be far more important with respect to the evidence of particular, mystical states and specific developmental points, than the more general developmental process will (because nearly all aspects of mystical experience contribute to the memory of mystical development). The developmental process may, on the other hand, have been subjected to more representational redescriptions, and the descriptions of it to more interpretations. In reality, mystical development has been intermingled with the processes of redescription and interpretation, implying that the more conceptual processes to some extent have become part of mystical development.

In the present context, the core of the matter is that John of the Cross has had to rely on the memory of the diverse elements in his mystical experience when redescribing it representationally and when describing it in written form. Accordingly, the processes of redescription, description, and interpretation must have been seriously constrained by the workings of memory. Due to the exceptional character of mystical experience and, in particular, of mystical states, it is not unlikely that the memory of it differs from the memory of other aspects of human experience. In this respect three general points (each involving one or more specific aspect) are relevant. The first point pertains to various aspects of the state of consciousness during which representations of information are stored in memory. The second relates to the way that information is retrieved from memory. The third point concerns the way that retrieved information is treated in working memory.

The first point is that the memory of something apparently is affected by the degree of emotionality (if any) in a particular state of consciousness. The memory of something is considerably (maybe even proportionally) enhanced with the amplification of emotionality, stress, pain (physical or psychological), and like factors (McCauley 1995). Damasio suggests that the explanation of this is that emotions work as a booster for working memory and attention because these are motivated by preferences (1987, 197-99). Increased attention to something means that more representations of that *something* will be added to the existing knowledge reserve, thereby easing the memory of that *something*.

The above concerns one of the more significant factors that can be expected to constrain the process of remembering aspects of mystical experience pertaining to the time during which there is consciousness of mystical conceptions or emotions (especially during actual mystical states of consciousness). Yet, the memory of something may furthermore be constrained by factors pertaining to the time of remembering something, that is, the retrieval of representations of information from memory, and this is the concern of the following two points, namely the second and the third.

The second point is that representations are retrieved from memory via a retrieval cue which requires that the cue overlaps the representations to be retrieved (Barsalou 1992, 133; Clark 1991, 98). In relation to most aspects of human experience, most representations of information about the world are highly redundant and overlapping. Cues for one thing can be useful as cues for something else. The more that representations of something overlap other representations, the easier the memory of that something is. In the context of mystical experience, the question is: does the apparent *exceptionality* of the experience imply that the representations of the information related to it *do not* overlap representations of information related to ordinary experience? Are the two kinds of experience sustained by two different reserves of knowledge, or the same? If mystical and ordinary experience arise out of the same store of knowledge then the relevant cognitive representations can be expected to be highly overlapping whereby the memory of mystical experience should not be particularly more difficult than the memory of other things. If, on the other hand, mystical experience is sustained by a specific reserve of knowledge, then evidently there will be less overlapping, or none at all, between the two kinds of representations, and the memory of mystical experience will be impeded. I would suggest that in the case of a mystic living the religious life within a monastery (like John of the Cross), for whom ordinary experience to a very great extent has been concerned with religious and mystical matters, there undoubtedly will be a continuation of the information about the two aspects of experience, inasmuch as the content of mystical states of consciousness derives from the mystic's general mystical ideas and can be part of wakeful consciousness as well.

The third point pertains to the amount of acquired knowledge of something. The point is that the memory of something is facilitated considerably when more knowledge about that something is accumulated both because it makes it easier to find fitting retrieval cues and because it improves the organization of representations (further easing the retrieval) (Barsalou 1992, 118, 120, 125-26 and 141; 1987, 117). And since the recurrence of more or less similar mystical states increases the store of knowledge, it seems likely that the memory of mystical experience in general improves as the mystical process advances.

Finally, there is a fourth point which concerns the issue of how retrieved representations of information are treated in working memory. This point relates to three aspects that may constrain the memory of mystical experience. The first aspect is that retrieved information normally is dealt with until it makes sense. If something is not fully remembered, then the missing information will be reconstructed by inference, typically working by the substitution of missing information with information from a seemingly related 'frame' or a 'script'.[10] This is because memory is designed to produce a sensible and integrated output whatever the problems of retrieval might be. The harder retrieval is, the more this will result in partial and defective information, and the more information will need to be inferred and filled in. The product of this process of retrieval and inference will then mostly be viewed as if it was actually remembered, even if it is to some extent recon-

---

10. Scripts and frames are models of possible organizations of information in memory (Barsalou 1987, 125). More generally they refer to the particular expectations of a subject.

structed (see Barsalou 1992, 141-42; Clark 1991, 89, 93, and 96). This is particularly significant with respect to the memory of early mystical experience as
this presumably will be harder to remember than the later mystical experience.
It is therefore predictable that a mystic has to rely on his/her expectations
about early mystical experience when attempting to remember it. More
concretely, this implies that descriptions of early mystical states, in particular,
will be modified by other aspects of the mystic's general knowledge.

A second aspect is that retrieved representations of information typically
are revised and new representations are added to the existing. If new information is added then it may either be mixed with the old information or it
may simply substitute it (Barsalou 1992, 130). According to A. Barsalou,
concepts are actually *constructed* in working memory on the basis of representations of information retrieved from long term memory (1987, 129). A
consequence of this is that representations stored (often without purpose) at
one point in time can later be used in new ways in creative thinking, as in the
process of constructing concepts for specific purposes. This aspect of the
workings of memory has far reaching consequences for the potentials of
imaginative creativity and thus for the cognitive products of the process of
representational redescription.

A third aspect constraining the treatment of retrieved representations is
that the most frequent foci of consciousness will be considered the more
typical (Barsalou 1992, 120; 1987, 117). This has specific relevance for the
memory of mystical states. In the concrete, it means that the more frequently
occurring mystical states (that is to say, distinct mystical states of some degree
of similarity) will be considered the more typical and contribute the most to
the constitution of the 'scripts' or 'frames' used to fill up missing representations of other mystical states. Consequently, the representational
redescription of particular mystical states will supposedly draw upon representations of the most common states to a much greater extent than representations of the less frequent states.

On the basis of all these factors constraining the workings of memory, it
should be manifest that John of the Cross' descriptions of the diverse aspects
of his mystical experience will hardly be *equally* reliable. In general, the
advancement of the process of developing mystically will ease the memory of
mystical experience as a whole. On the one hand, because of the continuous
expansion of the knowledge reserve, and on the other, because of the
increasing degree of emotionality displayed in mystical states. But the
expansion of mystical experience resulting from the progression of the
mystical process will, at the same time, blur the memory of some of the more
specific aspects of mystical experience, especially that of the earlier mystical
states and the least emotional states of the first and the second stage.

Furthermore, it can be expected, that the more frequent mystical states will be remembered the best and stand out as being the more typical.

The case of John of the Cross

When the general constraints on the workings of memory are related to John of the Cross' writings as evidence of his mystical experience it should be possible to draw various conclusions about the expectable reliability of the various constituents of this body of evidence. In general, the descriptions of mystical states will presumably incorporate traits from several mystical states typical of some specific part of the developmental process. As opposed to this, it seems less probable that characteristics of mystical states typical of one stage should be mixed up with that of another stage due to the greater dissimilarity of mystical states of different stages.

With respect to the varying degrees of reliability of John of the Cross' descriptions of mystical states it can be expected that descriptions of early mystical states do not provide dependable evidence of John of the Cross' particular, mystical states. His descriptions may, nonetheless, constitute fairly good evidence of his typical, early mystical states and very good evidence of mystical states typical of the beginning of the process in general (that is to say, as a mixture of his typical, early mystical states and those reported by other mystics). It is furthermore predictable that descriptions of mystical states are the more reliable, the more typical a particular mystical state is of a certain part of the developmental process and the higher the degree of emotionality in the state. This further implies that typical mystical states of a high degree of emotionality may tend to override atypical states of equal degrees of emotionality. Consequently, descriptions of mystical states can only be expected to provide dependable evidence of particular, mystical states of exceptional emotional character. Yet, it is not impossible that mystical states of a higher degree of emotionality than all previous mystical states, that is, mystical states initiating a higher degree of emotionality (e.g. a new stage) may acquire some salience because of their status as the first of a certain degree of emotionality. If this is the case, the mystical states initiating the diverse stages of the developmental process could, for instance, have been remembered somewhat better. It is hardly the case, though, that the descriptions of them will not have been blended with features of later, mystical states. Finally, it can be expected that the descriptions of the general process of mystical development are very reliable provided that one accepts that they simultaneously give evidence of John of the Cross' changing conceptualizations of his mystical experience.

Relating the theoretical predictions about evidence of mystical experience to the concrete works of John of the Cross, it should be considered how his descriptions of the various aspects of mystical experience match the expectations of the descriptions. In this respect, it is interesting that especially his descriptions of early mystical states do not correspond with what could have been expected. John of the Cross has actually described his early mystical states in rather a lot of detail. Repeating the theoretical anticipations, this aspect of his mystical experience ought to have been remembered rather poorly and therfore also have been recounted vaguely and imprecisely. But this is not the way it appears in the evidence. In spite of the very advanced developmental point at which he has written his works, he has actually attended to some of the early mystical states with unexpected descriptive precision. In order to explain this, John of the Cross' life as a Discalced Carmelite should be taken into account. I would suggest that the reason why he has been able to describe those early mystical states with reasonable precision is that the descriptions have not been based exclusively on his *memory* of the described. Evidently, this adds to the complexity of the evidence. The point is that John of the Cross, in his position as a spiritual confessor within the Discalced Carmelite order, had exceptional access to the testimonies of other mystics' mystical states. He never concealed the fact (and had no reason to do so) that he had drawn upon other persons' mystical experience, as a natural complement to his own, to the extent that it had seemed relevant. Continual encounters with persons going through a developmental process rather similar to the one he had gone through himself, presumably functioned as a repeated reminder of his own experience. Numerous accounts of nuns' mystical states worked as retrieval cues for his own mystical states and, at the same time, provided him with additional knowledge of the subject. There is also a fair chance that the majority of those reports on mystical states heard by John of the Cross concerned the pre-mystical stage, the first stage, and — to some extent — the second stage. The reason for this was that most of the nuns needing his spiritual advice were at the *beginner* stage of mystical development, because only a few of those who initiate mystical development go through with it. Additionally, it is at the beginning of the middle part of the process of mystical development that most consolation and guidance is needed.

With respect to the reliability of the descriptions in question, there is no reason to question that the reported characteristics of early mystical states are really typical of these. What is rather uncertain, though, is whether they are descriptions of this part of John of the Cross' own mystical experience. It seems most plausible that in his reports he has combined the memory of his own early mystical states with the reports of others; has redescribed this new blend of knowledge representationally; described the outcome of the redescriptive process in his writings; and then, finally, interpreted (and reinterpreted) this. If this is correct, the accounts of early mystical states in the works of John of the Cross do not relate particular or average mystical states of the beginning of his mystical development, but they do presumably provide very dependable evidence of average, early, mystical states, typical of this kind of mystical development.

In varying degrees, this probably holds for other aspects of John of the Cross' mystical experience as well. The mixing and revision of information are incessant, cognitive processes which means that all aspects of John of the Cross' mystical experience will have been subjected to these processes. The reason why I have considered the evidence of early mystical states in some detail is that it constitutes the more extreme case and thus serves to illustrate the point. Accordingly, the descriptions of the more advanced mystical states will presumably refer more directly to John of the Cross' own mystical experience and to a greater extent to particular, mystical states than the evidence of early mystical states. Similarly, it seems likely that the descriptions of the more advanced stages relate more specifically to this aspect of his experience than the descriptions of the less advanced stages.

V.   Historical introduction to John of the Cross

A preliminary comment

Before engaging in the attempt to outline the historical and personal background of John of the Cross, I wish to make a brief remark on the extent to which I deem this relevant at all. Numerous scholars have been at pains to trace and identify the roots and sources of John of the Cross' ideas and metaphors (e.g., Alonso who has devoted a whole book to the task, 1942; Crisógono 1929; Herrera 1966 to mention a few). Others, again, have ardently opposed the view that John of the Cross's more important ideas and metaphors should have been polluted with conventionality (Wilhelmsen 1980, 393 is a conspicuous example; but see also Mancho Duque 1982, e.g., 27). In my view, it is rather unlikely that either of these endeavours will contribute significantly to explain what John of the Cross' works document about his mystical experience and ideas.

On the one hand, it is plain that his ideas, his mystical experience, and his ways of communicating have been influenced more or less directly by both the cultural and religious traditions of his time. Hence, it is also important to pay due attention to these traditions and that is my motive for presenting an outline of John of the Cross' background. On the other hand, John of the Cross has evidently been selective regarding those ideas and metaphors which seemed most relevant to his purposes, just as he has contributed in some (minor or major) way to ideas and metaphors by elaborating and modifying them. The problem is that it is impossible to determine which specific elements from tradition he has mixed (and in which particular way) with his own contributions. In the light of that there is really no point in taking the trouble to link specific elements of his ideas, and ways of communicating them, with specific constituents from his cultural background. Yet, this is exactly what has received a great deal of attention in the scholarly studies of his works.

The spiritual environment in 16th century Spain

The Spain of the late 15th and the entire 16th century can be characterized as a time of intense spiritualness. An outstanding religiousness prospered within the numerous monastic orders, just as it flourished unrestrained within the church generally. The whole period was one of intense spiritualness and devotion, but the character of spirituality nonetheless changed considerably as the 16th century progressed. According to the Spanish historian M. Andrés, who has devoted specific attention to the issue, the epoch as a whole can be divided into four periods with diverging kinds of spiritualness. The ideas of one period were partially abandoned in the next, coincidentally with new ideas being elaborated. This does not mean, though, that the spiritual persons of one period reacted deliberately against tradition. In fact, the opposite is more likely to have been the case. This is presumably also one of the reasons why the periods overlap and the distinctions between them are relatively indefinite.

Inasmuch as the spiritual ambience should be correlated with the more general political and social tendencies, the whole issue becomes a little tangled. The problem is that the political environment of 15th and 16th century Spain was under the very strong influence of diverse kings, whereas the switches from one spiritual period to the next did not follow one king being replaced by another. Hence, it is a little difficult to uphold a sharp distinction of the spiritual periods. It appears that the political environment has indeed affected the spiritual, but that the effects have been delayed.

In spite of the relative indistinction of the spiritual periods, the variation between them is still so notable as to make discrimination relevant. Andrés identifies the specific characteristics of the periods as follows: The first period (1470-1500) is where the monastic orders were established. In the second period (1500-1530), the method of recollection (a way of meditating) and ways of approaching God were formulated. In the third period (1530-1559), the method of recollection and the spiritual 'ways' were elaborated further. In the fourth period (1556-1591), mysticism flourished and the orders were reformed (1983, 647).

In the following, I shall address the spiritualness of the epoch and correlate it with the relevant political circumstances and changes. I have chosen to keep to Andrés' distinction of the spiritual periods to the extent it seems pertinent, dealing with the periods in chronological order. In my view, the distinction of the two periods from 1500-1559 is somewhat superfluous and can be joined in one, inasmuch as the latter part consisted more of *constituting* and *confirming* than actually *renewing*. In general, the spiritual inventiveness of the epoch is unsurpassed in the history of Spain. It is the most incomparably important and most creative 120 years of spiritualness in Spain, wherefore the periods in combination give a pretty good insight into this aspect of Spanish history.

In the context of John of the Cross, it is the period from 1500 till 1559 that is of main interest, because the more influential spiritual persons of that period founded the fundament of the ideas of 16th century mysticism. In fact, it is quite uncertain if John of the Cross had had first-hand knowledge of any of the works of the recollection mystics, but the idea that the best way of approaching God was to follow specified 'ways', as well as the general vocabulary introduced along with the ideas, must have been commonly known in the religious orders. More specifically, John of the Cross had without doubt known a great deal about these ideas, since he had worked for a long time in close connection with Teresa of Jesus who knew the recollection ideas very well and was much inspired by them. From 1559 and onwards Spanish spiritualness was primarily marked by Teresa of Jesus and John of the Cross himself.

The period until 1500

Because of the Arabian occupation, the major part of Spain was isolated from the rest of Christian Europe for several centuries. For this reason, the Spanish church was secluded for a very long time from the power of the Pope. The power appertaining to the Pope in other European countries were therefore entrusted to the Kings of Spain. As a consequence of this, Spanish Catholicism developed in a slightly diverging manner and therefore came to differ on specific points from the remainder of Catholicism. In addition to that, the enforced situation of that time formed the basis of a tradition that enabled the Spanish kings to maintain exceptional power over the Church also after the conquest of the Arabs (Mackay 1977, 22 and 139).

Due to approximately 700 years of Arabic presence in the country, Spain became one of the Christian world's paramount sources of classical knowledge. The Arabs had studied the Greek philosophical and mathematical-astronomical works profoundly and had translated them into Arabic and provided them with extensive commentaries. Both the original translated works and the commentaries were then translated from Arabic to Spanish and other European languages, after which they soon were exported out of Spain, especially to England and France. Later on, the classical works spread to the rest of the Continent including Spain. In this way, the classical works came back to Spain again after having toured Europe, meaning that Spain did not profit at first from classic thought (Mackay 1977, 86 and ch. 4; Andrés 1983, 427).

The economical situation in 14th century Spain was not exactly prosperous. First the plague came to Spain in the middle of the century and thereupon a serious economical decline followed in its wake. In the last part of the century, insecurity and worries about the future were rampant. It appears that along with this, beliefs and ideas began to drift and stray in all possible directions. Thus, anti-Semitism, millenarian movements, eschatological and occult propensities trailed the depression, just as people looked to astrology for explanations of the social upheavals of the period, especially after Halley's comet in 1454 (Mackay 1977, ch. 8; Andrés 1983, 497, 541, 543, and 546).

In 15th century Europe, at the same time as there were strong reactions against ritualism and formalism in many countries, the Catholic Church was inordinately formalist and ritualist. Especially during the last 25 years of the century, reactions began to spread in Spain where they took the form of the foundation and extension of a myriad of new religious orders where interior spiritualness and devotion could be cultivated in replacement of the more external ritualism (Andrés 1975, 21; 1983, 609; A Benedictine of Stanbrook Abbey 1954, 8 and 135). In general, the new spiritual religiousness weighted austerity, asceticism, mortification, as well as observance of the rules of the orders, the rites, and the law of the Church and God. All of the orders shared the appreciation of religious devotion, mental prayer, penitence, hermitism, manual labour, all of which were combined with fairly simple doctrines and a focus on the Bible. The particular form that Spanish spiritualness took was probably inspired by the North European, spiritual movement, Devotio Moderna, that was particularly prevalent in the Netherlands (Andrés 1983, 672 and 1975, 22 and 384).

In Spain, the theology of the century was dominated by Christocentrism, with a specific stress on the suffering of Christ, going back to the two hundred years earlier Ramon Llull, who, in turn, had been inspired by Bonaventure. Like Bonaventure, Llull further insisted that creatures allude to God wherefore the entire world can be studied as a book that gives Man knowledge of God (Andrés 1983, 462, 465; 1975, 96). During this period attempts at internalizing religion were widespread which is also why both Franciscans, Benedictines, and Augustinians founded monasteries where very severe, religious precepts and rules reigned. Especially among the former two, a profound and spiritual religiousness began to prosper and thrive. Several Spanish historians count this period a first, Spanish Reformation (the second follows in the subsequent century) (Andrés 1983, 609).

Coinciding with tendencies towards the internalization of religion, the common tolerance towards other religions and forms of religiousness dropped remarkably. It appears that several factors affected this situation. Some of these factors were the constitution of the so called Catholic kings (Isabella and Ferdinand) in 1474, the institution of the Spanish Inquisition in 1480,[1] and the economical pressure on the people (due to the escalated war against the Moors

---

1. The Spanish Inquisition were established in 1480 as a response to inadequate Christianization of the converted jews. Yet, the Catholic kings had already in 1478 intensified the activities of the papal Inquisition (Lovett 1986, 282; Highfield 1972, 28).

in Granada) (Elliott 1963, 66; Highfield 1972, 248). Reversely, a fanatical intolerance within the Church and among lay people may, at the same time, have influenced the politics of the kings. Certainly, it had not been the case that the coexistence of Jews, Muslims, and Christians had been free of problems up until then, but in general Spanish Christianity had accepted the assimilation of people of other religions. A contributing factor to this relative tolerance may have been the fact that both Jews and Muslims had supplied the country with considerable economical resources (Lovett 1986, 257).

With the founding of the Spanish Inquisition, the Christianizing efforts were at first directed at the Jews. In 1492, all Jews were forced to convert completely to Christianity even in lifestyle, otherwise they would be banished. Later on, attention was directed at the Muslims. In 1492, after ten years of intense war, the Moors in Granada were finally defeated. In 1502, the Muslims were, like the Jews before them, obliged to convert or leave the country (Highfield 1972, 28; Lovett 1986, 19).

The period from 1500 to 1559

The Catholic kings deemed the uniformation of the Catholic faith highly important and, inasmuch as they had direct control over the Inquisition and there was no Pope to interfere with their business, they acquired considerable power over the Church and religion. In 1527, the Habsburgian Charles V was inaugurated as king. That did not bring about any major changes, though, since he was equally occupied with the reformation and unification of the Catholic Church and simply continued the political practice of the former Catholic kings. All in all, Charles V held resolutely onto the control over the Spanish church which his predecessors had procured (Lovett 1986, 59 and ch. 19).

The Spanish Inquisition became even more significant in the 16th century, although the goal of its activities shifted from non-Christians to unorthodox Christians. Certainly, the Inquisition must have been busy in the first 30 years of the century, because spiritualness was not only prospering within the religious orders (which could be bad enough), but also outside of the orders where it was completely out of control. One of the more explicit results of the spiritual initiatives of the period was the publication of numerous works on mysticism, Spanish as well as translated (Andrés 1983, 650).

One question that occupied spiritual persons throughout the epoch was the question of how a person could approach God. The Franciscans, in particular, were occupied with the development of an efficient method by which an individual could approximate God by mystical means. Two Franciscans were the first to formulate such a mystical method, namely Francisco de Osuna and

Bernardino de Laredo. The advice and precepts proposed by these two mystics were followed by all of the spiritual persons belonging to this early spiritual school of thought. Indeed, their ideas turned out to be very lasting, inasmuch as they formed the basis of the later Spanish mysticism, first of all represented by Teresa of Jesus and John of the Cross. Hence, it seems pertinent to take a closer look at the ideas presented by these two Franciscans.

The method suggested by the Franciscans was centred around the notion of recollection ('recogimiento'). Recollection designates a way to God or a method of how to move nearer to Him. More generally, the method of recollection can be delineated as a process during which the soul first enters into itself and thereupon ascends up above itself. The first step on this way to God is that the sensuous desires should be annihilated. This is at once a process of purification and destruction that reduces the person to nothing (*nada*). The soul participates actively in the purification of the sensuous desires through mortification and the like but God similarly needs to do His part. This part of the process is thus executed in joint cooperation of God and the soul. Through this internalizing process, the soul begins to enter itself whereby it gains knowledge of itself and its own condition. This knowledge is not a goal in itself, though, but only a means of acquiring knowledge of God.[2] The point is that when the soul reaches the depth or the center of itself it will find God, because that is where He really hides Himself. In this way, knowledge of God goes through knowledge of oneself. The next step on the way of recollection consists in a virtual transformation of the soul. This part is solely carried out by God, implying that the soul ought to remain completely passive in order to ease God's operations from this point forward. Accordingly, recollection is both a gift of grace and a result of one's own efforts, inasmuch as the final transformation is donated by God while human cooperation is a precondition for it (Andrés 1983, 657-61 and 679; 1975, 36, 90-93 and 124).

According to the recollection mystics, the process of moving nearer to God unfolds in three stages. The first, involves the mortification of the sensuous desires and is purely sensuous and corporal. The second, where the soul enters the center of itself, is rational (which means that it is both sensuous and spiritual). And the third, where the soul ascends above itself, is purely spiritual (Andrés 1975, 373). In agreement with the Christian tradition, and especially that of the Franciscan order, this new spiritual religiousness was Christocentric. Nonetheless, the idea of how an individual is supposed to relate to Christ diverged significantly from that of former ideas. The

---

2. According to Andrés, the Spanish notion of self-knowledge is not identical with the Socratic notion, because the method of recollection aims at going beyond (and not of finding) oneself in the encounter with God (1983, 673).

traditional view was that a person should *meditate on* the suffering of the human Christ. The recollection mystics, on the other hand, held that one should *imitate* Christ as human *and* God. More specifically, this advice implied that one physically should follow His life on earth (with labour, poverty, and penitence) whereas one spiritually should follow Him as God (by mystical means) (Andrés 1975, 127-29).

An essential element in the understanding of a person's nearing to God is the transforming power of love. The point is that mystical union of the soul and God requires similarity of the two (as far as it is possible for the imitation to resemble the original). In accord with the Christian tradition, love is capable of transforming the lover into the beloved. It is further in the power of love (of a certain kind) to suspend the understanding which engenders an unknowing requisite for the approach to God. In this way, love is a potent means for the alteration of the soul (Andrés 1975, 104 and 114).

It was not only within the Franciscan order that a new kind of religiousness flourished in the early 16th century, though. There was a whole number of religious groups that began to emphasize the importance of the individual and internal religiousness. In the previous period, religion certainly tended to become internalized, but it had not yet become individualized. The spiritual devotion of the end of the previous century demanded several hours of prayer every day, but it was a kind of vocal prayer that was exerted collectively, just as the value of the institutionalized rituals still were appreciated (Andrés 1975, ch. 1).

There were two main trends in the attempts to internalize Christian religiousness in the 16th century Spain. On the one hand, several groups were opting for the more spiritual kind of religiousness. Among these should be counted the recollection mystics, but also the less orthodox group named the Illuminates (*los alumbrados*) who did not belong to any religious order, although they had been closely connected to the recollection movement until 1523 when the two groups split up.[3] In 1524 the Franciscans condemned the Illuminates and the following year the Inquisition did the same (Andrés 1975, 40 and 356). On the other hand, Erasmism began to spread in Spain, especially among the higher layers of society, not least those connected to the Habsburgian king. Lutheran ideas also had some few followers but mainly in the Northern part of the country (Elliott 1963, 207).

---

3. The Illuminates searched for a direct and instantaneous way to God in order to elude the slow mortification and purification involved in the Franciscan method of recollection. For the Illuminates, recollection ought to be passive all the way through, which means that the whole work was entrusted to God (Andrés 1975, ch. 13; Elliott 1963, ch. 6).

The two religious trends diverged on major points. For the recollection mystics (Franciscans as well as Illuminates) internalization consisted in mystical approach to God, whereas the Erasmians strove to cut away the institutional ritualism. They shared the reaction against collectivism, externalism, and formalism, but their solution of how to do this differed fundamentally. As an example, Erasmus' view was that Christ should be followed morally, whereas the mystics recommended that he should be imitated both as a human and God. To put it somewhat squarely, the Erasmic understanding of internal religiousness was intellectual while the Spanish was mystical (or experiential) (Andrés 1975, 374).

In the early 16th century when the threats from Judaism and Islam had been eliminated, the Inquisition was free to engage fully in the job of expelling all kinds of possible heresy. The diversity of the endeavours of reforming the Church provided plenty of work for the inquisitors. Especially the Illuminates and the few Lutherans were pursued, possibly because these tendencies had special appeal to the common people which may have seemed to be a particular threat to the coherence of the ideas of the Catholic Church. In general, it seems to have been the popularization of religion (a fundamental aspect of Lutheranism) that the Spanish church resisted. Religion should be controlled by the institutions of the Church. Accordingly, religious ideas ought to be produced solely by theologians, and religious life was idealized by those living in the confirmed orders of the church. The fear of handing religiousness over to the common people was expressed in particular through opposition to the translation of the Bible into the vernacular. A loose prohibition of reading the Bible in Spanish had existed already under the Catholic kings but in 1551 it was forbidden explicitly (Elliott 1963, 218).

Still, it was not only the more popular ideas of the Lutherans and the Illuminates that were chased. All potential heresy was investigated by the Inquisition. Inasmuch as the inquisitors had little insight into the various religious directions, they lumped them all together with the justification that they all emphasized the more internal religiousness at the expense of the more external. The inquisitors had little interest in determinating whether a group of religious people reacted against ceremonies and religious orders or they simply emphasized a personal relationship with God. Actually, the recollection movement avoided to a great extent problems with the Inquisition, probably because the movement sprang from one of the religious orders, just as their formulations were inspired by traditional Catholic ideas.

In general, the traditional and the innovative tendencies of the period dissented throughout the first half of the century. The disagreements not only concerned spirituality and religious ceremonies but also the humanist and theological ideas. The humanist Renaissance had inspired many Spanish university theologians who began to advocate the more direct and scientific studies of Bible, language, and history (Elliott 1963, 208; Andrés 1983, 646; Baruzi 1924, 128). The conservatives, though, overcame the renewers in the end. To some extent, the outcome of the controversy was fostered by the new king's (Philip II) support of the conservatives. Philip II had succeeded his father in 1556 and exceeded both him and the Catholic kings in religious orthodoxy and intolerance, just as his control surpassed earlier control of the Spanish church (Lovett 1986, 156 and 279; Elliott 1963, 222). Towards the end of the 1560s, Spain was very closed and anti-reformist (Elliott 1963, 208). As opposed to his predecessors, Philip II mainly opposed the foreign attempts at reformation, whereas he approved the national endeavours to reform the Catholic Church (as his rather positive attitude towards the reformations of the religious orders shows) (Peers 1954, 33-40).

In the period between 1550 and 1560, the Inquisition intensified the efforts to expel the heretic tendencies. As mentioned, the prohibition of reading the Bible in Spanish was introduced in 1551. In 1558 (/1559), Philip II interdicted the import of foreign books and censured those published in Spanish. It was similarly forbidden to study in other countries. And in 1559 the major works on recollection were proscribed (Elliott 1963, 218; Lovett 1986, 292; Andrés 1975, 41). In this way, the country was isolated from foreign innovativeness at the same time as the propagation of Spanish published material was prevented.

The period from 1559 to 1591

The Council of Trent (1545-63), of which a major part of the delegates were Spanish, aimed at reforming the general, Catholic doctrine in order to take the consequences of the prevalent discontent with the formalism of the church. The decisions of the council were, in general, very beneficial for the spiritual life in Spain. The council had settled that hermits should belong to monasteries which resulted in a common acceptance of mysticism provided that the mystics belonged to one of the religious orders (Lovett 1986, 148; Peers 1954, 23; Elliott 1963, 237). For a long time, a widespread spiritualness had been latent, but the many prohibitions had managed to keep it down. Now that the prospects opened up, spiritualness and religious devotion began to prosper and thrive. In agreement with the general tendencies of the time, the Inquisition also acquired a somewhat looser politic from the middle of the 1560s. With the removal of the Grand Inquisitors, first in 1566 and next in 1573, a gradually more moderate course began to be led (Elliott 1963, 235; Andrés 1975, 49).

The spiritualness and internalized religiousness had been in progress from the beginning of the century and had become very prosperous towards the middle of the century, but then the Inquisition had tightened its grip and the internalization of religion had partially been brought to a standstill. The coincident liberalization of the attitude of both Church and Inquisition gave a very strong impetus to the spiritualness that had been impeded for quite some time. So, from around the early 1560s, spiritual life intensified and escalated into a second Spanish Reformation (in the view of some historians) (Andrés 1983, 609). The changes were particularly manifest within the many religious orders where more and more nuns and friars wished to live a simple life in poverty and solitude. Some of these took the full consequences of their religious aims and broke out of the orders and constituted reformed segments of the orders. These reformed orders were still subordinate to the authority of the orders from which they had chosen to be segregated, but in everyday life the nuns and the friars were attached to far more strict and severe rules.

Within the Carmelite order Teresa of Jesus initiated the foundation of reformed Carmelite houses, first for nuns and later also for friars (John of the Cross was one of the two friars inhabiting the first). In correspondence with the harsh rules, the reformed Carmelites wore no shoes and were called the Discalced (shoeless) Carmelites. There was a widespread interest in the reformation and the number of houses increased enormously (Peers 1954, 22). Predictably, the Carmelite order did not approve of the reform, though, and there were several serious conflicts during the years preceding the final complete separation of the reformed order from the unreformed order in 1580 (Peers 1954, 32-43; Crisógono 1975, 198).

Rid of the conflicts with the Carmelites, controversies soon appeared within the reformed order itself. In the middle of the 1580s (a few years after the death of Teresa of Jesus in 1582) a conflict that had for a long time been dormant broke out between two of the more dominant persons within the reform. The one, Gracián, is described as a charismatic and charming person and had been the favorite of Teresa of Jesus, whereas the other, Doria, seems to have been a very powerful and rational, but not particularly popular, person. Several others, among which were John of the Cross, were dragged into the controversy, because they supported one or other of the conflicting parties. The strife encompassed numerous facets. In principle, the disagreement concerned the organization and supervision of the order which was by then fairly large. Doria opted for a centralized authorization (with authority in his hands), whereas Gracián (and John of the Cross) preferred to maintain the more decentralized organization of the reformed order as Teresa of Jesus had started it. In practice, the controversy further concerned the guidance and supervision of the nuns and the friars where Doria wanted these aspects to be under the control of the superiors of the provinces (which would guarantee him considerable influence through the selection of superiors), whereas these matters had been dealt with locally and directly in the time of Teresa of Jesus (Peers 1954, 92; Crisógono 1975, 308 and 324). Apart from these more specific disagreements, there was also some controversy about the activities of the reformed order. Gracián championed a more extroverted expansion-style (mission into the new world, for instance), whereas others (like John of the Cross) favoured a more contemplative and spiritual direction (Peers 1954, 74).

The spiritual religiousness of 16th century Spain culminated with the mysticism of Teresa of Jesus and John of the Cross. Teresa of Jesus' ideas about mysticism were to a great extent inspired and influenced by the early Franciscan works on the method of recollection. John of the Cross, with his theological schooling, was additionally influenced by the academic trends of his time at the university.

Summary

In the 120 years from 1470 till 1590, Spanish religiousness became continuously more and more individualized. Focus shifted from the more collective to the definitely personal and individual relationship with God. Until 1500 there was an incipient reaction against the emphasis on the more ritualist element (regarded as the more external) in religion. The monasteries were considered the right place to devote oneself to religious life and the orders multiplied. Yet, it was still a highly collective form of religion in which the observance of the many rules and regulations of both church and orders kept the nuns and friars busy with activities that were considered profitable for religious life.

From 1500 till around 1525-30 the personal relationship with God was brought into focus. Spiritual persons began to develop methods and so-called ways that were supposed to aid a person's nearing God. Within the orders, the nuns and friars did not exactly resist the use of rituals or even consider them damaging in any way. They simply believed ritual to be fairly ineffective as a means of approaching God. The 'spirituals' outside of the orders regarded all forms of rituals as veritable hindrances to the approach to God. There were no major changes in the spiritualness of the period from 1525-30 up till 1559. During the first 20 years, news of the various spiritual ways and methods was dispersed and became commonly accepted in religious environments. However, in the last decade everything quietened down due to the ban on both Spanish and foreign spiritual books. In fact, the prohibition was very 'efficient' and had the undesirable effect of strongly impeding the spread of religious ideas.

From 1559 and on, the conditions of spiritual ideas and ways of living improved significantly, because of the more relaxed attitude towards minor variations in religiousness. In this period, many orders were reformed, so that the increasing demands on the conditions for spiritual life could be satisfied.

The personal background of John of the Cross

The aim of this section is to delineate some of the main features of the life and education of John of the Cross. It is far from the intention to go through all of the known details on the matter.

Upbringing and monastery life

John of the Cross (originally Juan de Yepes) was born in 1542 and died in December 1591. He came from a poor family and his father died when he (John of the Cross) was very young. From 1551 John of the Cross lived with his brother and his mother in the fairly large city of Medina del Campo where he attended a religious school the first couple of years, at the same time as he worked in a monastery church and later in a hospital for the poor. John of the Cross attended a Jesuit school from the age of 17 until he entered the Carmelite order in Medina four years later. After the first year, he moved to a monastery in Salamanca where he additionally matriculated at the university and studied for four years (Crisógono 1975, 23-69; Baruzi 1924, 75-98). During this period John of the Cross began to have a strong desire to live a more ascetical and contemplative religious life than that lived within the Carmelite order. By chance he became acquainted with Teresa of Jesus who had initiated the reformed Carmelite order some few years earlier. In 1568 John of the Cross joined the reformed Carmelites (at which point he also took the name Juan de la Cruz) (Crisógono 1975, 67 and 76; Baruzi 1924, 157 and 166).

John of the Cross' life as a Discalced Carmelite was not only contemplative, since he had much practical work as a confessor and spiritual counsellor, and he had also to travel much (by foot or by ass) as was common for the superiors within the religious orders. Hence, he did not have a great deal of time to nurture his own spiritual progress or writing. The only longer period when he was isolated from people and released from the duties of the reformed order was a period of nearly nine months of 'imprisonment' within the unreformed order. Since this period seems to have had considerable impact on John of the Cross, it is relevant to consider the episode a little closer.

Towards the end of the 1570s, relations between the reformed and the unreformed Carmelites turned into a regular conflict. Actually, John of the Cross does not seem to have been particularly controversial or personally involved in the strife, but for some reason or other, he was arrested towards the end of 1577 and held isolated under very miserable conditions for about nine months in a Carmelite monastery-prison in Toledo (Teresa de Jesús 1988, 1057; Crisógono 1975, 130-33; Baruzi 1924, 187).

In all probability, the period of isolation has encouraged John of the Cross as a poet, since the major part of his very large poem, the *Spiritual Canticle*, was written (or composed) in prison.[4] In addition to that, he has apparently confided to one of the nuns that he had received a very special and irreplaceable grace in prison (Baruzi 1924, 189). Hence, it is not impossible that the period of solitude was likewise particularly profitable for his mystical life.

Education

John of the Cross' education began at the Jesuit school where he presumably was taught basic linguistic disciplines like Latin and grammar (Crisógono 1975, 38; Baruzi 1924, 89). He received his academic education partly at the University in Salamanca, partly at the school belonging to the monastery where he lived, which means that he must have been introduced to diverging theoretical tendencies.

The University in Salamanca was fairly large with 7000 students and it was known for having many prominent professors. From the beginning of the 16th century, some pluralism was accepted at the Spanish universities which allowed Thomism and anti-Thomism to persist side by side. In Salamanca three of the predominant and disagreeing doctrines were taught coincidentally, namely the Scotist, the Thomist, and the Nominalist (Andrés 1983, 589; Crisógono 1975, 52-56; Baruzi 1924, 122). In this period, there was a considerable openness towards new ideas. Yet, under the authority of Francisco de Vitoria (d. 1546), the University in Salamanca little by little began to favour a more stringent logical and philosophical (primarily Thomist) method in the search of truth (Baruzi 1924, 126; Andrés 1983, 615; Wilhelmsen 1980, 6). During John of the Cross' time at the University, authority lay in the hands of Melchor Cano who strongly opposed heresy and Protestantism. Hence, he was also very suspicious of everything new and unknown and clung to a strict and rigid Thomism. The convergence of the former openness and the new style led to some controversies between the Thomists on the one side and the Humanists on the other side.

Really, the conflict at the University simply represented the paradigmatic

---

4. He may also have written other poems during this time, but there is much disagreement on the matter (see Baruzi 1924, 189; Crisógono 1975, 136; Ruiz, in Juan de la Cruz 1988, 6; Eulogio de la Virgen Carmen 1968, 80).

shift from Scholasticism to Humanism, where the encounter of the two directions had swept over Europe and had come to Spain at this time. More specifically, the disagreement of the Traditionalist and the Humanist doctrine further concerned the reading of the Bible. In accordance with Humanism, the Scripuralists argued for a literal reading of the Bible as a text, whereas the Scholastics argued for the traditional method of reading the Bible in continuation of earlier theologians (Baruzi 1924, 129; Wilhelmsen 1980, 6). From 1560 the Scripturalists surmounted the Scholastics on this point, wherefore John of the Cross followed the Scriptural reading of the Bible (Vilnet 1949, 21).

At the Carmelite school, the order's tradition of teaching Baconthorpe (a mainly Thomist Aristotelian) was followed.[5] Baconthorpe disagrees with Aquinas with respect to the acquisition of knowledge of God (as well as on other minor points), inasmuch as he believes that careful study of the Bible will lead to insight into the Being of God. Accordingly, he views the Bible, and not God's Being, as the genuine object of theological study (Crisógono 1975, 58; Wilhelmsen 1980, 24, note 12). Possibly due to the influence from Baconthorpe, the Carmelite order had a very strong tradition of meditating on the Bible (Vilnet 1949, 9).

In general, the University's environment and that of the monastery differed somewhat, but not to the extent that John of the Cross was confronted with two directly opposing doctrines. In both places, the Thomist-Aristotelian philosophy and theology were predominant. All in all, it can be asserted that he could hardly have left Salamanca without a profound knowledge of Aristotelian and Thomist ideas.

5. According to Herrera, John of the Cross' psychology (or more specifically, his understanding of the workings of the faculties of the mind) seems to have been strongly influenced by Baconthorpe (1966, 592).

VI. The conceptual development of John of the Cross as displayed in his *Spiritual Canticle*

An hypothesis of conceptual development

The processes of redescription and interpretation

In this chapter, I shall address the issue of how John of the Cross' works display his repeated redescriptions of cognitive representations of mystical experience. The concern here is not what the works reveal about his mystical experience. I shall address that issue in the following chapter. In this place the question is, first, what the works reveal about the processes of redescribing his mystical experience representationally, describing the experience in his writings, and interpreting the written and, second, the way that these processes have affected John of the Cross' understanding of his mystical experience. I would suggest that the processes of redescription and interpretation in combination yield a developmental product differing qualitatively from that of mystical development. To put it somewhat squarely, the recurrence of mystical states combined with various advantageous conditions yield mystical development, whereas the process of interpretation joins an already ongoing process of representational redescription, and these two, together, yield conceptual development. I shall put forward the following two hypotheses, namely;

(1) that John of the Cross' conceptual development, in particular, is revealed through the changes that he had undertaken in his *Spiritual Canticle*, and

(2) that this development had been triggered and advanced by representational redescription which, in turn, has been accelerated considerably by the more explicit interpretation.

The aspect of the hypothesis suggested in (2) is inspired by and supported by Karmiloff-Smith's theory and evidence of cognitive development, briefly presented in Chapter III. Here, I shall outline those points in her theory that have specific relevance for an understanding of John of the Cross' changing conceptualizations of his mystical experience. She theorizes that cognitive development from the beginning of life involves a process of spontaneous redescription of representations of information within particular cognitive domains. Due to this process, the knowledge within one domain becomes accessible to other parts of the cognitive system, at the same time as this knowledge is lifted from an implicit level to more and more explicit levels. Development commences with information storage and continues with several phases of redescription of the representations of the information. At the lowest explicit level there is neither conscious access to information nor linguistic expression. Later there is conscious access but no linguistic expression. The highest level is that of language (1992, ch. 1) or, to put it differently, the conceptual level, making explicit expression of the conceptualized possible. The process of redescription does not necessarily stop, though, just because an acceptable conceptual level has been achieved. An individual may keep on redescribing internal representations throughout life. Through this reflective process, a more and more abstract understanding of personal experience, ideas, and meta-ideas can be gained. In principle, there is no final upper level, although such a level can be identified at the textual level, just as the process naturally will cease with the death of the individual.[1]

The process of representational redescription refers to an aspect of development that primarily is conceptual and which is related to a more behavioural aspect of development. It is the process of representational redescription that relates the more performative and the conceptual aspects of development to one another. Conceptual development results from the representational redescription of the processes and products of all aspects of development, implying that the conceptual products themselves may be subjected to representational redescription. According to Karmiloff-Smith, it is the conceptual development that leads to continuous improvements of behaviour beyond that of the mastery of it.

Karmiloff-Smith provides convincing evidence that representational redescription in childhood is phased. Her theory concerns the development of fairly small children, but inasmuch as an individual may keep on elaborating his/her conceptualization of the world, the process of conceptual development resulting from representational redescription may extend far beyond childhood. At a more general level of description, it seems plausible that such potential development similarly will progress in phases, even if not necessarily going through the initial phases as in childhood (presumably a great deal of new knowledge is acquired directly at one of the higher levels). Furthermore,

---

1. Viewed from another angle, it should be stressed that conceptual development does not *necessarily* progress unendingly. As R.N. McCauley points out, most people do not develop models or theories beyond childhood knowledge for everyday activities, because such theories are not needed (1987, 305).

it seems plausible that the process also from the higher conceptual levels and onwards will leap forward at certain points. These points may in turn be identifiable through the conceptual products of the process wherefore conceptual changes will mark the transitions between developmental phases. This should be kept in mind when investigating the higher levels of conceptual development.

The conceptual changes displayed in the works of John of the Cross are the products of a long process of conceptual development. But, even more importantly, both the conceptual changes and the process leading to them have been influenced by the process of writing and reviewing his works. In my view, the process of writing and subsequently interpreting the written can be expected to give a veritable impetus to the process of representational redescription. Hence, I will argue that it is convenient analytically to differentiate between a process of internal redescription and a process of more explicit and concrete interpretation when dealing with written works. The products are at once the explicit outcome of the process of interpretation (which ultimately encompasses anything written and the related interpretations of it) and the more abstract, internal process of representational redescription.

Basically, the process of internal redescription is the more general of the two. The two processes are phased in the way that the process of interpretation at some point combines with that of the already ongoing process of representational redescription. Internal, representational redescription starts early in a subject's life and may continue for the rest of it. In this way, the process of interpretation is added to that of representational redescription. The process of writing serves as a powerful tool for the more internal process of representational redescription.[2] In the case of John of the Cross, the internal redescription of representations has started in childhood, continued with his theological training, been present during his first mystical state, and has continued for the rest of his life. The process of interpretation, on the other hand, was initiated with his first written work.

Interpretational levels and layers

Before turning to an analysis of John of the Cross' developing interpretations of his *Spiritual Canticle*, it seems pertinent to discuss the concept of

---

2. At the level of evolution, Clark speculates that the human exploitation of the environment — of which written representation is a conspicuous example — has triggered or formed the basis of the evolution of a high-level, logical way of thinking. According to this hypothesis, a particular mode of exploiting the environment by some generations has affected the minds of the later generations (1991, 134 and 140).

'interpretation'. In general, I employ the concept in a rather broad sense as referring both to John of the Cross' own interpretations of his written works and to anyone else's interpretation of his works. The latter, though, is irrelevant in the present context, inasmuch as the concern here is how John of the Cross' recurrent interpretations of his writings have affected his conceptualization of his mystical experience.

John of the Cross has repeatedly returned to interpret and amend some work or other. The process of interpretation has therefore unfolded over a fairly long period during which he has addressed works or problems more or less intensely at various points in time. Consequently, the process of interpretation has increased and decreased periodically where the more intense interpretational periods supposedly are loosely identifiable through the interpretational products, that is to say, the amendments. Accordingly, the periods of main interpretational concentration have yielded some traces which, I will suggest, should be appointed 'layers' of interpretation. In turn, it is these layers that display how the interpretational process in John of the Cross' case has leapt forward at diverse points in time. Thus, it should be possible to identify earlier and later layers of interpretation.

I will furthermore propose that John of the Cross has interpreted the *Canticle* at more than one level and that, at least two interpretational levels, namely a higher and a lower, can be discriminated analytically. In reality, however, it is more likely that there are several interpretational sub-levels in between the lower and the higher level. The lower level is first of all displayed in the concrete interpretations of the single verses in the *Canticle* whereas the most important evidence of the higher level is the reorganized poem coupled with the revised argument. The former relates mystical experience at the level of mystical events (narrated as love encounters). The latter, on the other hand, relates the mystical process in its entirety including mystical development (narrated as effects on the female main character in the poem) and the gradual nearing to God (narrated as the unfolding of the love-relationship). Borrowing a terminological distinction from connectionist theories (e.g., Smolensky 1986, 203-204, but see also Thelen and Smith 1994, who uses the terms in a similar way), the interpretational levels can be correlated with the levels of analyzing mystical development, namely at the micro-level (corresponding to the lower interpretational level) and the macro-level (corresponding to the higher interpretational level) respectively.

Analysis of the parts of the *Spiritual Canticle*

Introduction

Inasmuch as John of the Cross' works primarily document the interpretational process, it is this part of the general process resulting in conceptual development to which I shall attend in the following. Obviously, a description of this process must be based on an analysis of John of the Cross' works which (rather subtly) reveal the already completed processes of redescription and interpretation through the developmental products consisting in conceptual changes. It can be expected, though, that the interpretational process really has unfolded in continuous and gradual progression.

The developmental products (discontinuous in nature as they are) do not reveal the continuity of the processes of which they are the outcome. Consequently, the works of John of the Cross can be expected to demonstrate an interpretational process that has advanced in discontinuous leaps. Even if it is unfeasible to accurately map the unfolding of this process, it ought to be possible (at the textual level of analysis) to loosely identify aspects of it if major conceptual changes are somehow displayed. I would argue that this is the case in the works of John of the Cross and, in particular, in the *Spiritual Canticle*. The point is, that the *Canticle* as a whole has been elaborated upon in several phases over a period of many years. Every time he has taken up the work, to add or change something, he seems to have changed his mind about how to understand his mystical experience. Hence, he has undertaken fundamental changes which, in turn, have resulted in some minor or major inconsistencies (since he has not always taken a major change to the logical conclusion, i.e., executing all of the minor changes that would have been required for the preservation of full coherence and consistency of the work). For that reason, inconsistencies among the diverse parts of the work indicate at once the interpretational changes and the process that resulted in them. In short, the work gives evidence for the development of his conceptualization of his mystical experience. In the light of this, it is relevant to focus on the phases in which the *Canticle* has been elaborated and the changes that John of the Cross has made at various points in the process of composing the poem, commenting on it, and revising both poem and commentary.

In the following, I shall first present the phases in which the *Canticle* has been elaborated, then turn to an analysis of the changes and the resulting discrepancies between the parts of the work, and finally discuss what this reveals about John of the Cross' conceptual development.

The phases of composing and interpreting the Canticle

As mentioned above the *Canticle* has been elaborated little by little starting with the major part of the poem, then the rest of the poem and a commentary on it, and finally a revision of both poem and commentary.[3] Evidently, parts of the work have not been developed in discriminate phases that only need to be discovered. It is a highly subjective matter how one discriminates the work into separate parts that are considered to relate to distinct interpretational phases. In my view, it is relevant to distinguish three phases:

1. 1577-78   During this period when John of the Cross was imprisoned by the unreformed, Carmelite order for nearly 9 months, he composed the first two thirds of the poem (the first 30 or 31 verses),[4] although possibly not in written form.

2. 1579-83   In the years between 1579 and 1581, John of the Cross probably wrote the verses 31/32-34 and started commenting on the poem in dialogue with the nuns. In the period from 1582 till 1584, he wrote verses 35-39 (probably in 1583), the first commentary on the poem (finished in 1584), and two treatises, the Ascent of Mount Carmel and the Dark Night, about a person's approximation to God by mystical means.

3. 1584-86   In these years, John of the Cross revised the entire *Canticle* (finished in 1586). (Rodríguez, in Juan de la Cruz 1988, 549-54; Mancho Duque 1982, 30).

As can be seen, John of the Cross has progressed with his writings more rapidly in the intermediate period between the initiation of the first commentary and the termination of the revision of it, that is to say, somewhere in between 1582 and 1586. This seems to have been a period during which his conceptual development virtually has exploded. Presumably, this is the period when the rather intense writing-process seriously began to affect

3. Actually, the revision of the commentary seems to have been initiated already when he at some point read the original commentary, since he has added notes that anticipated some of the major changes.

4. J.V. Rodríguez, who has introduced a Spanish version of John of the Cross' collected works, argues that the first 31 verses have been written during the same period (in Juan de la Cruz 1988, 553). R.M. Icaza, who has analyzed the stylistic relationship between poetry and prose in the original *Canticle*, suggests that he initially wrote the first 30 verses and then later the last nine verses (1957, 1).

his understanding of his mystical experience. In particular, it seems to have been the process of commenting on his own poem, the writing of the two more theological and instructional treatises, and the revision of the *Canticle*, that have accelerated John of the Cross' conceptual development.

It should be pointed out that he has probably started out reflecting on the more concrete aspects of his mystical experience, i.e. particular mystical states or specific aspects of development. It is therefore predictable that there is some degree of coincidence between the diverse layers and levels of interpretation. Accordingly, the lowest layer of interpretation can be expected primarily to display the lowest interpretational level (hence, give the most direct evidence of actual mystical states), whereas the latest layer, reversely, can be expected to display the highest interpretational level (and therefore give more evidence of the developmental process in general).

Dissimilarities of the parts of the Canticle as evidence

The differences between the various parts of the *Canticle* indirectly display the process of interpretation and the conceptual changes that have followed from it. The numerous inconsistencies implicit in the *Canticle* will barely elude anyone who reads the work in its entirety, inasmuch as some of these inconsistencies are quite conspicuous. Since John of the Cross has written the *Canticle* over quite a long period, it is no surprise that there are some differences between the earlier and the later parts of the work. It appears that he at some point has changed his mind about his own mystical experience and therefore also about his writings, and that this change of mind has provoked him to amend the *Canticle*. In his final revision of the work, he has at once reorganized the poem completely and accomplished minor refinements and additions in the commentary on the poem.

Divergences can be pointed out both between the poetic and the prose part of the work, between the original and the revised commentary, within the original commentary, and even within the reorganized poem. Only the original poem seems to be free from actual inconsistencies. From my point of view, it is natural that interpretational incongruities have arisen as the process of interpretation has unfolded. Still, it is important to point out that John of the Cross does not seem to have overlooked the inconsistencies resulting from the changes he made, which means that he apparently has given higher priority to the changes than to upholding a perfectly logical and coherent work.

It is not my intention to go through all of the minor divergences at the various levels of interpretation. Truly, all changes in the *Canticle* do reveal something about the process of interpretation but some of them are far more significant than others. Inasmuch as John of the Cross considers every interpretation that can in some way or another be extracted from the poem to be equally valid, his interpretations often shift between sticking closely to the word of the poem, veritably departing from it, or reading into it. The method of embracing the poem as widely as possible inevitably generates some inconsistency between poem and commentary on specific points and even between one part of the commentary and another. Such cases are copious but actually they reveal more about the process of communication (through the movement from poetic to prosaic expression) than about the process of interpretation.[5]

Hence, I shall in the following concentrate on those changes and ensuing discrepancies that, in particular, give evidence of John of the Cross' process of interpreting his writings and therefore also of redescribing his mystical experience representationally. The most significant alterations are those that in one way or another indicate that John of the Cross has come to view some aspect of his mystical experience (and consequently of his writings about it) in a significantly different way. He has carried out three such changes, namely the reorganization of the poem, the addition of the general argument about the content of the poem, and finally a change in the argument.

The poetic part of the work

The story in the *Canticle*

Before turning to the relation of the original and the reorganized poem, a brief presentation of the poem and the narrative structure of it seems fitting. The poem is clearly inspired by the *Song of Solomon* and, like this, it portrays a passionate love-relationship.[6] The poem is mounted as a sort of dialogue between to lovers who speak alternately, although not necessarily directed at the other person. In some of the verses, the speaking person rather addresses some anonymous bystanders, sometimes speaking more like an actor turning to the audience for advice or in order to tell something important. The female, main character calls her lover the beloved ('el Amado'), whereas he in turn calls her the spouse ('la esposa'). Throughout the poem, the two persons are respectively passive and active by turns and often only one of them is present. Sometimes it is hard to identify which one of the two lovers is speaking in the specific verses. For that reason (I presume) John of the Cross has (retro-

---

5. See Luce López-Baralt for a more thorough analysis of some of the contradictions between commentary and poem (1978).
6. See Vilnet for a thorough investigation of the *Song* as a source of inspiration for the *Canticle* (1949, 106-13) and Orozco, who considers the *Canticle* to be a recreation of the *Song* (1959, 212).

spectively, it appears) pointed this out above those verses in which the acting persons shift. In the beginning of the original poem, she is searching desperately for her beloved, later on the story oscillates between intense union and separation of the two, and towards the end there is undisturbed happiness and pleasure between them. The middle part of the reorganized poem, on the other hand, does not involve the shift between union and separation but moves steadily from recurrent events where the lovers are separated towards the recurrence of more peaceful events of union of the lovers.

Delineation of the narrative in the original and the reorganized poem

I have divided the poem into thematic sections (focusing on events and their consequences) and I have arranged the two poems opposite one another. I go through the poem in clusters of verses instead of dealing with the verses one by one, because the events rarely are described in a single verse. Thus, in many cases an event is related in one verse, whereas the effects of the event stretch into several subsequent verses. In other cases, a couple of verses build up to the occurrence of an event:

The original poem (A)

1-11: *The spouse searches for her beloved.*

The first verse refers back to an earlier point in time when the lovers were together. Now he has left her alone and she yearns for him. Throughout verses 1 to 10 she alternately searches for him and complains about the suffering his departure has caused her. In the eleventh verse she exclaims her utopical wish of suddenly seeing his eyes in a spring into which she is looking..

The ongoing theme in verses one to eleven is the search for her beloved and her expression of suffering.

12: *His sudden appearance is overwhelming.*

The wish of seeing her beloved is complied with. But then she cannot stand it. His sudden appearance is far too much for her. She is so overwhelmed by the sight of him that she immediately takes flight. He, on the other hand, orders her back to him.

13-16: *Pleasure and intimacy.*

In verse 13 and 14 the spouse praises her beloved, their love, and the effects of that love. In the following verse she praises their mutual bed. In verse 16, she tells how *other* young women try to follow her beloved and the wonders he emits.

17-24: *Progress in pleasure and intimacy in retrospection.*

In verses 17 to 24 she describes some events of love and the effects that these events have had on her.

25-26: *Pleasure and intimacy but with the risk of being disturbed.*

In verse 25 there is some danger of the peaceful pleasure being ruined. In the following verse she tries to make the presence of her beloved even more

The reorganized poem (B)

1-12 (A1-11): *The spouse searches for her beloved.*

The themes of 1-12 are equal to those of A1-11, although verse B11 has been added. Here the spouse begs her beloved to disclose his appearance, since this is the only cure for her pain and her illness.

13 (A12): *His sudden appearance is overwhelming.*

13 is identical with A12.

14-15 (A13-14): *Pleasure and intimacy.*

14 and 15 are identical with A13 and 14.

16-21 (A25-26, 31-32 og 29-30): *Pleasure and intimacy but with the risk of being disturbed.*

In verse 16 there is some danger of the peaceful pleasure being ruined. In the following verse she tries to make the presence of her beloved even more noticeable (and in this way increase her pleasure). In verse 18 potential disturbers of the peace are staying close by the lovers, ready to intrude in their peaceful pleasure. The potential intruders are cursed not to move closer while the lovers are united in love. In verse 19 the beloved is urged to hide and to watch noticeable (and in this way increase her pleasure).

27-28: *Pleasure and intimacy together with description of happy event in retrospection.*

In verse 27 the danger is over and the lovers rest together. In verse 28 it is revealed that they have been wed during this restful time. In this verse the beloved retrospectively considers how and where they were married and how he cured her faults.

29-31: *Pleasure and intimacy. Approaching disturbers of the peace are cursed.*

The spouse is sleeping but apparently outsiders are ready to violate the peacefulness. In order to avoid such disruptions, the potential intruders are cursed by him. In the last verse, possible disturbers of the peace still stay close by the lovers, ready to intrude in their peaceful pleasure. At this point, they are cursed not to move closer while the lovers are united in love.

32: *He observes her from afar.*

The beloved is urged to hide and to watch the spouse (and her companions) while she is on a journey (this verse seems strangely out of place).

33-34: *Pleasure and intimacy.*

At last she has returned (to him?) and everything is pleasure. In verse 34 she looks back at the act of returning.

35-39: *She encourages future escalation of the pleasure.*

In the last five verses she encourages him to lead her further into their mutual love. She seems to be imagining how their love will develop and how he will treat her.

the spouse while she is on a journey. In verses 20-21 there is once again pleasure and intimacy and the spouse sleeps peacefully. But it is nonetheless necessary to curse approaching disturbers of the peace.

22-23 (A27-28): *Pleasure and intimacy together with description of a happy event in retrospection.*

Identical with A27 and 28.

24-35 (A15-24 and 33-34): *Progress in pleasure and intimacy (partly in retrospection).*

In verse 24 the spouse praises their mutual bed and in the following verse she describes how *other* young women try to follow her beloved and the wonders he emits. Verses 26 through 33 contain a description of some earlier events of love and the effects that they have had on the spouse. Verses 34 and 35 are identical with A33 and 34.

36-40 (A35-39): *She encourages future escalation of the pleasure.*

Identical with A35-39.

Summary of the changes in the poem

The addition of an eloquent verse (B11) enhances the coherence of the poem.

A verse describing the risk that the lovers' peacefulness is disturbed (A25/B16) and one describing the need to draw the beloved nearer (A19/B17) are transposed to an earlier point in the poem.

A verse describing the risk that the lover's peacefulness is disturbed (A31/B18) is transposed to an earlier point where it becomes the natural continuation of the previous two verses. A verse describing the separation of the lovers (A32/B19) is similarly transferred to an earlier point where it coheres much better with the neighbouring verses.

Two verses describing some potential disturbances (A29-30/B20-21) — expressed through the necessity to curse the potential disturbers of the peace — are transposed to an earlier point in the poem.

The two verses describing the marriage of the lovers and its profound effects on the spouse (A27-28/B22-23) are transposed to an earlier point in the revised poem.

Those verses describing the longest, uninterrupted period of progressive love in the whole poem (A15-24/B24-33) are transposed to a much later point. Furthermore, this change transfers an extremely influential and effectful event of love in a wine cellar to a later point (which furthermore is subsequent to the wedding of the lovers).

At first sight poems A and B are very alike. In both poems, the narrative structure reflects a love-relationship in progress. Initially the lovers are apart. There is no direct description of her emotional state but it seems evident that she yearns desperately for him. There is an implicit reference to previous pleasure and intimacy, implying that the relationship has declined temporarily. At the end of the poem she encourages or imagines their future escalating pleasure and intimacy. In spite of this apparent similarity, there is a basic difference in narrative structure apart from the beginning and the end of the poem, though. Altogether, the changes turn out to be very significant when examined more closely.

The narrative structure of the poem

Evidently, the narrative structure of the poetic *Canticle* is not indisputable, although the main lines probably are incontrovertible. Still, the structure of the poem can doubtlessly be classified in various ways according to the theory imposed on it. My delineation of the structure of the poem is, of course, in accord with the purpose of presenting it which is to bring out the major changes in narrative structure resulting from the reorganization of the verses in the poem.[7]

The original poem (A)	The reorganized poem (B)
1-11: Describe the spouse's yearning and searching for her beloved.	1-12: Describe the spouse's yearning and searching for her beloved.
12: Describes the appearance of the beloved.	13: Describes the appearance of the beloved.
13-32: Describe the oscillation between the lovers' peaceful and intimate pleasure and the danger that it will be interrupted.	14-15: Describe the lovers' peaceful and intimate pleasure.
	16-21: Describe how the lovers' peaceful pleasure is in danger that it will be interrupted.
33-39: Describe how the lovers' pleasure increases continuously.	22-40: Describe how the lovers' pleasure increases continuously.

Analysis of the crucial alterations in the poem

In my view, it is first of all two pivotal alterations in the poem that give a clue to an explanation of what the primary purposes of the reorganization of the poem have been. The changes in question are the inversion of the order of two of the central events in the poem and the compilation of the verses involving negative elements. Hence, I shall go through these particular changes in detail.

---

7. S. Lindhardtsen proposes an outline of the narrative structure (of the reorganized poem only) with a focus on the opposition between lack and abundance (1977, 25).

1) Compilation of verses relating problems for the love-relationship

Those verses that involve danger or risk that the peaceful pleasure is interrupted or which describe the separation of the lovers are scattered all over the middle part of the original poem, whereas these verses are assembled in one long sequence in the reorganized poem. Due to this particular alteration, a poem with a basically different narrative structure is created.

Hindrances to the love:
In verse A25/B16 there is danger that something wonderful will be destroyed. In verse A26/B17 a destructive force is ordered away while a constructive force is called upon. In verse A31/B18 some anonymous, potential disturbers of the peace are cursed. In verse A32/B19 the lovers are temporarily separated. In verse A29-30/B20-21 some anonymous, potential disturbers of the peace are cursed.

The compilation of the less positive elements in the poem (the lack of intimacy and the risk that the pleasure is interrupted and disturbed) results in the narration of a slowly but *steadily* advancing process. There is little doubt that one significant purpose of the reorganization of the poem has been to create a more regular and constant progression in the lyrical narration of the love-relationship. In the original poem the love-relationship oscillates between undisturbed peace and the danger that this peace is disturbed until a very late point. In the reorganized poem, pleasure and intimacy gradually intensifies throughout the poem. The reorganization of the verses has made the originally rather disorderly narrative structure very orderly. In the earlier version, the relationship also improves and intensifies but it does not do so in constant progression. In the later version, it is evident that the spouse moves steadily and continuously towards an apparently preconceived goal and that the relationship develops constantly. The goal is the same in the two versions but the way of getting there is not.

The progression of the love-relationship involves the gradual shift from considerable uncertainty towards reasonable certainty. It should be emphasized that the uncertainty does not derive from the risk that one of the lovers should leave the other. It is the love itself and the intimacy between the lovers that are in danger, because of external threats. Often the dangers are in the form of outsiders that are ready to attack and disrupt the intimacy. In the original poem, the uncertainty of the love is mixed up with periods of certainty which means that it stretches over a much longer period than in the reorganized poem where uncertain and certain periods are separated. Hence, the love is in danger in various ways until the 32nd verse in the original poem, so that only 7 verses narrate a truly peaceful and safe love. As opposed to this, the uncertainty comes to an end already in verse 21 in the reorganized poem, which means that 19 verses are left to peaceful intimacy with absolutely no risk that intruders will interrupt the peacefulness. Due to this structural change, the two poems give the reader rather different overall impressions of the love-relationship. The uncertainty and the suffering related to it are rather short-lasting in the revised poem compared to that of the original poem so that the change results in a stronger stress on the certainty of the love.

Coincidentally, this restructuring has had a side effect as regards the relation of the *Canticle* and the *Song of Solomon*. The narrative structure of the *Song* is much more similar to that of the original *Canticle* than to the reorganized poem. In the original poem and the *Song*, the love-relationship has its ups and downs throughout a very great part of the story, whereas the uncertainty related to this turbulence comes to an end briefly after the middle of the story in the reorganized poem. A result of the change is that the story in the original *Canticle* — in correspondence with the *Song* — is much more exciting and less predictable than in the reorganized *Canticle* (by this, nothing is said or indicated about other qualitative differences between the two).

2) The inversion of the order of two central events

In addition to the more general structural changes, John of the Cross seems to have assigned great significance to the reversion of the poem's two most central events and their consequences, namely the spouse's visit in the 'interior wine cellar' and the wedding of the lovers. Therefore, the sequence of these events and their consequences seem to be of major importance.

The visit in the interior wine cellar (A17-20/B26-29):

Event:	Effect:
The spouse drank from her beloved in a wine cellar, A17/B26.	She has lost her knowledge, A17.3-4/B26.3-4.
	She has given up her former pre-occupations, A17.5/B26.5.
There he gave her his breast, A18.1/B27.1.	She has acquired new knowledge, A18.2/B27.2.

She has conferred everything to her beloved, A18.3-4/B27.3-4.

They have been engaged, A18.5/B27.5.

She has surrendered both her soul and her possessions in his service, A19.1-2/B28.1-2.

She does nothing apart from loving him (now), A19.3-5/B28.3-5.

She does not mix with others anymore, A20.1-2/B29.1-2.

She has been won by the one she is in love with, A20.4-5/B29.4-5.

The wedding (A27-28/B22-23):

Event: **Effect:**

She entered the desired garden, A27.1-2/B22.1-2.

She reposes, reclined, towards her beloved (description of an earlier event), A27.3-5/B22.3-5.

                                            She has been restored, A28.4/B23.4.

There (apparently in the desired garden) they have been wed under the apple-tree where her mother had been violated, A28.5/B23.5.

First of all, the inversion of the two most central events means that the marriage occurs *anterior* to the one event, the visit in the interior wine cellar, that has the greatest impact on the spouse. Of course, the inversion also advances the wedding in the second poem, whereas the event in the wine cellar is postponed. This change coincidentally has a seemingly unintended consequence that appears to be rather inconvenient and which diverges from the general purpose of improving the structure and cohesion of the poem. The point is that the relocation of the verses concerned produces a striking irregularity which is that the spouse promises her beloved to be his spouse at a point when they have already been wed. It was during their meeting in the interior wine cellar that she gave her promise to him to be his spouse. It is not the inconsistency in itself that is of any significance, though, but the fact that it is highly improbable that John of the Cross should have been unaware of it but still has chosen to carry out the change. This indicates that the inversion of these two events has seemed very important to him.

Thereupon, the relocation of the central events (the transfer of the wine cellar event, in particular) generates a more general dissimilarity of the poems which is that the development of the spouse intensifies and escalates much later in the revised version than in the original. In the second version of the poem, the spouse develops steadily but very slowly from the 13th verse and on. It is not, though, until the first really effective event (the wedding in B22) that her development really makes progress. But then the second and even more effectful event follows almost immediately after (B26) implying that the most significant part of her total development unfolds in less than 7 verses (in between B22 and B29). Of course, her development continues after these two events but this is where the (seemingly) most important part of the developmental process is effectuated. In the original poem, the process is described as having unfolded in quite a different fashion. Verse A12 (=B13) is also here a turning point, inasmuch as this is where the *relationship* between the lovers begins to be realized in the poem. But unlike the reorganized poem, the greater developmental changes in the spouse take place in disparate leaps throughout the middle part of the poem.

Finally, the relocation of the events in question additionally produces a minor dissimilarity between the two poems regarding the *relation* of the two events. This point is not so much related to the succession of the events as to the period in between them. In the original poem, there is a fairly long period between the events, whereas they occur shortly after one another in the later poem. The difference is that in the first poem, there are no grounds whatever to associate the two events, while the second poem actually gives the impression that the two events are causally related, that is to say, that the occurrence of the event in the wine cellar *follows from* the fulfilment of the wedding.

Summary

The reorganization of the poem results in a few but very fundamental changes in narrative structure and a change of the succession of the most remarkable events. Firstly, the love-relationship progresses far more steadily in the second than in the first poem. In connection with this, the uncertainty of the love is originally weighted much more heavily than the certainty. The opposite is the case in the reorganized poem, so that the peaceful and safe love becomes much more salient and important due to the compilation of all of the verses involving risks and dangers. Secondly, the transformation of the spouse intensifies much later on in the revised poem. But once her development really gets started, it escalates dramatically. Thirdly, the occurrence of the deeply effective events is more spread out in the original poem than in the revised. In the latter, both events are put off for the last half of the poem which means that they occur with a very short interval giving the impression that they are causally related.

Purposes of the reorganization of the poem

The discrepance between John of the Cross' earliest representational re-description of his mystical development (presupposing that this is, at least partially, communicated in the most primitive poem in the *Canticle*, that is, in the original 30/31 verses) and his later redescriptions (revealed through the additions and the interpretational changes) comprises important evidence both of his mystical and his conceptual development. As documentation of this (and especially of his mystical development) the changes in the *Canticle* involve one problem that needs to be considered. The problem is whether the main motive for the reorganization of the poem has been to make it correspond with a new understanding of the developmental process or he has had some other intentions with the reorganization. One aim could have been to render the poem more pedagogical and comprehendable. Thus, the steady progression in the second poem more clearly narrates a process of gradually approaching a desired object and this might, in his view, have seemed to render the process of mystical development more intelligible. This may have been a point encouraging the reorganization of the poem but I doubt that it should have been the principal reason. The changes are quite fundamental after all. Another motive might have been the generation of a more coherent poem.

There is no doubt that John of the Cross has had aesthetical ambitions and has attempted to optimize the poetical expression in all possible ways. Yet, this has barely been the sole reason for the reorganization of the poem. The revised poem is both more intelligible and more coherent but it is in a way also less exciting. The dangers are eliminated much earlier in the second rendition and the reader has to wait much longer for the more exciting part, inasmuch as the prime love encounters occur later on. In general, the un-folding of the love-relationship is more predictable in the reorganized poem than in the original.

In my opinion, John of the Cross must have had some really good reasons for the more basic changes in the *Canticle* (among which is the reorganization of the poem). The case is that he regarded his poetry (and the best of his explanations of them) as having been divinely inspired (Juan de la Cruz 1988, Prólogo 1; Herrera 1966, 597). They were not simply products of his own mind. Therefore it is most likely to have caused him grave concern to change them. He hardly did so just for the fun of it. My suggestion is that one very good reason for carrying out the major changes was the discovery that the poetic form did not properly fit the object or the content to which his interpretation related. In other words, the structure of the poem no longer seemed to him to correlate suitably with that of mystical development. By this I do not mean to deny that other purposes have had some influence on the changes undertaken. My point is that he presumably would not have changed the poem so fundamentally, if it were not for this particular reason. Accordingly, I will suggest that John of the Cross has intended to reconstruct the poem to communicate the structure of mystical development better (that is, in accord with his changed conceptualization of it).

It appears that John of the Cross has come to see the poem as relating some aspects of his mystical experience inaccurately or even erroneously, doubtlessly pertaining to the structure of the developmental process. The problem is to identify which specific aspects of his mystical development he has wished to relate differently through the reorganized poem. As I have already pointed out, the seemingly most important changes in the poem pertain to the inversion of the order of the two most central events and the compilation of the verses describing more or less negative circumstances. Consequently, I shall concentrate my discussion of the possible motivations on these particular changes.

The motive for assembling the verses involving either risks that the peace-fulness might be disturbed or the lack of intimacy, seems to have been that the original poem gives the impression that John of the Cross' mystical develop-ment had unfolded in uneven leaps with several moves backwards (insofar as the poem is read in agreement with the general argument that it narrates the entire process of mystical development). Presupposing that the poem is read in accord with the revised general argument, the reorganized poem, on the other hand, depicts mystical development as having unfolded in steady progression, even if it has proceeded very slowly up to a certain point. This suggests that John of the Cross, in retrospection, has begun to see his development as a far more evenly and steadily progressing process than he did when he originally composed the poem.

The motivation for the transposition of the two most central and effective events is not exactly plain. Several possibilities should be taken into consideration. The first is that he mainly has aimed to invert the occurrence of the events as relating mystical states. The reason for this could be that John of the Cross, in close consideration of the event in the wine cellar, may have reached the conclusion that it actually concerns a more advanced mystical state than the wedding event. In retrospection, the wine cellar event may have seemed too advanced for the rather early point in the poem. If this is correlated with the first, concrete interpretation of the event (as initiating the third stage) and the point at which it is argued to occur (that is to say, in the middle of the second stage), this possible change of mind begins to make sense. Thus, he seems originally to have composed the verse as relating a very sublime mystical state around the end of the second or the beginning of the third stage. At that point the poem consisted of 30 or 31 verses, which means that the one relating the wedding event (A27-28) — obviously telling of the transition to the third stage — was one of the ultimate verses. Somewhat later, he then added 8 or 9 more verses (leaving 11 instead of 2 or 3 verses to tell of the time after the entrance into the matrimonial stage).

Interpreting the poem in detail, he has come to see the whole poem as relating the mystical process in its entirety wherefore he has divided it into parts relating definite stages. Reinterpreting the poem and the commentary even later on, he has more or less held on to both the general argument about the poem and his concrete interpretation of the verse concerned. But correlating the specific verse with the general argument when reconsidering the poem as a whole, it has become clear to him that this particular verse was misplaced. Consequently, he has transposed the verse to a more advanced point in order to make it correlate better to his new conceptualization of the mystical process. He may or may not have aimed to change the succession of the two central events. To put it differently, it is possible that he has intended to place the wine cellar event so that it related a mystical state in the third stage. The point is that this may have been the only way of combining the double aim of advancing the wine cellar event and producing a coherent poem (apart from the inconsistency of promising to marry one's beloved after having already been wed).

A second possibility is that the purpose of the relocation of the two central events has been to bring the structure of the poem into accord with a changed view of the progression of the mystical process. The point is that he additionally must have intended to modify the way that the poem (apparently) relates the progression or, to be precise, the speed of mystical development at the diverse points. Following the new structure of the poem, the developmental process is depicted as having progressed rather slowly for a very long time instead of taking a major leap a couple of times in the middle part of it. According to the reorganized poem, it is not until the highest mystical stage that the process seriously speeds up. Hence, the revised poem gives the impression that it is not until after the transition to the third stage that John of the Cross' mystical development has escalated. This change follows from the inversion of the order of the events *and* because of the transfer of the wine cellar event from the middle of the poem to the last quarter of it. The first point is that the (seemingly) more effective event occurs earliest in the original poem and the (seemingly) less effective event occurs latest. In the reorganized poem the opposite is the case, so that the (seemingly) less effective event precedes the (seemingly) more effective one. The second point is that the exceptionally effective event occurs at a very advanced point in the poem. This change might indicate that John of the Cross with time has concluded that the most effective mystical states have taken place much later than he originally thought. Yet, in fact such an explanation discords with his general teachings (which the reorganized poem can be expected to reflect) that the major developmental changes are brought out towards the end of the second stage and that only minor changes need to be undertaken in the third stage. Consequently, this may have been a disadvantageous side-effect of some other aim (the above mentioned, of producing a coherent poem, for instance) rather than a motive in itself. It is no surprise that the process continues also within the final stage but it is highly unexpected that it advances at the, until this point, absolute highest velocity. Altogether, he seems to have taken the rough with the smooth, in this case accepting the narration of an exponential escalation in the process within the highest mystical stage.

J.V. Rodríguez, who has taken care of the textual revision of John of the Cross' works in *Obras Completas*, similarly discusses the possible purposes of the reorganization of the poem. He reaches a rather similar conclusion. In his view, the more general aim of the reorganization has been to form the poem in such a way that it describes a *gradual*, mystical process. According to Rodríguez, the problem with the original poem is that it does not respect the graduality and steadiness of the process. The intermediate stage is praised excessively, and unreasonably highly favoured. Moreover, the last stage is given far too little attention and is even succeeded by perturbations (in Juan de la Cruz 1988, 649, note 11). Both of these points are improved in the reorganized poem. An effect of the inversion of the central events is that the highest stage is underscored whereas it was a little underplayed before. The compilation of the more negative elements, on the other hand, renders the process more steady and even.[8]

One or two poems?

In the light of the differences between the original and the reorganized poem, the question of how the two are related arises. This is an important issue because the relation of the parts of the *Spiritual Canticle* may affect the way of understanding the process of interpretation that has resulted in the work in this form. In the following, I shall present three diverging propositions of possible relationships between the original and the reorganized poem. The pivotal question is whether the *Canticle* contains two distinct poems or only one. It is far from certain, though, that it is possible to reach a final conclusion about this. The Danish poet S.U. Thomsen has proposed a theory that suggests two mutually exclusive solutions to the problem. According to Thomsen, a poem is no longer improvable once it has been finished (in principle, the final work is unchangeable).

Every work of art has an ideal form implying that the work is not finished until this form has been *found*. The ideal form is final and once it has been obtained, the work cannot be improved further (Thomsen 1994).[9]

In agreement with Thomsen's theory, there are only two possible relationships between poems A and B in John of the Cross' *Canticle*: either there is only one poem or there are two fundamentally distinct poems. Applying the first solution to the *Canticle*, there are neither two versions of the poem, nor two poems. Really, there is only one finished poetic work. Either poem B is the work and A is an unfinished form of it. Or poem A is the work and B is a deteriorated form. Hence, the poem exists in two editorial forms of which

8. As opposed to Rodríguez, I deem the two poems to be equally true to John of the Cross' mystical experience, even though they relate dissimilar components and in diverging perspectives.

9. In relation to this, I wish to emphasize that I disagree with Thomsen's theory that every work (of art) has an ideal or optimum form only needing to be discovered by the artist. If this theory is accepted, it ought to be no major problem determining whether the *Canticle* contains one poem in two renditions or it contains two distinct poems. It should only be a matter of identifying the ideal form. In my view, the ideality of form is a subjective matter. I believe that when Thomsen finds it rather unproblematic to make such clearcut differentiations it is because he bases his distinctions solely on aesthetical evaluations.

only the one is final. Determining which one of the two constitutes the finished work — which one is the work of art — is, of course, of major importance from an aesthetical point of view.[10] But for a scientific investigation of John of the Cross' conceptual (and mystical) development, this question will be of no concern. Hence, the view that the original and the reorganized poems are either unfinished or deteriorated renditions of the same poem need not eliminate the significance of the non-work edition for other than aesthetical purposes. The second solution to the problem would, in accordance with Thomsen's theory, be that the poems A and B are two finished and fundamentally different poems. Hence, they should be considered equally original and should be investigated as independent works. Neither of the two should be deemed more important than the other.

Disregarding Thomsen's general theory of poetic works, a third possibility should be considered. It may be that the *Canticle* contains only one poem but in two remarkably distinct versions. The one is not simply either an unfinished or a deteriorated rendition of the other. The argument for this proposition would be that there is indeed an unmistakeable continuity between poem A and B, since poem B is a reorganization of the verses in A (with only one additional verse that mainly has aesthetical significance). This argument would concede that there are certainly important differences but they are not so fundamental that A and B constitute two distinct poems. Each version has independent qualities and characteristics but they are much too similar to be distinct poems. The variations are important and are emphasized through the characterization of A and B as constituting two (more or less independent) versions, even if the insistence that there is only one poem lays a major stress on similarities and continuity.[11]

At this point, I would like to state how the theoretical problem concerned here may be affected by — and affect — my general hypothesis about the

10. And this has in fact concerned many (and not only purely aesthetical) studies of the *Canticle*. R.M. Icaza, for instance, argues that the original *Canticle* is the more authentic (1957). It is also quite common to prefer the revised version of the Canticle (poem and/or commentary) and sometimes without even pointing this out or arguing for such selectiveness (e.g. Lindhardtsen 1977; Wilhelmsen 1980).

11. In fact, this allows a reasonable (and very expedient) flexibility for theoretical determination, regarding the degree of variation. In the last instance, this view opposes a clear distinction between one work and another. The extreme consequence of this would be that on the one hand, there is never a finished work and on the other hand, there is always a finished work (this is exactly what Thomsen opposes). That is to say, at any stage in the creative process, a work can be claimed to have reached its final stage, simultaneously with this same work comprising the beginning of a new work. Whether the changes of it are improvements or not, is a matter of taste (a view that Thomsen similarly opposes).

Canticle as displaying John of the Cross' developmental processes or aspects of these. With specific respect to his conceptual development, the dissimilarities between the poems are far more theoretically important than the similarities. In fact, the argument that the *Canticle* contains two independent poems would form an attractive justification for my hypothesis that John of the Cross has undergone a conceptual development. The hypothesis, in turn, supports a strong distinction of the original and the revised poem. Still, neither of the other two possibilities would challenge the hypothesis that John of the Cross has developed conceptually (the changes would, after all, be the same notwithstanding the theoretical stance) but the degree of the changes might point in the direction of relatively more continuity in the developmental process. The argument that there are two poems, on the other hand, would indicate a conceptual development that has vaulted forward with more definite conceptual changes as the result.

The problem of delimiting one work from another does not only concern poems or works written bit by bit like the *Canticle*. On the contrary, it is a matter of general relevance. A similar dilemma concerns other (practically alterable) works, as well as thoughts and ideas. Basically, any work or thought takes its starting point in other works or thoughts using these as building bricks, so to speak. A web of existing works and thoughts make up tradition, at the same time, as tradition constitutes the fundament of inspiration or the point of departure for the construction of new works and thoughts. In the same way, a work or thought potentially contains the material for constructing a new work or thought. This implies that on the one hand, nothing is created from the ground but on the other hand, all creativity contributes with something new. At the micro-level of describing the creative process there will inevitably be continuity. But at the macro-level of describing existing works or thoughts, discontinuities are, of course, identifiable — otherwise it would be impossible to delimit any work or thought as distinct from others. At this level, the problem is to determine the exact point at which the dissimilarities are so great that one should no longer speak of gradual changes of an existing product but of a new product. And this is the problem faced in the *Canticle* both regarding the poetic and the prose part of the work.

Before discussing the possible ways of differentiating the *Canticle*, I would like to point out that it really is an intricate matter to resolve an issue like this decisively. The fact that two stories to a greater or lesser extent share a basic narrative structure, for instance, does not make them the same story in two versions. But does even the slightest dissimilarity in narrative structure make them two stories? And if so, can any alterations of some kind or other be carried out without resulting in the construction of a new work? The relation of the *Canticle* and the *Song of Solomon* illustrates these problems very well.

The narrative structure of the original poem is more than simply inspired by that of the *Song* but at the same time, it is far from being a mere imitation of it. The similarity is more like a recreation of a very similar structure. Yet, the reorganization of the *Canticle* has considerably modified this similarity. The original poem actually shares more of the *general*, narrative structure with the *Song* than with the reorganized *Canticle*. But, when it comes to the details both of narrative structure and of other elements, the poems in the *Canticle* are, of course, much more alike than either of them is with the *Song*.

Before suggesting an answer to the question, I shall briefly sum up the presented possibilities. Either there is one poem in two fundamentally similar editions, or there are two distinct poems, or finally, there is one poem in two more or less diverging versions (in that case the degree of variation should be determined in the concrete analysis according to one's theory).

Provided that the poem is taken to relate aspects of John of the Cross' mystical experience, implying that the single verses refer to mystical states, then the inversion of the wedding and the wine cellar event does not in itself seem to alter the meaning of the verses in any significant way. But the way that the inversion of the events affects the progression of the process of transforming the spouse actually alters the way that mystical development is related in the poem. In addition to that, the compilation of the more negative elements similarly modifies considerably the way that mystical development is related. What is even more important, though, is that these two changes reinforce one another, so that they in combination produce a poem describing a steadily, instead of an unevenly, advancing process. This rules out the first possibility that the original and the reorganized poem should be one poem in two fundamentally similar editions.

If Thomsen's theory is followed, the *Canticle* contains two separate poems. Inasmuch as they differ on such fundamental points they must be distinct poems. Yet, even though the structural alterations cause some fundamental dissimilarities, the revised poem is still made from the material of the original poem (with the addition of a single verse) changing the combinations of the parts only at the level of whole verses leaving the composition at the level of both words and sentences unchanged.

In fact, the similarities and dissimilarities are equally fundamental depending on what one focuses on. If the focus is on the poem as recounting the structure of the mystical process, then the differences are the more salient. If one focuses on the aesthetical coherence of the poem, then the differences similarly are quite remarkable. Yet, on just about all other points (in particular the way that mystical events are depicted), the similarities are by far the most conspicuous. All in all, it depends on the *focus* whether the similarities or the dissimilarities are deemed the more significant. Consequently, it does not make a lot of sense to let the degree of distinction follow as an inescapable consequence of the identification of some degree of dissimilarity. In fact, it is hardly feasible to settle the matter decisively in a case like this. In conclusion, it seems most sensible to distinguish two versions of one poem, if all aspects are taken into account. Still, as a report of the mystical process it really makes sense to discriminate two poems. For the present purpose, the degree of similarity/dissimilarity of the original and the reorganized poem should be determined on the basis of the way that they relate John of the Cross' mystical experience where the single verses relate mystical states and the poem in general reflects the developmental process either in fragments or in its entirety.

The prose work

Presentation

On the request of one of the Discalced Carmelite nuns, John of the Cross has taken on the project of explaining his poem. For various reasons, he has at a later point decided to reorganize the poem and to undertake a meticulous revision of his own commentary. Yet, his procedure in the revision of the prose work has basically been to copy the original commentary and to add points wherever it appeared fitting. Unlike his revision of the poem, he has primarily added to the concrete interpretations of the single verses without making any major changes in them. By and large, the second commentary is thus mainly an enlarged and improved edition of the first.

In the commentary, the topics described and discussed and the sequence of them sometimes seem a little arbitrary because they relate directly to the verses in the poem. Even if the commentary is not always much of an explanation of the poem (although this is what John of the Cross himself claims it to be) the former is still related to or inspired by the latter. Hence, neither the subjects discussed nor the sequence of topics are organized according to a predetermined scheme.

In John of the Cross' opinion the poem can be interpreted in numerous ways that are all equally valid. In accord with this view, he certainly has had no intentions of finishing the process of interpreting the poem. In fact, his intention has rather been to initiate this process. His commentary should therefore be taken as an example of how the poem can be, but not of how it ought to be, interpreted (Juan de la Cruz 1988, A/B Prólogo). L. López-Baralt accurately describes John of the Cross' procedure of interpreting his own poem as one of extension and addition but not of explanation (1978, 21).

The two general arguments about the content of the poem

In his original commentary on the poem in the *Canticle*, John of the Cross furthermore presents an argument about the general content of the poem. In the revised commentary, this argument is modified somewhat along with the revision of the concrete interpretations of the verses. These two general arguments (especially the original) have far reaching consequences for the relationship between the parts of the *Canticle*, because they generate considerable divergences between the diverse levels of interpretation. Hence, they also make up highly significant evidence of John of the Cross' conceptual development and deserve due concern.

In the original commentary, John of the Cross argues that the poem in the *Canticle* describes the stages of mystical development including the time anterior to the stages classified by himself (Juan de la Cruz 1988, Cántico A27: 2). The structure of the poem is thereby claimed to follow the structure of the process of mystical development. Each part of the poem is related directly to a particular mystical stage. Surprisingly, though, this argument of how to read the poem does not appear until the interpretation of verse 27 in the original commentary, which means that it is a bit more than two thirds into the work.

In the revised commentary, the stage *following* the mystical process has been added to the argued sequence of stages in the poem.[12] According to this new interpretation, the last five verses of the poem really deal with the eternal union with God that is expected to be obtained after natural death[13] (Juan de la Cruz 1988, Cántico B argumento and 22:3). At first sight, this may appear to be nothing but a slight modification of the argument that the poem delineates the process of mystical development. But in fact, it is a rather drastic change that could be based on a wholly new interpretation of the poem. If this is the case, the alteration implies that John of the Cross at one point should have expected some qualities of mystical states to be typical of an advanced point in the final stage, whereas later on he should have regarded these qualities as relegated in general to the eternal stage. The point is that inasmuch as the last five verses are the same in the two versions of the poem,

---

12. The addition of the final stage to the structure imposed on the poem is anticipated before the actual writing of the second version. During the process of rereading and correcting his own original commentary, John of the Cross has inserted some adjustments to the structure (this one, for instance), by adding some further comments in the margin (Juan de la Cruz 1988, Cántico A27:2, note 7-8).
13. Of course, John of the Cross does not claim that the description of this ultimate stage is based upon his own experience but only that he has imagined what that stage must be like.

the same verses are claimed to depict either the mystical states in the final mystical stage (or maybe a part of it), or the eternal union in the original and the revised commentary respectively. Still, the change could also primarily be motivated by the intention to contribute to the formation of a more harmoniously structured poem.

In the revised commentary, the general argument is presented twice. At the beginning of the commentary, the argument appears as a general guidance of how to read the poem. Here a shortened rendition of the original argument is offered, although the period prior to the stages of the process is omitted and the stage following the actual mystical process is added. The sequence of the stages are expressed in traditional Christian terms with which the nuns doubtlessly have been acquainted. Further on in the revised commentary, the original formulation of the argument is copied, although still with the addition of the eternal stage. Here a detailed treatment of the argument appears in the same place as in the original commentary which is in extension of the interpretation of the verse narrating the wedding event (A27/B22). At this point, the stages are classified in correspondence with the general (and traditional) metaphor in the *Canticle*, according to which the mystical process is a gradual fulfilment of the love between God and the soul.

It appears that John of the Cross gradually has developed his interpretation of the poem as covering more and more levels. He has started at the level of single verses (or groups of verses) viewing each in isolation and interpreting them as relating specific, mystical events. The considerations of the single verses have, in turn, occasionally inspired him to consider more general aspects of the process. Little by little he has then come to see the poem in a more general perspective as relating the entire mystical process. The fact that he originally included the pre-mystical stage and later included a post-mystical stage is irrelevant with respect to the interpretational *levels* but most important as evidence for a valuation of the significance of the stages *and* as evidence for his interpretation of the poem.

Secondary effects of the change in the argument

As could be expected, the alteration of the general argument has had some consequences for the revision of the rest of the commentary. In particular, John of the Cross has needed to adjust his interpretation of the last five verses to it. The change causes some confusion about whether the verses concerned refer to the highest mystical or the post-mystical stage.[14] In his introductions

---

14. B39:3-6 and 40:5-6 in the commentary deal with the highest mystical stage, for instance. In order to read this in concordance with the new argument, one needs to imagine that

to the concrete interpretations of each verse, he unfailingly manages to continue the thread of the new argument. Hence, it is primarily at the level of the interpretation of single lines that some unclarity arises.[15] Here it often seems almost as if the passages oscillate between talk of respectively the one stage and the other. Attending closely to the text, it turns out that this mainly is because his sometimes rather ambiguous expressions simply leave the meaning open. Hence, the interpretations can be read in the one way or the other. So, even though the new interpretation departs from the old on fundamental points, the expressive openness has made it possible for John of the Cross to copy most of the original commentary with only minor changes and some important additions. This has, of course, facilitated the work of revision.

In combination, the three major changes, namely the reorganization of the poem, the addition of the first general argument, and the change of it, have some consequences for the diverse levels of interpretation. Putting the relation of the parts a little squarely, one might say that the alterations of the parts of the *Canticle* are disproportionate in degree. The point is that the two versions of the poem are highly dissimilar, the two renditions of the argument less so, and the editions of the concrete interpretations even less so. Hence, some inconsistencies at the more concrete level of interpretation arise, because he has failed to adjust the revised interpretations of the single verses to the rather radical changes in the reorganized poem, whereas others arise because the revised interpretations of the single verses are not adjusted to the changes in the general argument about the poem as such. Accordingly, some such inconsistencies are revealed through the relation of the poem and the commentary while others are displayed in the relation of the concrete interpretations and the general argument in the original and the revised *Canticle* respectively.

Purposes of each of the two general arguments

In both the case of the first and the second argument it can be ruled out that John of the Cross has been moved by aesthetical motives to present the argument in the first place and to change it later on. As opposed to this, is seems rather certain that both arguments have had pedagogical and instruc-

---

even though the *verses* treat on the eternal union, John of the Cross has nonetheless chosen to talk about the matrimonial union.

15. In fact, it is no surprise that the introductions ('anotaciónes') fit the new argument better than the rest of the reinterpretations, since these introductions were not in the original commentary, but are written exclusively for the new edition.

tional purposes. Yet, this has barely been the main reason for coming up with the idea of how to interpret the poem as a whole. It is more likely that having had the idea, it dawned upon him that it would, at the same time, ease the understanding of the poem tremendously.

Taking a closer look at the instructional advantages of the first argument, he may have wanted to make sure that his readers did not miss the point that the poem actually relates the mystical process quite specifically. He has presumably taken it for granted that his readers (whom he took to be the Discalced Carmelite nuns and friars), at least at that point in the commentary, would have no doubts that the poem relates elements of mystical experience. Yet, by making it explicit exactly how the one relates to the other, he seems to have wished to enable his readers to get a better overview of the mystical process. It is obvious, though, that for the spiritual reader looking to the commentary for instructions on how to read the poem it would have been a greater help if the argument and the overview of the process had been introduced right from the start (this point is indeed rectified in the second edition of the commentary).

In my view, the fact that the argument is not presented in the beginning of the commentary is exemplary evidence of the process of interpretation. Primarily, it shows how John of the Cross gradually has changed and nuanced his understanding of the poem as recapitulating his mystical experience. He has started out commenting on the poem, verse by verse, without really making it very clear to himself what exactly the more general scheme of the poem was. It is not until the point of commenting on the verse interpreted as narrating how the third stage was inaugurated, that it has stricken him that the poem actually recounts the whole mystical process. Certainly, he has had a pretty good idea of what the whole thing was about. He has probably had something like a draft version of the idea in mind for a long time but it is not until at this point that he has worked it over and made it explicit. Secondarily, it indicates how he has commenced conceptualizing the process of mystical development in an increasingly more general perspective. Yet, the fairly sudden presentation of the argument only comprises partial evidence of this aspect of the unfolding of John of the Cross' conceptual development and should therefore be correlated with the other part of it.

This other part is the two more general treatises, the Ascent of Mount Carmel and the Dark Night. Since John of the Cross has written these two works and the commentary on the poem in the *Canticle* more or less during the same period of a couple of years, it is likely that the work on the treatises has influenced his work on the commentary. This work has most probably been highly significant for his conceptualization of the structure of the mystical process, inasmuch as this is one of the main themes in the treatises.

The work with the description of the mystical process in general is almost bound to have influenced his understanding of it. In my view, it is not unlikely that it is the process of making his reflections on his mystical development explicit that has made him aware that the poem in the *Canticle* really seemed to relate the stages of mystical development in detail.

Due to the concentrated reconsideration of the process of mystical development, especially in connection with the formulation of the Ascent and the Night, John of the Cross has acquired a far more general understanding of the process. Enriched with this new conceptualization of the mystical process, he has come to see the poem in a new light. Commenting on a verse that (with its reference to the wedding of the lovers) clearly seems to narrate the inauguration of the matrimonial stage (the third and final), it has stricken him that the poem (divinely inspired as he took it to be) truly related the entire mystical process from the beginning to the end and not only accidental bits and pieces of it. Hence, he has at that point presented this more general interpretation of the poem in his argument.

Turning to the modification of the argument, the purpose of it is not exactly plain. In fact, it is a little puzzling why he has changed his mind this way. I shall present three possible answers to the question. The first possibility is that John of the Cross, in reconsideration of how his mystical approach to God relates to the structure of the poem, has come to view the last five verses as somewhat exaggerated as descriptions of mystical states in the ultimate, mystical stage. Obviously, an easy solution to such a mis-relationship would be to argue that the verses really do not concern a mystical, but a post-mystical, stage. If I shall identify a possible element in the last verses of the *Canticle* that might, in retrospect, have seemed to recount some aspect of mystical experience falsely, it would be the mention of a flame that causes no pain (in union of love). Thus, he may have come to view this as an over-statement with respect to the mystical states in the ultimate *mystical* stage, but as fitting the imagined post-mystical stage perfectly.

One possible reason why John of the Cross, when reviewing the poem, may have come to regard his earlier description of mystical states beyond pain as exaggerated, could have been that this simply was his new and improved experience. Thus, it is possible that his poetical portrayal of painless meetings with God actually had been nourished by his expectations that such mystical states would become achievable as soon as his soul was purified. This presumption might in turn have been based on a preconceived scheme of the relation of human beings and God. It is not impossible that he for a long time kept on believing that such mystical states would soon make their entrance in his experience (although he had already at that point reached the third mystical stage). Much later when this still had not happened, he may have reached the conclusion that these expectations would not be fulfilled in mystical life and that his conception of either the cause of the pain or the degree of purity obtained were false.

The second possibility is that the new interpretation simply has been inspired by the tense of the verbs in the last part of the poem. The point is that the last five verses recapitulate something imagined and wished for. It is not unlikely that it has occurred to him that this might appear a little odd to the reader whereas the tense would seem logical, if the verses related a stage to come after the completion of mystical life.

The third possibility is that he has wished to divide the poem in order to relate the diverse parts of mystical life more equally and, furthermore, to relate the not less important post-mystical stage. The new argument actually contributes to that end (aided by the reorganization of the verses).

The core of the matter is that the change in the argument seems to have been motivated either by the content of the verses concerned (the first possibility), the form of the verses (the second possibility), or the form of the poem in general (the third possibility). As a starting point for an evaluation of the possibilities, they can be divided into two according to the basic motive for the change, namely his mystical experience or the communicative power of the poem. Both could have been justified incitements for such a significant change on the background of John of the Cross' considerable efforts to communicate his mystical experience.

It would seem that John of the Cross' actual mystical experience had been the best reason for changing the argument, though. In my opinion, it seems most plausible that John of the Cross really has come to the conclusion that it was an exaggeration to speak of a flame that causes no pain. As I see it, he has really *interpreted* the line in the verse (instead of remembering his ideas at the time of writing the line) and correlated this interpretation with his current conceptualization of mystical experience. And this is, in my view, the main reason why the two Canticles end up seeming contradictory at this particular point.

The essence of this is that he, with his original mention of the painless flame, has thought of the consummation of mystical states in the final stage. A couple of years later, he has interpreted the line in a slightly more general perspective. At that point, it has occurred to him that it was not quite correct to describe the final stage as completely free of pain. Having shifted the focus from specific mystical states to various more general aspects, he has no longer interpreted the flame as pertaining to the realization of a mystical state only, but additionally as describing the stage as such or, more precisely, the time in between mystical states.

I am getting to the point now. Composing the final five verses, John of the

Cross' imaginations of future mystical states have been based on the consummation of current mystical states. And they were free (or maybe almost free) from the otherwise common pain and this is what is reflected in the mention of the flame that causes no pain. Interpreting this expression later, he has deemed it an overstatement with respect to two points. Firstly, as regards the stage in general which is very painful due to the longing for the eternal union (presumably, this pain is felt only during the time in between mystical states). Secondly, as regards the strength and exaltedness of mystical love which seems to be harmful somehow even at that point (Juan de la Cruz 1988, Cántico B39:14).

Still, I do not think that this has been the sole reason for changing the argument. Whatever has been the primary motive, I think that John of the Cross has recognized several advantages to the change. Thus, he has presumably changed the original argument in order to make it fit both the impression that the poem gives anyway and his new (and slightly more general) interpretation of the verseline. As an extra gain, the poem has been classified more harmoniously.

One or two arguments?

This section should be intitiated with the question whether the change in the general argument makes it two arguments or two more or less dissimilar renditions or versions of the same argument. It is hardly as tangled an issue as in the case of the poem, since there are not a whole range of changes that should be taken into account. Thus, it is only the addition of a post-mystical stage to the argued content in the poem that has any significance, inasmuch as the omission of the period prior to the classified process in the initial presentation of the revised argument seems to be rather insignificant and maybe even accidental. He appears to have judged this rather unimportant and may not have taken the trouble to mention it in his presentation of the second argument. After all, he seems to have considered that very early period more as an indispensable precondition for the mystical process than to be actually part of it.

The issue is therefore to assess the degree of dissimilarity of the two arguments with respect to the final stage. When the original argument (presented in the interpretation of verse A27) is compared with the extended rendering of the revised argument (presented in the interpretation of verse B22) there are no basic differences (the change in argument is not yet relevant in relation to this verse which narrates the wedding event and announces the initiation of the third stage). Since the purpose of the argument is apparently to guide the reading of the *Canticle*, an evaluation of the dissimilarity following from the change really has to be based on the way that the reading is guided by the old and the new argument respectively. In the light of this, the change actually seems to have been rather insignificant when viewed in isolation from the alterations in the rest of the work. Segregated from the other changes, the new argument can barely be considered to diverge fundamentally from the old and should rather be deemed an extended version of it.

Accordingly, the degree of dissimilarity of the arguments corresponds more or less to that of the concrete interpretations where the most fundamental changes are those that are accommodations to the change in the argument, whereas nearly all other modifications are elaborations of the existing interpretations. Therefore, the shift in the way that the reader is directed to read the work mainly stems from the changes in the poem coupled with the argument adjusted to the reorganization of the verses. Consequently, the real importance of the changes do not come to the surface until the revised work is estimated as a whole.

Connecting evidence and hypothesis

How mystical experience is recounted in the diverse parts of the Canticle

Now we must address the issue of what the diverse parts of the work actually relate about John of the Cross' mystical experience as a basis for evaluating his conceptual development. In this context the first question is if the poem was originally composed with the intention of recounting the entire mystical process. A negative answer will further provoke the question of what the poem was then supposed to portray, whereas a positive answer will give rise to the question of what the original poem actually documents about the process.

The relation of the original and the reorganized poem tells us that the one component in the poem that first of all had appeared wrong to John of the Cross was the way that it depicted the progression of the mystical process (including the issue of the gradual improvement of mystical states). Two themes in the poem can be interpreted as recapitulating the mystical process, namely the gradual intensification of the love-relationship and the changes in the spouse. In the original poem, the major changes in the spouse are carried out around the middle of the poem (between A17 and 28) whereas the love-relationship increases and decreases recurrently in intensity and peacefulness until undisturbed peace finally is attained. Here it should be kept in mind that the poem only consisted of 30/31 verses at first. The cluster of verses around the wedding (27-28) is therefore located towards the very end of the most primitive poem. Accordingly, the original poem relates a developmental process that rather suddenly intensifies and vaults forward (towards the very end of what is related in the most primitive poem or in the third quarter in the completed, original poem) whereas the actual mystical states seem to improve in a rather disorderly manner.

Certainly, the structure of the original poem in the *Canticle* could primarily have been motivated by the structure of the *Song*. Supposedly, this actually has been the case. Yet, the structure of the *Song* could in itself have been one of the main reasons why John of the Cross chose to use it as a sort of model for his own poem. My point is that it is likely that one reason why the poem has appeared so inspiring to him is that it narrates the growth of a love affair seemingly corresponding remarkably well with the development of his own mystical relationship with God. One such parallel might have been the fairly disorganized structure of the *Song*. Hence, I do think that the disorganized structure of the original poem is inspired by the *Song*. But the reason why he has picked the *Song* as a model *and* the reason why he more or less has copied the structure of it is, in my opinion, that it captures something about his mystical experience as he understood it when composing the poem. And this something doubtlessly pertains to the way that John of the Cross' mystical development has progressed.

So, what is it that the original poem (as opposed to the revised) describes? I would suggest that the original poem recounts mystical development at the micro-level of description. This is the level of describing the actual progression of the process, where recurrent mystical states give impetus to the advancement of the process at the same time as diverse features of the mystical states themselves change very slowly, staggering forward while oscillating between more and less advanced states respectively.

Turning to the first version of the commentary, the concrete interpretations and the general argument should be considered separately. The concrete interpretations mainly describe the mystical process at the micro-level of particular mystical states, although sometimes shifting to the macro-level of selected, general aspects of the process. In his concrete interpretations, John of the Cross typically zooms in on what is already in focus in the verses of the poem, supplying more detailed descriptions of it. Occasionally, he shifts the focus from mystical states to more general aspects of the mystical process (often inspired by his own poetical metaphors) thereby switching to the macro-level of description. In general, the concrete interpretations give quite detailed accounts of selected topics of mystical experience, either particular mystical states or specific aspects of the general process. These occasional shifts between levels of description do not give rise to any major problems, though, as the process is not yet attended to as a whole.

Presenting the first general argument, John of the Cross attempts to describe the mystical process in its entirety at the macro-level. He switches his attention from the details to the totality, aiming to describe the mystical process form a very general perspective. In his argument about the content of the poem, John of the Cross simply divides the various verses and the corresponding interpretations into parts that are related to the developmental stages without accommodating the poem and interpretations to the switch-over to another level and focus. This actually generates considerable inconsistency between the various degrees of generality of the descriptions of the process. The problem is that at the micro-level of description, the process seems to have zig-zagged its way ahead which is what is related in the poem and therefore also in the concrete interpretations. When the process is considered from a more general perspective describing it at the macro-level, all the minor irregularities disappear and the process seems to have progressed steadily and without any apparent or real relapses, which is (more or less precisely) reflected in the argument. Consequently, the original *Canticle*, as a combination of poem, concrete interpretations, and general argument, is highly inconsistent due to the switch between the two levels of description.

Proceeding with the identification of what each of the parts in the *Canticle* really describes, the next is the revised work in which the most significant alterations are those in the poem. If the poem is viewed in isolation, the re-arrangement of some of the verses in itself affects the way that the poem will be read. Due to the various changes, the reorganized poem, unlike the original, narrates a love-relationship that gradually develops undisturbed towards intensification. It is not actually the case, that the reorganized poem expresses a less burdensome development of a love affair. The point is that the poem depicts a more steadily improving relationship. Contrary to the original poem, the reorganized poem therefore seems to delineate the unfolding of mystical development as it appears at the macro-level rather than at the micro-level. The extensions of the concrete interpretations, on the other hand, do not in themselves alter the way that the mystical process is related.

Estimating the argument in isolation, the primary change is the inclusion of the eternal stage. Yet, this does not affect the way that the process seems to have progressed according to the poem, inasmuch as the change is that the last five verses are claimed to relate a non-mystical stage subsequent to the process. Hence, the last five verses and the interpretations of them become relatively insignificant in relation to mystical experience. More specifically, a particular aspect (the pain) about mystical states or possibly the final stage is conceived of differently in each of the two arguments. Accordingly, the modification of the argument does not in itself change the way that the mystical process is presented but only a specific aspect of it.

Actually, the judgement of the revised argument should not be isolated but ought to be coupled with that of the reorganized poem and the corresponding interpretations. When the poem is deemed in combination with the argument, the revised Canticle evidently relates a far more undeviating, continuous, and harmonic progression of the mystical process. As a whole, the revised Canticle indisputably relates mystical development in a general perspective far better than any part of the original Canticle. But, at the same time, the revised Canticle completely neglects the micro-level of mystical development, that is to say, the progression at the level of mystical states, where the process seems to have relapsed once in a while.

Terminating this discussion, it should be pointed out that it is in the two treatises, the Ascent and the Night, that John of the Cross has systematized his idea of the structure of mystical development most elaborately. In these two works, he does not claim that the concrete process does not *seem* to relapse once in a while. Truly, what looks like regression to the subject is just God's way, though, of trying the soul.[16] His point is that the process does progress incessantly, even though it does not always appear that way. It is not unlikely that John of the Cross through repeated representational redescription of his mystical experience, and the interpretation of his own writings about it, has reached the conclusion that the mystical process may have seemed a little disorderly to him but that this was just because of his lack of insight. Later, when he achieved a better overview of the process, he came to understand that all parts of the process had each their purpose, even if it was sometimes concealed to himself. Consequently, he has considered the new understanding of the process to be the more realist. Still, it is not impossible that he has been aware that the original Canticle actually captured elements of his mystical experience from another angle, inasmuch as he apparently has made no attempt to destroy the original work in order to replace it with the new edition. Thus, he may have considered the new version to add to the old rather than substitute it.

The display of conceptual development in the Canticle

I initiated this chapter with the hypothesis that a process of interpretation joins an ongoing process of internal redescription of cognitive representations. The process of representational redescription in itself triggers and promotes conceptual development but this accelerates tremendously once the process of

---

16. In a rather similiar way, he describes the process as involving a worsening of the condition of the subject which he considers an apparent descension. He explains that this seeming descension is requisite for the improvement of the subject. Hence, it only *seems* as if one's condition deteriorates due to the mystical process. In reality, the decline simultaneously is growth.

interpretation additionally sets in. Thereupon, I proposed an analysis of how the process of interpretation, indirectly reflecting representational redescription, is documented in the *Canticle*. The task is now to combine hypothesis and evidence and show how the diversity of the parts in the *Canticle* reveals John of the Cross' conceptual development.

John of the Cross' conceptualization of his mystical experience has been facilitated and fostered by his written description of it and his interpretations of those descriptions. Writing thoughts down and subsequently reading the written work is an important help for thought itself. It eases the organization of ideas and concepts that may have started out rather disorderly. Basically, it is the process of representational redescription that causes conceptual development, potentially involving actual conceptual changes. But it is the process of interpretation that boosts this kind of development and pushes it forward. In this way, it is the combined processes of redescription and interpretation that have altered John of the Cross' way of seeing his own mystical states and development. Through consecutive explicit formulation and re-formulation of his ideas, first in spoken and then in written form, John of the Cross has diversified and generalized his understanding of his mystical experience.[17] Yet, it is the process of interpretation as it is displayed in John of the Cross' works that gives evidence of both the internal and the more explicit process. And

---

17. It should be emphasized that some scholars have argued that the motive for John of the Cross' more theological interpretations of his poems has been to accommodate contemporary theology etc. Thus, Lindhardtsen suggests that the purpose of interpreting his own poem has been to spiritualize the sexuality in the poem (1977, e.g., 28). This is, in my view, an absolutely preposterous suggestion. The manifest sexuality in the Canticle was already spiritualized by tradition and has barely surprised the contemporaries of John of the Cross in any way. Lindhardtsen does not overlook the tradition of interpreting the Song of Salomon in a spiritual context, but nonetheless suggests that John of the Cross has been capable of partially transgressing conventions and reading the Song in a double way, namely the *original* mythico-cultic and the contemporary politico-religious, which Lindhardtsen sees as the cause of a controversy or 'polemic' between the unitive view of the Song (where there is no distinction of poetry and religion, corporality and spirituality, or reality and text) and the dualist view (where there are such distinctions) (1977, 37-38). López-Baralt in a similar vein proposes the view that John of the Cross has felt morally obliged to interpret his poem theologically (1978, 24). Certainly, the more theological interpretations of the poem are plain and numerous. I have not focused on this part of the interpretational process, because I have deemed it less significant as evidence of John of the Cross' conceptual development. This is not to say, though, that it does not give evidence of conceptual development at all. In my view, the more theological interpretations of the poem, just as the other modifications throughout the work, are motivated by repeated reflection and interpretation that has enabled him to diversify and generalize his understanding of both his mystical experience and his own writings.

here the changes in the *Canticle* are far the most significant. Consequently, the uncovering of major changes in the *Canticle* give evidence of the conceptual development of John of the Cross.

Looking at the processes resulting in conceptual development as a whole, it is presumably the process of representational redescription that has motivated the process of interpretation. The earliest part of the *Canticle* (the original 30/31 verses of the poem) is at once the first explicit product of an already long process of redescription and the foundation of (and basically the initiation of) the process of interpretation. Hence, the earliest poetry is also the best documents of his most primitive, representational redescription. His later contributions to the original part of the poem, his first commentary and his later revision of both poem and commentary, give evidence of the conceptual advances gained through the joint processes of redescription and interpretation. The process of interpretation involves repeated reinterpretation of the written. The reinterpretation in turn has inspired a new conceptualization of the described and new ideas that similarly are described and reinterpreted etc. In short, from the moment of initiating the first written work, anything written (implicitly anything redescribed representationally) has affected any subsequent writing or redescription (jointly making up the processes of redescription and interpretation). In principle, the more obser-vable part of John of the Cross' process of interpretation included the original composition of the poetic *Canticle* (insofar as he may have interpreted and composed it more or less coincidentally), the formulation of a commentary on it, the writing of the two instructional treatises, and eventually, the reinterpretation and amendment of the first *Canticle*.

In general, the *Canticle* gives evidence of three points at which the combined processes of redescription and interpretation seem to have vaulted forward. The analysis of the parts of the *Canticle* indicates that John of the Cross has elaborated and changed his way of understanding his mystical experience three times at least. The first conceptualization is disclosed in the earliest part of the original poem and (to some extent) documents his more primitive representational redescriptions of his mystical experience. The second conceptualization and the first (major) conceptual change is revealed in the first argument about the structure and content of the poem and primarily concerns his understanding of this, but secondarily indicates how he has begun to see the mystical process in a more general perspective. The third conceptualization and the second (major) conceptual change is exposed in the revised *Canticle* as a whole but most noticeably in the reorganized poem. These changes indicate that John of the Cross has come to see the mystical process in a very general perspective.

If my suggestion is right that the 30/31 first verses of the poem give evidence of the process of representational redescription at a particular point, inasmuch as the process of interpretation still had had little significance (if at all), then the problem is to identify how this part of the work relates mystical experience in comparison with other parts. In my view, this most primitive part of the *Canticle* mainly refers to two aspects of mystical experience. On the one hand, the verses portray (averages of) selected (types of) mystical states and how they have affected John of the Cross. On the other hand, the poem renders fragments of the developmental process in flashes. The first point remains undisputed by John of the Cross whereas he contradicts the second in his arguments (inasmuch as he argues that the process is related *in its entirety*). Accordingly, the most original part of the *Canticle* indicates that he initially has apprehended the mystical process in a highly fragmented way, grasping only scattered bits and pieces of it.

John of the Cross' argument that the poem as a whole describes the mystical process from beginning to end has supposedly been motivated by a fundamentally new way of looking at the poem *and* a new way of understanding his mystical experience. In the argument, he outlines the unfolding of mystical development in a general perspective. He pins down the points at which the developmental process has advanced from one part to another, at the same time as he provides some clues to the specific character of the diverse parts. Apparently, the point at which John of the Cross presents the original argument is coincident with the point at which he has come to see the poem as not only describing segments of his mystical experience, but as actually delineating the entire mystical process. Since the parts of the poem appertain specifically to those of mystical development, the details of the process do not protrude until the poem and the argument (in the original *Canticle*) are correlated. When the two are associated, it becomes plain that the mystical process has progressed in a rather chaotic way. The duration and the significance of the parts of the process seem to have been rather disproportionate and asymmetrical. But that is not all. What seems to be even more important is that the process seems to have unfolded in a highly disorderly manner going up and down for a very long time.

I suggest that it is the work with the two more general treatises (for which direct and careful reconsideration and explicit expression of the developmental process must have been required) that has driven John of the Cross to begin to think of the process of mystical development in a very general perspective. And it is this work combined with that of interpreting the poem that has made it clear to him that the poem really describes the stages of mystical development in reasonable detail. The argument is thus an explicit product of the combined processes of representational redescription and interpretation.

The revised *Canticle* gives evidence of the second point at which John of the Cross' conceptualization of the mystical process seems to have changed significantly. The descriptions of mystical states are not altered in any significant way in the revised *Canticle* but the mystical process in its entirety is presented very differently in the two versions of the work. As a whole, the revised *Canticle* delineates mystical development as a steadily progressing process that has moved forward towards the ultimate goal from beginning to end. It is primarily the reorganization of the verses in the poem that engender the transformation of the work. The corresponding changes in the concrete interpretations of the verses and the adjustments of the general argument (disregarding the addition of the post-mystical stage which does not seem to have been motivated by an altered view of the unfolding of the process but by his understanding of a specific aspect of it) have mainly been auxiliary means contributing to produce a relatively coherent work.

Actually, he seems to have wrestled with his new ideas for quite some time before undertaking the actual revision of the work. Thus, he has already anticipated some of the changes in corrections and remarks added in the margin of the original commentary (in Juan de la Cruz 1988, Cántico A27: 2, note 7-8). Hence, it would seem as if it is the work on the two treatises, mainly consisting in generalizing the mystical process, that has nourished John of the Cross' proof-reading of his original *Canticle*, thereby helping him see both the work and the mystical process in a much broader perspective. I will suggest that John of the Cross has then digested and refined these ideas for some time after which they have come to completion and culminated in the revisioning work on the *Canticle*.

Layers of interpretation and stages of conceptual development

It seems fitting to link the results of the analysis of the *Canticle* and evaluate John of the Cross' conceptual development more generally. First of all, the analysis indicates that the process of interpretation has proceeded in intervals resulting in layers of earlier and later interpretation. These layers are further related indirectly to levels of interpretation pointing in the direction of an interpretational process that typically has started out on a fairly specific level moving on to gradually more general levels as the process has proceeded. The layers of interpretation are the products of the periods of interpretation (and of redescription) wherefore the identification of the former will give evidence of the latter. Still, the distinction is somewhat artificial which is also the reason why the layers arising from the interpretation of the *Canticle* only can be identified loosely based on the distinction of parts of the work. The very earliest evidence of John of the Cross' conceptual development is not really a layer of *interpretation* as it is the product of representational redescription. This earliest layer is displayed in the original 30/31 verses of the poem. The original poem and the concrete interpretations of it, on the other hand, document the first actual layer of interpretation and is the outcome of the earliest period of interpretation. The original argument documents the second interpretational layer and is the outcome of the second interpretational period (promoted by the writing of the instructional treatises). Finally, the revised *Canticle* as a whole gives evidence of the third interpretational layer and is the product of the third interpretational period. All in all, the *Canticle* displays four general layers indicating major changes in John of the Cross' conceptualization of aspects of his mystical experience.

Thereupon, it should be pointed out that the changes in the way of conceiving of the mystical process — exposed through the diversity of the parts of the *Canticle* — suggest that conceptual development is phased as hypothesized by Karmiloff-Smith. Inasmuch as conceptual development is triggered by redescription of cognitive representations and accelerated by the process of interpretation, it is the conceptual changes that give evidence of conceptual development through the layers of interpretation.

VII. Mystical experience as displayed in the works of John of the Cross

The method of approaching God mystically

General characteristics of the process

In extension of contemporary, Spanish spirituality, John of the Cross often speaks of the process of mystical development as a path 'senda' or a way 'camino' that has to be followed (see Mancho Duque 1982, ch. 3 for a semantic analysis of John of the Cross' use of these words). The mystical process is a path that leads the travelling soul from the natural to the supernatural, that is to say, from a worldly life of and with humans to a divine life of and with God. Eventually, the process will enable the subject to obtain mystical (and therefore temporary) unions with God. John of the Cross' explanation of why such a process is requisite for the achievement of that end springs from his understanding of the goal itself, that is, the union of God and the soul. The argument is drawn from the Aristotelian notion (commonly accepted in contemporary Thomist theology) that two contraries cannot exist in one subject. Hence, the union of two subjects (God and the soul) in one (the soul) presupposes equality of the two (Juan de la Cruz 1988, e.g., Subida 1.2:2, 2.16:7, and Noche 2.4:2). The equality of God and the soul is not attained through mutual alteration of the subjects to be united as might have been expected but only through a likening of the soul to God. Consequently, the aim of the process is to yield the soul sufficiently equal to God in order to permit union. According to John of the Cross, the mystical way that gradually will lead the subject to God comprises several stages. In very general terms, it can be said that the process altogether involves two elements, namely the process of conditioning the soul to the mystical union with God and the realization of the union with God of which the latter coincidentally is an end in itself and a further conditioning of the soul to the eternal union with God.

Two closely connected questions arise from this. First, how is it possible for the soul to become equal to God and what is it that needs to be changed in the soul? And second, how are these changes obtained through the process of mystical development or, in other words, what are the means of initiating and advancing the process?

The relation of Man and God

An answer to the first question takes its point of departure in John of the Cross' understanding of the way in which the soul differs from God. It is therefore necessary to consider the soul's natural condition and how this relates to God. John of the Cross' argument for the possibility of approaching God mystically is best understood in the light of the idea that the soul is capable of returning to a lost condition or state of the soul. This was the natural condition of the soul when humankind was created but was lost because of Adam's fall. The condition is regained by each soul in baptism but then again lost during the life of a person. In the initial condition the soul possessed a purity similar to that of God (although it also then differed from Him by its createdness, of course) (Juan de la Cruz 1988, Cántico A33:3 and A37:1/B34:4; Herrera 1966, 595). John of the Cross' understanding of the purity of the newborn is philosophically supported with the Thomist anthropology that the human mind is like a tabula rasa at birth. What the adult soul needs to do is to strip itself of acquired properties accumulated since the original purity. The alterations that the soul needs to go through consist in an undoing or elimination of the effects on the soul of all events in the life of a person. What is needed is a veritable deletion of memory. As John of the Cross explicitly states, the purpose of the process is to take the soul back to the tabula rasa state of mind (Juan de la Cruz 1988, Subida 1.3:3). This does not mean, though, that the process likens the soul to God in the fullest degree, as this would necessitate a total undoing of the createdness of the soul. The death of the mortal part of a person is required for that purpose. This is indeed what the mystical process initiates but only natural death can complete it. Yet, the mystical process actually has the effect of making the soul sufficiently equal to God already in this life in order to make *mystical* union with Him possible. During this union the likening of the soul to God can be fulfilled temporarily.

The elimination of the accumulated properties and knowledge is a purification of the soul. The main point is that the soul is purified of and freed from its sensuousness. This does not literally mean that the senses are purified or eliminated but that their activities are reduced as far as possible. A total elimination of the senses is beyond the means of the soul in this life. What is achieved through the process seems to be an ability to cut off the functioning of the senses temporarily[1] (Juan de la Cruz 1988, Subida 1.5:2, 1.11:1-2, and

---

1. Evidently, he does not suggest that a complete and lasting suspension of the senses occurs. What seems to be the case is rather that the subject gradually builds up a lasting condition that somehow enables a transient suspension of the senses during mystical states.

Noche 2.4:2). The mystical process executes a destruction, purification, and beginning death of anything in the soul that differs from God. The process is probably best characterized as a dehumanization of the soul. Everything that lives in the soul must die, little as much 'poco y mucho, chico y grande', as John of the Cross says (Juan de la Cruz 1988, Subida 1.11:8). Moreover, he repeatedly emphasizes the variability of the individual processes of purification and elimination. Since the process is supposed to purify and eliminate whatever there is in the soul to purify and eliminate, the actual process is contingent on the soul itself. His understanding of this is indeed very concrete. The duration of the process varies considerably as the time it takes to purify and expel the 'habits' of the soul depends on the condition of the soul when the process is initiated (Juan de la Cruz 1988, Noche 2.7:3 and 9:3).

The direction of the process

The question of how the process produces the needed alterations of the soul at once entails the issues of what the process actually is like and how it works. As a whole, the mystical way leading a subject closer and closer to God can only be characterized very generally, since the process gradually changes in character. It sets out with a purification of the soul dealing with gradually more and more internal components. At some point, the purification combines with an actual transformation that gradually intensifies and eventually takes over from the purification when this part is completed. In general, John of the Cross views the whole process as a continuous movement that simultaneously goes from the exterior to the interior and from the lowest to the highest (Juan de la Cruz 1988, Subida 2.17:4).[2] The direction of the process is determined by the conceived composition of the soul as containing both an outer and lower and an inner and higher part. It is first of all the outer and lower part of the soul that needs to be purified and annihilated as far as possible. The point of departure is a life in the outmost and lowest part of the soul and the endpoint is a life in the innermost and highest part of the soul.[3] Metaphorically, the mystical way leads from the outskirts of the soul to the centre of it which is where the union with God takes place.

At this point, it seems pertinent to present how John of the Cross himself conceives of the stages of the soul's transformation. Actually, he accepts various metaphors classifying the mystical process into stages. On the one

---

2. Andrés describes the direction as helical. This orientation of the mystical approach to God was commonly accepted among the spiritual Spanish of the 16th century (Andrés 1975, 815).
3. Evidently, this understanding is in accordance with the Franciscan recollection movement from the beginning of the century.

hand, he refers two traditional metaphors but without using them more generally or elaborating them any further. The first of these metaphors identifies ten mystical degrees on a stairway of love where the tenth degree corresponds to the heavenly stage (Juan de la Cruz 1988, Noche 2.19-20). This metaphor does not have major influence on John of the Cross' general understanding of the process, though. The second metaphor distinguishes three 'ways' presupposing one another. The first is purifying, the second is illuminating, and the third is unitive, altogether leading to the glorious stage. This scheme is presented in the *Canticle* in connection with his argument that the poem unfolds in parts corresponding to the stages of the mystical process.

On the other hand, John of the Cross divides the stages of the process in accord with two other conventional metaphors both of which he elaborates in much detail and uses very generally in his works. Firstly, he directly correlates the above mentioned metaphors of the ways with another traditional distinction based on the metaphor of the mystical process as a gradually intensifying love relationship. The general metaphor of love goes more or less explicitly through all of his works. According to the classification of the mystical process derived from this metaphor, the first stage is that of beginners, the second is where the espousal between the lovers is realized, and the third is where the matrimony is fulfilled (Juan de la Cruz 1988, Cántico B1:1-2 and A27:2/B22: 3; Mancho Duque 1982, 46). Secondly, he outlines a scheme of the stages of the process in his elaboration of the metaphor of the dark night according to which the stages of process of approaching God mystically is likened to three distinct parts of the natural night.[4] Inasmuch as John of the Cross offers his far the most detailed presentation of the stages of the mystical process through

---

4. In this connection, it seems fitting to refer to M.J. Mancho Duque who, in accord with M. Eliade, considers the metaphor of the stairway archetypical as opposed to the metaphor of the night which he regards as personal (1982, 27, 81, and 84). Mancho Duque's view is that John of the Cross has been inspired to elaborate the metaphor of the night by his own personal experience of imprisonment. There is no foundation whatever for such opposite identifications of the sources of the metaphors. Both belong to the Christian tradition and in fact, John of the Cross directly refers to Aristotelian philosophy and Pseudo-Dionysian metaphor as the sources of inspiration of the metaphor of the night (and there is no reason to doubt the truth of this) (Juan de la Cruz 1988, Subida 2.9:6 and 15:13; see Wilhelmsen 1980, 32 note 36 for an overview of John of the Cross' references to the Christian authorities). I cannot see Mancho Duque's distinction of the source of the metaphors as anything but a justification of the personality of John of the Cross' ideas as opposed to the archetypicality of others' ideas. E.C. Wilhelmsen similarly argues that John of the Cross' use of various metaphors is absolutely personal. They are unique and not even linked to conventionality (1980, 393). This equally seems to be just another attempt to save John of the Cross' metaphors from being inflammated with conventionality.

his metaphor of the dark night, I shall stick to this metaphor in an outline of the parts of the process.

The mystical process starts with a purification of the least spiritual element in the soul which is the senses. According to John of the Cross, the soul is liberated from the influence from the objects of the senses in this first stage through a deprivation of the taste or the appetite for sensory perceptions of any kind (which, in his understanding, includes imagination) (Juan de la Cruz 1988, Subida 1.3:2). Both perception and that which he identifies as natural imagination (as opposed to supernatural imagination) are negated and gradually eliminated in the first stage. Metaphorically, the purification results in a darkening of the sensuous part of the soul. In the next stage, referred to as the spiritual night, the more spiritual elements in the soul are purified. The primary remedy for the purification of the spiritual part of the soul is faith. It is faith that guides the soul through this stage or part of the night. At this point, the process aims at an elimination of any remaining natural fantasies and imaginations, as well as of the natural (but spiritual) understanding. During this stage, the soul needs to be purified of particular forms in general wherefore even those imaginations that, in John of the Cross' view, are super-natural should be renounced thereby gradually eliminating the soul's tendency to think in images and forms. Metaphorically speaking, this stage leaves the soul in total darkness (Juan de la Cruz 1988, Subida 1.3:2-3, 2.2:2-3, and Noche 1.8:1-2). In this part of the process, the soul goes through a final disposition for the mystical union with God. In the third and final stage, the soul is already so purified of its humanness that adaptation no longer consists in purifying the soul but quite simply in transforming it. In this stage, a basic enlightening of the soul takes a beginning through God's very frequent and intimate communication with it. By means of its natural faculties, though, the soul comprehends nothing of what is supernaturally communicated to it. Following the metaphor, the soul is no longer in total darkness, as it has reached the immediacy of the supernatural light of the union stage. Since the soul is now able to discern a little supernatural light it is similarly capable of grasping a corresponding proportion of the communicated knowledge (Juan de la Cruz 1988, Subida 1.2:4-5 and 2.2:1). Following John of the Cross' ideas about the gradual transformation of the soul, this means that the soul comprehends the communicated supernatural knowledge to the extent that it has been denaturalized and transformed. To put it differently, the soul understands — insofar as it has become capable — of temporarily taking on divine properties during mystical union.

Evidently, the soul has not become completely dehumanized in the union stage as it still carries a body along or is carried around by one. It is more as if the degree of purity corresponds to certain abilities which somehow inhibit or control those elements that John of the Cross identifies as nondivine (cf. Juan de la Cruz 1988, Subida 2.7:11 and Cántico A39:4-5/B40:4-5).

In his efforts to render his teachings of the mystical process more intelligible, John of the Cross often turns to the metaphors of the night and the way (and others as they are all closely interrelated) blending the metaphors to achieve optimum expressive strength. It is the second part of the night (where the spiritual part of the soul is purified) that basically constitutes the way, because it is this part of the night that leads to the mystical union with God. The first night (where the sensuous part of the soul is purified) constitutes the door that has to be passed for a soul to enter the second night but the first night (or the act of passing through the door) simultaneously constitutes the beginning of the way. In this way, the first night can be said to be at once the beginning of the way and not yet really the way. Speaking of the way in its entirety, as a way that aims at reducing the distance between a person and God, the first night constitutes the beginning of this way. But viewed as a way that leads a soul to mystical union with God, the first night is not yet part of the way (see Juan de la Cruz 1988, Noche 1.11:4 and 2.9:4).[5]

Surprisingly, John of the Cross claims that the ascension towards God coincidentally is a descension and that the descension is an ascension ('en este camino el abajar es subir, y el subir, abajar') (Juan de la Cruz 1988, Noche 2. 18:2; Mancho Duque 1982, 96-100). The explanation of this paradoxical statement is that the process takes the subject upwards *through* taking it downwards. Descension is the (only) means of ascension. So, although the process continuously brings the soul closer to its goal, its condition actually seems to be worsened before it becomes evident that it has been improved. Really, the

---

5. Elsewhere, he states that for the soul to pass through the door which similarly is Christ (an idea that implies a reference to his view that the process basically involves a need to consider and imitate Christ) it has to go through the first night (although Christ is also both the beginning of the way and the way itself) (Juan de la Cruz 1988, Subida 2.7:2 and 8-9). So, on the one hand, the passage through the first night takes the soul to the door which is Christ, leading to the second night which is the way. On the other hand, the first night is itself the door leading up to the second night. This may seem a little contradictory but primarily springs from the metaphors of Christ and the night mutually sharing the meta-metaphor of the way. In other words, the contradiction is brought out by my association of the two metaphors but is not actually inherent in John of the Cross' idea about the way. The metaphor of the imitation of the life of Christ as causing the requisite reduction in the opposition between a person and God is very fundamental for his teachings. It lies behind his whole interpretation of the process. But, as a metaphor, it is easily conquered by that of the night (not to mention the metaphor of fire of love) supposedly due to his evaluation of its communicative power. This is probably also the reason why the metaphor of the dark night is the most overall and most frequently used metaphor in his two instructional treatises, the Ascent and the Night.

soul does not get worse than it was before but it appears to be much worse. The purgation of the soul brings all its impurities and uglinesses out. Metaphorically, John of the Cross describes the soul as initially being disgustingly ugly, but becoming even uglier as the process proceeds (Juan de la Cruz 1988, Noche 2.10:2). In John of the Cross' view, the process is the soul's way of approaching God. Travelling this way, the soul moves closer to God. Considering the relation of God and the soul, there is no doubt that the process gradually lifts the soul from its most base state to its highest possible state. Since it is a continuous approach to God it is also the whole process that brings the soul higher and higher up. Hence, it is also ascension all of the way even if it looks like descension throughout a large part of it.

The processes of purification and transformation

It is important to understand how extremely concrete John of the Cross conceives of the mystical purification. I have already mentioned that the duration of the purification depends on the condition of the soul at the beginning of the process. Yet, additionally, the subject's attitude and receptiveness have some influence on this. There may be a greater or lesser need for purgation depending on the amount of bad habits in a subject, or the degree to which he/she may be receptive to the treatment (Juan de la Cruz 1988, Noche 2.9:3). One of the metaphors that John of the Cross uses to express how and with what the soul is purged of all its human impurities is that of the fire of love. In accord with this metaphor, God employs a special kind of fire to burn down all the impurities in the soul. This gives a very good impression of the considerable concretion and materialism of his idea. The materiality of his understanding is, in particular, illustrated through his comparison of the effect of the mystical love-fire and that of the fire in purgatory. The former is a spiritual fire with which God purges the soul while it is still in the body, whereas the latter is a material fire with which the soul is purged once the physical part of a person is dead. The mystical purification has an effect similar to the purification in purgatory although it is of another kind and works by means of love. This is also the reason why those that have reached the highest degree of mystical illumination and purity do not need to go through purgatory (this must indeed have been a strong incitement for John of the Cross' contemporaries to enter the mystical way) (Juan de la Cruz 1988, Noche 2.10:2 and 5.12:1 and 21:5).

As mentioned, the actual process of purification is initiated with the purification of the sensuous part of the soul which apparently leads to some kind of change permitting a temporary suspension of the senses. John of the Cross generally refers to this part of the process as the purgative way or the night of the senses. The commencement of the process is not controlled by an individual, since it is God Himself who decides to place a particular soul in the dark night (Juan de la Cruz 1988, Subida 1.1:5). In spite of that it is still advantageous for the soul to actively do its part to help start the process. First of all, the soul should imitate Christ in all possible ways in order to conform with the life lived by Him. In order to know how to do this, the soul needs to consider the life of Christ which means that His life ought to be estimated very highly and attended to very carefully. The next thing that the soul should do, of its own volition, is directly related to the first. In order to be able to imitate the life of Christ properly, it is necessary to renounce any tastes for sensuous things (unless they are for the honour of God). For the love of Christ, one should have no taste for the world of the senses just like He Himself had no taste for anything but doing his Father's will while living in the world (Juan de la Cruz 1988, Subida 1.13:3-4).

Having entered upon the way — or the night — leading a soul towards God, the purification of the sensuous part of the soul takes a beginning. The soul actively assists God in this process of purification although it is quite difficult to determine which part of the work that is supposed to be carried out by the soul itself and which part is the work of God alone. In fact, John of the Cross does not seem to consider such a distinction very important. That which needs to be stressed for pedagogical and instructional reasons is that the process of purification neither can be initiated, continued, or accomplished without God but that the soul also needs to be actively involved in the work. And the soul can do a great deal particularly in the beginning of the process (see Gaudreau 1976, 195, Fig. 3). In order not to delay the process the soul certainly should get started with doing what it can (even if it is little compared to what God does).

One of the most general characteristics of the mystical process seems to be that it is extremely painful. Furthermore, it is also a very slow and gradual process. The purification is one long suffering from beginning to end which is also the reason why very few people manage to go through with it. Explaining why the purifying process is so extremely painful John of the Cross bases his argument on the earlier mentioned philosophical dogma that two contraries cannot exist in one subject (the soul). Consequently, the imposition of the divine purification on the still very impure soul with all its evils inevitably causes it pain[6] (Juan de la Cruz 1988, Noche 2.5:4). In particular, the purification of the spiritual part of the soul is torturous and incomparably worse than that of the sensuous part. The more that the soul approaches God, the

---

6. The suffering may likewise result from a feeling of God's absence but that is another matter (see for example Juan de la Cruz, Noche 2.8:1 and his interpretation of the early verses of the *Canticle*, especially A1:2/B1:15, A1:10/B1:19 and A6:1/B6:2).

more painful the process becomes. The closer that the soul is to God, the more it feels the pain arising from its lowliness as opposed to his exaltedness. The reason why the pain intensifies is not that the opposition between God and the soul increases as the soul simultaneously improves as it approaches God. In fact, there is always a proper relation of God's distantness and the soul's current condition, as God takes care only to approximate the soul with due respect to its degree of impurity/purity.

In order to display how John of the Cross attempts to explain why and how the pain increases as the soul moves closer to God, it might elucidate his explanatory mode a little, first to take a look at his more metaphorically inspired ways of expressing the matter. In one place, he proposes a parable likening the mystical pain to the natural pain that gradually increases if one approaches the sun (while looking at it, it seems) due to the impurity and lowliness of human eyes. In a similar way the base human understanding is blinded by the excessive divine light that continuously increases in the process of moving closer to God (Juan de la Cruz 1988, Noche 2.16:11). This is further supported with another parable likening the purification of the soul to the fire in (a piece of) wood: as the fire enters deeper into the piece of wood, the fire grows more violent in its attempt to take possession of the wood, at the same time as the heat grows stronger. Similarly, the soul is gradually more violently inflamed by the fire of love as it approaches the divine source of love more and more (Juan de la Cruz 1988, Noche 2.10:6-7). Both of these parables escape an explanation, though, of why it is the case that the pain arising from the purification increases. Really, the parables are not in themselves particularly clarifying. Nonetheless, they do manage to illustrate in which way the purification and the resulting pain grow more intense.

It appears that one cause of the increasing pain is simply that the purifying process is intensified and speeded up. John of the Cross does suggest a more direct explanation of the increase in the pain, though. Along with the progression of the mystical process, the purification is internalized continuously, working itself deeper and deeper into the soul and addressing imperfections of more and more spiritual and intimate character. As a consequence of this, the pain changes in character and becomes gradually more spiritual and intimate (Juan de la Cruz 1988, Noche 2.10:7). Since this is presented as an explanation, it seems that the so-called spiritual pain is worse than the sensuous.

Accordingly, the pain increases for two reasons. Partly, because the purification grows more violent and vehement (due to an intensification of the burning) and partly, because the pain grows more spiritual and intimate (due to a change in that which is burnt).[7]

Specific methods of purification and transformation

Since the process of nearing God unfolds in several distinct stages, the means of continuation also varies according to the particular stage that a mystic has reached. At this point, it is not yet the actual stages that are in focus but the methods (to the extent they can be read out of John of the Cross' works) by which the process can be started and promoted. Dealing with the means of mystical progress one needs to keep the dynamic and altering character of the project in mind. John of the Cross does not instruct his readers in the very specific means of mystical advancement, but primarily reflects on various related issues in more general ways. The expressions of his views and teachings revolve around a number of conventional metaphors (although taken from diverging segments of tradition) which he elaborates for his own purposes. The metaphors he uses are nurtured by — and nurture — his general understanding of the means of mystical progress.

Supernatural death

Attempting to outline the general method of approaching God mystically, John of the Cross explains that the strategy of approximating God mystically consists in putting human nature to death. The mystical process is the slow dying of anything that lives in the soul. This understanding takes its point of departure in his view of a mundane life which is seen as the cause of the infinite distance between God and a person. It is the corporal life that hinders the (spiritual) life with God. Hence, it is life itself that deprives a subject of the joys of God's company. The natural life is death to the true, spiritual life (Juan de la Cruz 1988, Cántico A8:1/B8:2). For obvious reasons, a solution to the problem is to put all live elements in the soul to death (assuming that something will be left). Unfortunately, this is not easily done. Knowing that this is what needs to be done is not enough to do it, nor is the knowledge of how it can be done. The problem is that it is far beyond the means of a human being to put one's own nature to death in this way. The major part of the job

---

7.   In the *Canticle*, John of the Cross gives a third and diverging explanation of the cause of the pain felt in the first stage of the process, though. Here the pain is claimed to arise from the inconvenience of living two opposite lives, namely the corporal and the spiritual, in two opposite places, namely the body and God. The trouble about the situation is that the tormenting life (the corporal) deprives the soul of the pleasurable life (the spiritual) by inhibiting it. It is the deprivation of the life desired so desperately by the soul that makes it suffer (Juan de la Cruz 1988, Cántico A8:2/B 8:3). This kind of pain seems to be qualitatively different from the above mentioned and is doubtlessly felt generally in between mystical states.

of putting the human part of the soul to death mystically can only be accomplished by God Himself. Therefore, the subject wishing to go through with
this process can only hope and plead for God to terminate it. As John of the
Cross' metaphorical reasoning goes, the soul is sick, the cure for the sickness
is death, and death lies in the hands of God (the kind of death concerned here
is supernatural and not yet the natural, of course) (Juan de la Cruz 1988,
Cántico A9:1-2/B9: 2-3). The reason why a mystic has to plead for God to go
through with putting it to death, is not so much that He is unwilling to do it
and only selects a few persons,[8] but rather that the process is so slow and
painful that it seems never to come to an end.

The topic of dying is considered from varying perspectives and with the
focus on differing aspects. In one place John of the Cross expounds on what
it more specifically is that causes the soul to die. The soul slowly dies because
of an extremely profound, but at the same time incomprehensible, *understanding* of God that is felt very intensely and seems never to come to an end.
Realizing the interminability of the acquisition of this understanding is in itself
a very profound understanding. It is the sensation of being incapable of
understanding and fully feeling God's immense being that puts the soul to
death (Juan de la Cruz 1988, Cántico A/B7:9).

It is a biblical assumption that the sight of God is lethal for human beings.
At the same time, the sight of God is extremely potent and capable of transforming the soul. Seeing God means death to the body but the soul is able to
see Him.[9] The more the body dies, the more the soul becomes capable of
seeing God. And the more the soul sees of God, the more the body dies. As
long as the soul sees God's beauty, it is entirely absorbed and transformed in
that beauty. In this way, the sight of God possesses the power of *transforming*
the soul. Besides, the soul has, at that point, already gone through some
mystical training wherefore it already lives more in that other life where it
loves than in this worldly life where it lives (physically, that is). Accordingly,
there are three good reasons for the desirability of the lethality of seeing God
which can be summed up as follows: Firstly, it is only the body that dies
anyway. Secondly, the mystical dying of the soul is in itself a method of
reaching the end that it craves so much for, just as the natural death finally
will be. Thirdly, the death of the mortal part of the *soul* is hardly a loss at all
(since the soul in love with God already lives more in that eternal life) (Juan

8. When very few people actually manage to finish this dying it is due to their inability
   to bear the suffering involved in it.
9. This is a mystical interpretation of the New Testament promise of salvation going
   along with the declaration that the law of grace has taken over from the old law (see
   e.g., Gal. 2:16-21 and Rom.). Yet, even if the soul was not able to survive the sight of
   God, it still would not fear it: for anything God wishes, the soul in love with God
   wishes too (Juan de la Cruz 1988, Cántico B11:10, Subida 2.22:7-8 and Vilnet, 88).

de la Cruz 1988, Cántico B11:10). These statements do not so much form a logical and coherent approach to the theme of dying at the sight of God, as it is a rattling-off of varying aspects from dissimilar perspectives on the theme. It is rather typical for John of the Cross, though, that he regards comprehensiveness, inclusiveness, and varying perspectives as far more important than logic and coherence.[10]

Mystical death at once involves dying to the world and to oneself (Juan de la Cruz 1988, Llama A2:24/B2:28). Such death coincidentally necessitates the breaking of all links with the external world and of the destruction of internal life. Really, the two are one, though, as the former is achieved through the accomplishment of the latter. The relations to the world are gradually broken down by the equally gradual elimination of the soul's inner life (which is supposed to give room for God's work in there). Through the process of mystical dying, the soul slowly draws nearer to the goal which is God. Due to its mystical death, the soul gradually approximates God, resembling Him more and more as the process progresses. When He visits it in its most interior parts, the soul little by little gets a foretaste of what is to come (in the eternal union, that is). At some point, the soul's human nature is destroyed to such an extent that the soul is capable of actually possessing God in perfect love which is spiritual life to the soul. The logic of this metaphor of the mystical process is that through losing its corporal and natural life, the soul gains spiritual life (which is much to be preferred) (Juan de la Cruz 1988, Llama A2:28-29/B2:32-33). Certainly, the aim of the mystical advance to God is to be united with Him in love, even if only temporarily so. But the ultimate goal, the goal of life so to speak, is achieved through the natural death which, for a soul in love with God, is an exceptionally desirable and sweet event. This is no wonder, of course, as natural death takes the soul that has been purified mystically directly to the eternal union with God which is not only infinite but also even more perfect than the mystical union (Juan de la Cruz 1988, Llama A1:24/B1:30).

Reduction of sensory activities

The particular purification needed for the approximation of God in earthly life consists in maximum elimination of the activities of the senses and a complete elimination of the taste (or the appetite) for the things of the world. John of

---

10. It should be mentioned that John of the Cross holds two fundamentally diverging views of the transforming power of seeing or looking in the context of God. In the poetic *Canticle* it is God's gaze that has the power to transform. In his interpretation of the verse, John of the Cross follows the Christian tradition more strictly taking the sight of God to be transforming.

the Cross generally speaks of this eliminating process as a mortification or a negation of the senses and the appetites, which gradually result in the beginning of the emptying of the mind. Metaphorically, this process leaves the soul 'in darkness and with nothing' ('a oscuras y sin nada') (Juan de la Cruz 1988, Subida 1.4:1-2). Due to the process of mortification and negation, the soul is deprived of its appetites for the pleasures of the senses. This is meant in the extremely concrete sense that the soul actually loses its capacity to take pleasure in sensuous perceptions of any kind whatever. Neither the sense of feeling, seeing, smelling, tasting, or hearing something that normally would be a pleasure of the senses is enjoyable for the soul any longer (Juan de la Cruz 1988, Subida 1.4:2). The soul enters into a vacuum where nothing can satisfy it as it is incapable of delighting in worldly pleasures, while the non-worldly pleasures are still out of reach.

The process of gradually making still the activities of the senses[11] seems to result from a technique of conscious renunciation of perceptual pleasures. John of the Cross employs the traditional terms of his time when referring to the techniques promoting the process of mortifying the senses and the appetites. He borrows the word recollection from the Franciscan, spiritual movement of the century which he presumably has known very well from Teresa of Jesus. John of the Cross does not use the word recollection in exactly the same way as the Franciscan mystics, though, for whom recollection is a term actually defining the way taking a soul to God.[12] John of the Cross' more general understanding of the way of approaching God is in agreement, though, with the Franciscans' understanding of recollection, and both involve an emptying of oneself or of one's humanness in order to make room for God's work in the soul. In the works of John of the Cross, recollection more specifically signifies inattentiveness to the events of the external world through concentration of attention within the soul itself. In recollection everything without exception is forgotten or, rather, recollection consists in forgetting everything (Juan de la Cruz 1988, Subida 3.39:2). It is recollection that, in his terms, strips the soul naked of the things of the world (Juan de la Cruz 1988, Subida 3.40:2) and it is also recollection that later disposes the soul for the mystical reception of God in its interior regions (Juan de la Cruz 1988, Noche 2.11:3). In the metaphorical language of the *Canticle*, the soul should step out from the things

---

11. In his general treatment of the process, John of the Cross does not specify, if the process aims at continuous or temporary suspension of the senses. In his more specific considerations of particular events of union (mystical states), the suspension of the senses is evidently only temporary, though.
12. According to Andrés, recollection initially referred to a specified mode of proceeding towards God (a 'way') while later (with Teresa of Jesus) it came to refer to a mode of inner meditation (1975, 36).

of the world and enter its inner self which really is where God hides Himself (Juan de la Cruz 1988, Cántico A1:4/B1:6 and 9).

From the terminology of Christian spirituality in general, John of the Cross borrows the terms meditation and contemplation. The difference between the two techniques, which might both be called meditative in the terms of our time, is that contemplation is a totally passive condition of receptiveness involving no conscious concentration whereas meditation, on the contrary, is active and focused (Juan de la Cruz 1988, Noche 1.10:1 and 10:4; A Benedictine of Stanbrook 1954, chs. 1 and 4). In John of the Cross' scheme, the technique of meditation appertains to the period anterior to the night and should be replaced with the technique of contemplation once the night is entered. Contemplation should then be practiced throughout the two first stages of the process until the final stage of union is reached. This further means that the active renunciation of sensory pleasures actually precedes the classified stages of the process. Once the actual mystical purification starts one should mainly take up a position of passive disposedness and receptiveness all of the time.

The core of John of the Cross' teachings is that an absolute precondition for searching for God is that one is emancipated from the things of the world. Even the slightest attachments to the world are impediments to the spiritual *nakedness* ('desnudez') required to follow the mystical way to God. The procedure to be followed by a subject in search of God initially consists in active mortification of its appetites through spiritual exercises and penitence after which passive contemplation takes over at some point (Juan de la Cruz 1988, Cántico A3:3-4/B3:4-5). The method of active mortification should be observed in the very beginning of mystical development (mainly prior to the classified stages) whereas such behaviour is directly obstructive later on. The value of active exercises, and, in particular, the more external of these, diminishes gradually as the process proceeds. Proportionally with this, the importance of God's work in the soul — during which the soul itself remains passive — increases. Hence, the soul that has obtained the highest mystical stage ought to invest all of its time in simply loving God and doing nothing else (Juan de la Cruz 1988, Cántico B29:1-3).

The suspension of imagination

John of the Cross follows the Thomist psychology that the senses comprise the only interface between the human mind and the world. It is this connection with the external world that the mystical process aims at cutting off thereby helping the mind return to its supposed original tabula rasa state.[13] This view

13. John of the Cross does not specify whether the return is temporary or continuous. Apparently the point is that during union with God (the mystical states, that is) a

is further related to the idea that the faculties of the soul, which in accord with the Thomist theory are constituted by understanding, memory, and will, are only nourished by whatever enters through the senses. Hence, the starvation of the senses will eventually lead to the equally necessary emptying of the faculties. In particular, John of the Cross dwells on the necessity to still the faculties of understanding and memory (and the elimination of their content of forms and images) as it is impossible to approach God by means of these. The approximation of God necessitates conformation with Him and He is beyond form and mode. Hence, the mind should be emptied of all its former knowledge, lose its former mode of comprehension, and avoid all sorts of imaginations. In short, anything that has form should be expelled. The reason for this is that God does not fall within particular knowledge and understanding, both of which should therefore be destroyed. According to John of the Cross, a *non-understanding* or *knowledge-less* state (implying that one is unable to understand due to an *emptiness* in the faculty of understanding) follows from non-imagination. Hence, the pacification of imagination will eventually lead to an elimination of the understanding. The mystical union of God and the soul necessitates equality of the two. And since God is beyond image and form the soul needs to attain a condition in which it is so pure and simple that it is equally free of limited forms or images (Juan de la Cruz 1988, Subida 2. 16:7 and 9).

The issue of what it is that the mind more specifically should be cleared of, and the method of doing this, is mainly treated in respect to each of the faculties of the soul.[14] With regard to *understanding*, John of the Cross only considers in rather general terms the *methods* of emptying the mind. Thus, he advises that one should not attempt to understand things of some kind or other[15] and that one should rather travel the way to God unknowingly than knowingly. Still, he does not tell his readers *how* to do this. He argues that the reason for this is that the entire wisdom of the world is pure ignorance in comparison with the infinite wisdom of God (Juan de la Cruz 1988, Subida 1. 4:4). Anyone holding on to some particular knowledge is therefore totally ignorant in front of God. It should be emphasized that the damaging knowledge and understanding includes anything, without exception, that can be known about *natural life*. It is human understanding that hinders the reception of true, divine knowledge and it is the presence of human knowledge in the

soul can return to its original tabula rasa state and become equal to God (apart from its createdness). Yet the continual renunciation of sensory pleasures *and* the repeated mystical states also have some more lasting effects in this respect.

14. In his view, thought belongs to understanding, images to memory, and appetites (for sensuous pleasures) to willpower (Juan de la Cruz 1988, Subida 1.9).

15. This is indeed the mystical, as opposed to the theological way, although the two are claimed to complement one another.

soul that hinders union with God (Juan de la Cruz 1988, Subida 1.4:5 and 2. 4:4-6).

John of the Cross deals in various ways with internal representations or images which could be harmful. He distinguishes between representations that either are related or not related to external objects. The latter type can further be divided into those having particular form and those being free of form. The question about internal representations is particularly important for memory but similarly matters for that which he identifies as understanding. The first type of internal representations are those that have the external environment as their source. As the purification of the sensuous part of the soul aims at maximum reduction in sensory perceptions the subject wishing to go through the mystical process obviously ought not to cling to perceptions whether from vision, smell, hearing, or taste (e.g. Juan de la Cruz 1988, Subida 1.4:2 and 2. 4:4). In general, such representations should be renounced the sooner the better.[16]

16. In this context it seems relevant to consider John of the Cross' view on the use of religious pictures and the like. He treats the issue in rather much detail, partly (it seems), in response to his readers' specific concern for the matter, and partly because of the position such pictures had in the Catholic Church of his time. The Church recommended the use of religious paintings and the like to promote personal devotion (a practice that was vehemently opposed by several of the contemporary religious trends fanatically hunted by the Spanish Inquisition) as a help to evoke proper emotions and as a reminder of the focus of Catholic Christianity (Juan de la Cruz 1988, Subida 3.35:3). John of the Cross did not mean to contradict the use of pictures recommended by the Church. Not only would that be heresy but he would furthermore renounce his often stated submittance to the Catholic Church and its authorities. It would, in other words, have had to be based on trust in his own natural way of understanding things and thus be nothing but arrogance. Obviously, this is far from his intention. Furthermore, he evidently wanted to distance his own teaching from that of the Protestants, the Illuminates, and like heretics (from the point of view of the Catholic Church). Accordingly, John of the Cross admits that religious pictures used in the right way can be fruitful, but he also warns his readers against exaggerated use of such pictures. He acknowledges that pictures and the like can help evoke devotion for God or remind one of God and the saints. However, the good that pictures do is rarely very much, and besides they are often used in a very unfortunate way. What John of the Cross viewed as *misuse* of the religious pictures was the apparently not so uncommon adoration of the pictures themselves instead of that which they represented. He warned very strongly against confusing the means with the goal by taking pleasure in mere pictures. Any love of the pictures subtracts in equal proportion from the love of God. It is such exaggerated uses of religious pictures that he reacts against (Juan de la Cruz 1988, Subida 3.15:1-2, 35:1-3 and 38:2). The danger of mistaking religious pictures for the goal itself is similar to the danger of other sensory perceptions. They all nourish the natural appetite that should rather be starved to death in order to empty it. Like all other perceptions they affect memory negatively by leaving their respective traces in it. It is exactly these traces that the memory needs to be purified and emptied of, inasmuch as they hinder and

The second type of internal representations encompasses various kinds that may derive from either God or the devil. According to John of the Cross, it is quite common that persons following the mystical way begin to understand supernaturally through one of the corporal senses (including taste and feeling) and such representations are equally sensuous, in his view. These often extremely delightful representations occur in the second stage of the process which is where the spiritual part of the soul is purified in addition to the sensuous part (Juan de la Cruz 1988, Subida 2.11:1). John of the Cross speaks of this kind of supernatural imaginations or fantasies as imaginary visions (whether related to vision or not). He claims, that although they are super-natural, they belong to the natural senses just like natural perceptions of diverse kinds. Anything having form is sensuous whether supernatural or natural. In his view, such imaginary visions therefore include all supernatural representations of images and forms (Juan de la Cruz 1988, Subida 2.16:1-2). Generally, they affect the soul negatively because they contribute to fill up both understanding and memory, thereby obstructing the ongoing process of emptying them. The representations adhere to the soul's faculties that were supposed to be as free from particular form as possible in order to allow and ease the union of God and the soul (Juan de la Cruz 1988, Subida 3.7:2). As John of the Cross repeatedly stresses, God is beyond form wherefore the soul should strive for a condition of total formlessness. To obtain this, one should take care that the images and forms do not take residence in the faculties of the soul and this is done by renouncing and negating all kinds of imaginations (Juan de la Cruz 1988, Subida 2.16:10).[17]

The representations referred to involve, additionally, a more specific danger, i.e., that their sensuousness in itself indicates that they most probably derive from the devil rather than from God. And the intentions of the devil, motivated as they are by jealousy, are to impinge on the soul's nearing to God. Still, what John of the Cross wishes to emphasize is that they all equally impede the process of emptying the faculties, no matter what their source is. Besides, there is no reason to believe that representations of more or less sensuous character should contribute to an illumination of the soul. In fact, such a belief is an insult of God who has revealed everything without excep-tion in Christ (Juan de la Cruz 1988, Subida 2.22:5). There is nothing more to reveal and seemingly God does not repeat Himself over and over again. The

impede the goal of uniting mystically with God (Juan de la Cruz 1988, Subida 3.7:1-2). John of the Cross' general advice concerning memory is that no images should be preserved there.

17. Provided that this advice is followed and the supernatural imaginations are negated, although those that are from God may have a more general positive effect on the soul by enhancing its love, understanding, and softness.

trouble is, of course, that His wisdom is beyond the means of human understanding. All in all, there are many good reasons to make an effort to expel all representations in spite of their agreeability (Juan de la Cruz 1988, Subida 2.11).

In addition, John of the Cross deals with other kinds of supernatural representations that are non-sensuous and purely spiritual. Unlike the earlier mentioned supernatural representations, these are understood by means of certain spiritual senses corresponding to the physical (or corporal) senses (except that he omits the tactile sense) (see Juan de la Cruz 1988, Subida 2.24: 3 including note 1). These representations are without form and occur to the more advanced mystics. In the terms of John of the Cross, such representations are offered to the understanding and communicated to the soul while it remains totally passive (Juan de la Cruz 1988, Subida 2.23:1 and 4). There are four types of such non-sensuous representations, namely visions, revelations,[18] auditions (*locuciones*), and spiritual feelings, each related to spiritual senses. In a way, they are all spiritual visions, though, as they all are comprehended by the understanding which he refers to as the spiritual eyes of the soul. To understand is to see, as he expresses it. Anything comprehended causes a spiritual vision in the soul. Accordingly, the soul receives a form- and image-free understanding or spiritual vision by supernatural means. These purely spiritual representations are much more profitable than the sensuous representations (and besides, they are much safer as they presumably are from God) (Juan de la Cruz 1988, Subida 2.23:2-4). There are two reasons why this is the case. On the one hand, they are without form (due to their non-sensuousness) and therefore do not diverge the soul from the aim of conforming to God. On the other hand, they do not require any activity on the part of the soul which is important at the later stages in the process where it is very important that the soul remains passive and lets God work in peace.

The transforming power of love

I have earlier mentioned that John of the Cross often supports his arguments with reference to the authorities of the Christian tradition more or less generally accepted by his contemporaries. His argument that the dissimilarity of the soul and God needs to be reduced is thus based on the Aristotelian doctrine that it is impossible for two contraries to co-exist in one subject. His explanation that love is a means of carrying a soul to God is similarly supported with the authorities and likewise takes its point of departure in an

---

18. Revelations are received and understood in a manner comparable to something perceived through the sense of hearing without actually hearing it (Juan de la Cruz 1988, Subida 2.24:3).

Aristotelian sentence. John of the Cross points out how important it is to be aware of the direction of one's love, as love possesses a certain power that is effectuated through the act of loving. This is the power to equalize the lover with the beloved and even subject the former to the latter. And the greater the affection, the stronger this power is (Juan de la Cruz 1988, Subida 1.4:2-4). The moral (and the logic) of this is, of course, that the more one loves *creatures* (the created), the more *creature* one becomes and the more one submits oneself to creatures. This aspect of the explanation is primarily aimed at those who are still fighting with their human desires before entering into the dark night. Once the process of purification sets in, love very slowly begins to effectuate its positive power of weakening and eventually eliminating the sensuous love while simultaneously strengthening the spiritual love. The former is the human way of loving and the latter is the divine way of loving. Love slowly transforms the soul, subjected to mystical purification, into the longed for conformity with God (Juan de la Cruz 1988, Noche 1.4:7-8). Even if one manages to reduce one's love for other creatures, it is certainly not in the power of a human being to enhance one's love of God. It is only God Himself that can make the soul love Him. Inasmuch as God neither loves anything external to Himself, nor loves anything more base than Himself (which, in principle, excludes anything but Himself) He does not love anything created for what it is in itself. So, for God to love the soul, He absorbs (or places) it within Himself in a certain manner thereby making it equal to Himself. Through this feat, God manages to love the soul with the same love as He loves Himself.[19] It may take a little faith to accept this rather tautological argumentation but faith has barely been a scarcity among the contemporary readers of John of the Cross. The core of this teaching is that it is the love of God that bit by bit transforms the soul from its humanness to similarity with God, but this love is monopolized by God and is therefore beyond the means of a person. God shares this love as he pleases, but due to His infinite love and compassion it pleases Him to share it.

John of the Cross underscores that ardent love and desire for God typically are followed by His visits in the soul (Juan de la Cruz 1988, Cántico A12:1/B13:2). It seems that if the subject strives arduously and incessantly for its mystical aims, these will almost certainly be granted it bit by bit. The reason why this should be the case is not that the soul can develop such love and desire itself and thus attain these goals by its own efforts, but rather that God Himself desires the growth of the love-relationship between Him and the

---

19. As this is expressed in a sublime manner it should be cited: 'Por tanto, amar Dios al alma es meterla en cierta manera en sí mismo, igualándola consigo, y así ama al alma en sí consigo, con el mismo amor que él se ama.' (Juan de la Cruz 1988, Cántico B 32:6 which is nearly identical with A23:5).

soul wherefore He induces the desire in the soul (Juan de la Cruz 1988, Cántico A27:1/B22:2). John of the Cross' view that God Himself takes delight in the soul and its virtues is further supported by his statement elsewhere that the best thing that the soul can do for God is to offer itself and its virtues to Him (Juan de la Cruz 1988, Cántico B16:1).

So far, I have presented John of the Cross' argument that love causes the desired alterations of the soul making it gradually more similar to God. He further attempts to explain how love works in the soul although he mainly does so aided by (more) metaphors. One of the conventional metaphors that John of the Cross elaborates for his own purposes is that love sets a subject on fire. Through the inflammation of the sensuous part of the soul, all of the contrasting impurities are displayed and burnt up. In the second stage of the process an inflammation of the spiritual part of the soul is initiated and this feels rather different from the earlier inflammation. It hurts and touches all of the soul's properties and appetites enhancing the desire to be satisfied by this divine love. The more disposition and room that God finds in the soul to burn it and unite with it, the more are the properties and appetites estranged from worldly affairs. Such divine love is received passively and causes a very strong passion and insatiable desire as the soul is satisfied neither by worldly nor by divine love. At this stage, the fire of love already has some of the properties of the later union. When God inflames the spiritual part of the soul with the fire of love in this way, He disposes the soul for the later union at the same time as He begins to give this union to the soul. John of the Cross claims that the true, mystical union is so forceful and violent that the soul needs to be strongly fortified in order to be capable of receiving it. Yet, when the soul finally reaches the stage of union and is united with and transformed in God, this union and transformation is fulfilled by means of the same love-fire with which it was previously purged (Juan de la Cruz 1988, Noche 2.10-11).

The metaphor of fire of love actually condensates the fundament of John of the Cross' teaching that a person is capable of approximating God mystically to the point of union. The expressiveness of the metaphor of love-fire draws its power from the source of the metaphor that is to say, fire: The fire of love works in a manner similar to that of fire. Fire consumes by inflammation, hence love of fire consumes by inflammation. When fire of love burns in the soul, anything consumable (and needing to be consumed) is indeed consumed. This is also why the love-fire is a very safe remedy, as it burns up all that needs to be burnt, leaving the incombustible remainders pure and clean.[20]

---

20. The fact that fire normally leaves incombustible parts black and seemingly impure has evidently been useless for his explanation and is therefore also left out of the metaphorical mapping.

Metaphors of the approach to God

The mind as container

I wish to draw attention to an interesting relationship between (1), John of the Cross' interpretation of the mystical process; (2), his 'theory of mind' (or psychology); and (3), a general metaphor of the mind as container, common at least in the western world (see Johnson's treatment hereof 1987, ch. 2). The psychological theory that John of the Cross embraces is closely connected to, if not directly based upon, the metaphor that the mind is like a *container* that can be *filled* up with *content* and *emptied* again thereby enabling a *refilling* with more attractive content. An individual only has partial control over the process and it furthermore takes a lot of effort to execute the controllable part of the process. Somewhat more specifically, the metaphor (in John of the Cross' version of it) proposes that there is an overall container (the soul) that contains minor containers, i.e., the faculties of the soul, namely understanding, memory, and will. Each of these faculties can be filled, emptied, and refilled of and with content by means of procedures suitable for their particular natures. The filling of the faculties normally unfolds during ordinary development, the emptying takes place during the beginning of mystical development, and the refilling during the completion of mystical development. Each of the faculties are further divided in two, each respectively *inhabiting* an *outer and lower part* of the soul (the sensuous) and an *inner and higher part* (the spiritual). Hence, the movement goes from the outside to the inside and from beneath to above. In John of the Cross' understanding, the process consists of an emptying of the faculties' own (acquired) nature followed by a refilling with God's nature. Hence, he generally speaks of the process as executing a conformation with God: memory and understanding are conformed with God's formlessness and willpower with his will.

It should be evident from this brief outline of the metaphor underlying John of the Cross' psychological understanding of the mind that, in spite of the spiritual aims of his teachings, they take their point of departure in a very concrete and material, metaphorical understanding. What I intend to point out by mentioning the relation of the metaphor, the psychological understanding, and his mystical teachings is that the metaphor (in a form synthesizing Thomist psychology and Dionysian mysticism) has contributed to John of the Cross' conceptualization of the process of mystical development. Furthermore, it has facilitated his endeavours to communicate it in a form comprehensible to his readers.

The mystical process as a journey

The general scheme of John of the Cross' teachings is similarly nurtured by the metaphor of the developmental process as a journey. He seems to have appreciated this metaphor very much as he has elaborated on several versions of it, some of which cover the entire mystical process and others a specific part of it.

1) A first journey metaphor is based on a mapping of the ascent of a mountain to the process of mystical development from beginning to end. Like most of John of the Cross' metaphors, it is initially presented in a poem that later is interpreted in detail (this particular poem plays only a minor role in his works in general, though). The metaphor outlines a journey taking the traveller up the Carmel mountain. Here, the duration of the journey obviously (that is to say, in correspondence with the metaphorical source) depends on the traveller and his/her condition. Among the more concrete advice of how to ascend this high mountain, John of the Cross suggests the procedure of stripping oneself of worldly things and affairs and turning oneself into a *nothingness*, as this is the precondition for achieving everything (see Juan de la Cruz 1988, 129). In his more detailed instruction, John of the Cross departs from the metaphorical source and shifts to the metaphor of the relation of God to His creatures, according to which His creatures are nothing and God is everything. For some reason, he makes no effort to fuse the two metaphors (presumably he has deemed it unnecessary for the communication of the idea),[21] but simply uses them as a couple complementing one another. In accord with the metaphors, the procedure of ascending the mountain is thus the departure from mundane everything, passing through nothingness, eventually entering into divine everything.

2) John of the Cross proposes another journey metaphor which covers the earlier part of the process only.[22] According to this metaphor, mystical

---

21. Although he might have done this by focusing on the particular aspect of the source domain that has to do with the relative ease or difficulty the ascension of a mountain involves depending on the weight carried by the person ascending it. Mapping this onto the target domain through the reasoning that the deprivation of everything would turn the person into nothing and make the person lighter, one would get the metaphor that the closer a person is to nothingness, the easier is the approach to everything.

22. This metaphor seems to be closely tied to or inspired by the contemporary conception of the possibility of approaching God spiritually through the interiorization of one's life. The techniques of this strategy were developed by Spanish Franciscans earlier in the 16th century.

development can be illustrated as a process during which some experiencing Self, conceived of as the soul,[23] travels through this same soul from the periphery to the centre. Relating this variant of the journey metaphor to the more concrete procedures of the process, the method of initiating and promoting the first steps of the movement inwards is to empty memory and understanding of their content. The actual means of carrying out the beginning of this (admittedly exhausting) journey, is to negate one's interests in (or appetite for) worldly things and to renounce all kinds of sensuous representations entering the faculties of the soul. In short, John of the Cross' general instruction in the method (the vehicle, so to speak) is that it consists of annihilation, elimination, and destruction of content, whereas his more specific advice is that renunciation and negation constitute the means of going through with this. The process further involves a veritable transformation of the faculties of the soul but this part of the process is not covered by the metaphor.

3)   Finally, John of the Cross employs a third journey metaphor which he elaborates at two levels, covering a part of the mystical process and the entire process respectively. In general, the metaphor encompasses the whole mystical process from beginning to end. But actually, the focus of the metaphor is more specific as it primarily is elaborated to describe the purifying part of the process. This is the already mentioned metaphor of the process of mystical development as a dark night (*noche oscura*) of the soul. It is probably the most comprehensive of his metaphors and the one that best expresses his conception of the mystical process in its entirety. It is a metaphor that is developed in much detail with respect to the earlier stages of the process and it plays a major role in his more instructional treatises. In accord with this metaphor, the aim of the journey is to take the traveller from one day to another day. Inescapably, the journey lasts throughout the night between the two days. In practice, the metaphorical night may extend over a shorter or longer period, though. Evidently, this discords with the source of the metaphor (the natural night), but actually it accords with the subjective experience of a night (it may seem longer or shorter).

Due to the important position that this metaphor has in John of the Cross' works and teachings, it seems appropriate to attend more closely to it. As

---

23.   This is particularly evident from his own interpretation of the *Canticle* that the spouse (the main, female character in the description of this sublime loveaffair and to whom everything occurs) is the soul itself. Accordingly, it is the soul which narrates its mystical encounters with God in the poem.

mentioned above, the metaphor of the night is elaborated in most detail with respect to the purifying and eliminating part of the mystical process. Indeed, *the night* specifically refers to this particular part of the process. But the metaphor is intended to cover the whole process and actually conveys much insight into his more general understanding of the process. Yet, as a metaphor of the whole process (including both the point of departure and the ultimate endpoint) it is not developed very thoroughly as some aspects are expressed almost in passing or actually implied in the general scheme of the metaphor. Still, with time the metaphor seems to have begun to underlie, permeate, and not the least influence, his conceptualization of the developmental process.

The metaphor of the purifying and eliminating part of the process is elaborated very meticulously in passages that are spread out over his two instructional treatises. From beginning to end, the soul's nearing to God, as it is expressed through the metaphor of the night, is a movement from natural light, through supernatural darkness, towards supernatural light at the end. Little by little the soul begins to 'see' a very little supernatural light that gradually grows stronger and at some point is like the light intensity of dawn. In its entirety, the mystical process can therefore be likened to the passage from day to night and day again.[24]

The soul's point of departure is the world supplying it with natural light. The philosophical base of the metaphor is that this light is knowledge which, in agreement with John of the Cross' Thomist psychology, enters through the senses. In the language of the metaphor, the senses are the window to the light of the world which means that once this window is darkened through the pacification of the senses, the soul is left in darkness (Juan de la Cruz 1988, Subida 1.3:3-4). As soon as the night is entered, a gradual darkening of the soul takes a beginning. During the passage through the first part of the night the senses are darkened by means of the annihilation of the sensuous part of the soul (Juan de la Cruz 1988, Subida 1.3:2-3).[25] This eventually leads to what he considers to be a total erasure of the soul's previous knowledge (described with the Pseudo-Dionysian concept of unknowing and the Thomist concept of a tabula rasa state of mind respectively).

Passing through the second part of the night, the spiritual part of the soul is purified through the complete negation of the spiritual properties (like

24. The metaphor, though, actually contains a minor inconsistency concerning the second full day which is claimed coincidentally to correspond to God Himself and to the eternal union (which is the mapping that produces a coherent metaphor as it describes the terminal point of the *process*). Furthermore, God is also likened to the mystical union (which simultaneously corresponds to dawn) (Juan de la Cruz 1988, Subida 1.2:5, Subida 2.2:1 and 3:5; Mancho Duque 1982, 128).

25. Generally this part of the night is referred to as the night of the senses or simply the first night.

understanding) and appetites (for knowledge that in no way contributes to the process, for instance). In this stage, faith darkens and empties the understanding (*how* it works is not explained directly as the knowledge of this is seemingly taken for granted). Similarly, hope darkens and empties the memory and love darkens and empties the will (Juan de la Cruz 1988, Subida 2.6:1). In the second part of the night, corresponding to the middle (and darkest) part of the natural night, the soul is left in pure faith and absolute darkness (Juan de la Cruz 1988, Subida 1.3:3 and 2.2:2).[26]

The third part of the night is the beginning of the perfect union during which God intimately communicates secrets in the most interior part of the soul. This part of the night corresponds to the early (natural) dawn when some light is discernible. This part of the night seems less dark than the previous parts due to God's incipient illumination of the soul, even though, with respect to the natural understanding, this part of the night is much darker than the former two parts of the night (Juan de la Cruz 1988, Subida 1.3:4 and 2.2:1). The mystical process ends when natural death takes over transferring the soul from the dawn of the mystical union to the full daylight of the post-mystical stage of the eternal union with God. Hence, the mystical process continues until natural death after which the soul is finally united essentially and substantially with God in the beatific union (which is not supernatural and mystical but *natural*) (Juan de la Cruz 1988, Subida 2.5:1-4).

Mystical states develop and cause development

The relation of mystical states and development

Initiating this section it should be stressed that, in accord with John of the Cross' writings, mystical states occur in a developmental process. Hence, both the intensity and the character of mystical states change as a person develops mystically. John of the Cross discusses the means of development at two levels. On the one hand, he tries to describe how the individual who is following the mystical way should behave in order to promote progress. At this rather general level he mentions imitation of Christ, mortification of the senses, love of God, and the like. On the other hand, it is implicit in all John of the Cross' treatments of the matter (once in a while even stated directly) that from some point and onwards, it is mainly the mystical states themselves that have an effect on the subject and hence give an impetus to mystical development. Therefore, his occasional attempts to characterize some of the various

---

26. This part of the night is generally referred to as the spiritual night or the second night.

mystical states are important for the understanding of his development.

Thus, it seems to be a general characteristic that mystical states give a strong impetus to the development of a mystic. To a great extent it is the mystical states that change the condition of the soul. In this way, there is a close relationship between actual mystical states and the continuous mystical development. On the one hand, mystical states affect the mind of the mystic, thereby simultaneously promoting the developmental process and yielding an immediate developmental product. There would be little or no mystical development without mystical states. On the other hand, the products of the developmental process seemingly cause mystical states to change. Mystical states may therefore change in various ways as mystical development unfolds.

The connection of mystical states and mystical development is also evident from John of the Cross' own treatment of both, where one aspect is often commented on simultaneously with (and indistinctly from) the other. Especially in the *Canticle*, John of the Cross' reflections on mystical states, immediate effects, and development, are often so deeply entangled that they all float together.

Throughout the developmental process, mystical states constitute a main cause of mystical development. Consequently, it seems that one way in which a mystic can contribute to promote the process is by facilitating the induction of mystical states (to the extent that this lies in the hands of a person). The realization of mystical states, promoted by one's own efforts will then give an impetus to the process of mystical development. Bringing about conditions that will ease the induction of mystical states is easier said than done, though. The condition of a subject is so bad at the starting point of the developmental process that it is very difficult to get the process started at all. The trouble seems to be that the furnishing of the proper conditions requires a considerable amount of self-control which the person does not yet possess due to the soul's condition and all its bad habits. The condition of the soul is therefore bound to impede the initiation of the process. As the subject improves and learns how to ease the occurrence of mystical states he/she also acquires some minimum degree of control over the induction of them. Surprisingly, though, this does not seem to be an aspect that can be learned beyond a certain point. It seems rather that the control of the induction of mystical states actually reduces in the more advanced stages in which mystical states apparently occur quite unintentionally. Hence, it seems that along with mystical development a person gradually loses the ability to influence the realization of mystical aims.

Yet, as the mystical states become gradually more frequent and spontaneous in the more advanced stages of the process, so the reciprocal influence of mystical states and mystical development also grow far more momentous.

In this way the process becomes more and more self-promoting which means that there no longer is any need for the subject to make any efforts, just as there really is no way of doing anything to advance the process.

Presentation of the developmental stages

It seems relevant briefly to present how the stages of the mystical process interrelate. John of the Cross' distinction of the stages of the process seems to be based on characteristic differences in either the quality or the quantity of consciousness in mystical states. As opposed to this, it seems that the effective processes generally stretch over more than one stage. Thus, it does not seem to be the case that the effective processes of one stage are discontinued when a new stage is entered. However, new operations may join in with those already in progress. In the first stage mystical adaptation consists of an initial reconditioning of the functioning of the senses, which breaks down the subject's normal attachment to the external world. In the second stage, the subject undergoes adaptational operations aiming at a pacification of internal cognitive processes that have no immediate relation to sensory inputs. In the third stage, the subject begins to receive a certain kind of exceptional knowledge or starts to understand in a new way. This initial enlightening or instruction is apparently a foretaste of the real illumination that is expected to be characteristic of the post-mystical eternal union with God. Some of the operations in the earlier stages do come to an end at some point in the process, but the transformational operations intensify continuously right to the end. Even though John of the Cross discriminates several stages, he simultaneously views them as being combined into one integrated process. This is also the reason why the mystically advancing soul resembles God more and more, along with a slow but steady detachment from worldly affairs. Similarly, he believes that the soul continuously becomes more closely united with God as the process progresses.

More specifically, the first stage of the mystical process consists in a 'destruction' of what John of the Cross identifies as the sensuous and more 'exterior' part of the soul. The internal processes in the first stage involve an internalization of attention and a gradual stilling of the normal activities of the senses which in combination begin to break down the subject's connectedness to the external environment. As a result of these processes, the direction of attention gradually switches from the external to the internal world.

In the second stage, the internal processes of destruction and annulment are continued but now additionally address more 'spiritual' abilities than before. At that point, the subject further is exposed to what is described as something like an erasure of existing memory content, which ruins the ordinary way of understanding (as mentioned earlier, John of the Cross himself considers memory and understanding to be separate properties). Moreover, the subjective willpower is similarly suspended which results in a sort of indifference and imperviousness conceived of as conformation with God's will.

Some of the operations already in progress continue in the third stage while others seem to be discontinued. In this stage, a new and exceptional manner of understanding very slowly begins to be build up in the mind. John of the Cross views this as an initial supernatural illumination of the soul with which God communicates divine secrets, even though it still is incapable of grasping the content of these secrets. In this final stage of mystical development, the mind has already attained a suitable state of emptiness and imperviousness as the processes effectuating this condition have been fulfilled. Yet, other alterations of the mind that were initiated in the previous stage are continued and strongly intensified. At this point, an apparently exceptional and extraordinary cognitive capacity is constructed in the mind, causing the subject to understand in an entirely new manner.

Together, the first two stages have two purposes. The one is to develop the subject in such a way as to enable him/her to obtain the particular kind of mystical states characterizing the ultimate, mystical stage. The other purpose is to condition the subject properly in order for the subject to be capable of enduring and persisting such mystical states at all. Accordingly, the process of mystical development modifies the soul in two ways. On the one hand, the soul is likened to God in order to eliminate the opposition between them as far as possible which is a precondition for union. On the other hand, the process fortifies and strengthens the soul in order to yield it strong enough to stand the overpowering and overwhelming union with God.

Addressing the problem of mystical states

John of the Cross has not himself organized his descriptions of the diverse mystical states into a coherent system (as opposed to the stages of mystical development). This means that the analysis of the variability of mystical states inevitably involves noteworthy problems, because of the disparate character of the works in which John of the Cross reflects on mystical states. The considerable interval between the initiation of mystical development and the time at which the works have been written has further increased the inconsistencies in the descriptions of mystical states. Hence, the descriptions of mystical states cannot necessarily be expected to constitute reliable documents of particular mystical states both because of the incoherence of the descriptions and the distance between his mystical experience and the time of writing about it. With respect to the relative inconsistency of John of the Cross' descriptions, one of the more specific problems is that his considerations of mystical states apparently often are motivated by his own poetic metaphors. He typically interprets the metaphors as designations for God's diverse ways of visiting the soul. Therefore, his point of departure in trying to explicate the character of a particular mystical state is often a metaphor. This means that in many cases a metaphor reminds him of something which may of course be a certain kind of mystical state, but it might as well be a certain idea that he sees his chance to develop, but which he presents as a description of a certain (type of) mystical state. In general John of the Cross' works are very ambiguous due to the rather diverging character and purposes of the works combined with their more or less coincident topics. The problem is that similar issues are addressed with the use of disparate terminology and metaphors. This means that both the interpretation of the distinct descriptions of mystical states and the untangling of the various contradictions among the descriptions involve difficulties.

In order to display the uncertainties resulting from these problems, it is necessary briefly to attend to the actual character of the works. All of John of the Cross' prose works relate to a poem which he intends to explain. How faithfully a prose work relates to a specific poetic work varies considerably, though. The two treatises, the Ascent of Mount Carmel and the Dark Night are both related to the poem titled Dark Night. The former does not actually deal with the single lines of the poem, though, whereas the latter only deals with the first two verses. In neither of these works does the poem comprise a primary source of inspiration (except as a source of the basic metaphors elaborated in them). Together, the treatises offer a relatively systematic handling of the two first stages of mystical development. Yet, the *Spiritual Canticle* is no doubt the one work rendering most difficulties: on the one hand, because the prose work is a very direct commentary on the poetic work wherefore the issues considered, and the order of issues, often seem arbitrary and disorganized; on the other hand, because the work in its entirety, including poem and commentary, exists in two renditions that on some points are highly dissimilar and sometimes even contradictory. The *Living Flame of Love* relates to the poem of the same name. The description in the *Flame* appears to be inspired directly by the poem, although each of the concrete interpretations are elaborated much more meticulously (from all points of view, that is) than in the *Canticle*. The *Flame* focuses, in particular, on the third stage of mystical development. Like the *Canticle*, the *Flame* exists in an early and a later rendition. Yet, the revision of the *Flame* has not been aimed at a reorganization of the poem, as in the case of the *Canticle*, but only on further specification and elaboration of the concrete interpretations of the verses.

The problems arising from the unavoidable distance between the incident of a mystical state and the subsequent reflections on it, is that the little which is known about John of the Cross' particular mystical states, is filtered through his own representational redescriptions of them. Any description is therefore the product of a long process of representational redescription and mostly also of interpretation. Hence, the descriptions supposedly tell more about averages of (types of) mystical states than about particular states, just as they probably have been influenced by his more recent mystical states, development, and later reflections. On this background, John of the Cross' works cannot be regarded as authentic and direct testimonies of his mystical states. Reservations are therefore pertinent with respect to the possibility of partial inaccuracy and unreliability. Certainly, this is not a problem that solely pertains to the works of John of the Cross as it will be involved in all such evidence. There is nothing better to do than to take the inevitable uncertainties into consideration and make due reservations.

The fact that John of the Cross was fully developed mystically when he began to write about the mystical process entails several aspects to be considered. Firstly, he has presumably remembered the latest incidents of mystical states, that is, those that are typical of the last stage, better than the earlier mystical states. Secondly, John of the Cross' considerations of his mystical states indicate that he rarely has attended to one particular mystical state and concerned himself with a meticulous description of it which means that there is little evidence of particular, mystical states in his works.[27] Much of the evidence rather concerns average or typical states. Thirdly, it can be assumed (strongly supported by recent theories in cognitive psychology of the workings of memory) that John of the Cross has been unable to avoid mingling distinct mystical states. Supposing, as I do, that mystical states are indeed very variable, John of the Cross is apt to have fused features from dissimilar states. In short, a particular characteristic of a mystical state or a type of mystical state may be mixed with characteristics from other mystical states. I do not intend to let these problems keep me from analyzing specific aspects of mystical states, though. But it will keep me from being able to connect the various specific aspects with particular mystical states.

27. This is no surprise, of course, as specific descriptions of one mystical state without any interfering memory traces of other more or less similar states as a minimum would have required that John of the Cross had written his descriptions down almost immediately and this has not been his style. Even if he had, any mystical state would have been compared with and related to earlier states.

The diversity of mystical states

Before addressing the issue of the character of mystical states in the various stages of mystical development, it seems fitting to estimate the relative diversity of mystical states. Viewing conscious states from a general perspective, it does not make a lot of sense that there should be any fundamental difference in the variability of the various kinds of states. I would therefore expect that mystical states potentially are as variable as wakeful states, for instance. If the cognitive makeup allows variability of distinct wakeful states, then this is probably the case with distinct mystical states as well. This point supposedly holds good for variations at all levels, even if in varying degree, between cultures, within cultures, and even within individuals. It is likely that the states of consciousness typical of different cultures varies considerably and that the potential states of consciousness, ordinary or extraordinary, are to some extent culturally determined.[28] States of consciousness common for one individual can similarly be expected to differ from those common for other individuals.[29] And finally, the discrete states of consciousness of an individual can similarly be expected to vary depending on internal and external circumstances. The writings of John of the Cross strongly indicate that mystical states vary not only between developmental stages but also within a stage.

With Greenfield's theory of consciousness as the point of departure, it should therefore be possible to approximate an understanding of the potential diversity of mystical states. There are several factors that jointly constrain the variability of consciousness. With respect to the quality of a mystical state, a particular focus of consciousness, an epicentre, triggers a certain amount of associations and in this way the epicentre, itself constituted by a small group of neurons, serves to aggregate a larger group of neurons (activated by the associations) forming a gestalt generating consciousness at a particular time. The content of a mystical state is thus contingent on the focus of consciousness. The quality of consciousness is further affected by the degree of connectedness of a sequence of consciousnesses and the relative smoothness in the shift from the consciousness of one thing to that of another thing. The quantity and the duration of a particular consciousness is contingent on the size and the maintenance of the neuronal gestalt generating the consciousness. This in turn is conditioned by the strength of the epicentre (determined by the amount of associations it triggers and the cognitive value it has for the person

28. This is supported by and explainable with the earlier presented theories of epigenetic development.
29. Apparently, psychological distinctions between classes of 'temperaments' (see Wulff 1991, 53) are based on such variations.

concerned) and the degree of arousal at the particular time. Considering the immense number of possible combinations of different epicentres and neuronal groups that vary in size and duration in time, it should be clear that although there is not an infinite amount of possible conscious states, there must be a very high degree of potential diversity. In the case of mystical states, the amount of possible states is considerably reduced, though. The reason for this is that the range of potential epicentres and the associations they are able to trigger is limited to those related to mystical conceptions and emotions. Furthermore, the variability of mystical states will presumably change in the course of mystical development. In the beginning of the developmental process, a certain amount of cognitive representations of mystical relevance will constitute the foci of mystical consciousnesses. As the mystic advances in the process of mystical development, some of these representations will be considered superior to and more precious than other representations. Those that are estimated as being the more advantageous (and therefore also have greater cognitive value) will more and more often constitute the foci of mystical consciousnesses while the rest of the representations will be neglected or suppressed. In this way, certain epicentres will be cultivated and strengthened very much while others will lose in relative power and thus in competitiveness. Consequently, both the actual amount of different consciousnesses and the degree of dissimilarity of distinct mystical states can be expected to decrease as mystical development progresses, because of the reduction in the number of epicentres activated from time to time.

A discussion of the relative dissimilarity or similarity of mystical states should be initiated with the very general statement that ultimately every single mystical state of consciousness probably is unique in some way or other. This is not to say, though, that two such unique mystical consciousnesses may not resemble one another very much. Indeed, it seems likely that most mystical states have something in common and that many have very much in common. On the other hand, some mystical states will most probably be very dissimilar to some other mystical states. To be somewhat more precise, I would suggest that in general a particular mystic's mystical states in a delimited period in the developmental process will share several features with one another while each of them will differ considerably from those of another period in the process. All in all, some fundamental traits will be characteristic of (nearly) all mystical states that a mystic has in a lifetime. In the case of John of the Cross all mystical states seem to have involved varying degrees of conceptions and emotions of mystical love. In his case, emotions of mystical love appear to have become absolutely dominant in mystical states in the more advanced part of the developmental process. In fact, all of those more advanced states seem to have been minor variations of emotions of mystical love.

Mystical states in the stages of mystical development

For the purpose of investigating how John of the Cross' mystical states and mystical development are related, some aspects are particularly significant as evidence of an explanation. One such aspect is the differences between the mystical states of the diverse stages. A coupling of mystical states and particular points in the developmental process necessitates a distinction of the particular traits of the various mystical states in the diverse stages (as far as such traits can be identified). The problems involved in this revolve around certain questions. What (if anything) is specific for the mystical states of each of the stages of mystical development? And which traits do the states of one stage share with those of the preceding or subsequent stages?

The pre-mystical stage[30]

It seems that the very early states (whether they are considered mystical or wakeful is mainly a matter of definition) are highly pleasurable but unfulfilled.

In connection with John of the Cross' explication of the very first verse in the poetic part of the *Canticle*,[31] John of the Cross states that God visits the soul in numerous ways, one of which he refers metaphorically to as 'touches of love' which again cause 'wounds of love'. Apparently, it is simply the female's exclamation that she was wounded or lacerated ('herido') in the poem which he in his commentary develops into the metaphor *lacerations of love* ('heridas de amor'). According to John of the Cross, God's purpose with these visits in the soul is really to inflict pain on it. God's aim is to augment the soul's love, desire etc. for Him which He does by briefly visiting it and inflaming it with love after which He abandons it. And it is this that lacerates the soul (Juan de la Cruz 1988, Cántico A1:10/B1:19). As John of the Cross informs his readers, the soul constantly suffers God's absence, but the suffering and the desire is tremendously increased when God visits it so briefly and momentarily. The touches of love can therefore be likened to arrows of fire,

30. In agreement with the original *Canticle*, the first four verses in the poem narrate the stage prior to the classified stages of mystical development. Yet, in the revised work this stage is left out of the argument about the content in the poem (Juan de la Cruz 1988, Cántico A27:2/B22:3). Whether these states and those of the beginning of the first stage actually are mystical or wakeful depends on the definition of mystical consciousness, just as the descriptions can be interpreted in various ways. If complete inattention to the external environment is considered an absolute criterion for mystical states, then these early states are not necessarily actual mystical states. If not they may be deemed weak mystical states.

31. Which in the general argument is said to treat of either the stage preceding the actual process of purification (Juan de la Cruz 1988, A27/B22) or the first stage of purification (B argumento 1-2).

just as the way that they affect the soul can be likened to the way that arrows of fire are capable of setting something on fire. The touches hit and penetrate the soul instantaneously and transiently, inflaming it with love and leaving it entirely on fire. Due to this, the soul is so completely kindled that it simply burns up, virtually departing from its natural self and entering into a new way of being.

Somewhat less metaphorically, John of the Cross further explains that the way the soul is inflamed with the fire of love is that it is granted a sample, but only that, of the pleasures of divine love. It is shown a wonderful delight that immediately is taken away from it again. In spite of the transience of the feeling, it lasts exactly long enough to intensify the soul's painful yearning for God. And this really is God's intention with these touches of the soul, that is to say, He wishes to enhance its desire for Him by briefly pervading it with love. This is altogether a most pleasant experience, so even though the spouse (the female main character in the poetical *Canticle*) complains about the wound or laceration, she ought to be highly pleased (cf. Juan de la Cruz 1988, Cántico A1:8-10/B1:16-19). Still, it may be that such a mystical state is extremely pleasurable, if weighed in isolation. But at the same time, it is because of the joy of the feeling that extreme suffering ensues from it. Partly, because the joy of the feeling makes the ensuing loss of it so much worse. Partly, because the evanescent character of the feeling does not permit it to culminate.[32] In other words, as a result of such states, the subject seems to be left frustrated and hungering for more.

---

32. A little later on in the commentary, John of the Cross contradicts himself concerning the cause of this type of love laceration. He does so in the context of distinguishing it from two other types of wounds. Here he claims that the laceration of love is caused by the reference of God's creatures to Him, whereas no visit of God is said to be involved at all (Juan de la Cruz 1988, Cántico A/B 7:2). This new interpretation is hardly intended to be an elimination of the previous and more detailed one. It is more likely that it is an inconsistency that arises because the disparate claims about the cause of this type of state appear in connection with his interpretation of two different verses. The claim that creatures' reference to God causes the laceration helps produce a coherent interpretation of verse 7, and this is most probably the reason for the alternative interpretation (Cántico A/B 7:5). Of course, it could also be that he had forgotten his explanation of the metaphor. And it could be that he, in his alternative interpretation, sticks closer to the poem and lets his interpretation — like the poem at this point — continue the Christian tradition going back to Bonaventure more stricly viewing *creatures* as signs referring to God.

The first stage of the mystical process

— The beginning of the first stage

In his interpretation of one of the verses, which in both commentaries is argued to recount the beginning of the first stage of mystical development, John of the Cross refers to mystical states that work very much in the same way as the inflaming love-touches. It is the unfulfilment and incompletion of the states that augments the craving for more (Juan de la Cruz 1988, Cántico A6:3-5/B6:4-6). It is difficult to say whether he simply deepens out his explanation of the mystical states described as touches of love in other metaphorical ways (a favoured strategy of his) or he considers a slightly different (kind of) state. It seems most plausible, though, that the two (kinds of) mystical states are very similar even if there are minor differences. The effects of the mystical states concerned are the same and no real differences are pointed out.

At this early point in the mystical process, it is the incompletion of a mystical state coupled with the highly pleasurable character of it that causes desire for and love of God in the subject. Such mystical states seem to be very brief and furthermore incomplete in some way or other.

A brief comment on the description of the stage prior to the classified mystical process and the beginning of the process seems pertinent. One of the verses that are argued to relate the first mystical stage is interpreted as describing a mystical state quite similar to those prior to the first stage, and this actually questions the reliability of the identification of the initiation of the process. Why has John of the Cross interpreted the first four verses in the *Canticle* to depict the pre-mystical period and the following to depict the first mystical stage, if he at the same time describes them rather similarly. Indeed, this indicates that his later interpretation of the poem, presented in his second argument about it, is more true to his mystical experience which means that the descriptions of highly incomplete mystical states all pertain to (the beginning of) the first mystical stage.

— The first stage in general

According to John of the Cross' descriptions, the mystical states of the first stage of mystical development are characterized by two traits. The first is that a certain kind of dying fertilizes the soul. The second is that union with God generates a feeling of losing oneself.[33]

33. John of the Cross has described his early, mystical states in fairly much detail in the *Canticle* (provided that this work delineates the whole mystical process as argued by

Fertilizing death:

John of the Cross further proposes an alternative metaphor that is intended to help explain how mystical states in the first stage of mystical development actually work in the mind. He returns to the metaphor of God's touches as *arrows of love* that are sent into the heart of the lover by the beloved. These mystical states appear to be rather momentary, since they are, in the language of chivalry, arrows of love going right through the soul. Nonetheless, they virtually fertilize heart and soul with divine understanding and love in such a way that the soul can be said *to conceive* by God. John of the Cross claims that this divine conception consists in comprehending the beauty, highness, wisdom, and virtues of God. Moreover, he asserts that the reason why these particular mystical states are capable of impregnating the soul is that they have a lethal effect on the soul and little by little will take its life. The fertilization of the soul with the love of God thereby actually follows from the soul's loss of its life (Juan de la Cruz 1988, Cántico A8:3-4/B8:4-5).

As mentioned, John of the Cross discusses two more kinds of wounds as metaphors of mystical states, although only the more serious wound is discussed in detail. This metaphor is taken from the language of medicine and may be translated as an open, running wound (*llaga afístolada*)[34] or, following his explication of the metaphor, it may be translated as dying simply and purely. The touch of God causing this type of wound is not very much and does not last very long because, if it did the soul would break away from the body. The actual character of such a mystical state is not discussed any more precisely, since John of the Cross mainly concerns himself with the effects of the state. His general account seems to imply, though, that it is a rather violent and forceful (kind of) mystical state, and this is further supported with his treatment of the effects. Inflicted with this immaterial wound, the soul lives 'dyingly' as love slowly puts it to death, transforming it into love. In accord with his general style of accumulating explanations, John of the Cross suggests an additional and more general cause of the death of the soul. Not only does the soul die from love, but it furthermore dies because this dying seems never to come to an end (Juan de la Cruz 1988, A/B7:3-4).

John of the Cross' treatment of the diverse kinds of wounds, briefly mentioned in connection with verse 7, is reconsidered in the interpretation

---

himself). As I have mentioned before, the descriptions of early mystical states can be expected to be made up from a blend of memories of several mystical states and of other persons' descriptions of their mystical states.

34. This is a particular kind of (physical) wound that is narrow, deep, running and disinclined to close (Juan de la Cruz 1988, 601 note 1).

of verse 9. Here he considers the cure of the wound. It is not explicitly stated which types of wounds a cure is sought for, but indirectly it seems that the cure primarily concerns the wound of dying. The only cure is to finish the already initiated putting the soul to death with love. A little more subtly, he explains how this is to be accomplished. God's absence is the cause of both pain and wound, wherefore his presence is the cure. Implicitly, it appears that it only is God's *continuous* presence that can cure the soul, because otherwise the soul would be cured every time God visited it in one way or another. What seems to be the point is that the cure for dying is the eternal union with God (and evidently, this would cure all the other wounds as well) (Juan de la Cruz 1988, Cántico A9:2/B9:3).

The topic of mystical states causing (some degree of) a certain kind of death in the soul is mentioned specifically in connection with the first stage of what John of the Cross himself identifies as the mystical process. He views the entire process as a gradually progressing death that will culminate with the incident of natural death. The death of the human elements in the soul is considered to be a precondition for true mystical life (identical with recurring but transient divine life). That the death of the soul simultaneously will fertilize it and thereby prepare it for another kind of life is therefore predictable on the background of the conceptual scheme of the process. The reason why the death of the soul is fertilizing is that only an annihilation of the natural contents of the faculties of the soul will give place for God to do the constructive and transforming work in it.

Thus even though the mystical states concerned (somehow) cause a process of dying that again (somehow) causes fertilization of the soul, this is not necessarily the immediate benefit gained from these mystical states. It seems that dying is just one method of emptying the faculties of the soul. Seemingly it is emptiness (or incipient vacuity) that can be interpreted as a condition of fertility. Nor an empty (and thus fertile) soul is an end in itself, though. An empty and fertile soul is only powerful when it facilitates the commencement of the constructive process of transforming the soul. The processes of dying and emptying do have partial ends (fertilization of the soul, for instance). But these are only ends insofar as they ease the display of other processes. In general the mystical process (like other developmental processes) involves a very long chain of processes and products. Each part of the process certainly has an end but not necessarily an end in itself. Often it is just a partial end preparing for the processes to come next. Hence all of the partial ends aim at the ultimate end and all either initiate or advance the achievement of this end.

In this way the process of putting the soul to death is merely one of the initial steps towards the ultimate goal as are the processes claimed to empty the soul by burning it and the like.[35] I would suggest that the reason why dying fertilizes the soul is that it works towards the same partial end as other ways of emptying the soul of its contents. Consequently, dying is an early purifying process that like the other (and later) purifying processes prepares the soul for the transforming processes.

It seems nonetheless that the more specific effects of mystical states causing this kind of dying actually differ somewhat from the purifying effects of the more advanced mystical states. In agreement with John of the Cross' descriptions of mystical states, it is rather certain that the kinds of mystical state having the described deadly effect (that again have a fertilizing effect) are exclusively characteristic of the first stage of mystical development. In the later stages, mystical states have other effects on the subject.

A feeling of personality loss:

John of the Cross explains that while there is union of the two lovers, God and the soul, the two live in one another. The union is so profound that it can be said that they are one and the same. This condition is attained because each lover gives possession of her-/himself to the other during the union (Juan de la Cruz 1988, Cántico A11:6/B12:7). Interpreting this, it appears that during mystical states a subject loses his/her sense of being a delimited person. In accord with John of the Cross' statements, which are of course highly personal, it seems that one loses the feeling of being oneself during mystical states but in return one gains the feeling of being someone else. In some form or other, this trait appears to have been involved in all of John of the Cross' mystical states, inasmuch as they all have involved some degree of union.

The (rather hypothetical) joining of two (equal) persons ought to involve a mutual absorption of the parties involved, that is to say, of the one in the other and the other way round, wherefore the process equally ought to imply the dissipation of both persons' boundaries and the emergence of a mutual circumference. It is not the union of two equal persons that John of the Cross aims to explain, though, as the one person is far superior to

35. A brief remark seems relevant here. I take the fact that John of the Cross consistently shifts from one metaphorical expression to another when considering the effects of mystical states (regardless of whether he speaks of dying, burning, or the like) not only to be a sign of stylistic innovativeness, but likewise to be an indication of real (even if minor) variations in the content attempted communicated. In short, when he speaks of dying in connection with some of the early states, but unfailingly turns to speak of burning in connection with some of the later states, I find it reasonable to assume that real differences underlie the differences in expression.

the other. Therefore it is only the bounds of the inferior person that disappear, just as the union implies only the inferior person's absorption by the superior person. In this way, the feeling of being or possessing someone else (God) is gained in exchange for the loss of oneself as long as the mystical state lasts. Afterwards the feeling of loss persists but that of gain disappears.

The feeling of losing possession of oneself (or one's heart as John of the Cross would say) seems to go far beyond the mystical state itself. In the earlier stages of mystical development this causes a feeling of immense emptiness. The loss and the resulting feeling of emptiness generate a continuous hunger and craving in the subject. It could have been expected that the subject would long to regain what was lost (oneself or one's heart, that is) but this does not seem to be the case. On the contrary, the subject wishes to attain that which temporarily substituted the loss during the mystical state. And the hunger drives the subject incessantly to try to reach this end (Juan de la Cruz 1988, Cántico A 9:5 and B9:6). In John of the Cross' interpretation of this, the mystic does not strive for God to visit the soul again, but simply craves for God Himself whom he/she expects to be capable of filling in what was lost.

All in all, this aspect of early, mystical states has two effects. One is actualized during the mystical state and part of it remains after the state. The other aspect *results* from the remaining part of the first effect. During these mystical states the person has a feeling of being absorbed by God which produces a feeling of losing one's own personality. After the state, the former feeling disappears while the latter stays on. This, in turn, causes an immense yearning for God.

Summary of the first stage

It is now time to return to answer the questions posed at the beginning of this section. The task is to discriminate the specific characteristics of early mystical states from those of later states. I have discussed three features that John of the Cross has described as characteristic of early mystical states. To sum up briefly, the issues are the following: Mystical states are delightful but incomplete and unfulfilled. Mystical states generate an initial dying in the soul that fertilizes it (presumably through emptying it). God and the soul reciprocally surrender all possessions to one another in mystical states which gives the soul a sense of losing itself. Without exception, all of these immediate effects cause a feeling of emptiness that again causes extreme desire and hunger for God.

Apparently, all of the (diverse) internal processes in early mystical states end up causing an insatiable yearning and hungering for God. This issue is considered rather meticulously in connection with the initial part of the developmental process and not in connection with the subsequent parts. Moreover, the whole first quarter of the poem in the *Canticle* tells of the spouse's (alias the soul) longing and searching for her beloved (alias God). The scrupulous attention to this particular effect of mystical states in the context of very early development indicates that this is where it matters the most. This certainly makes sense, inasmuch as the initial part of the process is a point at which the relationship between God and the soul is still rather undeveloped, wherefore the distance between God and soul still is at its highest, just as the mystical states are both weak and infrequent.

Yet, early mystical states seem to have some traits in common with later states. Thus, the capacity to cause a certain kind of emptiness is not only common for mystical states in the initial but also in the middle part of the mystical process. In addition to that, it is a general characteristic of mystical states throughout the process that they generate a feeling of being united with God which again provokes the mystic's complete surrender to God.

The second stage of the mystical process

— Initiation of the second stage

According to John of the Cross' interpretation one of the earlier verses (A12/B13) in the poetic *Canticle* narrates a particular mystical state during which the engagement of the lovers takes place. In accord with his general argument about the poem, this is further interpreted to be the state that realizes the transition to the second stage referred to as the espousal stage (corresponding to the spiritual night or the illuminative way). In his view the verse describes (the first incident of) a kind of mystical state that is rather typical of (the beginning of, I presume) the second stage. John of the Cross specifically focuses on two features of this (type of) mystical state, namely that it generates a sensation that the soul departs from the body and that the love actualized in the state causes resemblance of God and the soul.

With respect to the first aspect, the point is that this (type of) mystical state generates the sensation that the soul is withdrawn from the body and virtually departs from it. The subject is deprived of both activities and sensations in and of the body. Even though severe physical pains and bodily damages are generated in such a mystical state, these are not felt (that is, if one can call it pains if they are not felt). John of the Cross explains that it is because of the suspension of the senses that the pain is unnoticed (Juan de la Cruz 1988, Cántico A12:3-5/B13:4-6). It appears that he has been aware of the incapacity to move and perceive during the state and of the feeling of detachment from body and mind. Contrary to that, he has apparently been unaware of the pains and the bodily damages during the mystical state.

When these aspects are interpreted in connection with one another, it seems that the declarations about these mystical states correlate different points in time, namely during such a mystical state and some time after it. The sensation that some part of oneself departs from the body seems to be what John of the Cross has been aware of during the state. The same holds good for the loss of sensory perception and the inability to move. But if he did not feel any pain or other physical devastation during the mystical state, then he must have gathered from later pain and damage that it had been generated during the state. Thus, the presumption that the mystical state has been painful must have been motivated by his later notice of pain and damage, presumably supported by the experience of other mystical states during which pain has been felt.

The second point is that the love generated in the mystical states in question produces such equalization of the lovers involved in the act that the one resembles the other. This is presumably the inception of the process that eventually will transform the soul completely into God. The completion of this will not be realized in terrestrial life, though (Juan de la Cruz 1988, Cántico A11:6-7/B12:7-8).

— The end of the second stage

Towards the end of the second stage of the mystical process, a most expedient type of mystical state, referred to as 'touches of union', sets in. Since God is without any form whatever, it is convenient for the attainment of touches of union that one helps empty the faculties of the soul. A touch of union occurs quite unexpectedly and is a kind of mystical state that has a very powerful effect on a person. John of the Cross considers these mystical states in connection with a general instruction in how to treat the faculty of memory. Hence, he focuses on the way that these states specifically work on memory as secluded from understanding and willpower. During the touches of union God is completely united with memory. This very deep union has several consequences.

First, these divine touches free the soul from both imagination and fantasy whereby memory begins to be liberated from specific and distinct knowledge (Juan de la Cruz 1988, Subida 2.32 and 3.2). Thus, on the one hand, John of the Cross advises that the emptying of the faculties of the soul disposes the soul to receive these touches of God. On the other hand, it appears that the mystical states themselves contribute efficiently towards that end. Second, he argues that total insensitivity, inescapably goes along with the suspension of imagination. In John of the Cross' view, the ability to perceive is dependent on the ability to imagine. Hence, the subject is no longer capable either of imagining or perceiving anything at all. Third, a very substantial, supernatural knowledge and understanding is infused in the soul, although the knowledge really is incomprehensible by natural understanding. In this way, the loss of natural knowledge is replaced with a fill-in of some kind of divine knowledge. In connection with the reception of this new knowledge, John of the Cross stresses that it is very important that the soul stands by during those divine touches, if it wishes to profit fully from the infusion of knowledge. Otherwise, the soul will interrupt the reception of knowledge with its natural (and limited) abilities. This is because the supernatural knowledge received in such a mystical state is so frail that it is easily disrupted, if the soul intervenes with its activities (Juan de la Cruz 1988, Subida 2.32:4). Such mystical states are effectuated purely by God wherefore the subject can contribute nothing to them, except negatively. Fourth, a striking forgetfulness remains for quite some time after a touch of union. Deprived of specific knowledge, which is the means of remembrance, the soul for a long time following such a state is left in such forgetfulness or confusion that it involves great pain for it to remember anything. The forgetfulness resulting from the claimed elimination of specific knowledge lasts for quite some time after such a mystical state has come to an end. Hence, one forgets to attend to ordinary things like eating, drinking, and the like (Juan de la Cruz 1988, Subida 3.2). In fact, the effect remaining after such mystical states sounds more like a sort of distractedness or confusion than actual forgetfulness.

A brief remark on the character of these mystical states seems relevant here. The suspension of imagination coupled with the declared elimination of knowledge could be an indication that the natural tendency to represent cognitively is affected somehow. Even if the issue remains quite inconclusive, I would suggest that the more specific and conceptual cognitive representations change into emotional representations. In my opinion, it is likely that it is the processes contributing in various ways towards the reduction of the generation of the more specific and conceptual representations that John of the Cross interprets as the emptying of the soul's faculties. Similarly, it is the products of this process, that is to say, the resulting reduction in the more specific cognitive representations during mystical states that he takes to be the destruction of specific and natural knowledge.

In this context, it seems relevant to mention the way that this significant forgetfulness caused by these mystical states appears in the developmental process. While most of the alterations resulting from development unfold continuously through steady increase or decrease of some feature, the forgetfulness or distraction differs from most of the other products of mystical development in that it apparently sets in at a certain point in the process and then disappears again. I would suggest that the explanation of why mystical states exclusively produce such confusion and distraction in a specific part of mystical development is that it is a (inconvenient) side-effect of mystical states for which some basic development is requisite. Hence, some development is the precondition for the display of what seems to be the avoidance of the generation of the more specific conceptual representations which, in turn, causes the subsequent distraction. The reason why these efficient mystical states occur in the middle (and not in the beginning) of the process is that the unfolding of them presupposes a certain degree of mystical development. In other words, the touches of union require a certain cognitive capacity to be brought out and this capacity is provided by mystical development. Yet, further development is needed in order to avoid or overcome the rather disadvantageous subsequent distraction or confusion following from a mystical state.

Summary of the second stage of the process

It is not possible to give an undifferentiated picture of the specific characteristics of mystical states in the second stage of the process as the mystical states of this period seem to be quite disparate. The mystical state claimed to initiate the stage apparently suspends the senses and produces a sensation that the soul withdraws from the body. This mystical state is said to involve physical pain and devastation that is not noticed until the state has come to an end. This mystical state further generates a kind of love that has the power to cause semblance of the soul and God. The sensation that the soul departs from the body is not described explicitly in connection with other mystical states, but the suspension of the senses (claimed to cause the sensation) seems to be common in mystical states at least from the second stage and onwards. Hence, it is possible that this is the first mystical state suspending the senses completely. This particular effect may also be that which has motivated the identification of this state as the initiation of the second stage. The remaining elements in the mystical state concerned are seemingly part of most mystical states in varying degree. The feeling of love increases continuously as the process advances, although it seems that the more significant aspect of the transforming effect of love does not set in before the initiation of the second stage. The physical pain and bodily devastation are not mentioned specifically in connection with other kinds of mystical states but it seems that, at least in the third stage, mystical states are free of all kinds of pain.

As representations of the more advanced part of the second stage, the mystical states referred to as 'touches of union' are described in most detail. The most significant characteristic of these mystical states is that which John of the Cross regards as elimination of specific (identical with worldly) knowledge (in his view, due to the suspension of imagination) and the substitution of this with divine knowledge. They are furthermore followed by a serious confusion or forgetfulness. The temporary elimination of specific knowledge seems to be tantamount to a stilling of the generation of more specific and conceptual cognitive representations and it seems that this has not been possible until the developmental point permitting the touches of union. It further seems that the reception of new knowledge is enabled because of the absence of the more specific, cognitive representations which means that this similarly has not been part of earlier states. Yet, the emphasis on the frailty of the received knowledge would indicate that the more specific cognitive representations may at that point still interfere and take over.

The third stage of the mystical process

— The transition from the second to the third stage

The *Canticle* is quite uncertain as evidence of various kinds of mystical states, because some of the more significant of these are ascribed to more than one point in the developmental process depending on which part of the work one follows. Thus, he distinguishes three (types of) mystical states that alternatingly are claimed either to occur in the second stage, initiate the third stage, or to occur in the beginning of the third stage. The cause of this ambiguity is partly that the group of verses relating the mystical states concerned have been transferred from the middle of the original poem to a more advanced point in the reorganized poem and partly that his concrete interpretations of the verses concerned are incongruent with both of his general arguments. The descriptions of these mystical states in the commentary are inspired by three metaphorical expressions in the poem, namely the touch of the spark, the spicy wine, and the spouse's drinking from her beloved in a wine cellar. The narrative structure of this particular sequence of verses is divided into three parts. According to John of the Cross' interpretation, the story in the first two verses culminates in the third verse in a very sublime event having some very remarkable effects that are related in the subsequent verses of the sequence.

The sequence of verses in the poem, according to John of the Cross' interpretation, relates mystical states that are connected because they are typical of the same period in the developmental process. As mentioned, it is highly uncertain, though, of which period they are typical. Furthermore, the descriptions of these mystical states in his commentary strongly indicate that they really are not typical of the same period and that he mainly has connected them because of the poetic connection of the metaphors inspiring the descriptions. For that reason, I have deemed it irrelevant to follow directly any of his couplings of the mystical states concerned at the diverse points in the developmental process. I do take his claims in the commentary as a point of departure, though (as this is where the more detailed descriptions of the various mystical states appear), but I shall evaluate the reliability of his interpretations on the basis of a comparison of his descriptions of the mystical states and his more general statements about the developmental process.

I wish to underscore that it is essential to identify the typicality of the mystical states of one stage as distinct from those of other stages and match the diverse mystical states and stages as precisely and correctly as possible, inasmuch as this is indispensable for an understanding of the process resulting in mystical development. If characteristics of mystical states typical of the one developmental point are erroneously ascribed to another point, this will render the distinct characteristics of the mystical states of the diverse points in the developmental process highly inconclusive. It is therefore important to cautiously estimate the developmental points of the described mystical states.

— The event in the interior wine cellar

In the poem, the touch of the spark and the spicy wine led up to the culmination in the interior wine cellar where the spouse has been drinking from her beloved. Yet, as mentioned these mystical states primarily seem to have been connected because of the connection of the metaphors in the poem. It is rather clear, though, in John of the Cross' more concrete interpretations of the verses that he elaborates his more general conceptualization of some of his most advanced mystical states. Thus, the metaphors seem to have triggered the memory of different mystical states that were not necessarily connected in any specific way.

The event in a wine cellar is not claimed to describe a type of recurring mystical states. It is, on the contrary, related as one specific event, that is to say, one particular meeting between the two lovers.[36] This does not rule out the possibility, though, that mystical states like this one have actually been typical of a more, or less, extended period.

Metaphorically, the spouse's act of drinking from her beloved corresponds to the concrete union of God and the soul. Each of the soul's faculties is affected by this mystical state as sweet love is infused into the willpower, divine wisdom into the understanding, and memory is recreated and diverted with the reminder and *feeling* of the glorious stage. The whole soul without exception participates in the state which he likens to a drink penetrating and intoxicating all of the limbs of the body thereby justifying the metaphor. The intoxication suspends imagination and empties the soul of all specific knowledge. In replacement for the lost knowledge, the soul is filled with divine knowledge.

The subsequent group of verses telling of the effects of this mystical state portray a heavily drunken spouse stepping out from the wine cellar. It appears that this mystical state truly brings about a significant alteration of the mind. Without exception, all worldly knowledge is erased and substituted with divine wisdom. As long as the soul is absorbed in the union of love all particular forms vanish. It is not the case, though, that former knowledge and habits really disappear, not even during the union. The point is rather that the soul's worldly knowledge is so absorbed in the divine wisdom that it is just as if any other knowledge has disappeared.

Natural knowledge vanishes and is replaced with divine knowledge both because the soul is so immersed in the union that it cannot relate to anything else and because the soul is so transmuted in God that it totally conforms with his simpleness which is completely free of forms and images. Accordingly, there are two reasons why the subject is deprived of forms and images during this mystical state. The one is that the mystical state is so overwhelming that there simply is no room for specific forms anymore. The other is that the state has the capacity to strip the subject of specific knowledge and of particular forms. It is a temporary switch of knowledge, though, that occurs during the mystical state, although it does persevere for some time after it (Juan de la Cruz 1988, Cántico A17:11-12/B26:13 and 26:16-17). An additional effect of this mystical state is that

36. Indeed, it seems perfectly natural that he has interpreted the verse this way irrespective of whether it relates a single incident or a condensation of several more or less similar mystical states. The point is, that his primary intention has been to interpret a particular verse which, in correspondence with the composition of the poem, evidently relates a specific event. In the *Canticle*, he takes his point of departure in the poem and whenever he digresses from it, as he often does, he does so on purpose maybe because some idea or viewpoint is triggered by either the reading of the poem or the writing of the commentary.

knowledge of the world begins to appear like pure ignorance in comparison with divine wisdom. The two kinds of understanding — the
mundane and the divine — are inversely proportional, so that knowledge-
ability of the one means ignorance of the other.

Of course, as there is no chance of staying in the mystical state, the
subject sooner or later returns to mundane reality. But the reinstallation in
temporality does not in itself return the natural properties or behaviour to
the subject. Just as the effects of the act of love endures, so does the unknowing (the emptiness of memory and understanding) as John of the
Cross expresses it. As a consequence of this, the soul becomes totally
alienated from anything that is of the world. This causes a certain indifference towards the external world that again results in an inability to
judge or estimate the affairs of the world. His explanation of the cause of
this total indifference is that the soul no longer contains the knowledge by
which human matters are measured (Juan de la Cruz 1988, Cántico
A17/B26).

All in all, a mystical state like the wine cellar event shares major characteristics with the mystical states referred to as touches of union that are
typical of the end of the second stage. Like them, this particular mystical
state suspends imagination, empties the soul of specific knowledge, and
provides it with divine knowledge. There is one major difference, though,
which is that this state, unlike the touches of union, apparently does not
produce forgetfulness or confusion (causing the subject to forget to eat,
drink, and the like), but instead produces a lasting feeling of estrangement
towards the external world. Yet, alienation is actually claimed to be a
general effect of the mystical process wherefore this aspect need not be of
major import. The similarity of these mystical states indicates that either
this mystical state (the event in the wine cellar, that is) is simply an incident of a more or less coherent group of mystical states classified as
touches of union or it is a state that is quite similar to these.

It is now time to couple the mystical state referred to as an 'event in a
wine cellar' with a specific point in the developmental process, as this is
very important for an evaluation of the developmental process in general,
because this (kind of) mystical state seems to have been very influential.
According to the original poem, this is the mystical state that has initiated
the second stage.[37] Correlating the original poem and the first general

37. It is relevant to consider how this interpretation corresponds with the transition to
the second stage, though. The transition to the second stage is not pointed out in the
concrete interpretations of the single verses which means that it does not appear until
the presentation of the general argument in verse 27 in the original *Canticle*. Hence,
the concrete interpretations need to be coupled with the general argument to make

argument, on the other hand, this (kind of) mystical state seems rather to have occurred in the middle of the second stage. Yet, according to the revised *Canticle*, on the other hand, it has occurred in the first third of the final stage. Complicating the matter further is that John of the Cross, in his concrete interpretations of the verses concerned actually associates the descriptions in the verses with mystical states characteristic of the third stage.[38] It could thus have initiated the second stage, have been typical of the middle of the second stage, or it could have been typical of the beginning of the third stage (possibly contributing to the initiation of this). As this is a matter of major importance, I shall discuss the evidence supporting each of the possibilities.[39]

There is really no evidence supporting the original argument, according to which the mystical state poetically described as an event in a wine cellar has taken place in the beginning of the second stage (and even less that it should have initiated it). As opposed to this, the similarities of the event in the wine cellar and the touches of union may support the concrete interpretations of the original poem and the view in the revised *Canticle* in general that this particular mystical state has occurred in the beginning of the third stage. The point is that the mystical states described as an event in a wine cellar and as touches of union respectively have much in common, but the former is better, more intense, and characterized with an additional, positive effect in comparison with the latter (whether they are

this point explicit. In the general argument, verse A12 is interpreted as relating the transition to the second stage. This leaves only five out of 39 verses to describe the entire second stage (and the second stage is otherwise given major attention in his two instructional treatises). There is nevertheless, no direct conflict between the concrete interpretation of the verse relating the transition to the third stage and the general argument that the transition to the second stage is narrated in verse A12. The conflict is between verse A17-18 and the interpretation of verse A12.

38. Actually, John of the Cross has not changed this view in the concrete interpretation in the revised commentary but the change of context (resulting from the re-organization of the poem and thus the concrete interpretations) justifies an altered interpretation in better harmony with the context wherefore further changes may have seemed superfluous to him. The concrete interpretation of the verse as telling of the entrance into a new stage is therefore far more salient in the original *Canticle*, although it similarly is implicit in the concrete interpretation of the verse in the revised *Canticle*.

39. I wish to underscore that I do not intend to display how John of the Cross contradicts himself. I take it for granted that the contradictions are brought out because of the editorial changes undertaken at various points in time. Presumably he has intended to convey dissimilar meanings at the diverse points in time. But, inasmuch as he mainly has changed the meanings simply by shifting the contexts of the original poetical expressions, it is only natural that contradictions arise here and there.

all of the same type or not is less important). Furthermore, the event in the wine cellar is free from the effect of subsequent confusion characteristic of the touches of union which may also be taken as evidence that it is a more advanced state, inasmuch as John of the Cross asserts that this effect is not produced in later mystical states. Thus, the mystical state described in the verse as drinking in a wine cellar is presumably more advanced than those referred to as touches of union (it could, for instance, be an advanced variety of them). Since the touches of union are typical of the end of the second stage, the wine cellar event might have occurred in the beginning of the third stage (as claimed in the revised *Canticle*). The exceptional developmental changes resulting from this (kind of) mystical state indicate that this mystical state is transitional in some way or other. Hence, it seems plausible that this mystical state has played a major role in the passage from the second to the third stage.

There is no chance of reaching a decisive conclusion of the matter but some points seem fairly certain. Inasmuch as this particular state apparently is rather similar to, but slightly more advanced than, the mystical states referred to as touches of union (typical of the end of the second stage), it seems most plausible that it has been later than the touches of union. With respect to the more specific point at which this mystical state has occurred, two possibilities seem most reasonable. It may have contributed to the transition to the third stage without actually constituting *the* mystical state marking a shift from the one stage to the other. It would thus have occurred towards the very end of the second stage. Such an interpretation actually disagrees with John of the Cross' interpretation in his original commentary on the verse and neither agrees nor disagrees directly with his revised commentary. If this is nonetheless the case, then the (kind of) mystical state described as an event in a wine cellar would be one of a number of mystical states contributing to the transition from the second to the third stage. The interpretation that the wine cellar event narrates a mystical state in the beginning of the third stage would, on the other hand, correspond with the revised *Canticle* in general. This suggestion is contested by the apparently very strong influence that this (kind of) mystical state has, which strongly indicates that it has occurred before the final stage of the process, inasmuch as John of the Cross generally teaches that the fulfilment of the fundamental changes in the soul is a precondition for entrance into the ultimate stage.

Connecting the evidence, it seems most plausible that the mystical state in question has been involved in the fulfilment of some major developmental changes that may have been brought forth around the termination of the second stage and the initiation of the third (according to John of the

Cross' classification of the stages). The period in between the two stages may or may not be considered transitional. The main point supporting this solution is the exceptionally strong impact that this (kind of) mystical state has on the subject which suggests that it has occurred around a turning point (which may have stretched over a fairly long period) in the developmental process. John of the Cross' writings indicate that the process of mystical development speeds up towards the end of the second stage. It appears that the developmental process has taken a turn during the period towards the very end of the second stage and that the mystical states of this period have had rather drastic effects producing some major changes. This is the period during which the ultimate *perfectioning* of the subject is carried out (which does not mean that development comes to an end but only that the more fundamental changes have been completed).

Accepting the above as evidence that the wine cellar event refers to a (number of) mystical state(s) that has (have) occurred during a more or less extended (transitional?) period at the end of the second stage, it seems reasonable to relate this (kind of) mystical state to the 'touches of union'. My suggestion is that the mystical states referred to as touches of union are less advanced than that depicted as the spouse's drinking from her beloved in a wine cellar. It is furthermore not unlikely that there is some degree of alternation either of the diverse kinds of mystical states or of the diverse aspects of them in varying combinations. The more specific relation of the mystical states concerned aside, they all seem to be typical of the same period around the end of the second stage (and possibly stretching into the beginning of the third stage). Additionally there is the problem of untangling the relation of the mystical states described as an event in a wine cellar and as the wedding of the lovers respectively. My suggestion is that both of these mystical states have occurred (and maybe recurred) during a period of intense development just around the end of the second stage and the beginning of the third. One might speculate that a mystical state like the one described as an event in a wine cellar is slightly more advanced than the states referred to as *touches of union* and that this mystical state has contributed to the termination of the purifying part of the mystical process whereas the wedding event is (remembered and identified) as the first mystical state typical of (the beginning of) the third stage.

It seems pertinent at this point to relate the discussed parts of the *Canticle* to one another in order to give an overview of the way that the work relates the issue of connecting specific mystical states apparently described in the poem with specific developmental points. When composing the poem, John of the Cross may not yet have correlated the diverse mystical states narrated in the poem with exact points in the developmental process. In the concrete interpretations of the single verses in the original *Canticle*, he has related the single verses more explicitly with specific mystical states and, in some few cases, furthermore correlated them with specific developmental points. He does not seem to have viewed the content of the poem in a general perspective until the presentation of the general argument in verse A27. In the first general argument he considers the issue of how the various verses relate to specific points in the developmental process, but without integrating this with the concrete interpretations of the verses. In the reorganized *Canticle*, he connects both the verses in the poem and the concrete interpretations of the verses with specific developmental points.

— Initiation of the third stage

In the *Canticle*, John of the Cross presents his general argument that the poem delineates the stages of mystical development in connection with his interpretation of a particular verse (A27/B22) said to describe the mystical state that has at once realized the wedding of God and the soul and initiated the final stage of mystical development. The event is poetically depicted as the spouse's (playing the role of the soul) entrance into the desired garden. It may have been a singular event or the first incident of a type of mystical states that are typical of the third stage. According to John of the Cross, mystical states become very frequent as soon as this final stage is entered.

The mystical state depicted as the wedding of God and the soul is praised in exalted tones, although the possibility of accounting for it simultaneously is denied in his claim that it is a mystical state beyond expression (or, beyond that which can be said or thought, as he expresses it) (Juan de la Cruz 1988, Cántico A27:3/B22:5). Two specific features are claimed to be typical of this state, namely one effect that exclusively is actualized during the state and one that seemingly persists. The first is that during the state there is such union of the human and the divine nature that both resemble God even though the soul does not change its being. The second point is that this mystical state is capable of eliminating the very last deficiencies still left in the subject thereby 'repairing' the soul as John of the Cross expresses it in the verse (Juan de la Cruz 1988, Cántico A27-28/B22-23). This aspect might be taken to support the singularity of the state, inasmuch as the very last defects cannot be destroyed over and over again. Yet, this point should hardly be emphasized too strongly as he similarly interprets the event in the wine cellar as the mystical state bringing about such ultimate refinement in the soul (Juan de la Cruz 1988,

Cántico A17/B26). This strongly indicates that the final developmental changes are carried out gradually in several mystical states. This further supports the suggestion that the wine cellar event and the wedding event jointly work towards this end in around the same period of the process.

In accord with the revised *Canticle*, it seems to be due to this final modification of the soul that there will be no more distractions whatever during mystical states from this point and onwards which means that the soul can get the very best out of all subsequent mystical states. Hence, this and the following mystical states should be completely peaceful and beyond the risk of being interrupted. Yet, the original *Canticle* actually portrays potential disturbers of the peace waiting to disrupt the peace in the verses following the narration of the wedding. This indicates that the risk that the peace in mystical states is disturbed really is not eliminated *for good* at any point or that it has not been eliminated completely at the point concerned.

If it is the case that transition from one stage to another consists in *living through* a mystical state of a particular kind different from those of the former stage and common in the new stage (as implied in the intepretation of some of the verses that particular mystical states have initiated the second and the third stage respectively) then the mystical state depicted as a wedding can be expected to be the first (or only) of a better and more sublime kind than all earlier mystical states. If this is correct, then transition from one stage to another may be considered instantaneous. Another possibility is that the passage from one stage to another (or, more precisely, from one part of the process to another) takes place more gradually in which case the later *identification* of a point at which a subject can be said to have entered a new stage is founded on the memory of what is taken to be the first incident of a mystical state of a more advanced kind (see e.g., Juan de la Cruz 1988, Cántico A12 and 27:3/B13 and 22:5).

— The third stage in general

John of the Cross considers the issue of mystical states typical of the final stage of mystical development both in the *Spiritual Canticle* and in the *Living Flame of Love*. Unfortunately the *Canticle* is a little problematic as evidence of the most advanced mystical states, because John of the Cross has changed his mind on several points with respect to the connection of mystical states and the developmental stages. In the original *Canticle* the ultimate mystical states are described towards the very end of the work. In the revised rendition the states ascribed to the third stage are those referred to as the touch of the spark, the spicy wine, and the event in the interior wine cellar. The states described towards the end of the work are, on the other hand, ascribed to the beatific stage.[40]

In general the *Canticle* and the *Flame* do not seem to actually disagree on any points, though, which indicates that also the evidence in the *Canticle* is quite dependable with respect to the third stage. The characteristics of the kind of mystical state referred to as 'spicy wine' are not mentioned in the *Flame*, though, which means that the unanimity of the *Canticle* and the *Flame* more specifically pertains to the mystical states related in the ultimate verses in the *Canticle*. This furthermore supports the view that these descriptions do concern the final, mystical and not the post-mystical stage. Yet, even if the last verses in the *Canticle* do refer to the post-mystical stage, then John of the Cross' imaginations about this stage are based on his experience of mystical states in the final mystical stage which means that the verses and the related interpretations give equal evidence of that stage anyway. More specifically four features seem to be characteristic of the diverse mystical states in the third stage. Firstly, some mystical states intoxicate the subject as a strong wine would. Secondly, a flame of love is ignited in the soul and it is this that works in these mystical states. Thirdly, there is such conformity between God and the soul that a reciprocal love emerges during the mystical states. Fourthly, there is always more to be learned in mystical states.

Intoxication with a strong wine:

Commenting on two expressions in the poem, the *touch of the spark* ('toque de centella') and the *spicy wine* ('adobado vino'), John of the Cross interprets these as metaphors of two kinds of mystical states. He claims that they are rather similar and mainly differ in the duration of the actual mystical states and their effects. Actually, they are described as working by rather different means, though, as the one type inflames the heart with love-fire that burns up the soul, whereas the other type works in a manner rather similar to that of intoxication with a strong wine. In fact, nothing sustains his claim that they are similar or even associated in any way. Inasmuch as he furthermore stresses that those referred to as spicy wine are typical of the third stage, as is maintained in both of the concrete

---

40. John of the Cross has been perfectly aware that it might appear a little strange to his readers that he considered himself capable of describing events to come after death. He explains that the reason why this has been possible for him is that a mystic in the mystical states in the final stage gets a foretaste of the eternal union (Juan de la Cruz 1988, Cántico A38:4/B39:5-6).

interpretations of the verses, it is rather clear that he only associates these mystical states because the metaphors inspiring them are connected. Also, it is only the metaphor of the spicy wine that is elaborated into a detailed description of a certain kind of mystical state.

The mystical state referred to as 'spicy wine' intoxicates the subject just like a sweet, spicy, and strong wine would (Juan de la Cruz 1988, Cántico A15-16/B24-25). Such a mystical state rapidly causes the subject to love, desire, honour, and praise God. It is these feelings that, in turn, affect the soul positively by comforting and healing it. During this kind of mystical state, God furthermore grants the soul presents and virtues at the same time as communicating wisdom and secrets to it. All this beautifies and enriches the soul, so that its virtues are rendered absolutely perfect. Following John of the Cross' interpretation, the soul's love, desire, and honour of God are expressed as *emissions of divine balm* ('emisiones de bálsamo divino') in the poem[41] (Juan de la Cruz 1988, Cántico A16:7/B25: 8).

The intoxication with spicy wine in a mystical state of this kind may last up to several days, even if not constantly in the same degree. Such mystical states and their effects typically last over a span of time which John of the Cross defines with the word 'harto' which may be translated as *ample, sufficient,* or *satisfactory.*[42] Thus, mystical states like the spicy wine sometimes last for one or two days, sometimes for satisfactory or satiating ('hartos') days (which appears to be more than two). He stresses that a state persevering for such a relatively long period does not do so in the same degree and intensity. The intensity of such mystical states increases and decreases spontaneously and uncontrollably throughout the entire state (Juan de la Cruz 1988, Cántico A16:7/B25:8 but see also Subida 2. 5:2-3 and 32:2-3).

In a more general perspective, John of the Cross' commentary on verse 16 in the *Canticle* is an excellent example of how it seems to be a single word — or more precisely, his own *commentary* on that word — that triggers an association which then inspires a brilliant metaphor of the distinction of earlier and later stages of mystical development. Along with the presentation of the metaphor, he also nuances a distinction involved in it. Commenting further on the earlier mentioned expressions in the poem, the

41. The fact that in the poem certain girls (souls?) are looking out for the touch of the spark and the spicy wine apparently leading to the emissions of divine balm emanating from the beloved (alias God), does not seem to restrain John of the Cross' interpretation that the divine balm emanates from the soul.

42. Covarrubias' dictionary of the Spanish language states that 'harto' as an adverb refers to that which is sufficient and necessary whereas it as an adjective (as in Cántico A 16:7/B25:8) means satisfied (with food) (1943).

touch of the spark and the spicy wine, John of the Cross dwells on the latter, explaining that the wine has been boiled with spices, it is, in other words, boiled wine ('vino cocido'). Boiled wine is mature ('añejo') wine and contrasts with new wine. The differences between matured and new wine serve as a metaphor of the differences between the stages of mystical development, the later and earlier stages respectively — a metaphorical mapping he mediates by another metaphor which is that of old and new lovers. The expression as a whole is interpreted metaphorically to mean that the love given by God to the perfectly developed already has been matured in their souls at the same time as it has been spiced with their virtues (Juan de la Cruz 1988, Cántico A16:7-10/B25:8-11).

The soul is burnt with love-fire:

During the extremely delightful states of union typical of the third stage, a particular kind of flame (of love) is ignited in the soul. It has the unusual capacity to both consume the soul and transform it into God (Juan de la Cruz 1988, Cántico A38/B39). In the *Flame*, John of the Cross describes a fire that burns so strongly in the soul that it actually sends its flames out (bathing the soul in glory). The love-fire burns so thoroughly in the soul that it itself causes flames to arise[43] (Juan de la Cruz 1988, Llama 1:3). This poetical description, though, is not directly correlated with a particular state. Hence, it might instead refer to a more lasting condition of the subject achieved through mystical development.

A reciprocal love is engendered:

The love generated in the most advanced mystical states has the further effect of generating such conformity between the soul and God that a reciprocal love is formed. This mutual love founds the basis of a shared possession of equal, divine substance or essence (qualities, one might say). As there is no mention of an exchange of these qualities, it is more as if the state itself creates so complete conformity that it produces similarity of the parties involved. The soul only possesses the divine essence temporarily, though, just as the shared fruition of this consummate love only lasts as long as God exerts this transforming act in the soul (Juan de la Cruz 1988, Llama A3:69/B3:79). This means that the qualities and the delight only

---

43. According to Mancho Duque who has analyzed John of the Cross' general uses of various metaphors including that of flame and fire, the fire always goes in the direction from God to a person as opposed to the flame that always goes from a person to God (1982, 189-90 and 218-20).

persist during the mystical state and do not characterize the stage in general. Indeed, it is the transience of these feelings that constitutes the principal difference between the mystical states in the third stage and the post-mystical stage. A core notion in John of the Cross' teachings is that a stage, basically not unlike the states in the ultimate mystical stage, follows natural death. He believes that there are two differences between the mystical states in the third stage and the post-mystical stage, namely that the latter is even more sublime and that it is permanent.

Infinite learning:

Towards the very end of the *Canticle*, John of the Cross further considers an aspect of mystical states which is particularly illuminating with respect to the possible completion of mystical development at the same time, as it imparts something about the mystical states themselves. The point he makes is, that there is always more to be learned in mystical states which actually is the same as saying that there is no end to development. John of the Cross explains to his readers that new mysteries keep turning up because the divine source of wisdom is inexhaustible. There is always more to comprehend (Juan de la Cruz 1988, Cántico A36:2-3/B37:3-4). There are two kinds of learning that will continue to the very end of the mystical process. The first is that there is always more to understand about God because He is an infinite source of knowledge. The second is that the soul is capable of continuous advancement in the ability of loving God.

The skill in loving God is particularly interesting in a developmental context. In the most advanced mystical states, God teaches the soul how to love Him as much as He loves it. Such perfection in loving God mystically will not be obtained until then. The way that God will instruct the soul in loving Him is by showing it how to do it (by loving it thus, it seems) (Juan de la Cruz 1988, Cántico A37:2-3/B38:2-4). One of the minor differences between the two versions of the *Canticle* is that John of the Cross originally has some reservation about the extent to which the soul will learn how to love God: it will indeed become capable of loving God as much as He loves it, whereas it is impossible for the soul to love Him as much as He loves Himself. In the revised commentary, where this instruction in love is relegated to the eternal union, the reservation is omitted (Juan de la Cruz 1988, Cántico A38:3).

Apparently, there is no longer any need for the more fundamental developmental changes in the final stage of the mystical process. At this point, it is solely the specific, mystical capabilities for divine love and knowledge that can be improved. Through the attainment of a developmental state, seemingly enabling a state of stillness (or what comes closest to that) over certain cognitive activities, the mind of the subject is completely adapted to mystical aims. Inasmuch as this ability seems to be a main factor in the more basic mystical development, these properties are supposedly so well developed that they do not (or almost do not) need to be further perfected once the final mystical stage is reached. But the very specific mystical aptitude in loving God can still be enriched it seems. It appears that John of the Cross has believed the refinement of the proficiency in mystical love to be virtually interminable.

Although it is also in this case ambiguous, if John of the Cross has expressed these views concerning mystical states in the third stage or as imaginations of what would be characteristic of the eternal union with God, the issues concerned doubtlessly characterize mystical states in the third stage. Even if John of the Cross has imagined this to be characteristic of the post-mystical stage, it would obviously be equally characteristic of the stage preceding it since his imaginations are based on actual experience.

Summary of the third stage

The issue of the difference between mystical states in the final stage and earlier mystical states entails several aspects. First, there is the intoxication with a strong wine. The effects of this kind of mystical state actually resembles that of the one depicted as the spouse's drinking from her beloved in the wine cellar. Indeed, it seems likely that these mystical states are very similar in the way that they work, even if the spicy wine metaphor refers to a more advanced and therefore also more persevering mystical state than the wine cellar event does. Second, there is the fire burning and transforming the soul. Correlating this with the more general aspects of the mystical process, it appears that similar cognitive processes are generated in several (types of) mystical states, that is to say, that it is the same kind of love-fire that works in the soul. On the other hand, it seems that these processes or this love-fire affect(s) the mind or the soul differently at the various points in the developmental process, just as it doubtlessly varies in intensity. Third, there is the issue of the generation of reciprocal love causing semblance of God and the soul. In varying degrees, this is presumably part of most mystical states from the beginning of the second stage and on. But it is not until these very perfect mystical states that the love is so strong that the soul takes part in God's *divine essence*. Fourth, there is the issue of undisturbed peace in mystical states. Earlier, the mystic was susceptible to all kinds of distractions, attacking him/her from external and internal sources. Apparently, the elimination of this potential commotion is tantamount to purity of the soul. The purification is carried out gradually throughout a major part of the developmental process, but comes to an end at some point around the termination of the second stage or the beginning of the third. Once the purification is completed and all of the potential disturbances have been stilled, a person is in a much better position to profit fully from mystical states. Finally, there is the point about the continuous instruction in the ability to love and in divine knowledge. The significance of this is that improvement in mystical abilities is infinite. More specifically, the reception of this divine knowledge seems to be common from the end of the second stage and on.

The actualization of love seems to be one of the most typical characterstics of mystical states at least from the second stage and onwards. Therefore, it seems that the mystic from that point and onwards gradually learns how to love God and become better at loving Him during mystical states. With respect to the acquisition of new knowledge it does not seem to be the case that all mystical states provide the subject with new knowledge. The acquisition of divine knowledge seems to be typical of mystical states in the later part of mystical development, but not of those in the earlier part.

Mystical states as catalysts of mystical development

I have argued that mystical states and mystical development are closely connected and mutually affect one another. Having attended to the issue of how mystical states vary and change as the stages of development take over from one another, it is now time to reconsider the findings. In the first place I shall present an overview of how the effects of mystical states change as the process progresses and thereupon attempt to explain how mystical states are capable of influencing or even causing mystical development.

In order to give an overview of the changing ways that mystical states work, it is necessary to consider each of the respective parts of the process. In the period prior to John of the Cross' classified stages of the process, mystical states may or may not occur.[44] If not, then wakeful states of mystical content will nonetheless contribute to forward mystical development. However, it is certain that a person has to invest considerable efforts in the promotion of mystical development. Thus, it seems that the developmental process to a

44. Evidently, this would have to be judged on the basis of John of the Cross' descriptions correlated with the definition of mystical consciousness. But inasmuch as there are no *dependable* descriptions of actual states of consciousness from this period, it is impossible to make sure if John of the Cross has had mystical states already at that point or the initiation of the first stage can be identified as the developmental point of mastery of mystical states (permitting mystical consciousness to be realized). In my view, the latter seems more plausible.

great extent is fostered by meditation aided by deprivation of various kinds of sensory stimulation which jointly seems to prepare the way for mystical states of consciousness. The first step on the mystical way is to enable and facilitate the induction of mystical states. In accord with John of the Cross' teachings, the proper behaviour working towards this goal consists in the renunciation of the pleasures of the senses. Once this practice is mastered fully, a mystic is ready to get started with the actual mystical process (as it is classified by John of the Cross).

Already from the beginning of the first, classified stage and onwards, it is exclusively the mystical states that advance development. In the beginning of the stage, it seems that mystical states have not yet become really effective, though, but mainly work through the enhancement of the desire for God thereby encouraging the mystic to go on with the project in spite of the suffering involved in the process. This indicates that motivation in itself disposes a person for mystical states. At this point, one of the main components of mystical states seems to be a very insufficient and unfulfilled love. It is the incompletion of the love in these early mystical states that causes emptiness and frustration. Consequently, this emptiness and frustration can only be filled and satisfied with more love, that is to say, with more and, in particular, better mystical states.

In the second stage, mystical states work in various ways. First of all, it appears that the already activated mystical love is implemented in a new way. Mystical love begins to transform the soul, emptying it in a new way in addition to the already ongoing way of emptying it. Furthermore, some mystical states typical of the more advanced part of the stage cause a suspension of both sensuousness and that which is identified as imagination which, together, radically foster the required emptiness of the soul. The emptiness resulting from the mystical states of the first stage is not yet of the kind produced during the more advanced mystical states. Apparently, this early kind of emptiness is not brought out during the actual mystical states, but rather results from the unfulfilment and the termination of them. As opposed to this, the emptiness described in the context of the more advanced mystical states of the second stage is generated during the realization of mystical consciousness and disappears immediately or soon after the state comes to an end. Furthermore, it seems that the first kind of emptiness is a feeling of loss, namely the general loss of worldly pleasures and the immediate loss of God's love and presence. The more advanced kind of emptiness seems, on the other hand, to be identical with the gradual reduction in the generation of the more specific and conceptual cognitive representations.

In the third stage of the mystical process, mystical states are incomparably more powerful and efficient than ever before. In this stage, mystical states work by means of love only and at this point the transformation in love goes into yet another stage and is implemented in a new way. It seems that the realization of love in itself improves the love by easing the unfolding of it. At this point, it is mainly the expansion of the proportion of the emotional aspect of mystical love that is developed.

Summing up the gradual alteration of developmental catalysts, it appears that prior to the initiation of the process described as a dark night, a mystic contributes to the incipient purification by behaving in certain ways and by reducing the amount of sensory inputs. The general purpose of the purification is to allow and facilitate the induction and the unfolding of mystical states by gradually enabling the unawareness of first the external world and later of the more specific and conceptual internal representations. These efforts are, in turn, encouraged by states of consciousness that may either be deemed weak mystical or wakeful states of mystical content. In the first stage of the night it is the mystical states that promote the process of purification but at a very slow pace. In the second stage mystical development is driven forward by mystical states that intensely work on the purification and transformation of the soul. In the very last stage mystical states work on the further refinement the soul even more and, in particular, on the improvement of the proficiency in mystical love. Going through innumerable mystical states the mystic gradually builds up an ability to elude certain disturbing cognitive representations, initially those that are related to sensory perception and later, those that are related to imagination. It seems that this ability is a precondition for the full display of mystical love.

In order to provide a better overview of the gradual changes in the purifying and transformational processes and their respective products, it seems relevant to present these changes more schematically. The advantage of a schematical presentation is that it will render John of the Cross' conceptualization of his mystical development more transparent. The intention is to bring out the relation of the processes and products of purification and transformation. The diagram (see p. 210) is a condensation of my interpretation of his more generally used metaphors of the mystical process.

The Processes and Products of Mystical Purification and Transformation According to John of the Cross

Preparation for the process	Sensuous purification	Sensuous and spiritual purification	Mystical union	Eternal union
Day (supplying natural light*).	Early night (supplying little natural light).	Midnight (no light).	Dawn (supplying little supernatural light).**	Day (supplying natural but divine light).**
Meditation on the life of Christ.	A purifying and transforming love-fire empties the soul of its appetites for the things of the world and increases its desire for God.	A purifying and transforming love-fire empties the soul of worldly knowledge and at some point begins to fill it up with divine knowledge.	A transforming love-fire fills up the soul with divine knowledge.	A transforming love-fire will fill up the soul with divine knowledge.

*   Light is a metaphor of knowledge.
**   In John of the Cross' understanding, the mystical unions of God and the soul are supernatural, whereas the eternal union with God is natural inasmuch as the soul at that point is permanently freed of its createdness. It is thus one divine nature that is united with another divine nature.

Altogether, mystical states are the principal catalysts of mystical development. Without them a mystic is bound not to get very far. The question is how this can be explained. How do mystical states produce mystical development? For an explanation of this, the presented evidence of the factors giving an impetus to mystical development can be supported with psychological and neurological theories of ordinary development and of consciousness respectively. It is rather generally accepted among cognitive theories of psychology that development is triggered by experience. Development may be predisposed (or maybe even predetermined to some extent), but it is experience that provokes and precipitates it. In agreement with this neurological theories of epigenesis suggest that the neural phenotype of an individual at any point in time reflects the experience of that individual. The theory is that the structure of the neural system changes constantly as a result of neuronal activities. The neuronal activities are, in turn, contingent on the very concrete experience of the subject. In the light of this, it begins to make sense that mystical states condition the cognitive system in certain mystical ways, with mystical cognitive functions as the result.

With Greenfield's theory of consciousness it should furthermore be possible to identify the specific neuronal activities in mystical states more precisely. In agreement with Greenfield's theory, consciousness emerges from the activities of neuronal groups of a certain size. The deeper and more extended a particular consciousness is, the more neurons are activated in the generation of the consciousness. The potential size and durability of a neuronal group recruitable by a particular epicentre is, first of all, contingent on the strength of the epicenter (which is dependent on the subject's earlier experience related to that particular epicentre). The greater the number of active neurons, the greater also the number of synaptic connections of neurons strengthened by the activities. Yet, the degree of the effects of particular neuronal activities is in itself delimited by the strengths of the synaptic connections in the neuronal group concerned (as this sets the upper limits of the amount of electricity within the group of neurons). Thus, the stronger the synaptic connections within the neuronal group, the more the synaptic connections are strengthened (and the strengths of the synaptic connections are, like the strength of the epicentre, dependent on the subject's earlier experience related to the content of the generated consciousness). In short, the prior experience of the subject delimits the total amount of electrical activity involved in the generation of a particular consciousness and this, in turn, determines the effect it has on the existing neural structure.

Applied to mystical states, this means that the quantity and the duration of the connected consciousnesses of a mystical state determine the degree of the developmental effect of the state. The content of consciousness, on the other hand, determines the very specific changes in the synaptic connections resulting from the neuronal activities. Consequently, the *quantity* and the *duration* of consciousness determine the degree to which development influences mystical states, and the *quality* of consciousness determines the more specific *way* in which it influences them. In general, one might say that mystical states condition the cognitive system appropriately for mystical experience.

An overview of the process resulting in mystical development

In John of the Cross' works, mystical development is described as involving two distinct kinds of change, namely the purification and the transformation of the soul. These changes are effectuated, though, by processes that basically are the same throughout the developmental process, even if the processes vary in intensity and more specific character, just as the cognitive abilities affected by the processes apparently shift considerably in the course of development. It is thus the same processes that have dissimilar effects on a person. The essence of all the processes somehow contributing to mystical development is mystical love. Mystical love, in some form or other, is the fundamental cause of the kind of mystical development revealed in the works of John of the Cross. As I have already pointed out in more than one context, the effective processes of mystical love consist in consciousness of cognitive representations of conceptions and the responding emotions of mystical love. Hence, even the earliest wakeful states of consciousness of conceptions of mystical love will have some minor developmental effect as it initiates the acquisition of knowledge of mystical love that later may be the source of actual mystical states of consciousness focused on mystical love. The stronger the effects of the consciousness of mystical love, the greater the quantity of consciousness. This means that the effects of mystical states inevitably will amplify as the mystical process advances, because the gradual accumulation of mystical experience enables mystical consciousness to become deeper, more extended, and more lasting.

In spite of the fundamental similarity of the processes of purification and transformation, there are some quite significant differences, though. Focusing on the more specific products of the combined processes of purification and transformation, namely the purity and the transformation of the soul respectively, the dissimilarities protrude at the same time, as the similarities are evident. The purity of the soul consists in the ability to avoid various other specific cognitive representations. The essence of transformation is, on the other hand, the ability to generate mystical emotions of love to such a degree that they overpower all other kinds of cognitive representations. Yet, this presupposes a certain degree of purity towards which transformation itself contributes considerably as representations of emotions of mystical love gradually take over the dominance of consciousness from representations of conceptions of mystical love. Purification and transformation thereby contribute to one and the same end which is the expansion of consciousness of mystical emotions at the expense of various other specific conceptions. The processes of purification and transformation differ to the extent that they contribute more to the one aspect than to the other.

As mentioned, it furthermore seems that the cognitive abilities affected by the processes of purification and transformation change at various points. In the pre-mystical stage, the effective processes work through the internalization of attention enabling an increasing unreceptiveness to sensory inputs. In the first two stages of the actual mystical process (as it is classified by John of the Cross) the effective processes are directed at the generation of more specific cognitive representations that are cognitively derived.

Distinguishing the two stages more specifically, the developmental processes of the first stage are mainly directed at cognitive representations that are more directly related to the person's attachment to the external world. So far, one kind of specific, cognitive representation is simply replaced with another kind. Consequently, this part of the process does not yet produce the kind of emptiness that will permit the more emotional representations to take the place. In the second stage, other kinds of more specific cognitive representations (presumably those related specifically to conceptions of mystical love) are suppressed, which gradually gives room for the more purely emotional representations to take over the dominance of consciousness. In the final stage, the effective processes are solely directed at the augmentation of cognitive representations of emotions of mystical love. In general, the process seems to be a gradual intensification of the emotional aspect of mystical love, implying that it is this aspect that gradually overpowers all other aspects.

For the purpose of furnishing a general overview of the process of mystical development as it is documented by John of the Cross, it seems pertinent to present my explanation of these processes and the resulting products in a compressed and more schematical form (see diagram, p. 214).

An explanation of the processes and products of mystical development

The effective processes:

Pre-stage	First stage	Second stage	Third stage
Internalization of attention by means of meditation and sensory deprivation.	Suppression of various kinds of more specific cognitive representations and incipient generation of emotional representations of mystical love during mystical consciousness.	Suppression of cognitive representations of conceptions of mystical love and increasing focus on emotions of mystical love during mystical consciousness.	Increasing focus on emotions of mystical love during mystical consciousness.

The products:

Pre-stage	First stage	Second stage	Third stage
Internalized attention and reduced processing of sensory inputs.	Shift in the predominance of consciousness from one kind of specific cognitive representation to the predominance of another kind of such specific cognitive representation and now with awareness of emotions of mystical love during mystical consciousness.	Shift in the predominance of consciousness from representations of conceptions of mystical love towards emotional representations of mystical love during mystical consciousness.	Predominance of emotional representations of mystical love during mystical consciousness.

On the basis of these two diagrams, it should be clear that there are no fundamental differences between the processes purifying and transforming the soul
mystically. They may nevertheless be conceived of as highly dissimilar (as
John of the Cross seemingly has done) if the conceptual and the emotional
aspect of mystical states are segregated. Following such a reasoning, the two
processes yield each their developmental product. It is the purification of the
soul that produces mystical purity which, in turn, will permit the already
ongoing process of transformation to be brought out with full power. With
respect to the resulting mystical purity and transformation, the case is a little
different. The point is that mystical purity refers to a developmental state permitting the realization of mystical states differing considerably from all
anterior mystical states (as these are restrained in varying degree by various
degrees of mystical impurity). Mystical purity is therefore the cognitive condition enabling mystical transformation to be fulfilled. This further implies
that the main difference is that of purity and impurity and not of purity and
transformation.

The relative stability of the cognitive changes

At this point it seems pertinent to discuss the relative stability or instability
of the cognitive changes resulting from mystical states. John of the Cross does
not always distinguish sharply between transient changes occurring during a
single mystical state and more permanent developmental changes. He often
refers to changes without stating explicitly if they are abiding or transient,
leaving it to his readers to detect this from the context. John of the Cross often
speaks of the effects of mystical development as virtues and the further
development of them as growth of the virtues. As in many other matters he
typically prefers metaphorical expressions as descriptive means. The virtues
are like flowers and just as flowers take root in the soil, so do the virtues take
root in the soul. The virtues are in the process of ('se van') taking root
('cogiendo'), being acquired ('adquiriendo'), and taking seat ('asentando').
Once they have taken root, seat, and have been acquired, they are like a
festoon of flowers that beautify and decorate both the soul and God (Juan de
la Cruz 1988, Cántico A21:5/B30:6). This is mentioned in connection with the
espousal stage in the original commentary in the *Canticle* and in connection
with the matrimonial stage in the second commentary.

Elsewhere John of the Cross similarly makes use of the metaphor of virtues
like flowers, but here he focuses specifically on the fragrance of flowers.
Flowers, as he points out, are to some extent fragrant all the time once they
have blossomed. But as long as they are buds, the fragrance cannot be sensed.
He furthermore notices that when flowers are touched and moved they spread

their redolence much more abundantly so that the fragrance both increases and is felt increasingly. These qualities can be likened to the development of the virtues in the soul, he claims. God has granted virtues to the soul so that it constantly possesses them. But in worldly life the virtues are scentless like flowers in bud, except when touched, moved, and renewed by God. Only then are the virtues really felt and enjoyed by the soul (Juan de la Cruz 1988, Cántico A26:4/B17:5). This parable appears in the context of the espousal stage in both of the commentaries in the *Canticle*, but he presents it as a characteristic of worldly life in general.

John of the Cross further attempts to define, in more theological terms, the achievements of the mystical process at any given point. He states that once a soul has reached spiritual matrimony it remains in the stage. But the soul is not constantly in *actual* or current union with God. According to John of the Cross, the actualization of mystical union cannot possibly be continuous in this life (Juan de la Cruz 1988, Cántico B11:3). The statement further implies the possibility of a continuous union in another life, that is to say, ensuing natural death (Juan de la Cruz, Cántico A17:9 and B26:11). Even though the distinction is made concerning spiritual matrimony, the more general definition of mystical states as actual union presumably applies to all of the stages.

How does this correspond with the theories of consciousness and epigenetic development? Apparently, the virtues that John of the Cross speaks of are lasting changes of the cognitive system — resulting from meditation, sensory deprivation, and, in particular, from mystical states — that pave the way for more and better mystical states. These developmental changes are not very useful for anything but the facilitation of mystical consciousness. They may have some minor affect on wakeful consciousness, but their main significance concerns the subject's gradually improving proficiency in having mystical states, especially with consciousness focused on emotions of mystical love. More specifically, the core of mystical development is tantamount to the acquisition of knowledge of mystical love. It is the gradually expanding knowledge of mystical love that has the major impact on the ease of having mystical states of consciousness.

As I have pointed out in the earlier presentation of Greenfield's theory of consciousness, it is the strengthening of epicentres and the extension of relevant associations related to both the conceptual and the emotional aspect of mystical love that first of all enables mystical states to expand in depth, extension, and duration. Going into a little more detail with the explanation, the knowledge of mystical love is build up during the recurring consciousness of conceptions and emotions of mystical love. Whenever there is consciousness of some aspect of mystical love, the involved epicentres are strengthened, supposedly because the representations of that of which there is consciousness are stored in the strengths of the synaptic connections of the neuronal group constituting the epicentre.

Returning to the issue of the relative variability or immutability of the developmental changes, it seems most plausible that the changes typically (but not necessarily) accumulate very slowly. In extension of this, it seems likely that the developmental state at any point in time will be relatively stable, although the knowledge (stored in the strengths of the synapses) only lasts until new knowledge modifies the existing knowledge (by readjusting the synaptic strengths). The experiments of Merzenich, et al., further suggest that the synaptic strengths will reduce, or maybe even that the synapses will disappear, if the neurons are inactive (if there is no consciousness of mystical conceptions or emotions, for instance) for an extended period of time.

With respect to the relation of the more lasting developmental changes and the transient changes of state of consciousness (corresponding to John of the Cross' metaphor of the noticeability of the virtues as flowers' varying fragrance and spread of fragrance) it should be stressed that the temporary change of consciousness is at once the immediate cause of the more lasting developmental changes and the incipience of these changes. The point is that it is while there is mystical consciousness that the neuronal activities affect the synaptic connections of the active neurons (which supposedly is the neural foundation of the cognitive development of proficiency in having mystical states). Inasmuch as it must be the immediate changes in neural structure that remains afterwards then mystical consciousness itself constitutes nascent, mystical development.

VIII. An explanation of mystical states and mystical development

Purity and love — mystical states in development

Introducing the subject

In the following, I shall address one of the more enigmatic issues involved in the exploration of mystical experience, i.e., the question of the specific quality of mystical states. The quality of mystical states changes, however, in the course of mystical development, whereby this issue is closely associated with that of the products of mystical development. What are the changing contents of mystical states of consciousness like, and what are the developmental products giving rise to the changes? Some contents of mystical states change more radically than others, which further means that the developmental products permitting the changes are more distinct and therefore also more easily identifiable. In John of the Cross' works, evidence of the character of mystical states is just as often found in the poems as in the commentaries on these. Much of the evidence comes in poetic metaphors and some of it is indeed quite obscure and ambiguous.

In accord with John of the Cross' works, it seems that one of the most significant contents of mystical states is that which is referred to as 'love'. Mystical love is one of the components that continues throughout the process of mystical development, even if it is very immature — sort of embryonic — in the beginning of the process. From a developmental perspective, though, some of the components in mystical states undergoing more drastic changes are equally significant, although they barely constitute mystical ends in themselves. In this respect, it is the cognitive representations which are considered to be *damaging* that are particularly important. However, significant changes in the feeling of pain also contribute to the changing quality of mystical consciousness. Finally, recurrent mystical consciousness has a further general side-effect, which is a gradually increasing estrangement from the world.

Proficiency in mystical love

What the metaphor of love communicates about mystical states

It is barely possible to examine the distinctive qualities of mystical states in depth. And it is certainly not possible to penetrate the very specific properties of mystical states to such a degree that they can be comprehended completely. Still, it is, in my opinion, feasible to acquire considerable insight into the distinctive properties of mystical states. I have no expectations of resolving the matter in general, though. My intent is to propose an hypothesis of the distinctiveness of specific qualities of mystical states to the extent that John of the Cross gives evidence of the matter in his writings.

In John of the Cross' works, evidence of the specific kind of emotionality typical of mystical states is presented in a highly metaphorical form. Aiming to inquire into the nature of the mystical emotions and feelings, one should look to the metaphor of love. A question that may strike the reader of the *Canticle* and the *Flame* is why John of the Cross repeatedly speaks of love. And heart. What has the particular motivation for selecting love, heart, and the like as metaphors of some of the feelings generated in mystical states been? Moreover, the use of metaphors of love as expressions of aspects of mystical states is not specific for John of the Cross, but can be found among Christian mystics in general. Obviously, the conventionality of the metaphor of love has been one good reason why John of the Cross has used it. This aspect of the metaphor is not at stake at this point, though. Here, the question is whether the poetical expressions of love communicate anything about the internal processes in mystical states. Are mystical states described in metaphors of love because elements in them resemble aspects of other kinds of human love? And, if so, which aspects of ordinary love have seemed to parallel mystical love? This is a matter of which the metaphors of love can be illuminating.

John of the Cross' general metaphor of the relationship between a particular soul (his soul) and God is that of love. The metaphor of the general unfolding of the relationship takes its point of departure in the theological doctrine that God initially loves the soul. The next step is for Him, God, to infuse love in the soul in order to make it love and desire Him. This He does by touching it gradually more and more intensely and forcefully eventually uniting Himself with it (in it). Very slowly, at the speed of the particular soul, God teaches it how to love Him in the same way as He loves it. At some point, the soul is so well versed in the habit of loving (in this special way) that it is capable of loving God reciprocally in the same degree as He loves it, at least as long as He shows it how to do this.

The metaphors of the actualization of the love-relationship, the exertion or the act of love, so to speak, is at once much more romantic and far more sexual than those referring to the more general process. Accordingly, the metaphors of the actual events of love are deeply passionate as opposed to the fairly unemotional character of the metaphors of the development of the relationship. It is during the mystical states that mystical love is realized. For that reason, it is the metaphor of the love in mystical states that is of concern in the present context. Originally, the mystical states are narrated poetically (coupled with coincident narration of the developmental process) which means that the metaphors initially have been presented in the poems. Many of the poetic metaphors are then later transferred to the interpretations in prose and sometimes elaborated further. I mention this only to give an idea of how the metaphors meet the reader in John of the Cross' works. I do not intend to identify some specific point in time at which John of the Cross has taken the (already existing) metaphors into use as opposed to another point in time at which he has begun or continued the elaboration of the metaphors. Such an attempt would be pointless and futile.

The metaphor of love as evidence

Before turning to the discussion of the character of those internal processes that give rise to mystical love, it seems pertinent to consider the character of the evidence of these processes with due respect to the relative ambiguity of it. Various uncertainties should be taken into consideration. One such is the issue of how John of the Cross' metaphors of love relate to their source domain which is human love. The point is that he hardly has drawn upon personal experience when using the more sexual aspects of love as a source of the metaphors. Literary testimonies of sexuality have been copious, though, so inexperience has supposedly been no hindrance. No doubt, one of John of the Cross' primary sources of information of the matter has been the *Song of Solomon*. In fact, the lack of experience may have been an advantage for poetical inventiveness as it may have permitted greater freedom in the metaphorical mappings of the source. The supposition that John of the Cross has been sexually inexperienced may seem trivial but needs to be emphasized, because it means that there is reason to assume that even though some of his poetical metaphors apparently correlate physical love it is conceivable that they simply relate to other *descriptions* of physical love. John of the Cross' access to the reality of this part of the metaphorical source domain has probably been mediated by literature. Evidently, he has supposedly had personal experience of other aspects of the source domain, that is, of other aspects of human love.

The significance of this is that there is no justification for a presumption that the erotical metaphors indicate that John of the Cross' mystical states truly have included aspects directly resembling sexual passion. Obviously, this does not rule out the possibility that mystical states do involve elements resembling elements in sexual states. If there is such similarity of aspects of sexual and mystical states, the likeness may either derive from similarity of the internal processes involved in the two kinds of conscious states, be mediated by existing metaphors (in which case it relates to the resemblance of John of the Cross' *readings* of the (metaphorical) descriptions and his own mystical emotions), or it may simply be accidental.

Further incertitude stems from the prevalent ambiguity of whether some specific part of a poem communicates something about an actual mystical state or a preceding/succeeding state. Yet, it seems plausible that poetical narration of the presence of both of the lovers concerned in a verse or a group of verses is an indication that the description refers to the actualization of a mystical state (still keeping the reservation in mind that elements from a number of states may be blended). The reason why the description of the lovers' mutual participation in an event indicates that it concerns the realization of a mystical state is that John of the Cross generally asserts that mystical love exclusively is consummated temporarily, that is to say, during mystical states.

With respect to the ambiguity of the relation of the source and the target domain of the metaphor of love in general, I do not think that the incentive for choosing the traditional metaphor of love has been some real similarity between the part of the source domain that relates to physical love and the target domain of the metaphor. In spite of this initial scepticism, I take it to be very plausible that there is a real resemblance between the actual point of departure for John of the Cross' elaboration of this aspect of the metaphors (which is the literary and conventional accounts of the source domain) and the target domain. It seems likely that the various renderings of sexuality have seemed to John of the Cross to portray feelings very similar to some of those typical of his own mystical states. Hence, he has formed an impression of what physical love is like (probably justified by and supplied with personal experience of other elements of human love) and deemed it a highly valuable metaphorical source of certain mystical emotions and feelings. His understanding has, in turn, clearly been supported by the conventional, metaphorical expressions of mysticism. More specifically, I will suggest that the motivations for taking the conventional love-metaphor into use is triple:

1) Conventionality has made this metaphor useful through securing communicative power. Additionally, the conventional use of the metaphor has supported its value as expressions of mystical experience. Tradition has supplied the metaphor with authority. This motive is not exclusive for the metaphor of love but holds for all of the metaphors used by John of the Cross as they all are traditional.

2) The more or less erotical aspects of human love (of sexual intercourse and post-coital feelings as John of the Cross has known about them from

literature and other sources) may indeed have seemed comparable to various elements in mystical states.

3) The value of the more sexual metaphor of love has supposedly, in his view, been supported by the more romantic metaphor of love (painful longing for the beloved and the like) which may have seemed to parallel feelings resulting from the lack of mystical states, that is to say, feelings of mystical love displayed during wakeful states and stemming from a longing for union with God.[1]

As evidence of the specific cognitive processes that can be defined as mystical in one way or another, several aspects of the metaphor of love should be taken into account. First of all, there is the question about where the internal processes giving rise to the various aspects of mystical love are located. The point is that John of the Cross seemingly has identified one or more physical location(s) or organ(s) as the focus of sensations of mystical love. Thereupon it is relevant to consider the quality of mystical love. More concretely, the concern is what the emotions of love are like. In this respect, I have argued that there is no guarantee of even the slightest similarity of this particular part of the source (physical love) and the target of the metaphors. But I have also pointed out that resemblance is not unthinkable. With respect to other parts of the source (other aspects of human love) one may, on the other hand, assume that the metaphorical mapping is based on personal experience.

Locating the feelings of mystical love

John of the Cross' poetic metaphors of love are very varied and apparently refer to distinct aspects of mystical experience. One question is how heart relates to soul in the more metaphorical uses of the words. This is a significant issue because heart and soul often are used synonymously. Thus, in his prose works John of the Cross sometimes shifts unreservedly between the two words without further explanation (see, e.g., Juan de la Cruz 1988, Cántico A8:3-4 and 9:5/B8:4-5 and 9:6). I do not hereby intend to argue that John of the Cross uses the words inconsistently (although that may indeed be the case). What

---

1. Whether such feelings are mystical or ordinary is a definitional matter. Feelings of mystical content (love of God) should be defined as mystical, even if they are not brought out in mystical states. This does not necessarily entail that mystical feelings or emotions are the same when brought out in mystical and wakeful states, though. The quantity of consciousness will doubtlessly affect the way that feelings are experienced by the subject. Furthermore, mystical feelings will supposedly be mystical in the sense that they influence the process of mystical development no matter whether they are realized during wakeful or mystical states.

I want to say is that there might be a reason for his use of both words and possibly also for his way of using them.

The shifting applications of the words *heart* and *soul* and the (frequent) interchangeability of them may contribute more specifically to an understanding of concrete mystical states. In this respect, the poetic expressions are most significant. In the poetic *Canticle*, the main female character is hit by arrows (verse 8) whereby she is wounded in the heart (verse 9). In this place John of the Cross supposedly narrates a mystical event. The heart is in focus which could be an indication that the emotions or feelings produced in the state are centred around the heart. In the *Living Flame of Love*, on the other hand, she is hurt in the most profound centre of the soul (verse 1). This idiom equally seems to refer to a particular mystical state. As opposed to the former expression, the latter indicates a mental focus of events. In each case, the choice of the one word at the expense of the other could also simply be poetically motivated. Or it could be accidental (although expressive fortuitousness is not typical of the works of John of the Cross). Eventually, the female is guided by a light in her heart in the poem entitled Dark Night (verse 3). This expression is a little tricky, though, as it simultaneously can be interpreted to relate to the induction of an incident of a mystical state and to refer to the more general guidance through the mystical process. The latter corresponds with John of the Cross' own interpretation of the poem in its entirety. All in all, there is a whole number of possible motivations for the alternating uses of the words *heart* and *soul*. I shall begin with a brief presentation of the possibilities and then discuss them one by one.

1) The first possibility is that the shift from the use of the one word to the other is motivated by experience and theology respectively. He might have considered the word *soul* to correspond better with his theological views (primarily expressed in the commentaries) than *heart*, whereas he may have seen *heart* as corresponding better with his actual experience of mystical development and/or of mystical states. In other words, it could be that only the word *heart* relates to mystical experience, whereas the word *soul* only has theological relevance. This explanation is contradicted by both evidence (indicating that mystical states affect the mind) and the theories of consciousness and emotions. As evidence of this, John of the Cross' common references to specified mental faculties like memory and understanding in descriptions of mystical states could be mentioned.[2]

---

2. More specifically, there is also his description of a mystical state in which God touches the memory whereby it suddenly gives a jump in the brain where it (memory) is seated (Juan de la Cruz 1988, Subida 3.2:5).

2) A second possiblity is that he simply has had literary motives for the various uses of the two words. Thus, it is not impossible that John of the Cross has viewed the word *heart* as the more poetical word while he has deemed the word *soul* more scientific. This would explain the tendency towards a more frequent use of *heart* in the poetic works as opposed to the more common use of *soul* in the prose works. Yet, it would not explain the relative indistinction of his use of the words. One would still have expected that the words had been applied stringently in two dissimilar ways.

3) A third motivation could have been that *heart* and *soul* are equally relevant with reference to all aspects of mystical experience because all mystical processes are centred equally in the heart region and the mind in some indistinguishable way. In this case, *heart* and *soul* really can be used interchangeably. The occasional indiscrimination of the words certainly supports this explanation. Yet, the many discriminate descriptions of aspects of mystical states indicate that diverse aspects can indeed be separated from one another. I would take this to be an indication that the locations of the distinct internal events would similarly be identifiable.

4) A fourth possibility is that John of the Cross typically speaks of *soul* when referring to the stages of the process and to his relationship with God in general, whereas he speaks of *heart* when referring to particular events of intimacy. Such consistency cannot be documented, though. It would be a logical explanation but one for which there is little evidence.

5) A fifth possibility is that *heart* is relevant in connection with specific aspects of mystical states (emotionality, for instance) while *soul* is relevant with reference to other aspects (conceptions of mystical love, for instance). This would mean that some aspects of mystical states are centred in or around the heart, whereas others are centred in the mind.

6) And finally, a sixth possibility is that *heart* is most relevant in relation to some mystical states while *soul* is most relevant in relation to others. This latter possibility would imply that when John of the Cross prefers *heart*, it is because the focus of mystical processes in a particular state has been the heart region and the other way round when *soul* is preferred.

The latter two possibilities involve one problem, though. The trouble is that if the respective uses of the words correspond with variations in the focus of mystical processes (5) or in distinct states (6), then this would presumably be

developmentally conditioned. If that was the case, I would expect an application of the word *soul* in connection with earlier mystical states substituted
with the use of *heart* in relation to later and more developmentally advanced
mystical states.[3] But this is not the case. As an example, the word *soul* appears
in the poem entitled *Living Flame of Love* which narrates (mystical states in) the
last stage of development.

   To sum up, the changing uses of the words *heart* and *soul* could have been
motivated either aesthetically (2), or experientially and theologically (1). Or it
it could have been motivated by the experience that mystical love seems to be
generated coincidentally and indistinctly in both heart and soul (3). Yet, it is
also possible that the alternation of the words, on the contrary, reflects actual
differences in mystical experience in one way or another (4-6). Furthermore,
it should be stressed that the possibilities not are mutually exclusive.

   I shall now turn to a discussion of the above presented possibilities and
correlate this with the earlier presented theories of consciousness and emotions, respectively. First of all, I wish to point out that for John of the Cross
the strongest weighing motive has presumably been how well the words in
question corresponded with his mystical experience, inasmuch as he has
deemed it of utmost importance to be as true as possible to that which he
believed to be direct experience of divine truths. Motives that he has recognized as going against his experience would therefore have had to be very
strong. Nonetheless, various theological, aesthetical, (etc.) conceptions and
expectations, have of course influenced the way that he has construed his
experience. On the basis of John of the Cross' writings alone, it would indeed
be very difficult to settle upon a final conclusion of the matter.

   With respect to mystical experience as the motive for the shifting uses of
the words heart and soul, it is clear on the basis of Damasio's theory that
mystical emotions of love must be located somewhere in the body. It could
therefore be expected that when John of the Cross speaks of heart in the
context of actual union with God it is because mystical states (or at least the
mystical state in the context concerned) has involved internal processes located
in the heart or other bodily organs close to the heart. Greenfield's theory of
consciousness may, on the other hand, contribute to solve the issue of how the
word soul may have had experiential relevance to John of the Cross. In the
light of her theory, it is obvious that conscious experience of something is a

---

3. This expectation is based on the changes in mystical states resulting from deve-
    lopment, namely the increase in the feelings referred to as *love* (which presumably
    would be related to the word *heart*) coupled with the gradual reduction of
    representational specificity (which presumably would render the word *soul* less
    relevant as this is where the faculties of memory and understanding are believed to
    be located).

cognitive event.[4] It should therefore also be clear that the word soul is suitable to designate the experience of mystical love. The possibility that only heart had experiential relevance while soul only had theological relevance (1) can therefore be ruled out. Similarly, the possibility that the word heart refers to mystical states and the word soul to the developmental process (4) cannot be supported (neither with evidence, nor with theory).

Having stated that the words soul and heart really can be expected to be equally relevant as reference to mystical experience, the next point is to consider what has motivated his selections of the one word rather than the other in the diverse particular contexts. As I have already pointed out, there seems to be no stringency in his way of using the two words. Thus, there is no specific evidence that the words heart and soul refer to dissimilar aspects of mystical experience (5) or that they refer to different types of mystical states (6). Considering John of the Cross' works in general, both of these two suggestions can be supported, though, just as it would correspond with my application of the theories of consciousness and emotions respectively. Thus, it seems likely that the word heart refers mainly to the more purely emotional aspect of mystical love which supports the possibility that the two words refer to different aspects of mystical experience (5). It furthermore seems plausible that these aspects are displayed in different degrees in the diverse mystical states of the parts of the developmental process thereby supporting the possibility that the two words are not equally relevant with respect to all mystical states (6). This still leaves the problem, though, of why he has not used the word in any systematic way. It is not impossible that the more emotional and the more conceptual aspect of mystical states experientially have mixed into one (supporting possibility 3), so that there has been no point in distinguishing the two sharply. This would explain why he has not seen any need for a systematic application of the respective words. This leaves me with the suggestion that he mainly has had aesthetical motives for the selective uses of the words heart and soul.

In conclusion, I suggest that the most realistic explanation of the matter is that the use of both words has, in fact, been motivated by actual differences in aspects of mystical states (which may truly have undergone some changes in the process, even though this is not expressed through the shifting uses of the words *heart* and *soul*). At the same time, it seems that John of the Cross primarily has had literary motives for the concrete uses of the words. I suggest that John of the Cross' indiscriminate uses of *heart* and *soul* (common in both prose and poetic works) justify that mystical states typically involve cognitive

---

4. This may indeed seem trivial but needs to be stressed as John of the Cross' works in isolation could be interpreted as evidence that some mystical states mainly are bodily events.

representations of events in both heart and brain. In general John of the Cross provides evidence that the internal events generated in mystical states are very varied and encompass several distinct components. Neurological theories support this point as conscious experience emerges from a web of closely interrelated internal processes operating in both body and mind.

A possible similarity of mystical and sexual states

Inquiring into the properties of mystical love, the poetical accounts of the matter are important. In some cases John of the Cross actually depicts a deeply erotical intimacy in his poems. In the poem entitled Dark Night the breast of the female is blooming as she caresses her sleeping lover (verse 6). In the *Canticle* we hear about the lovers' mutual bed which is elaborately ornamented (verse A15/B24). Elsewhere the same poem tells of how she, the female main character, rests on the soft arms of her beloved (verse A27/B22). These fragments of John of the Cross' poems seem to express or more indirectly refer to feelings that strikingly parallel post-coital feelings. Evidently the events have appeared extremely intimate to the experiencer. More specifically these metaphorical expressions seem, on the one hand, to relate feelings of tranquillity, calm, and imperturbability, and on the other hand, to refer to the wondrousness of the events concerned. Other poetical expressions have more explicit metaphorical reference to sexual intercourse. The poetic narration of the event in the interior wine cellar in the *Canticle* is a salient example of this. In the verses relating the event, the female tells how her lover gave her his breast in a place where she drank from him (verse A17-18/B26-27). Especially, the metaphor that she drank from her beloved could be interpreted as having elements of the physical act of love as its source. The crucial (and tangled) question is which information the poetical expressions presented above communicate (presupposing that they communicate anything relevant at all).

The possibility that qualities of the specific constituents of mystical states (the realization of the love between God and the soul) resemble sexual sensations (like orgasm and subsequent feelings) is not easily checkable. Ultimately, the probability of it falls back on the ability to communicate certain kinds of experience to others that are inexperienced (in this context, of sexual experience to John of the Cross).[5]

The poetic descriptions of intimate closeness between the lovers coupled

---

5. Is it likely that literature and other sources has provided John of the Cross with such a good idea of the properties of sexual experience that it is an impression of sexual sensations that John of the Cross has utilized as a metaphorical source? Or, is it, on the contrary, more likely that the literature concerned has inspired other imaginations (corresponding with his experience) that has nothing at all in common with sexuality?

with perfect calm strongly indicate that the portrayed feelings of mystical love really do resemble feelings typically succeeding orgasm. In my opinion, the poetry renders very good evidence that the specific aspects of mystical states related in the poetic expressions concerned resemble feelings of post-coital calm somehow. As opposed to this, nothing indicates that there similarly is an element in mystical states that essentially resembles orgasm. Consequently, it appears that if there is something to the coincidence of aspects of mystical states and sexual sensations, then it is mainly the feeling of satiety and calm.

Evidently, it is still highly uncertain whether the two kinds of states really have anything in common. In isolation, the evidence furnished by the works of John of the Cross remains uncertain. Hence, there is reason to correlate this body of evidence with the theory of consciousness and evidence of sexual states. According to Changeux, neurological research has provided evidence that (electric) stimulation of specific points in the limbic system of the brain (primitive neural structures that are involved in the production of emotional feelings)[6] generates pleasurable sensations. Apparently, a partial explanation of this is that specific electrical stimulation of neural centres (in parts of the limbic system) releases or activates the neurotransmitter dopamine. Dopamine is known to initiate a series of processes causing a not further specified feeling of pleasure. Apparently, it is not dopamine itself that generates a feeling of pleasure, though, but the release of enkephalins (endogenous morphinelike neurotransmitters) *provoked* by dopamine. Changeux suggests that the feelings produced in orgasm similarly arise out of indirect stimulation of the specific neural centers mentioned above. It is furthermore known that orgasm simultaneously results in a very high level of the content of enkephalins in the blood and releases enkephalins in the higher cognitive centres of the central nervous system (where messages received in codes are processed and analyzed).

The question is how enkephalins affect consciousness. Principally it seems that they inhibit the transfer of messages of pain from the spinal cord to the brain. Hence, enkephalins (and other similar endogenous and exogenous neurotransmitters) cause unawareness of physical damage. Changeux further suggests that the post-orgasmic presence of enkephalins in the CNS is the cause of other contented feelings typical of such states (see 1985, ch's. 4 and 5). Thus, it seems likely that a more localized liberation of enkephalins in the spinal cord primarily relieves physical pain, whereas a more general release in the blood and the higher brain structures account for the less definite

6. Changeux emphasizes, though, that a whole group of nerve centres participate in the generation of emotions. More concretely, he states that emotions arise from a dialogue between various neural systems, especially the hypothalamus, the limbic system, and the cerebral cortex (1985, especially 110 and 158).

feelings of pleasure. Both of these effects may be relevant with respect to the potential similarity of aspects of feelings in mystical and sexual states respectively. John of the Cross' repeated descriptions of the feeling of pleasurable tranquillity could be quite similar to the not further specified pleasurable feeling and contentedness. Thus, it is not impossible that specific emotions and feelings of mystical love actually do resemble those typically following sexually induced pleasure (descriptions of which John of the Cross may have recognized) because both involve the release of enkephalins.

There is one big problem with this suggestion, though. This is that enkephalins apparently affect consciousness in a way that corresponds very badly with the evidence of mystical consciousness. According to Greenfield, the analgesic effect of enkephalins (and morphines) can be explained with their inhibition of the growth of neuronal gestalts (Greenfield 1995, 172). As I have pointed out, evidence of mystical states strongly indicates that they are characterized with a sequence of deep and enduring consciousnesses of closely associated conceptions and emotions emerging from large and connected neuronal gestalts. The descriptions of mystical states seem to have most in common with depressive states with respect to the quantity of consciousness. Thus, both kinds of states seem to be characterized with highly reduced sensitivity to the external environment, little or no physical movement, and enhanced sensitivity to pain (although the latter is a tricky issue to which I shall return in a while) (see Greenfield 1995, 183 and Damasio 1987, 147). Furthermore, the perseverance of some mystical states suggest that consciousness in such states can grow very deep. John of the Cross' descriptions of those mystical states metaphorically referred to as spicy wine where the degrees of consciousness seem to increase and decrease in intensity for several days are particularly illustrative in this respect. In light of Greenfield's theory of consciousness, the only plausible explanation of the extraordinariness of the degrees of intensity of mystical states is that it is the outcome of very large and enduring neuronal gestalts. Consequently, it does not seem very likely that mystical states involve a general release of enkephalins or that the feeling of satiety and calm should stem from a high level of the content of enkephalins in the blood and the CNS, as this simultaneously would inhibit the formation of large neuronal gestalts and produce rapid shifts among disconnected consciousnesses. Consequently, it seems that even though the descriptions of the feelings of satiety and calm characterizing mystical states resemble those characterizing sexual states, nothing indicates that the cause of these feelings are similar in the two kinds of states.

This does not render the similarity unimportant, of course, but it means that it barely derives from an actual similarity of the internal processes from which conscious experience emerges. I would suggest that the satiety and calm generated in mystical states are related to other emotions than those giving rise to the feelings following orgasm. After all, such feelings characterize various kinds of states and, as the above discussion has shown, this is the only similarity of mystical and sexual states that John of the Cross' writings document. In fact, it is not improbable that the similarity of this particular aspect of mystical and sexual states has become more conspicuous because John of the Cross has been inspired by descriptions in the *Song of Solomon* of what seems to have been physical love. I would suggest that feelings of mystical love have little in common with sexual feelings, but that they have very much in common with other human feelings of love. Furthermore, the explanation of this could be that they are generated in the same way, that is, in response to similar cognitive representations of love (except that mystical love is oriented towards God and is based purely on imagination).

What is mystical purity?

Pain

It seems to be quite common for mystical states to cause the subject involved various kinds of pain. Yet, this is an element that changes fundamentally with the progression of development. Mystical states in the early stages are typically characterized with physical pain and bodily damage, whereas those in the final stage are free of all pain whatsoever (even if this point is a little ambiguous).

John of the Cross treats of the topic of pain in mystical states in great detail in connection with the mystical state supposedly constituting the transition to the second classified stage. This particular mystical state is claimed to cause the subject very severe pain and considerable physical damage. But it is a pain and physical damage that is not felt during the state. In fact, it is not quite clear how John of the Cross has been able to identify the pain, if it is not felt during the mystical state. Actually, he indicates that he has concluded that the state was painful on the basis of the paralysis also characterizing the state concerned. Thus, he seems to have reasoned that it is because of the severity of the pain that the soul temporarily departs from the body. Yet, it is not impossible that this inference has been supported with his notice of some kind of physical damage once the mystical state has come to an end, combined with diverse kinds of pain felt in other mystical states.

However, it appears that some kind of pain is quite common in mystical states in the first two stages of the classified process. Contrary to that, it seems that mystical states in the third stage are free of the pain typical of the earlier stages. In general, he claims that the most advanced mystical states are free of pain (even though he actually contradicts this once in connection with his reflections on the differences between the eternal union and the mystical unions) (see Juan de la Cruz 1988, Cántico A12 and 38:11/B13 and 39:14; Llama A/B4:12; Noche 2.21:5).[7] All in all John of the Cross provides clear evidence of a significant change in the character of mystical states with respect to pain of some kind or other.

In John of the Cross' view, pain arises when the soul's impurity is confronted with God's purity. He regards it as a natural phenomenon that pain results from the meeting of two such extreme opposites. Thus, John of the Cross identifies the factors upon which mystical pain is contingent to be the impure condition of the soul and the pure ditto of God. A natural solution to the problem would therefore be to change the condition of either God or the soul. Predictably, John of the Cross suggests a purification of the soul. A logical consequence of his conception of the cause of the pain felt in mystical states coupled with the process of purification is that it is indeed possible to alter the phenomenon. In accord with John of the Cross' understanding of the matter it could therefore be expected that the physical pain produced during a mystical state will either reduce or disappear as mystical development progresses.

His conception of the causal relation of impurity and pain is further developed in his discussion of those mystical states referred to as the 'touch of the spark' and the 'spicy wine', where he discusses how a subject is affected differently by (similar) mystical states at dissimilar points in the mystical process. His point is that mystical states, although similar, affect the subject differently, which means that it is the *condition* of the subject that varies while the effective processes are the same. The difference is that mystical states cause considerable harm to undeveloped subjects (or new lovers, as he calls them) but no harm at all to developed subjects (old lovers).

Correlated with his understanding of the mystical process as a process of purification this begins to make sense. John of the Cross claims that as long as the soul is not completely purified and conformed with the spirit as he says, mystical states are usually accompanied by an intense pain and physical damage. It is not until the soul is completely purified that mystical states do not inflict more or less severe pain on a person. In the final stage of mystical development, the soul is so purified that pain no longer goes along with pleasure in mystical states as was the case in the earlier parts of the process. This is because there is total conformity (due to the soul's recently gained state of purity) between God and the soul at this point (Juan de la Cruz 1988, Llama A/B4:12 and Cántico A38:11).

---

7. In the revised commentary on the *Canticle*, John of the Cross maintains that it is impossible ever to avoid pain in mystical states and that painless union with God is restricted to the beatific stage (Juan de la Cruz 1988, Cántico B39:14).

Why are mystical states painful in the major part of the developmental process? And why do they cease to be painful in the final part of the process? I would suggest that both pain and pleasure are products of the extreme quantity, combined with the specific quality, of consciousness in mystical states, whereas the change from the one to the other is contingent on a gratification in the quality of consciousness. More specifically, it seems that already at the point when a mystic begins to have mystical states (presumably when the actual mystical process as it is classified by John of the Cross is initiated) a mystic has undergone considerable development conditioning him/her for mystical states. Very early mystical states therefore already involve consciousness of considerable depth. Yet, at that point the mystical conceptions of love have not yet been cultivated to such a degree that the responding emotions of love are generated to any significant degree. Hence, consciousness is dominated by various mystical conceptions (not necessarily of love alone). Greenfield states that a very deep consciousness (as in depressed states) enhances awareness of pain. With more specific respect to the physical pain, I would suggest that this really is what happens in mystical states in a large part of the developmental process. Consciousness is so deep that awareness of already existing pain is enhanced. Physical pain is not engendered in mystical states but the degree of consciousness of pain is increased.

In addition to this, it furthermore seems that the first two stages of the process involve another kind of pain that supposedly is restricted to wakeful states and thus is relieved during mystical states. Considering John of the Cross' more general (and conventional) religious ideas of the relation of a person and God, according to which the soul is base and sinful while God is compassionate and generous and loves the soul in spite of its lowliness, it is not impossible that a more psychological pain arises from the intense consideration of the immense distance between oneself and God and of the cause of it (which is one's own sinfulness and baseness). The point I am making is that it seems likely that it is very painful to recognize (a) the lowliness of oneself, and (b) the implications of this, i.e., that the distance to God is enormous and will take plenty of time to exceed. Thus, it is not impossible that the continual meditation of these unpleasant thoughts may produce something like a depression with a mystical focus. If this is the case, then the depression is simply overcome because the mystic believes that the mystical endeavours have born fruit in the form of a change in his/her nature and a reduction of the distance to God.

Turning to the question of why the more advanced mystical states do not involve physical pain, I would suggest that the answer lies in the growth of the emotions of love. As I have pointed out before, the degree of consciousness of the emotions of mystical love (generated in response to conceptions of mystical love) in mystical states increases gradually throughout the entire developmental process, although this aspect of the developmental process accelerates at some point in the process. The main point in this context is that the cognitive representations of emotions of mystical love expand continuously and sooner or later begin to dominate consciousness to such a degree that they eventually cause an unawareness of pain. The cognitive representations of the pleasurable body states (in the form of emotions of mystical love) simply override the representations of the painful body states.

So far I have explained why mystical states in accord with John of the Cross' writings normally are painful and why they apparently cease to be painful in the final stage of mystical development. Yet, it still needs to be explained why John of the Cross contradicts himself regarding the possibility of having painless mystical states. Why is it that he in one place (in the original commentary in the *Canticle*, see Juan de la Cruz 1988, Cántico A38) maintains that union with God is free of pain in the third stage of the mystical process, and elsewhere claims that union with God always will involve pain in this life (thereby relegating painfree union to the eternal stage) (in the revised commentary in the *Canticle*, see Juan de la Cruz 1988, Cántico B39).

I would suggest that the contradiction regarding the possibility of having painless mystical states arises out of an ambiguity in expression which further has to do with the changes in the argument about the last verses in the *Canticle*. The verse-line concerned mentions a flame that causes no pain. In the original version of the work, John of the Cross argues that the verse refers to mystical states in the last stage of the mystical process. In the revised version, he has changed his argument on this point, claiming that the verse refers to the eternal union with God. I would suggest that the denial of the possible avoidance of pain in the third stage really does not concern actual mystical states, but refers more generally to the ultimate mystical stage. If this is correct, then both of his claims may be true to his experience in each their way. Thus, his original claim that the pain will be eliminated pertains to the physical pain felt in mystical states and the more generally felt psychological pain related to the recognition of one's lowliness and the remoteness of God. His later statement that pain cannot be avoided in mystical life seems rather to refer to the painful yearning for God during wakeful states.

Cognitive representations

One of the points vehemently asserted by John of the Cross is that the more advanced mystical states are completely free of forms and images. The images and forms involved in earlier mystical states should be suppressed until the point of elimination. Yet, the elusion of images and forms during the union of God and the soul requires that the soul attains a state of purity beyond such forms and images (a purity that is conceived of as some sort of emptiness of memory and understanding). So when the generation of forms and images in mystical states changes drastically in the course of mystical development, this is believed to follow from the gradually increasing purity of the soul.

In John of the Cross' works, those cognitive representations that can be subsumed under his notion of images and forms (and which can be classified as the more specific and conceptual representations of mystical love) presumably constitute the main content of consciousness in earlier mystical states. In the works of John of the Cross the more specific representations are (indirectly and metaphorically) presented as potential disturbers of the mystical love. In the more advanced mystical states, these more specific representations compete with other kinds of less specific and more emotional representations (that in John of the Cross' view are more desirable). In the most advanced mystical states of the third stage the less specific and more emotional representations seem to be dominant while the more specific representations apparently have become insignificant. This explains why such representations are considered to disturb the peace or to pose a threat to the fruition of some of the 'touches of union' typical of the end of the second classified stage. Furthermore, the potential danger that the tranquillity of mystical love is interrupted is *completely* eliminated when the last stage is reached and mastery of mystical love is attained.

In this place, the concern is the relation of the earlier mystical states that clearly involve images and forms and those of the final part of the mystical process that, in John of the Cross' view, do not involve such images and forms. Since John of the Cross himself considers the aspect of mental representations, it seems pertinent initially to present his considerations of the issue. He distinguishes mental representations according to two points, namely their relation or non-relation to external objects and their form or formlessness. The distinction furthermore implies an evaluation of the degree of the relative undesirability of the representations. The most damaging representations are those that are related to external objects and have specific form. Less damaging are the representations that are not related to external objects, although they are endowed with specific form. Then there is a certain kind of formless representations that are unrelated to external objects. Such representations are not exactly damaging. Neither of these representations are characteristic, though, of mystical states typical of the more advanced points in the developmental process. As the mystical process proceeds, representations produced in mystical states become gradually more purely related to internal events and more formless until they, in John of the Cross' view, eventually disappear entirely. His argument that the more advanced mystical states are free of forms and images seem to indicate that nothing is represented in the mind, neither from external nor from internal sources. Still, these mystical states do not seem to be comparable to, e.g., dreamless sleep states, inasmuch as something is 'communicated' and 'knowledge' is received in some way or another in spite of the form- and imageless character of such mystical states.[8]

Following the writings of John of the Cross, an individual going through the entire mystical process is enabled to achieve temporary states of consciousness that are liberated from forms. Apparently, the developmental state enabling the subject to have such mystical states is that which John of the Cross construes as a condition similar to the original purity of the tabula rasa state of the soul (Juan de la Cruz 1988, Subida 1.4:3 and Cántico A39:1/B40:1). Developmentally this state is obtained as soon as the purifying part of the mystical process has been completed. It seems that, in John of the Cross' understanding, it is the purification of the soul that prepares it for the consummation of mystical love. Mystical love, in turn, realizes the equally requisite transformation joining the purification at some point. Each of the two parts of the process executes whatever is needed in order to reach its own end, but thereby simultaneously contributes to the general process of moving towards the ultimate end.

An explanation of the change in the cognitive representations in mystical states might proceed in either of two ways. One possibility is that absolutely nothing is represented cognitively in the most advanced mystical states. If this is the case, then the reason why such mystical states are accounted for as free of forms and images is that they are non-representational. John of the Cross himself, if he had the chance to participate in a debate on the issue, would hardly have objected to such an explanation. Another solution to the problem is that the two kinds of mystical states involve different kinds of cognitive representations or, at least, that the earlier mystical states involve kinds of representations that are absent in later mystical states. In this case, John of the Cross' testimony that some mystical states are liberated of forms and images does not imply that nothing is represented, but that nothing is represented in a form identifiable by himself. Concluding that the mystical states in question involve no internal representations at all on the basis of the argued imagelessness (as in the first possibility) implies the dilemma of explaining *what* it is that the mystic reports from such states. If one presumes that consciousness requires the generation of internal representations, then the hypothesis of non-

8. Thus, God wordlessly instructs the soul in his hidden and secret wisdom in the most advanced mystical states. The instruction is carried out in complete silence and without engaging either the corporal or the spiritual senses (according to John of the Cross' distinction) (Juan de la Cruz 1988, Cántico A38:9/B39:12).

representational states could (tautologically) be refuted solely on the basis of the existence of reports on such mystical states. Thus, if mystical states are non-representational then they are also unconscious. If they are unconscious then they cannot be reported. John of the Cross has reported his mystical states. Hence, he has been conscious and has generated internal representations during his mystical states (assuming that his writings are not pure fiction).

These considerations should be correlated with the widespread contention among scholars of mysticism that mystical states are completely void of content (see my discussion hereof in Ch. II and Almond 1983 part I, for a summary of the theories concerned). Assumptions that mystical states are contentless are typically based on claims like those proposed by John of the Cross that (some) mystical states are free of forms and images. The supposed contentlessness requires that there are no representations whatever including emotional representations. Considering the evidence of John of the Cross' mystical states, I would definitely not subscribe to an understanding of these as contentless (and hence unemotional). John of the Cross' *Canticle* is, in particular, striking evidence of the extreme emotionality of all mystical states without exception (in fact, the degree of emotionality increases along with the claimed decrease and eventual disappearance of internal representations).

In conclusion of this, I would suggest that those cognitive processes that are typical of mystical states in the later developmental stages are mainly or exclusively of emotional character. The content of mystical consciousness in the more advanced parts of mystical development does, in my opinion, consist of cognitive representations of emotions of an exceptional intensity that may be distinctive for mystical states. I have already mentioned that John of the Cross' works indicate that the more conceptual aspect of mystical states gradually diminishes and eventually seems to disappear as mystical development progresses. The question is if the emotional representations are generated in all mystical states without exception or whether this aspect similarly is involved in a part of the mystical process only. In my view, it seems most plausible that the feelings of mystical love intensify and increase little by little throughout the entire developmental process. It appears that both the quality and the intensity of the feelings of mystical love are enhanced as a result of mystical development.

It would seem natural that the coincident generation of the more conceptual and the more emotional representations in a mystical state would make it seem more impressive and intense than one with only the one kind of cognitive representations. Yet, this does not seem to be the case. On the contrary, the reason why the mystical states of the later stages of the process are far more exciting and impressive than the earlier mystical states is that they are free of the forms and images which I identify as the more specific and conceptual representations of mystical love. Following the works of John of the Cross, it seems that the more specific and conceptual representations in mystical states are quite insignificant, even if they can be extremely pleasant. Accordingly, it seems that, in his view, it is the emotional element of mystical states that matters. I would suggest that the reason why the more specific and conceptual representations subtract from — rather than add to — the value of mystical states, is that they tend to overshadow or distract from the emotional representations.

The importance of this is that mystical development, as described by John of the Cross, results in the continuous reduction of the representations of conceptions of mystical love in mystical states of consciousness. This aspect of development seems to result from the aspect of the developmental process that John of the Cross himself identifies as a gradual purification and emptying of the soul (particularly that of memory and understanding). The purifying part of the process is, in fact, discontinued after the second stage which seems to support an identification of this as the point at which mastery of mystical love (identical with optimum purity in John of the Cross' understanding) is attained. It is the state of optimum purity that permits the initiation of a stage where all mystical states are dominated completely by representations of emotions of mystical love. It is because the reduction of the more specific and conceptual representations in mystical states presupposes a certain kind of development that the (almost) purely emotional mystical states are restricted to and typical of the later part of the process. Therefore it also seems that the more specific quality of a mystical state is contingent on the developmental point at which it occurs.

The state of perfect, mystical purity

Having attended to the issue of what actually goes on in mystical states, it is time to draw some conclusions about the more general outcome of mystical development. The most important products of mystical development are the attainment of a state of perfect purity and proficiency in mystical love. Interpreting John of the Cross' writings, it is the process of purification that leads to mystical purity and the process of transformation in love that leads to mastery of mystical love. The purifying process is completed at some point, whereas the transforming process continues throughout the entire process of mystical development, also after a mystic has become proficient in mystical love. In reality, the two processes are inseparable, though. Purification is the means permitting and easing the flourishing and prospering of mystical love. In this way, it appears that perfect purity is only a partial goal of mystical development and that which leads to mastery of mystical love. What the *actual* goal of mystical development is depends on the perspective from which one identifies the goal. With respect to the life of a mystic, the goal is to master mystical love (although the refinement of this skill actually is interminable). With respect to the more general relationship between God and the soul, the final goal is the entrance into the eternal union with God without intermittent purification in purgatory.

In light of the relation of mystical purity and the ability to love mystically, it is germane initially to reconsider what mystical purity really is. John of the Cross states that purity results from the complete stilling of the faculties of the soul (that is, memory, understanding, and willpower).[9] This implies that it is the mystical purity that enables the avoidance of images (the more specific and conceptual representations) and various kinds of pain during mystical states.

Having reached this pure condition, a mystic is enabled temporarily to elude the otherwise disturbing relations to the external world (including those relations that are mediated by memory). Mystical purity seems to permit a complete, but temporary, detachment from the world.

In general, it appears that the major advantage of mystical purity is that the prevention of (or reduction in the dominance of) the more specific representations of diverse conceptions (of mystical love) enables a mystic to be more fully conscious of representations of emotions of mystical love. This explains why the state of optimum mystical purity is a precondition for the perfect realization of mystical love. If mystical purity is the precondition for mastery of mystical love, this further explains why the point of terminating the former will coincidentally be the point of achieving the latter. And this point seems to be somewhere around the completion of the second stage and the commencement of the third. Still, mastery of mystical love does not seem to preclude further improvement in the ability of loving God, though, even if the process will slow down once proficiency in this skill is attained.

Another effect of the attainment of perfect, mystical purity is that the mystically pure soul is constantly beyond ordinary emotionality of feelings of

9. To be precise, John of the Cross seems to believe that the ability to avoid the more specific cognitive representations is the outcome of the purification of memory and understanding, whereas the avoidance of pain in mystical states follows from the purification of willpower (more generally referred to as conformation with God's will). Accordingly, it is not impossible that he implicitly has discriminated a purity, consisting in the pacification of memory and understanding, facilitating the consummation of mystical love and one, consisting in conformation with God's will, enabling painless (mystical) union with God.

pain, pleasure,[10] compassion and the like (Juan de la Cruz 1988, Cántico A29-30:6-10/B20-21:9-16). John of the Cross describes this insensitivity as a very positive imperviousness that enables the subject to remain in constant equilibrium. This profound estrangement from the external world seems, however, to be a developmental side-effect more than an end in itself. Along with this alienation goes an increasing inability to find satisfaction in the affairs of the world. Ultimately this makes the soul incapable of taking pleasure in anything but God. Alienation and inability to find satisfaction are both caused by the gradual denaturalization and nascent divinization that, together, lead to a veritable retreat from the external world and the escape to the interior of the soul where God eventually is found. In the words of John of the Cross, the process bit by bit causes the soul to cease living where it lives (Juan de la Cruz 1988, Cántico A8:2/B8:3) thereby transferring its life from the body to the spirit. The result of this seemingly very concrete departure from material life is that mundane things and affairs no longer satisfy the soul. Material satisfaction is truly replaceable with spiritual satisfaction but such replacement does not really become noticeable until a person is well into the mystical process. Since the subject no longer relates to either things or people, God becomes the subject's sole companion. And as the subject is only occasionally favoured with God's visits (the frequency seems to amplify very slowly) it is, in general, a very lonely process[11] (Juan de la Cruz 1988, Cántico A3:6, 6:2, 9:5 and 10:3/B3:7, 6:3, 9:6 and 10:6). Just as the bonds to the world begin to break as departure from it proceeds, so does a feeling of not belonging to the world set in. Apparently, the feeling is generated by an alteration of the way of perceiving the external environment. The subject gradually loses the common way of sensing and understanding. Consequently, objects and people are perceived in a basically different manner and appear strange and outlandish (Juan de la Cruz 1988, Noche 2.9:5).

The ceaseless striving for God leads to a total alienation of the subject from the surrounding world. The soul has already lost its interest in the things and people of this world, even though it still searches for God in them. Naturally, when the soul does not find Him in either people or things, and when it realizes this, people and things really begin to molest and harass it. Having to deal with the business of the world interferes with the soul's project and is

10. He speaks of worldly and of various *spiritual* pleasures, but obviously not of the soul's very intimate pleasures of being with God Himself. The cause of the insensitivity to all emotions that do not stem from God directly is that the soul at this stage constantly contains all riches and joys in itself (Juan de la Cruz 1988, a brief reference in Cántico A29-30:8 and otherwise B20-21:11-13).

11. The loneliness of the process is the theme of verse A 34/B 35 in the *Canticle* and of the commentary on it where the loneliness is considered to be both a precondition for and a means of achieving intimacy with God.

really very inconvenient for the improvement of its relationship with God. Since worldly occupations of any sort are impediments to the mystical development they are also extremely tormenting to the subject (Juan de la Cruz, Cántico B10:1-2 and 29:1-2).

The development of mystical consciousness

In the following I shall discuss how selected cognitive (mainly neurological) theories jointly may contribute to explain mystical development. The intention is to explain some of those cognitive processes that in interaction yield a set of products in the form of cognitive changes that together can be subsumed under the notion of mystical development. This really is a question of major significance for the understanding of mystical experience and should be addressed with due concern.

As I have pointed out before, John of the Cross' works more than indicate that there is a reciprocal causal relationship between mystical states and mystical development. Having a mystical state somehow produces some changes in the mind of the mystic. These cognitive changes, in turn, affect subsequent mystical states in various ways. In isolation, the cognitive changes resulting from a single mystical state of consciousness may indeed be rather insignificant. But as mystical states recur, the changes accumulate and together engender mystical development. Accordingly, it can be said that every minor cognitive change resulting from a mystical state of consciousness somehow contributes to the bits and pieces making up mystical development. At the same time, every minor developmental advance will, in principle at least, have some (mostly unnoticeable) effect on any following mystical state.

Competition of potential consciousnesses

So, how can this process be explained cognitively and neurologically? I shall take Greenfield's theory of consciousness (presented in Ch. I) as a starting point for the joining of selected aspects of a number of theories that in concert may throw new light on the subject of mystical experience resulting from an interactional process of mystical states and mystical development. It is evident from Greenfield's theory that whenever there is consciousness, there is consciousness of something. And while there is consciousness of that something, there cannot *simultaneously* be consciousness of other things. Hence, there will be competition among the current consciousness of something and the potential consciousnesses of other things. Which ones lose and which one wins in this competitive game is contingent on a whole number of factors as already mentioned in connection with the presentation of the theory.

Basically, the main factors are the strength of the epicentres (competing to form a group of neurons large enough for the generation of consciousness) and the degree of arousal. The higher the level of arousal is, the weaker an epicentre needs to be and the other way round (since arousal increases the sensitivity of neurons). But for the formation of a large gestalt (and the generation of a deep consciousness) time is needed. And when arousal is high, so is competition of neuronal groups because all neurons are very sensitive and therefore responsive to even minor stimuli. Hence, consciousness shifts rapidly from one thing to another. Medium arousal is therefore the best condition for a gestalt to grow. But this much only explains that the degree of competition varies according to the level of arousal, whereas it explains nothing about the dissimilar odds of the competing groups of neurons. So far, odds seem to be equal for all potential consciousnesses. This is rarely the case, though, because epicentres (made up of small groups of neurons) do not have equal strength. The strength of an epicentre relies partly on the degree of potential communication within the epicentre (which, at the neurological level can be described as conditioned by the number and the sizes of the neuronal synapses) and partly on the cognitive value[12] (as Greenfield terms it) of the epicentre. Furthermore, already active neuronal gestalts (assembled around an epicentre) generating consciousness get a head start, so to speak, because active neurons are more sensitive to inputs than inactive neurons. This means that once consciousness has managed to grow to some depth it simultaneously grows in relative competitive power simply because of its current activation and the size of the neuronal gestalt. A large group of active neurons is hard to compete with for a small group of inactive neurons.

All in all, this means that the optimum conditions for the formation of a very large gestalt in the first place is a relatively low (or medium) level of arousal and a very strong epicentre. With a strong epicentre, even a low level of arousal permits the formation of a gestalt large enough for consciousness to occur. And when arousal is low there is less competition among neuronal groups. If a gestalt formed at a low level of arousal gets the chance to grow reasonably large, then its further chances of growing very large and lasting for a considerable amount of time are very good. So, for a very deep consciousness of something to occur, a relatively low level of arousal and the existence of a very strong epicentre related to that something are the ideal conditions.

12. I would suggest that the cognitive value of something can be described as the total sum of associations of that something. This includes emotional associations which further can be identified as the reserve of emotional representations previously generated in response to something. These emotional representations will associate to anything which seemingly resembles the something that originally caused the emotional response.

As mentioned before, mystical consciousness seems to be a very deep consciousness of mystical conceptions and/or emotions unaffected by sensory
inputs. With respect to the quantity and imperviousness of consciousness,
mystical states seem to resemble depressive states very much. Indeed, the
conditions potentiating depression are a low level of arousal and very strong
epicentres (of whatever constitutes the focus of the depression) (Greenfield
1995, 183-84, but see also Damasio 1987, 163). The level of arousal in mystical
states may therefore similarly be very low but it might also be moderate (as
in concentrated wakefulness).

    As mentioned before, the level of arousal is controlled by shifting com-
binations of neurotransmitters flooding diverse parts of the brain and modu-
lating the degree of neuronal sensitivity. It appears, though, that the more
specific effect of neurotransmitters on neuronal activity is a very complicated
matter. It seems that the function of neurotransmitters simply is to regulate the
way that the mind works at any point in time. As an example of the complexity of the matter, a more general release of the neurotransmitter dopamine
is apparently associated with an enhanced general level of arousal, for instance, easing the formation of competing neuronal gestalts (which may
impede focused attention) (Greenfield 1995, 152). As opposed to this, a more
specific availability of dopamine in specific areas in the brain facilitates
focused attention and controls the orientation of attention. With more specific
respect to mystical states, I have mentioned before that mystical states seem
to resemble depressive states regarding the quantity of consciousness. And the
generation of depressive states is favoured by the general release of the neurotransmitter serotonin which eases the growth of neuronal gestalts by reducing
the level of arousal and thus the neuronal competition (1995, 152). It is
therefore possible that mystical states (in varying quantities) are similarly
favoured by the nueral release of serotonin and the resulting low level of
arousal. Yet, the main reason why mystical states (especially the more advanced ones) are very deep and connected is presumably that selected epicentres
(those of mystical relevance) have been cultivated excessively and thus have
grown exceptionally strong, thereby securing a very deep state of consciousness with smooth shifts from the consciousness of one thing to another.

Mystical consciousness defeating wakefulness

Having addressed the isssue of how neuronal groups compete for dominance,
it is now time to deal with the way that the competitive relation of epicentres
may change as a result of mystical development. At this point it should come
as no surprise that I will suggest that the way mystical development may
foster the generation of mystical states is through a strengthening of the

epicentres of mystical love and the related associations. Yet the problem is to explain how mystical epicentres grow stronger and extend the net of associations thereby gaining in competitive power.

I have pointed out that the evidence in the works of John of the Cross strongly indicates that there is a reciprocal causal relationship between mystical states and mystical development. I have suggested that the recurrence of mystical states produces some changes in the mind of the mystic and that these changes, in turn, facilitate the induction and the fulfilment of subsequent mystical states. It appears that simply being conscious of something affects the mind. Cognitively, this can be explained as resulting from changes in the reserve of cognitive representations. Whenever there is consciousness of something, the cognitive representations of that something or of something that is somehow related to it will increase in number. The quantity and the duration of consciousness determines the degree of the expansion of the relevant cognitive representations, whereas the quality of consciousness determines which cognitive representations that will be affected. This implies that, on the one hand, the epicentre concerned will grow in strength and, on the other hand, the amount of associations related to it will expand.

The consciousness of something emerges out of the activities of a neuronal gestalt centred around a small group of neurons constituting the epicentre of the particular consciousness. A neurological explanation of how neuronal activities are capable of influencing the strength of an epicentre and the associations related to it requires a return to the earlier presented theories and evidence that the structure of the brain is modifiable by experience. The activities of a group of neurons consist in electrical and chemical communication among the neurons and is processed in the synapses connecting the neurons. The total sum of the different weights of the synapses of a neuron delimit the possible degree of activity of that neuron. Similarly, the sum of all of the synaptic connections within a group of neurons sets the upper limit of activity of that group of neurons. What is important for an understanding of the modification of neural structure is that the activities of a group of neurons extend the net of interneuronal communication by increasing the number and the weights (or strengths)[13] of the synaptic connections of the neurons. The more that the synapses are used, the more efficient they become as a result of their increasing strength. This further implies that the more that neurons communicate, the easier communication becomes (see especially the works of Changeux 1985; Changeux and Dehaene 1993; Greenough et al. 1993; Jenkins et al. 1990 (a) and (b): Merzenich 1990; Recanzone et al. 1992 (a) and (b), but also Greenfield 1995, 41, 123, 155 and Damasio 1987, ch. 5).

13. The words 'weight' and 'strength' are used synonymously as descriptions of the potential power of synapses.

With respect to the possible changes in neural structure resulting from mystical states, the evidence from Merzenich, Recanzone, and Jenkins' experiments with monkeys is particularly important. What their work shows is that very intense neuronal activity of a specific kind (in the cases concerned various specialized uses of the hands) produces an actual enlargement of the neural areas in question. The expansion of neural areas may involve the generation of new synaptic connections and/or the strengthening of existing synaptic connections. Both changes produce a heightened capacity for interneuronal communication or, more specifically, a stronger electrical response to all subsequent input. The diverse consciousnesses of mystical conceptions and emotions are barely related to equally specific areas in the brain, but may nonetheless have a similar expanding effect on neural structures. It seems most likely that a number of specific (groups of) neurons distributed over the brain will be affected, so that certain (groups of) neurons gradually become specialized in matters of mystical relevance. In the present context, the main point is not whether *specific* or *varying* (groups of) neurons are affected by mystical consciousnesses, but that they are affected. At the cognitive level, the process may be described as a strengthening of epicentres of conceptions and emotions of mystical contents (using the terminology of Greenfield), or as the accumulating storage of memory traces (borrowing a term from connectionism, see McClelland and Rumelhart 1987, 174) of microfeatures of representations of conceptions and emotions of such mystical contents. In a somewhat more general perspective, it is the combination of various kinds of goal directed behaviour and the intermittent mystical states that produce the changes in neural structure that can be subsumed under the notion of mystical development.

Mystical development fosters the conditions of mystical consciousness in the mind of the mystic. Due to the strengthening of epicentres of conceptions of mystical love, the neuronal groups constituting those epicentres gain in competitive power in relation to other such groups of neurons. Consequently, consciousness of mystical conceptions and emotions emerges more easily because the formation of the neuronal gestalts generating it is facilitated. Furthermore, mystical consciousness is enabled to grow deeper and last longer, inasmuch as the neuronal gestalts will be enabled to grow larger and more lasting as competing neuronal groups will have more difficulty in overpowering them (cf. Greenfield 1995, 83-84). In this way, the entertainment of certain ideas and the responding emotions is at the same time, a cultivation of the competitiveness of all similar or related ideas and emotions.

John of the Cross' works strongly indicate that mystical development additionally changes the mutual competitive relationship between the (more or less specialized) neuronal groups generating consciousness of the more conceptual and emotional cognitive representations respectively. As the developmental process proceeds, the predominant consciousness in mystical states changes in quality shifting from more conceptual and specific representations to purely emotional representations of mystical love. In the light of Greenfield's theory of consciousness, I will suggest that the explanation of this is that John of the Cross' persistent attempts to nourish the emotions of mystical love — probably during both mystical and wakeful states — gradually has strengthened those synaptic connections storing the emotional representations of mystical love at the expense of all other synaptic connections (including those storing the more conceptual representations of mystical love) thereby sustaining the competitive capacity of the emotional aspect and maybe even weakening that of the conceptual aspect (as synaptic connections not only gain in strength when active, but apparently also lose in strength when inactive). Due to the gradual shift in the competitive relationship between the emotional and the more conceptual aspect of mystical consciousness, the former will gradually begin to take up an increasing amount of the neuronal activities (as a whole encompassing the number of activated neurons, the strengths of the synaptic connections, and the duration of the neuronal gestalts) involved in the generation of mystical consciousness. To put it differently, the degree of mystical consciousness dominated by emotional representations will gradually expand in both extension and duration along with a corresponding decrease in the degree of awareness assigned to the more conceptual representations.

So far, I have considered how the recurrence of mystical states affects mystical development and I have mentioned that the intentional attempts to internalize attention similarly plays a role as a cause of mystical development. At this point, I wish to draw attention to another factor that may influence some aspects of mystical development due to the contribution to a strengthening of selected epicentres and an extension of the net of associations. This factor is the continuous redescription of the representations of mystical experience. Representational redescription does not simply involve the substitution of existing representations of something with new representations of that something. It involves the addition of new and more abstract representations to the existing representations. This means that representational redescriptions enlarge the total representational reserve. It is not unlikely that this further means that the potential size of neuronal gestalts assembled around a mystical epicentre can be extended, inasmuch as the number of associations that can be triggered by an epicentre will increase. In the first place, this can be expected to ease the unfolding of mystical states during which the foci of consciousness are diverse mystical conceptions. Yet, representational redescription may additionally affect the unfolding of mystical emotions during mystical states. If it is the case that various mystical emotions of love are generated in response to various representations of mystical conceptions of love, then an increase in the supply of the latter may boost the generation of the former. Accordingly, it is not impossible that different cognitive processes contributing in each their way to augment the store of representations of mystical conceptions and mystical emotions respectively work in concert to optimize and facilitate the realization of mystical emotions.

The progression of mystical development

There is ample evidence in the works of John of the Cross that it can be very difficult to get the mystical process started. The reason why one may have troubles initiating the process is that this lies in the hands of God. It is good to prepare oneself for the process, but the actual processes of purification and transformation (consisting of the three stages classified by John of the Cross) are granted by God. It appears that, although a mystic does not control the initation of the process nor the completion of the process, a mystic still needs to get ready for it, though. The pre-mystical stage is not the issue treated in most detail in the works of John of the Cross, but it is nonetheless clear that meditation, in particular, does much to facilitate the initiation of the mystical process. As could be expected, the issue is treated most carefully in the two instructional treatises, namely the Ascent of Mount Carmel and the Dark Night, dealing with the way of following the mystical way.

A person who wishes to enter the mystical way needs to understand that Christ constitutes the door to that way or the way itself. One should consider (or contemplate) Christ in whom everything is revealed and imitate His life (Juan de la Cruz 1988, Subida 2.22:5-6, 1.13, and 2:7). In John of the Cross' understanding, the two general insights that can be extracted from the consideration of Christ are that one should rid oneself of the pleasures of the senses and that one should love God. The reasoning behind this is that union with God presupposes likeness with Him. The elimination of sensuousness is a prerequisite for the likening of the soul with God. Love is a means of likening the lovers to one another. In the pre-mystical stage, the trouble is to reduce sensuousness and engender love of God. The general stress on the importance of negating all kinds of sensory pleasures probably not only incorporates an advice of not enjoying sensory perceptions, but also of actually reducing them. Loneliness and meditation are some of the more specific ways of achieving the required non-sensuousness and love. Meditation involves internalization of attention with concentrated focus on selected topics like the life of Christ and His (God's) love. Or, as John of the Cross expresses it, one should meditate and make discursive activities and exercises with the imagination (Juan de la Cruz 1988, Llama 3.32) and one should extract knowledge and love from God (Subida 2.14:1-2). Loneliness is advantageous for the necessary concentration on the love of God. Loneliness means distancing oneself from loved persons and things. The love of the things and the persons of the world subtracts in equal proportion from the love of God. More concretely, loneliness also refers to the beneficiency of staying in lonely places. The best conditions for meditation are lonely (and not too pleasant) places. Pleasant places, on the contrary, are most inconvenient for meditation, the focus (or temple) of which is the soul itself (e.g., Juan de la Cruz 1988, Subida 3.39:2-3 and 41:1, Cántico 34:35). Furthermore, John of the Cross' repeated poetical and metaphorical references to darkness (as in the general metaphor of the dark night of the soul and the poem that inspired it) can be interpreted to mean that he has considered darkness to be expedient for the purpose of having mystical states. This interpretation is supported by contemporary testimonies that John of the Cross appreciated the night very much and considered it the best time for meditation (Peers 1954).

Before turning to an explanation of why certain behaviour and conditions are beneficial for the initiation of the mystical process, it should be pointed out that the relation of goal directed behaviour and convenient conditions, on the one hand, and the promotion of mystical development, on the other, is that certain behaviour and conditions improve the chances of having mystical states. And the occurrence of mystical states constitutes the initial goal of getting the process started just as it promotes the progression of the process. What needs to be explained is therefore why certain behaviour and external conditions are propitious for the generation of mystical states.

The reason why the negation of sensory pleasures are profitable seems to be that a reduction in perceived external events eases internalization and focus of attention and, furthermore, that a negation of the pleasurability of perceptions eases the concentration of affection on non-worldly things. Meditation is beneficial for the generation of mystical consciousness for several reasons. Firstly, because the internalization of attention in itself helps shut off the external world. Secondly, because prolonged focused attention permits the growth of the neuronal gestalts generating consciousness of shifting content. Thirdly, because the focus on conceptions of God's love generates emotions of love. And finally, it is not unlikely that meditation secures the most expedient level of arousal. Loneliness works very much like the general negation of sensory pleasures, and like that, it has a double advantage. It reduces the risk of distraction from focused attention and it eases the concentration on the love of God. Darkness is, more specifically, convenient because it eases the elusion of visible objects. Besides, the darkness concerned is primarily that of the night which means that the risk of distracting events and noises presumably has been very little at the time and in the surroundings of John of the Cross. It should be clear from this extended interpretation of the points made by John of the Cross that sensory deprivation plays an important role with respect to the improvement of the cognitive conditions for mystical consciousness. Supposingly, this is because sensory deprivation facilitates meditation, that is, the fully internalized and concentrated focus on conceptions of love of God that further generate emotions of that love.

On the basis of Greenfield's theory of consciousness supplied with Damasio's theory of emotions, it should be possible to explain how a non-mystic manages to initiate the process of becoming a mystic by providing the optimum cognitive conditions for it. Let me first line up the developmental state of a religious, non-mystic aspiring to become a mystic. The epicentres related to conceptions and emotions of mystical love are weak. Numerous epicentres related to worldly things and persons are stronger than those pertaining to conceptions of mystical relevance (and the responding emotions). Cognitive processes are constantly restrained by sensory inputs except during sleep states. Consequently, the epicentres competing to recruit a neuronal group generating consciousness of conceptions of mystical quality (and possibly some weak responding emotions)[14] have to compete both with other (and stronger) cognitively derived epicentres and with far more competitive externally derived epicentres. Odds are really bad for the mystically relevant epicentres.

In order to change these unfortunate circumstances within the cognitive system, the person can make an attempt to influence several factors constraining cognitive processes. Firstly, the person may try to train him/herself to affect the level of arousal in order to facilitate the formation of large neuronal gestalts. It is not unlikely that meditation is a powerful exercise in this respect, because the subject makes an effort to avoid rapid shifts between unrelated consciousnesses (characteristic of a high and inconvenient level of arousal). This is a point that may have both an immediate, but transient, and a slower, but more lasting, effect. Secondly, the person may strive to internalize focused attention in order to eliminate competition from externally derived epicentres. This probably requires some training (for which meditation obviously is an efficient means) and can doubtlessly be aided by various kinds of sensory deprivation. The internalization of attention may be facilitated immediately by providing the proper external conditions (darkness, loneliness, and the like), but it will presumably take quite a while to succeed with it. Finally, the person may nourish the reserve of cognitive representations related to conceptions of mystical quality thereby strengthening the relevant epicentres in order to

14. Consciousness of conceptions and/or emotions of mystical love is not necessarily mystical, since the definition of a mystical state of consciousness followed in this book requires that there is a certain quantity of consciousness implying that it is unrestrained by sensory inputs.

render them more competitive. Supposedly, the strength of the epicentres will be affected continually whenever the person dwells on the germane conceptions. Also in this respect, meditation will inevitably be a very efficient means. In the beginning of the mystical process, the strengthening of epicentres can be expected to proceed very slowly. But as development progresses, this aspect of the developmental process will inevitably accelerate. In particular, the process of further strengthening the epicentres will speed up once the representations of mystical emotions really begin to take root.

The reason why combinations of changes in the level of arousal, the direction and the degree of focus of attention, and the strengths of specific epicentres will influence the quality and quantity of consciousness is that it affects the interactions and the relative competitiveness of the competing neuronal groups. I wish to stress that the three factors are closely connected implying that a change in one factor will affect the other factors. Different combinations will have different effects. The coincidence of internalized attention and a reasonably low level of arousal, but with only relatively weak epicentres of mystical relevance, is more apt to produce a dream state or a daydreaming state (depending on more specific internal processes) than a mystical state. As opposed to this, very strong mystical epicentres will be capable of affecting the other two factors, so that a mystical state can be induced in numerous ways once the epicentres are strong enough. An actual mystical state is therefore dependent on the availability of relevant epicentres of some degree of strength.

This leads me to the issue of the changing speed of mystical development. In this context, the developmental process should be considered in its entirety, that is, from the pre-mystical period during which a person strives to initiate the process and until development has been fulfilled (ultimately development does not end before the person dies). The need for strong and mystically relevant epicentres in the mind of a person provides an explanation of why it can be very difficult to get the developmental process started.[15] The problem is that the strenghtening of epicentres not only takes time, but also focused attention to the due conceptions. Yet, focused attention to something can be difficult as long as the epicentres of that something are weak, since attention easily will be distracted (because of competition from stronger epicentres).

Before suggesting why the developmental process accelerates as it progresses, it seems pertinent to repeat the explanation of how the competitive power of epicentres is fortified. The process of strengthening an epicentre of something can, at the cognitive level, be described as the storage of cognitive

---

15. The mystical development of Teresa of Jesus is a salient example of this and her bibliography, in particular, gives ample evidence of the troubles she went through in this respect (Teresa de Jesús 1988, Vida).

representations more or less directly related to that something. At the neurological level, the process can be described as a strengthening of existing synaptic connections or the generation of new connections among neurons that from time to time are recruited by the epicentre concerned. Somewhat into the developmental process, but still in the rather early part of it, the process will already begin to speed up, because focused (internalized) attention to mystical conceptions will be facilitated, inasmuch as the epicentres in question have become relatively more competitive than they were before. A little further on in the developmental process, other factors will additionally begin to have some impact on the speed of the process. When the epicentres have become reasonably strong, the neuronal gestalts generating mystical consciousness (that is to say, consciousness of mystical quality and in mystical quantity) will become larger and more durable (and mystical consciousness deeper and more lasting). As a consequence of this, more neurons will be involved in the generation of mystical consciousness and the neurons will spend more time with that particular activity which means that the synaptic connections also will be strengthened correspondingly more. Accordingly, the realization of mystical states will in itself begin to have a far stronger impact on the developmental process.

A final point affecting the changing speed of mystical development arises out of the quality of mystical states. This is the gradually increasing degree of the emotions of mystical love generated in mystical states. Evidence of the workings of memory provided by psychological and neurological theories demonstrates that emotions have a very strong effect on the subsequent memory of something. The higher the degree of emotionality going along with the consciousness of something, the better that something is remembered. Damasio suggests that the reason for this is that working memory and attention are motivated by preferences and that feelings in general give value to something represented cognitively. Emotions, especially, function as boosters for continued attention and working memory. In this way, feelings influence experience by 'the automated assigning of *varied degrees* of attention to *varied contents*' (Damasio 1987, 199). Accordingly, it seems that objects, events, thoughts, etc., require subjective value for a person from their capacity to affect that person emotionally. In the present context, it is not only the degree of attention allocated to something or the subsequent memory of it that is at stake, but also the immediate effects on the cognitive system and the resulting cognitive changes.

Damasio explains that the cognitive system is equipped with a preference system innately biased to avoid pain and seek potential pleasure. This preference system is modified by experience throughout the life of an individual (although the fundament is layed out in the course of childhood development) and enables the subject to behave sensibly in relation to the particular surroundings (Damasio 1987, 179). Whenever something pleasant or unpleasant happens to an individual, this modifies the system in such a way that later seemingly similar incidents will generate a certain (emotional, for instance) response causing the behaviour suitable to either avoid the pain or seek the pleasure that the incident is expected to produce.

In the light of Greenfield's and Damasio's theories, in combination, it appears that the higher the degree of emotionality, the more the activated epicentres are strengthened. Following Damasio it seems that an emotional response to something eases the attention to that something. And according to Greenfield the duration of a single consciousness is constrained by the degree of focused attention (which, in turn, is restrained by the level of arousal). If attention is unfocused, consciousness shifts rapidly and without connectedness. The more that attention is focused on something, the better the conditions are for the neuronal gestalt concerned to grow and to persist. The larger and more durable the neuronal gestalt, the more the synaptic connections of the activated neurons (and thus the epicentre) are strengthened.

I am now getting to the main point concerning the relation of degrees of emotionality in mystical states and the speed of mystical development. It is clear from the writings of John of the Cross that the degree of emotions of mystical love (the love of God) realized during mystical states increases continuously in the course of mystical development. The growth of love between the soul and God really is the ultimate goal of mystical development. The general strengthening of epicentres of mystical love facilitates the generation of mystical emotions of love, thereby further reinforcing the strengthening of the synaptic connections storing the representations of emotions of mystical love which, in turn, will ease the subsequent display of emotional representations of mystical love. Accordingly, the expanding depth and duration of mystical consciousness (whether predominantly conceptual or emotional in quality) can be explained by the coincidental and mutually reinforced strengthening of the synaptic connections which store the emotional and the conceptual representations, respectively, as a result of recurring mystical states. Moreover, this explains why the process accelerates continuously along with the increase in the emotional aspect of mystical states.

All in all, it appears that the various aspects of mystical development — and especially that of mystical emotions — have a snowball effect on the developmental process where any degree of mystical consciousness facilitates subsequent mystical consciousnesses *at an escalating speed.*

The changing quality of mystical states

Heading for mastery of mystical consciousness

In this place the concern is how the shift in the competitiveness of neuronal groups may affect both the induction and the realization of mystical states eventually resulting in mastery of having mystical states of consciousness. In accord with the works of John of the Cross, the way that a wakeful state shifts to a mystical state changes considerably in the course of development. Mystical states are induced much more easily in the more advanced stages of the process. In John of the Cross' understanding, God discloses great wonders to the soul very frequently and with great facility in the third classified stage of the mystical process (Juan de la Cruz 1988, Cántico A28:1/B23:1). More specifically, this can be interpreted to mean that mystical states occur more spontaneously, more effortlessly, or both. Presumably, the word 'facility' (*facilidad*) implies a reference to both. Thus, it appears that mystical states occur more suddenly, just as the subject need not devote any efforts in order to enter into a mystical state. Moreover, John of the Cross claims that the soul initially contributes to the process, after which God gradually takes over, could be interpreted as an indication that personal behaviour affects the immediate induction of mystical states in the early part of development, but not later on. This further seems to imply that increased control of inducing mystical states does *not* follow from mystical development. In fact, the opposite appears to be the case. The little control that one may have in the beginning of the process disappears as a result of development. And if it was initially possible to contribute to the transition to a mystical state through one's behaviour or otherwise, then this is lost in the course of development.[16] From a developmental perspective it seems that a mystic has some influence on the induction of mystical states in the beginning of the mystical process, less so as the process advances, and not at all in the last stage. In short the greater facility with which mystical states are obtained in the last stage of development suggests that the shift between dissimilar kinds of conscious states at this point takes place without any efforts on the part of the subject which, at the same time, indicates that this was not so previously.[17]

16. This is, in fact, a little surprising. Especially when this evidence is compared with that of other types of extraordinary states like possession states, for instance. A subject achieves gradually more and more control of the induction of possession states as he/she has been possessed more and more times. Apparently, a person learns how to become possessed by reacting to certain stimuli (say, a specific drum rythm) and learns how to control possession (although the musicians and the priest(s) involved in a ritual also hold a great deal of control) (Walker 1972, 30 and 76).
17. A further perspective on the problem: John of the Cross' general view that mystical states (unions) are granted by God directly opposes the probability that it is possible

With respect to the realization of mystical states, it is clear from John of the Cross' writings that mystical states improve in various ways as a mystic develops. In the beginning of the developmental process, mystical states are incomplete and unfulfilled. From around the second classified stage onwards, this is no longer a problem. Furthermore, mystical states improve throughout the entire process, just as they tend to be more lasting in the more advanced parts of the process. It is not necessarily the case that every mystical state is better and more enduring than the preceding state, though. The point I am making here is that there is a general improvement in the capacity for mystical states of consciousness.

It seems pertinent to consider whether it is possible to explain *why* it is difficult to induce and hold on to a mystical state in the beginning of the mystical process, whereas mystical states occur spontaneously and effortlessly and are also better and more persistent in the more advanced part of the process? An explanation of this should indeed be within reach in light of Greenfield's theory of consciousness and the competition of neuronal groups. One possibility that needs to be considered is that meditation trains the subject to control the level of arousal (possibly by means of the disciplination of focused and internalized attention). This would ease the formation of large neuronal gestalts. But for this to work in the desired way, the existence of relatively strong mystical epicentres would still be requisite for the generation of a mystical consciousness of some depth. To be precise, a relevant epicentre would probably need to be very strong before an actual mystical state of consciousness could be generated (and not simply a wakeful state of consciousness of mystical content) as mystical consciousness must be of considerable depth to secure the required degree of imperviousness to sensory inputs. And this presumably necessitates a certain quantity of consciousness in order to secure the requisite degree of internalization of focused attention.[18] Accordingly, the induction of a mystical state of consciousness seems to be dependent on the existence of strong epicentres of mystical love, although a

to affect the induction of a mystical state. Considering the theological implications in this view (that God solely approaches the soul) it actually constitutes rather uncertain evidence of the mystical process. Especially when it is correlated with the evident contradictions between originally expressed view in the poem in the *Canticle* that he (alias the female in the poem) had approached God (the male) and the later interpretations of the poetical expressions (see Juan de la Cruz 1988, Cántico B22:1 and the related note).

18. In reality, a clear-cut distinction of a wakeful state of consciousness of mystical content and a mystical state of consciousness is mainly a definitional problem as they probably are related along a continuum where it is the quantity of consciousness that sets the bounds between the two kinds.

moderate or a relatively low level of arousal also will be advantageous once the epicentres have grown strong enough.

Combining this with the evidence in the works of John of the Cross, an explanation of why mystical states are obtained more easily, effortlessly, and with less control on the part of the mystic as the developmental process advances, I would suggest that in the very beginning of the process focused attention to diverse mystical conceptions (aided by meditation and sensory deprivation) may, at some point, grow so strong that it culminates in such a degree of consciousness, with internalized attention, that the subject will be completely unaware of the external world. With considerable effort, the subject has then achieved the inducement of a mystical state of consciousness. Much further into the developmental process, the relevant epicentres have become so strong that numerous objects, events, and thoughts, etc., are apt to trigger the recruitment and maintenence of neuronal gestalts constituting mystical consciousness. At that point, no efforts will be requested on the part of the subject in order to enter into a mystical state, just as he/she will have no control of it at all. The epicentres of mystical love will have grown so strong that the net of associations will be so extended that numerous objects, events, ideas, etc. may trigger an epicentre that, in turn, will induce a mystical state.

In John of the Cross' case two dissimilar kinds of mystical mastery can be identified, namely the mastery of having mystical states and the mastery of emotions of mystical love. The two kinds pertain to the quantity and the quality of mystical states respectively. Following John of the Cross, there are two distinct skills to be learned in the course of mystical development and these are the realization of mystical states and the display of mystical emotions of love. In his own conceptualization of the matter, the first is a conditioning of the soul, by which it is stripped of its humanness, and the second consists of learning *how* to love God.

With respect to the mastery of having mystical states, this is at once a matter of the quantity and the quality of consciousness. In general, a proficient mystic can be defined as a person who is able to have conscious states of mystical quality in such quantity that he/she temporarily is completely detached from the external world.

Neurologically, the proficiency in having a mystical state necessitates the existence of a relevant epicentre of such strength that it enables the recruitment of a group of neurons that is not only large enough for the generation of consciousness, but also for the defeat of competing groups of neurons and for the recruitment of another closely associated epicentre that can take over from the first (and so on for some time) to form a connected sequence of consciousness. Cognitively, it requires that a state of consciousness is of such depth that focused attention to associated mystical conceptions can be internalized to such an extent that the external world is shut off completely (for some time). Correlating this with John of the Cross' works, the developmental point of achieving mastery of mystical states seems to be identical with (and is presumably the reason for) his own identification of the initiation of the actual mystical process. This implies that the first stage is initiated once a mystic begins to have actual mystical states at all, that is, as soon as focused attention to mystical conceptions (and emotions) can be internalized to such a degree and consciousness attain such depth that there is unawareness of the external world. His identification of the initiation of the second stage may, on the other hand, be based on a turn in the improvement in the proficiency in having mystical states enabling much deeper, more extended, and more lasting consciousness of mystical love.

Turning to the second kind of mystical mastery, the mastery of emotions of mystical love, it is evident from the works of John of the Cross that a consequence of mystical development (insofar as the goal is mastery of emotions of mystical love as in John of the Cross' teachings) is that the competers of the desired mystical consciousness shifts from various non-mystical conceptions (externally or cognitively derived) to conceptions of mystical love. Going into a little more detail, the point is that already from the first classified stage and onwards, external events and objects are no longer much of a problem, inasmuch as attention already has become highly internalized. That which should be suppressed in the major part of the first stage are therefore primarily those cognitively derived internal representations that are considered sensuous or otherwise inappropriate by John of the Cross. Throughout the second stage (the part where a mystic heads more directly for mastery of emotions of mystical love), the cognitive representations (cognitively derived, of course) that should be attacked and subdued are mostly of a kind considered to be more spiritual but still disadvantageous.

At the neurological level of describing the matter, it appears that in the course of the second stage of mystical development, the emotional representations of mystical love gradually take up an increasing proportion of the total sum of representations stored in the strengths of the synaptic connections within the neuronal groups constituting the epicentres of mystical love and the related associations. In the beginning of the stage, the more conceptual representations of mystical love strongly outnumber the emotional representations which, at that point, still have not had that much impact on neural structures. It seems likely, though, that the emotional aspect is strengthened relatively more than the conceptual aspect giving rise to the change in the proportion of the two. In general, it seems that conceptions of mystical love generate emotions of mystical love which means that feelings of mystical emotions go along with consciousness of conceptions of mystical love in mystical states (and — in less quantity — in wakeful states). Yet, this ought not in itself change the proportion of the synaptic strengths that the two kinds of representations occupy. How can it be explained that, following the evidence in the works of John of the Cross, this relationship seemingly changes so fundamentally? It seems most likely that the reason for this is that the display of the more conceptual and the emotional representations respectively do not have equal effects on neural structures. In agreement with Damasio's theory of emotions, it appears that the display of emotions will boost the effect that the activation of a group of neurons has on the synaptic connections of the activated neurons. This coincidentally reinforces the strengthening of both aspects of mystical love and mainly may explain how the strengthening of epicentres of mystical love is accelerated through the display of emotions of mystical love. Joining Damasio's theory and the evidence in John of the Cross, I would suggest that the particular synaptic connections, modified by representations of *emotions* of mystical love, are modified relatively more than those modified by *conceptions* of mystical love. When the emotional representations gradually begin to dominate mystical consciousness to a greater and greater extent, the effects on neural structures of the emotional aspect of mystical love will obviously be fostered even more (with an escalation of the developmental speed as the result).

At some point in the developmental process (toward the end of the second stage where the touches of union appear), the proportion of the emotional aspect of epicentres of mystical love has grown so strong that the emotional representations occasionally are permitted to dominate mystical consciousness. The emotional aspect has not yet taken so much over from the conceptual aspect that the former can be sure to beat the latter. Hence, the more conceptual representations still have very good chances of overpowering the emotional representations during a mystical state (which seems to be what may happen in the mystical states referred to as touches of union). As mentioned above, a mystical consciousness dominated by representations of emotions of mystical love will promote the further strengthening of the emotional aspect of epicentres and associations of mystical love very much and thus give a very strong impetus to the progression towards the mastery of emotions of mystical love.

John of the Cross' writings do not give an unambiguous picture of the way that the change in the degree of dominance of the more conceptual and the emotional aspect of mystical love in mystical states has progressed. The original poetic *Canticle* indicates that the two aspects have been equally competitive for an extended period. Neurologically, this implies that during this period the conceptual and the emotional representations respectively have occupied a more or less equal amount of synaptic strengths of the epicentres and associations concerned. If the original *Canticle* is followed it seems, in other words, that there has been a strong competition between the two aspects of mystical consciousness for quite a while. The revised *Canticle*, on the contrary, indicates that the emotional aspect has taken much longer to become really competitive. Yet, when it finally did grow sufficiently competitive, the representations of emotions of mystical love shortly began to dominate mystical consciousness completely (throughout all mystical states, that is). This further implies that there has been no strong competition between the two aspects of mystical love for a prolonged period of time.

As I have mentioned before, John of the Cross' works are also highly uncertain documents of the exact point at which he has reached a developmental state enabling that which he has conceived of as an undisturbable mystical state and which I consider to be the point of reaching mastery of emotions of mystical love. Of course, it is not a matter of identifying an exact point in time (which evidently is impossible as well as it would be trivial). The trouble is that the two versions of the *Canticle* relates the early part of the third, classified stage differently concerning this point. Following the revised *Canticle* (which I deem the more relevant in this particular context), mastery of emotions of mystical love is that which instantiates a mystic in the third stage. The original *Canticle*, on the other hand, defers this developmental state to somewhat into the third stage (whereby it is no longer this developmental change that has motivated the identification of the transition from the one to the other stage).

Mastery of emotions of mystical love is achieved when the competitive power of the emotional and the conceptual aspect of mystical love (or the sum of the synaptic strengths storing each of the respective representations) has been inverted so that the emotional aspect, which was previously the weaker one, has grown stronger than the conceptual aspect of mystical love. Becoming a master of emotions of mystical love means that the subject is not only able to realize mystical consciousness dominated by emotions of mystical love, but furthermore that he/she is capable of exclusively having this kind of mystical state. The master of emotions of mystical love thus no longer has mystical states that are dominated by the more conceptual mystical contents.

The difference between conceptions and emotions of mystical love

Since mastery of mystical love is the developmental point marking the qualitative discontinuity between the more conceptual and the purely emotional mystical states documented by John of the Cross, a more detailed explanation of the distinction of the two kinds of states will be a natural extension of the above discussion. Greenfield's theory of consciousness is useful for an explanation of the way that the content of mystical consciousness changes from conceptions to emotions of mystical love. Damasio's theory of emotions, on the other hand, serves to explain what emotional content actually is at a more general level. One of the main points in Greenfield's theory of consciousness is that only one consciousness prevails at a time. She suggests that the reason for this probably is that it is not possible to form two neuronal groups sufficiently large for the generation of two consciousnesses at the same time (1995, 89). It is thus not possible simultaneously to be conscious of more than one thing. But the consciousness of something does not necessarily entail that there is equal awareness of all of the associations that the epicentre of that something triggers. In this way, there may be varying degrees of consciousness of the associations triggered by something (Greenfield 1995, 95). At the level of neurons, this seems to imply that although all of the neurons aggregated around a triggering epicentre contribute to the consciousness of something, it is not necessarily the case that all of the neurons give rise to equal degrees of awareness of the associations of that something. Presumably, the degrees of consciousness will be contingent on the varying strengths of the synaptic connections and the distance between the diverse neurons and the recruiting epicentres. Greenfield's theory implies that there can be simultaneous consciousness of both emotions and conceptions of mystical love, but that there will not necessarily be equal degrees of consciousness of both. Actually, the degree of the one or the other may be so low that there is no awareness of it (see Greenfield 1995, 95 for an example).

Furthermore, the point that a *state* of consciousness spans several consciousnesses of more or less closely associated foci should be taken into account in an explanation of the dissimilar contents of mystical states and the gradual change from the one to the other. Thus mystical consciousness can be expected typically to shift slowly and smoothly from one aspect of mystical love to another closely associated aspect of such love.

Turning to the theory of emotions, Damasio points out that emotions are triggered by something non-emotional. Connecting this point with the varying degrees of consciousness, it seems likely that epicentres of mystical consciousnesses generally (or maybe exclusively) relate to conceptions of mystical love. The activation of one such epicentre then triggers various amounts and proportions of associations of mystically relevant conceptions and the responding emotions. in the beginning of mystical development an epicentre will trigger more conceptual than emotional associations, just as the former will be more 'central' to consciousness than the latter. Yet the proportion of the amount of the two kinds of associations as well as their relative centrality will change gradually as the process advances. At some point very few (or maybe even none) of the more conceptual associations will be triggered and these will furthermore be relegated to the periphery of consciousness. Hence there will also be varying degrees of consciousness of the two kinds of content in the diverse parts of the developmental process. To be specific, there may be little awareness of the emotional representations in early mystical states. At that point the emotions are felt although they do not dominate consciousness.[19] As mystical development progresses there will be increasing awareness of the emotions (as the synaptic connections of the neurons concerned gain in strength). Towards the end of the second stage in John of the Cross' classification of the process, mystical consciousness may be fully dominated by emotional representations either with unawareness of or with a complete overriding of the more conceptual representations. The shifting mystical consciousnesses of a mystical state in this part of the developmental process may all be equally emotional in quality or they may shift between the two kinds of content.[20] Apparently, it is mystical states with such shifts in the consciousness of the more conceptual representations and emotional representations that John of the Cross metaphorically has described in a whole number of verses in the *Canticle* as diverse peaceful situations that are disturbed — or at the risk of being disturbed — by various intruders. Similarly, it is apparently these less smooth shifts in consciousness that have motivated his descriptions of the touches of union where a very fragile and easily ruined kind of knowlegde is received. In the final part of the process, mystical states will all exclusively be dominated by emotional representations (it is also at this point uncertain whether there is only unawareness of the more conceptual associations or there are no such associations in these mystical states).

John of the Cross' ranking of the value of emotions over conceptions of mystical love could have been motivated by various points. One of the more specific reasons why mystical emotions have appeared so much more attractive to John of the Cross than mystical conceptions could be that he has believed them (the emotions, that is) to correspond more truly to his goals of

19. It seems pertinent to stress that I understand a feeling of some emotion in the light of a combination of the theories proposed by Greenfield and Damasio respectively, whereby there can be various degrees of conscious awareness of a feeling, and a feeling is the representation of an emotion juxtaposed to the something that triggered the emotion.
20. It is thus not impossible for consciousness to shift from the one to the other in the course of a mystical state. John of the Cross' writings indicate that consciousness in mystical states have shifted only from the one to the other (from mystical emotions to mystical conceptions) and not the other way round. It is impossible to determine whether this actually has been the case or this unbalance simply follows from his preferences, as he may have considered it irrelevant to mention a desirable shift from consciousness of mystical conceptions to that of mystical emotions but absolutely pressing to describe the disastrous shift in the opposite direction.

approximating God. Still, it could also be because they have been exceptionally pleasant. Or it could be a combination of both. The first possibility is supported by his conception of God as being without form and of the importance of conforming with His formlessness. Since union is believed to take place in the soul of a person, the soul must be free of forms before union is possible (inasmuch as two opposites cannot exist in one subject in John of the Cross' Aristotelian understanding). This would indeed make sense of his preference for those mystical states that he considered to be formless. In fact the uncovering of his motives for giving a higher priority to emotions of mystical love than to the conceptions of that love is a little more intricate than this, though, as it is equally possible that it is the pleasantness of the mystical emotions that has convinced John of the Cross (and other mystics before him) of the divineness of this kind of consciousness. And that it is this conviction that has rendered the philosophical theory plausible and relevant. Yet, his uncompromising preference for the emotional content in mystical states must have been based on his experience that the more conceptual content of mystical states actually subtracted from the more emotional content. It seems most plausible that the reason why he has considered the coincidence of the representations of the two kinds of mystical content to be so utterly disadvantageous and harmful is that he has known that awareness of any kind of the more conceptual representations *reduced* the degree of emotionality in a particular state.

The quality of emotions of mystical love

It is now time to consider what emotions of mystical love are from the general perspective of Damasio's neurological theory of emotions. Initially, it seems germane to discuss the way in which the emotions displayed in mystical states are mystical. I wish to stress that I do not believe that the emotions of mystical love have anything in common with ordinary emotions of love. Yet, unlike ordinary emotions of love, the emotions in mystical states are generated in response to conceptions of the mystical love between God and the soul. This should be the point of departure for an evaluation of the quality of emotions of mystical love.

In Damasio's definition, feelings are direct perceptions of bodily events in the form of representations of changes in the structure and the state of the body (where body refers to heart, lungs, guts, and muscles as distinct from the nerve tissue constituting the brain). The content of a feeling is the state of the body. Most of the time it is simply the bodily states securing the perpetuation of life that are represented in the brain, giving rise to what Damasio refers to as 'background feelings' (the feeling of life itself). One of the points that

Damasio underscores repeatedly is that the representations of the body states are juxtaposed with the representations of something else (which is not part of the body but may — or may not — be part of the brain) and that feelings give quality of goodness (pleasure) or badness (pain) to that something (evidently, both kinds of representations are cognitive as they both occur in the brain). Accordingly, the representations of body states and the something else (within or outside of the brain) are separate. Furthermore, he stresses — and this is very important — that the representations of body states appear after the other representations, which means that changes in body states respond to (are triggered by) mental processes (Damasio 1987, especially ch's. 5 and 7).

Once in a while, something (within or outside of the brain) triggers an emotional response giving rise to the feeling of emotions (replacing the background feelings). According to Damasio, emotions are a collection of a whole number of changes in the state of the body (including externally visible changes like that of skin colour, body posture, facial expression, for instance) generated in response to thoughts, objects, or events. But once the emotional responses (the changes in body state) are triggered, they, in turn, modulate further brain processes (by the transmission of various neurotransmitters — affecting the level of arousal for instance — or hormones) (Damasio 1987, 139). As in the case of background feelings, the feeling of an emotion is the juxtaposition of the representations of body state and the representations of whatever triggered the emotions in the first place.

This theory provides an explanation of emotions and their relation to brain processes that may throw new light on both the emotional aspect of mystical states and its relation to the more conceptual aspect. I shall start out with the issue of how emotions of mystical love arise. Joining Damasio's and Greenfield's theories, it seems that in the more advanced part of mystical development, a number of epicentres of emotions of mystical relevance are reasonably strong (the specific strength depending on the exact developmental point) so that various aspects of the life of an individual in one way or another are related to these emotions and therefore activate one or more of the relevant epicentres. To be very concrete, this means that in the life of a mystic living in the religious surroundings of a monastery and among religious people (as in the case of John of the Cross) a great deal of everyday life is somehow related to religious, and often mystical, conceptions. This means that just about any object, event, or thought is apt to trigger some degree of emotions of mystical love. Whenever other conditions in the cognitive system are expedient (like inactivity and a propitious level of arousal), an epicentre of mystically relevant conceptions gets the chance to recruit a neuronal group large enough for the generation of mystical consciousness (thereby inducing a mystical state). In the light of Damasio's theory, it is clear that along with a mystical state of more conceptual quality, emotions of mystical love are generated in response to the conceptions of that love. So, although consciousness in such a case will not be dominated by emotional representations, the emotions will nonetheless be represented cognitively and thus *felt*. The emotions will furthermore affect the more conceptual representations in mystical consciousness.

In the final part of mystical development, the quality of mystical states become purely emotional (it seems). However, as Damasio makes clear, it is still something else that gives rise to the emotions. This something would supposedly be mystical conceptions of some aspect of the love between God and the soul. At this very advanced developmental stage, almost anything would probably be associated with such conceptions in some degree or other, so that numerous mundane occurrences would trigger a wakeful consciousness of mystically relevant conceptions. Wakeful consciousness of such conceptions would in many cases give rise not only to the responding emotions, but to mystical consciousness of such emotions (that is to say, a certain and very large quantity of the consciousness concerned). It would thus be the wakeful consciousness of mystical conceptions that had induced a mystical state of emotional quality. Following John of the Cross, the mystical state would be focused on emotions of mystical love right from the start implying at the same time, that the representations of mystical conceptions had terminated.[21]

Correlating the theories of emotions and consciousness respectively with the evidence from the works of John of the Cross, it strikes me that the purely emotional content of his more advanced mystical states may be rather special (maybe even unique) to this kind of conscious state. In wakeful states it appears that one is conscious of something and feels the corresponding emotions (whenever there are such emotions). It seems likely that the proportions of the two kinds of representations may vary somewhat, even if the more typical case is that the quantity of the two is balanced more or less so that they increase and decrease in correlation.

21. In this place it seems suitable to point out, that I generally have preferred the term emotions for feelings because the definition of feelings proposed by Damasio requires that the emotional representations are juxtaposed to the representations of the something that triggered them. Since the evidence in the writings of John of the Cross indicates that there is little or maybe even no awareness of the more conceptual representations triggering the emotional response, it seems likely that the juxtaposing representations similarly are relegated to the periphery of consciousness, at least during the major part of the mystical state. Hence, my preference for the term emotions does not imply that I believe that there is no juxtaposition at all but that I deem the degree of it highly uncertain (it may be rather insignificant).

Addressing the issue of what mystical emotions of love are from the perspective of Damasio's theory of emotions, I would suggest that they are pleasurable changes in body state generated in response to mystical conceptions of the love between God and the soul. The content in mystical consciousness focused on such emotions is the cognitive representations of the emotional changes in body state. With John of the Cross' accounts of mystical states as evidence, it is manifest that the pleasantness of mystical emotions more specifically consists in their being contented, sedate, and serene. Furthermore, it appears that these emotions are relatively varied in quality.[22] It does not seem unlikely that the emotional representations will seem to be free of form and images (as John of the Cross has described them) to the subject, and that this is the reason why such mystical states often are described as being contentless. In my view, this is the most plausible explanation of how conscious experience of *something* that seems like *nothing* is possible.

The unfolding of mystical development

Apparent discontinuity but actual continuity

Introducing this section, I shall first restate my view on the general relation of mystical development and other kinds of human development. In my opinion, mystical development is on many points comparable to the normal development of children. Still, on various points, it can also be expected to differ significantly from child development. The principal justification for assuming comparability of the two kinds of development is that they presumably capitalize on the same resources. The human mind is highly flexible and adaptive due to its complexity. The same resources can therefore be employed for numerous purposes. However, there is at least one fundamental difference between mystical and normal development. In general, psychologists seem to agree that the early development of the human mind is directed at various specific, cognitive domains. In agreement with Karmiloff-Smith's theory, the initial development of cognitive domains presumably involves the coincident specification of the domain and the acquisition of the knowledge sustaining it. This is hardly the case with mystical development. Mystical development, typically initiated in adulthood, is a further development of already developed cognitive structures. Hence the development leading to mastery of mystical states barely involves a specification of

---

22. When this is less obvious, it is because the variations in the descriptions need not necessarily be motivated by variations in the described as they could be the product of expressive creativity, presumably motivated by his wish to communicate and not only express his experience.

domains. It is more likely that it entails a more general development or conditioning of cognitive abilities.

Furthermore, it is appropriate to distinguish the levels of analyzing human development. As pointed out by Thelen and Smith, development seems sequential and discontinuous at the macro-level of describing the process, although there really is continuity at the micro-level. In this way, development simultaneously involves continuity and discontinuity (1994, 31). As an example, the relation of mystical states and mystical development can be said to correspond to that of the micro-level and the macro-level. At the micro-level, the process of mystical development can be described as progressing from one mystical state to another, each leaving its minor traces of development in the mind of the mystic. At the macro-level, mystical development can, at any point in the process, be described in its entirety as a composite of cognitive changes.

With more specific respect to the progression of the process that has resulted in the mystical development of John of the Cross, it is relevant to make a reservation concerning the credibility of his descriptions of the diverse aspects of the process. The point is that, at the time of writing his works, John of the Cross had already redescribed his general mystical experience representationally. In general, personal testimonies of experience have unavoidably been filtered through several representational redescriptions making them a mixture of the redescriptions and the redescribed. Obviously, this means that the experience is not documented directly and that the evidence is not necessarily reliable. Apart from this universal problem facing scholars of human experience, John of the Cross' testimonies of his mystical development entail a particular problem that has to do with the character of his works. The reason for this is, that there is a striking incongruity between the original poetic part of the Spiritual *Canticle* and the later versions of it. Presupposing that the work relates mystical development, John of the Cross seems to have changed his mind about the unfolding of it. Seemingly, he has gradually imposed a more and more rigid structure onto it. Thus, it is not impossible that he initially has regarded the developmental process as rather disorderly, whereas he later on came to see it as a fairly organized process. Accordingly, some of his later conceptualizations of the process suggest that the developmental process has progressed steadily in a predetermined and fixed sequence of stages.

As opposed to evidence in John of the Cross' works, the evidence supporting psychological studies of ordinary development generally derives from researchers' more direct observations of developmental changes.[23] Hence,

___

23. One of the disadvantages of such evidence is, on the other hand, that the data often are produced artificially (in laboratory experiments) and therefore may be incon-

theories and evidence of the normal development of children may contribute to throw light on the way that mystical development has advanced. In the following, I shall therefore estimate John of the Cross' description of the unfolding of mystical development in a general perspective and relate it to evidence and theories of child development. With respect to the details of developmental leaps, theories disagree on major points. It seems germane to point out that the divergence of cognitive theories of child development implies that psychologists, in many cases, draw contrasting conclusions on crucial points sometimes even based on the same data. Human development is a field of study that leaves many points open to interpretation.

With respect to the way that human development unfolds, Karmiloff-Smith and Thelen and Smith disagree, for instance, on fundamental points. Karmiloff-Smith suggests that ordinary, domain-specific development evolves in phases and not stages. By this she intends to emphasize that the development of a domain takes place recurrently and at different times within various micro-domains. More specifically, she proposes an hypothesis that various micro-domains of a cognitive domain are developed in phases and that the domain as a whole is developed repeatedly (1992, ch. 1). With respect to this latter aspect of the hypothesis, her point is that development is rede-scribed representationally by the subject. In the present context, the main point of interest is the relative flexibility and non-rigidity of the theory. The theory implies that the termination of one developmental phase and the beginning of a new does not necessarily mean that a domain (or a cognitive ability) is fully developed. Far from. It simply means that one little step towards the development of the particular domain has been taken. Ultimately, her theory suggests that development is unending.

On the basis of systems (or complexity) theory, Thelen and Smith delineate a general theory of development supported with evidence from their empirical study of the way that children learn to walk.[24] They advance a general hypo-thesis of the stages of the ordinary development of children suggesting that development at the more general macro-level is linear, qualitative, and irrever-sible, whereas development at the more specific micro-level is disorderly, non-linear, and reversible. Moreover, they suggest that development is modular[25]

gruent with more natural conditions of development (a point often made by U. Neisser, e.g., 1987, his introduction). Moreover, many actual changes may be much too subtle to observe while other changes (as in the case of walking studied by Thelen and Smith) may be easily observable.

24. It is important to point out that Karmiloff-Smith's theory draws on evidence of the more conceptual aspects of development while Thelen and Smith specifically support their theory with evidence of the more behavioural aspects of development.

25. The use of the term 'modular' is not unproblematic in the context of cognitive theory, where modules conventionally denote informationally, encapsulated input-processing

and heterochronic which means that structures and functions do not develop synchronously and simultaneously (1994, xiv-xvi). Like Karmiloff-Smith, Thelen and Smith regard development as a highly flexible process that is unpredictable and (often) disorderly.[26]

The theories proposed by Thelen and Smith and Karmiloff-Smith respectively converge on at least one point which is the ambition to construct a theory that will account for the flexible and often disorderly progression of the development of children. In this respect, both theories suggest that development is asynchronous and segmented. The theories may jointly contribute to explain diverse aspects of the evidence of the unfolding of John of the Cross' mystical development. Both theories support the evidence that mystical development, at the macro-level of description, has unfolded in phases and/or stages (where a phase concerns selected aspects of development and is part of a more general stage that, in turn, concerns more general changes brought out in the course of development).

I shall now turn to the more concrete evidence in John of the Cross' works. The original poem in the *Canticle* indicates that John of the Cross' mystical development has not always unfolded in straight and orderly progression. If the structure of the poem really relates anything about the progression of mystical development, then it seems that the process has been rather disorderly. To the extent that the original poem relates mystical development, the structure of the poem indicates that mystical development is apt to relapse once in a while. An advance achieved through development may temporarily be lost. If this is correlated with Thelen and Smith's theory, the relapses should only occur within a particular phase or stage, though, and not between them. If this holds good for mystical development as well, then the original poem in the *Canticle* provides a false picture of the progression of the developmental process, inasmuch as it indicates that relapses may transgress the stages.

In relation to the above, John of the Cross' works further provide evidence

---

units (see Karmiloff-Smith 1992, 6). Hence, it should be stressed that the term in their use denotes that cognitive domains are developed in parts (basically, the term is rather similar to Karmiloff-Smith's microdomains).

26. Apart from this, the two theories diverge on various points of which the most fundamental concerns cognitive representations. In Karmiloff-Smith's theory, the redescription of cognitive representations play an important role for the promotion of development. Once a specific behaviour is mastered, development is further promoted by recurrent redescriptions of cognitive representations of the knowledge sustaining that behaviour. It is this that keeps on pushing development forward (1992, ch. 1). Thelen and Smith, on the contrary, completely deny the importance of cognitive representations for development (1994, 42, see Karmiloff-Smith and Johnson 1994 for a critique).

of the developmental relation of various kinds of mystical states and it is possible that this will explain the occasional regressions in the process. From a general perspective, mystical states do seem to have improved steadily throughout the whole process. More specifically, it seems that the progression of mystical states has been less regular, though. Thus, in accord with the original poem in the *Canticle*, it looks as if mystical states that are either inferior or superior to one another (on all or some points) may occur interchangingly through a fairly extended part of the process. Probably, such a part would be within the limits of one of the stages distinguished by John of the Cross or maybe even delimited to specific substages. In the long run, it is rather certain that mystical states do improve in various ways. But during the progression of the process, occasional exceptions to the general progress may not have been uncommon. In my view, this clearly supports the relevance of analyzing development at two levels, as emphasized by Thelen and Smith. Likewise, their characterization of development at the macro-level (at which it is linear and irreversible) and at the micro-level (at which it is non-linear and disorderly) respectively seems to parallel the difference between the progression of mystical development in general and the progression at the level of particular mystical states.

The differences between the first and the second poem in the *Canticle* additionally contribute to elucidate the question about how mystical states change as a result of mystical development. There is little doubt that both renditions of the poem recount the realization of selected mystical states. The poetical variation with which they are expressed makes direct comparison of the described states very difficult, though. On the basis of the poem alone, it is therefore not easy to identify if and how mystical states improve. Yet, there are no reasons to question the point that mystical states improve in various ways. This does not necessarily mean, though, that all mystical states at some point in the process are entirely superior to all earlier mystical states. Inasmuch as the improvement of mystical states is closely connected to the unfolding of the process, it is no surprise that the two poems give highly diverging accounts of this issue as well. It is not an uncomplicated matter to discriminate the variations in mystical states potentially underlying the diverse lyrical accounts of love encounters. It is therefore also difficult to compare the descriptions of mystical states in the various parts of the *Canticle* but it seems, nevertheless, that the accounts of the improvements in mystical states are significantly dissimilar in the two renditions of the *Canticle* (including both the poetic and the prose part of the work). Thus, it is rather certain that the reorganized poem describes a more steady progression in mystical states than the original poem does, at least regarding the aspect of the external conditions of the love encounters (the mystical states, that is). In the reorganized poem, the external conditions are depicted as improving continuously. The meetings between the lovers grow continuously more peaceful and undisturbed. This is far from the case in the original poem where it is evident that potential disturbers of the mystical peace still constitute a considerable danger rather late in the poem, that is to say, in the verses A29-31. In particular, it should be pointed out that these external dangers are described in direct continuation of the narration of the mystical state supposedly initiating the final stage when all the potential disturbances ought to have been eliminated.

This particular discrepancy between the original and the revised poem suggests two points. First, it seems that the risk that potential disturbers (which I interpret as references to the more specific and conceptual cognitive representations) will interrupt the mystical peace, does not diminish in continuous and uninterrupted progress throughout mystical development. It is rather certain that a mystic develops an ability to avoid (the dominance of) undesirable cognitive representations in mystical states. Yet, the evidence strongly indicates that, in reality, it is rather accidental whether mystical consciousness dominated by emotional representations in a specific part of the developmental process suddenly shifts to mystical consciousness dominated by more conceptual representations (thereby interrupting the emotional peace), whereas an entire mystical state of equally emotional quality in the same part of the process seemingly remains free of the more conceptual aspect. This is, in fact, both explainable and predictable on the basis of Greenfield's theory of competing consciousnesses, because some randomness is the natural result of competitive processes. Second, the original poem seems to document that the more specific cognitive representations still comprise a danger in the beginning of the final stage. This challenges either (1) John of the Cross' own claim that absolute purity is the requisite condition for entrance into this stage (presupposing that it is correct that purity is tantamount to the avoidance of [the dominance of] the more specific cognitive representations), (2) his claim about the point of transition to the stage, or (3) his argument of the correspondence about the developmental stages and the verses in the poem.

I would suggest that the issues of the alternation of the more and less advanced mystical states and the occasional developmental relapses pertain to the one and the same aspect of mystical experience, although described at the micro-level and the macro-level respectively. Mystical development apparently produces some permanent changes (like estrangement and indifference towards the world), but the most significant change is the development of proficiency in the realization of mystical states. Going through a more advanced mystical state (with respect to various factors) will therefore be a sign of incipient developmental progress. As a consequence of this, having mystical states that are less advanced will from then on seem like developmental deterioration. But, in fact, it seems likely that it is normal for development to proceed this way. It seems plain that just because a mystic has had a very sublime mystical state of emotional content without the otherwise disturbing more conceptual cognitive representations this does not necessarily mean that he/she has developed proficiency in this kind of mystical state. Probably, developmental progress will at that point still only be nascent which means that it may take a long time for it to take root (to borrow an expression from John of the Cross). And while development is just beginning to take a step forward in this way, occasional backslides are predictable.

Transition between stages

At the macro-level of description, one of the crucial questions related to the unfolding of development concerns the passage from one phase in the process to another. What is it that makes a system in development shift from minor to major changes at some particular point thereby causing a developmental bounce? Two closely connected problems are involved in this, namely the cause of transition and the point at which it occurs. To put it differently, the issue of what it is that provokes development to depart from one phase and pass on to another simultaneously encompasses the problem of identifying the developmental point at which this occurs. Surprisingly, Karmiloff-Smith and Thelen and Smith propose contrasting hypotheses of the matter setting off the uncertainty about the relationship between theory and evidence.

In Karmiloff-Smith's theory, representational redescription plays a major role as a cause of further development. She opposes the (widespread) conviction that development is prompted by conflict (between something desired and the ability to achieve it, for instance). The idea that conflict is the cause of developmental progress implies that developmental phase-shifts are provoked because the system gets into trouble and needs to find a solution to the problem, so to speak. In Karmiloff-Smith's view, the opposite is more often the case. Change is typically driven by representational redescription which is driven by itself. Her point is that systems also change when they are in equilibrium (1992, 172-73). Development does not presuppose conflict and conflict does not necessarily advance development. According to her theory, the development of a cognitive domain sooner or later leads to mastery of some ability. Behavioural mastery is achieved when a part of the system functions efficiently and the whole system is in stability. Once an ability is mastered fully, the knowledge sustaining the ability is redescribed representationally and it is this that gives a further impetus to development. Consequently, transition occurs somewhere in between the achievement of behavioural mastery and representational redescription (1992, 24, 58, and 155).

Contrary to Karmiloff-Smith, Thelen and Smith believe that it is the need for developmental progress that causes further development. They suggest that transition from one stage to another occurs when mastered strategies have become insufficient (1994, 43). Their understanding of developmental transitions is based on systems (or complexity) theory and, according to this view, transition involves several steps. The first is that the stability of a system decreases in periods leading up to transition. Thereupon, instability and chaos take over from stability and order in the actual period of transition. Only thereafter can the system enter a new period of stability and order (1994, 63).

Taking Karmiloff-Smith's theory as a starting point, it would seem that the fulfilment of one phase can be the achievement of behavioural mastery (resulting from the development of a microdomain) while another and subsequent phase can be initiated with redescription of the cognitive representations of that behaviour. During the period of representational redescription there will typically be some degree of instability. Somewhat schematically, the transitional point between two phases would succeed behavioural mastery. In agreement with Thelen and Smith, behavioural mastery will be achieved somewhere in the middle of a phase/stage. Following their theory, the system will remain at the same developmental stage as long as cognitive abilities correspond with the subject's desires. It is not until changes are requisite (for the obtainment of desired events or objects) that changes are provoked. In their theory, minor fluctuations of a system is a symptom that it approaches transition, and severe instability is a symptom that it is in transition.

I have presented the two contrasting hypotheses of developmental transition in order to discuss them in relation to John of the Cross' accounts of the matter. He explicitly offers his view about the points of transition in mystical development. He indicates that certain mystical states have formed the passages between the stages of the mystical process. This is my formulation, of course, and is a fact with modifications. Actually, it seems to be the beginning of new stages that have been inaugurated with the occurrence of a new kind of mystical state. He presents this idea in his interpretation of the particular verses in the *Canticle* interpreted as descriptions of the particular mystical states constituting points of transition.[27] It would therefore seem that new types of mystical states have begun to occur from the beginning of each new stage. This does not, of course, document much about the end of the preceding stage or a potential period in between stages. But it does indicate

---

27. It is a little uncertain, though, to which extent this interpretation is reliable. Yet, in all of the parts of his interpretation of the poem he maintains that specific mystical states narrated in particular verses have been points of transition between stages. He has, on the other hand, changed his interpretations about which particular verses it is that describe the transitions.

that the period preceding a new stage prepares the subject for transition. This point is supported by his description of the mystical states referred to as 'touches of union' that contribute importantly to the fulfilment of the purifying part of the process and which are typical of the end of the second stage. This is a sign that the part of mystical development effectuated in the second stage has built up mastery of a cognitive ability that John of the Cross describes as mystical purity.

John of the Cross has specifically addressed the issue of the preconditions for transition from the second to the third stage of mystical development. He states that the last mystical stage will be entered once the faculties of the soul are completely emptied of specific forms and images. Actually, John of the Cross expresses it the other way round, that is to say, the specific knowledge will be lost when the subject arrives at the stage of mystical union (Juan de la Cruz 1988, Subida 3.2:8). This information is indeed very illustrative. It points out that the third stage will be entered as soon as one is ready for it. This further implies that one will be ready when the developmental processes belonging to the second stage have been fulfilled. Or, to put it differently, it indicates that transition is identical with the termination of a part of the developmental process. Elaborating the interpretation of the statement, it reveals that transition will not await some conflict or other need for it to occur. The mystic constantly rushes towards the goal at the end of the process. It demonstrates that the completion of some developmental product, say, the mastery of some ability is requisite for transition. It furthermore indicates that, towards the end of the second stage, a mystic undergoes a final development completing the stage and refining this partial product of development. Consequently, John of the Cross' understanding of his mystical development strongly supports Karmiloff-Smith's hypotheses about the developmental point of transition and about self-promoting development.

The composition of changes

So far, I have discussed the progression or the formation of the developmental process and the passage from one part to another in order to explain how mystical development unfolds in a more general perspective. In addition to these points, it seems relevant to consider the composition of the developmental changes. In the present context the principal concern is how the changes are constituted within the diverse phases or stages. This is primarily a matter of theoretical interest and an issue on which lack of evidence is predictable.

The phases and stages of development presumably relate to two aspects of change in the cognitive system. On the one hand, development presumably does not set to work on all parts of the mind at the same time. If the human mind incorporates several sub-systems, as is generally assumed by cognitive theories, then it seems unlikely that all of the sub-systems are developed simultaneously.[28] On the other hand, it is not unlikely that the same sub-systems go through distinct changes at different times. The point is that the diverse *parts* may be subjected to *various* changes at diverse points in time.

In the following I shall discuss how the changes underlying performative improvements can be explained. In this context, an abstract outline of potential modifications within limited stages or phases may be illustrative. If development leads to alterations of a specific system or sub-system consisting of numerous components, alterations might involve (1) change in the exploitation of selected components, (2) enlargement and/or alterations of selected components, (3) rearrangement of components, and (4) expansion of the net of inter- and/or intra-systemic communication. In reality, these potential changes presumably combine and complement one another over time so that complexes of changes may be classified into phases and stages.

I shall initiate the point with a further interpretation of the earlier referred evidence from the work of Merzenich et al. that there is a phased relation of performative improvements resulting from the learning of a strategy and from the enlargement of specific areas in the brain. Combining this with the theory that acquisition of knowledge results in and is identical with modifications of synaptic strengths, this leads to the inevitable conclusion that the learning of a new strategy does not require new knowledge. How can this be explained? I would suggest that the learning of a new strategy is at once an example of

---

28. This particular aspect of human development supposedly has basic traits in common with biological evolution. There is weighty evidence of similarity at one point at least which is piecemeal progression. Both advance step-by-step towards some unknown end. This implies that neither of the two unfold along a predetermined scheme and that both are phased or piecemeal. The process always progresses towards some nearby end which is an end in itself (not only as a partial end towards the ultimate goal). This means that a process may terminate on various points along a process following a certain route at the expense of numerous others. The route will only be identifiable in retrospection and the end remains unknown until it is reached. In principle, there is hardly any ultimate end to such a process. See Clark for a discussion of this aspect of evolution (1991, ch. 4). In the case of human development, physical and cognitive constraints will eventually terminate the process, of course. In fact, John of the Cross' understanding of mystical development supports the issue that development is piecemeal, although he took the mystical process to be the potential progression along a predestined course. Thus he maintains that it is more common to go only part of the mystical way than to go through with it. The mystical process is marked with limiting points or ends at which the subject going through the development may stop. Ultimately, a person may stop anywhere but, if doing so, he/she will only have obtained a developmental state according to the fulfilment of this limited part of the process.

the kind of change suggested in (1), (3), and (4). More specifically, it involves a change in the exploitation of selected components (1) which can be specified as the application of existing knowledge to a new field (or the mapping of knowledge from one field to another). Furthermore, it presumably involves a rearrangement of components (3) due to the transfer of knowledge from one field to another. Finally, it is the product of an expansion of the net of inter-systemic communication (4). Predictably, these changes will indeed modify neural structures. Supposedly, the structures modified will be more general and more moderate than those specifically related to the behavioural change which, in the case concerned, is a change in the use of the hands and this may be the reason why the changes in neural structure have not been identified in the experiments.

Yet, what about the enlargement of the neural areas (involving the streng-thening of existing synaptic connections and the generation of new synaptic connections resulting from the acquisition of new knowledge) specifically related to use of the hands? How do these changes correspond to the general outline of potential modifications within stages or phases. This change can be explained as the result of the acquisition of new knowledge related to the behaviour concerned. The strengthening of existing synapses illustrates the kind of change suggested in (2) as more specifically can be expected to result from the coincident enlargement and alteration of the synaptic connections. This is because the strengthening of a synapse at once involves an increase in the size of the synapse (its weight) and a modification of the prior synaptic strength. The generation of new synaptic connections is, in turn, a case exem-plifying (4) inasmuch as this change entails an expansion of the net of intra-systemic communication.

In the light of the discussions above, it seems likely that the mystical development of John of the Cross has been quite a bit more complex and compound than the stages classified by himself suggest. By this I do not mean to say that he has misconceived of his mystical development (whether he has or not is trivial in the present context), but rather that his general outline of the process is oversimplified.

For an understanding of the internal components of cognitive develop-ment, it is significant to consider how the various kinds of change relate to the developmental phases and stages identifiable in concrete developmental processes when they are viewed from a general perspective. For the purpose of explaining this aspect of developmental processes, it will be useful to combine the above hypothesis of various kinds of change with Karmiloff-Smith's theory of representational redescription.

In agreement with Karmiloff-Smith's theory, it appears that the deve-lopment of the diverse cognitive domains in children starts out with the

coincident specification of a domain and the acquisition of knowledge (synonymous with the storage of representations of information) related to that
domain. From the point of obtaining behavioural mastery, the process of
redescribing the representations specific to the domain concerned sets in. In
various kinds of adult development, the processes of knowledge acquisition
and representational redescription can be expected to proceed rather differently. In the case of the development of new ways to use the hands, for instance,
it seems that the developmental process starts either with the direct mapping
of already acquired and redescribed knowledge to a new field, or with the
further redescription of that knowledge. In either case this results in greater
cognitive flexibility with respect to the use of the specific knowledge. Accordingly it is the exploitation of existing knowledge (possibly enabled by means
of further representational redescription of it) that has enabled the elaboration
of a successful strategy. It is not until the strategy is mastered fully that the
acquisition of new specific knowledge takes a beginning. I would suggest that
at least part of mystical development corresponds more or less precisely to
this. It seems likely that the development in the pre-mystical stage results from
the elaboration of a strategy (of meditation, it seems) easing the induction of
mystical states, possibly aided by the representational redescription of some
unidentified knowledge. The first and the second stages of mystical development seemingly involve the acquisition of knowledge of mystical love
permitting the realization of mystical states of consciousness. It may also entail
incipient representational redescription of the acquired knowledge but this is
more uncertain. The beginning of the third stage is where both mystical states
and the emotional aspect of mystical love is mastered and this is the point at
which the representational redescription of this (new) knowledge really takes
a beginning. This is presumably also the point at which John of the Cross has
composed his very first work which (apparently) is the most primitive version
of the poetic *Canticle* (including the first 30/31 verses of the later poem). Yet,
it is not until the somewhat later initation of the process of interpretation that
the process of representational redescription has accelerated.

    With respect to the elaboration of useful strategies, it is important to stress
that the development of adult humans generally differs significantly from the
development of adult monkeys. The adult human initiating a new kind of
development typically learns a great deal from other people's experience.[29] The
point is most conspicuous concerning the use of written works but may
addditionally apply to other ways of learning from other people. With the
mystical development of John of the Cross as an example, the fact that he has

---

29. Actually, monkeys may similarly learn from other monkeys or even from humans.
    This aspect of learning, however, plays a much greater role for humans than for
    monkeys.

been able to draw upon written works about mystical experience implies that he has been able to acquire knowledge about strategies that had already been put to the test and had proven to be useful for the initiation of the mystical process. John of the Cross has only needed to acquire this knowledge (which he seemingly has done through conversations with Teresa of Jesus) and then adapt it to and integrate it with his other knowledge (a great deal of which he has acquired in the monastery and the university).

Terminating this chapter, it is pertinent to emphasize that developmental change in general is not restricted to the points of transition separating the diverse phases and stages. The shifts between phases and stages only mark the points at which change has taken a leap (wherefore it is also more easily identifiable). But change is continuous throughout the whole process. Within the diverse phases change supposedly occurs gradually, although not always evenly and at a constant speed.

IX. Conclusion

Following Lawson and McCauley's definition of a definition as a compression of a theory, I have suggested that a mystical state, on the basis of Greenfield's theory of consciousness and Damasio's theory of emotions, can be defined as a conscious state with internalized attention focused on mystical conceptions and possibly the responding emotions, during which consciousness is so deep that there is an unawareness of the external world. In Christian mysticism, the content of mystical consciousness can further be identified as various conceptions and the responding emotions of mystical love which is the love between God and a particular soul. Mystical development can be defined as the specific kind of development that arises out of the repeated and very deep consciousness focused on conceptions and emotions related to mystical matters. This further means that mystical development is initiated long before a person begins to have mystical states of consciousness. The point is, that some degree of mystical development is a precondition for the realization of mystical states. Mystical states and mystical development — springing from mystical ideas —together make up the core of mystical experience. Yet, the concept of mystical experience additionally encompasses a conceptual develop-ment resulting from the recurrent representational redescriptions of the knowledge sustaining mystical states and mystical development.

With respect to the prospects of identifying an intersection of all kinds of religious, extraordinary states, not to mention the chances of distinguishing an intersection of all kinds of extraordinary states, I have suggested that there are no reasons to be too expectant. In fact, I doubt that all of the various kinds of extraordinary states have anything in common but their extraordinariness (which in turn may be due to their common extreme quantities — either very small or very large — of consciousness). In spite of this initial scepticism, I do believe that it is possible (and presumably also fruitful) to identify common properties of selected kinds of extraordinary states. Yet, it is not impossible that there are better chances of identifying such intersections across the border separating the religious from the non-religious extraordinary states. The reason for this is that common properties of extraordinary states supposedly originate in the shared quantities of consciousness (to be specific, I could mention the apparent similarity of the quantities of mystical and depressed states of consciousness). The quality of consciousness does not in itself make a con-scious state extraordinary. With respect to the quality of consciousness, an extraordinary state can therefore be expected to share more with an ordinary state of similar quality (a mystical and a wakeful state focused on mystical ideas, for instance) than with another kind of extraordinary state (a mystical and a shamanist state, for instance).

In light of the above, the accomplishments of theories of mysticism and extraordinary states respectively should be estimated anew. I shall begin with an assessment of the argument of contentless and culturally transcendent mystical states. The theory of mystical experience proposed in the nearby work does not in any way support the argument about contentless mystical states. Yet, this does not necessarily mean that there is nothing at all to the ideas proposed by the theorists of contentless mystical states. It is true that the apologetic aims of many of these theories have been to save mystical states from the contamination of convention thereby sustaining the credibility of the argument about the divine source of mystical states. This aside, there may nonetheless be something to the idea that a certain kind of mystical states to a considerable extent transcend the more specific ideas of the religious traditions. The essence of the point I am making is: it is not completely impossible that some degree of similarity exists between the more developmentally advanced mystical states belonging to different religious traditions (it should be needless to say that no distinct mystical states are identical). It could even be that they are more similar than the more and the less advanced mystical states of the same person. In this respect, I would like to make a prediction that can only be verified on the basis of comparative studies. On the condition that (1) the essence of the mystical ideas of a number of religions all are variations of the theme of love and (2) the emotional aspect of mystical love is given the higher priority, then it is likely that the content of the more advanced mystical states of these traditions will have very much in common, inasmuch as they presumably will all be focused on a mystical version of human emotions of love which, in turn, can be expected to be fundamentally similar in all individuals.

Turning to the theories that the content of mystical states to a considerable extent is determined by the religious traditions within which they occur, these can evidently be supported with the theory that the content of consciousness derives from the cognitive reserve of knowledge of a person. Thus, it seems plain that a person's knowledge of religious matters will be strongly influenced by the particular religious tradition within which it is built up (although this is a point that may be changing with the new and more individually synthesized religions of our time, at least, it may be harder to trace the traditions of the synthesized ideas).

Finally, it is germane to estimate the theories of extraordinary states that the changes of consciousness can be explained with specific changes in the autonomic nervous system (or secondarily responding changes in hemispheric dominance) that typically are generated in response to specific kinds of stimulation. With the mystical states documented in John of the Cross' writings as the example, the theories and evidence of consciousness and emotions provided by Greenfield and Damasio respectively support the suggestion that this kind of mystical state (which presumably is typical of Christian mysticism in general) is dominated by representations of conceptions and the responding emotions (in varying proportions) of mystical love. It is not impossible that the changes in the autonomous system contribute to the body states constituting the emotions of love, of course. However, it is rather unlikely that they purely and simply are the emotions of love in this kind of mystical state. The reason for this is quite plain. The emotions of love (at least the kind of emotions documented in the works of John of the Cross) are generated in response to conceptions of love. The changes in the autonomous system are, on the other hand, generated in response to a great variety of behaviours and conditions. This simultaneously sets off the shortcomings of the theories concerned. If the differences in the diverse kinds of extraordinary states of consciousness can be explained with the diverse behaviours that, in the first place, generated the response in the autonomic system, then these changes do not account for the change in state of consciousness. If, on the other hand, these changes (or the secondarily responding changes in hemispheric dominance) account for the changes in state of consciousness, then the dissimilarities of states of consciousness are left unexplained.

I have argued that evidence and theories of other kinds of development, in particular evidence and theories of the normal development of children, may contribute to explain the developmental aspects of mystical experience. Mystical experience emerges from the capitalization on the same cognitive resources as other kinds of development. It is therefore likely that the processes resulting in dissimilar kinds of development are nonetheless essentially similar. Obviously, the extraordinary (mystical, for instance) development of an adult differs from the normal development of a child, though, on at least one fundamental point, which is the point of departure. In this respect, the main point is that the development of childhood presumably starts out with the coincident specification of the diverse cognitive domains and the acquisition of knowledge sustaining the respective domains. This is clearly not the case with any kind of development initiated in adult life. The present theory of mystical experience suggests that mystical development involves processes of knowledge acquisition, processes of applying knowledge from one domain to another, and processes of representational redescription and interpretation. Basically it is thus only the initial process of the specification of cognitive domains that mystical development definitely does not share with the normal development of children.

For the explanation of both the conceptual and the mystical development involved in mystical experience, Karmiloff-Smith's theory of the cognitive development of children has proven to be very useful. The essence of this theory is that it is the recurrent redescription of representations of information that drives cognitive development beyond the point of behavioural mastery. Karmiloff-Smith's theory additionally contributes, though, to explain the cognitive processes leading to behavioural mastery, through the distinction of the dissimilarities of the two kinds of developmental processes. However, it is the combination of Karmiloff-Smith's theory and the neurological evidence and theory of the development of adult monkeys provided by Merzenich and his colleagues that has enabled the application of her theory, including that of development until the point of behavioural mastery, to the mystical development of John of the Cross. Thus, the combination of the evidence and theories of childhood and adult development suggests that, in adult life, the mastery of some particular behaviour (which is not obtained during the normal development of children) can be reached without the acquisition of any new knowledge simply through the application (or mapping) of knowledge from one field to another (possibly through a further representational redescription of the knowledge).

The neurological theories of epigenetic development combined with Greenfield's theory of consciousness have helped explain the more specific neuronal processes resulting in the mutually dependent mystical states and mystical development. On the basis of these theories, I have suggested that it is the recurrent consciousness of certain mystical ideas and the responding emotions that modifies the synaptic connections storing the knowledge of mystical matters thereby giving rise to mystical development which, in turn, affects all subsequent conscious states of similar ideas and emotions.

In accord with the epigenetic theories of development, it is the very specific developmental processes that determine the developmental products. It is, in other words, the very specific experience of a person that determines the neural structure of a particular brain at any point in time. The neural structure does, in turn, constrain the cognitive abilities of that person at that point in time. In addition to that, the theories in question point out that the very specific way that particular synaptic connections are modified is contingent on the existing neural structure at the time of the neuronal activities causing the changes. To put it differently, the existing neural structure (at any point in time) determines the outcome of the neuronal activities at that point in time. In light of this, it should be clear that the general experience of a person will constrain the person's subsequent experience in various ways. In this respect it should be underscored that it is impossible to predict the way in which a person's general experience will influence that person's subsequent experience.

In the case of John of the Cross there are two identifiable factors that, in particular, seem to have contributed to the fact that he has developed mystically at all. The one factor is the exceptionally prosperous (even if fluctuating) spiritual tendencies of his time. The other factor is his very early introduction to and continuous training in religious life. This has already been initiated when he was a child with his religious schooling, his work at a monastery church, and at a hospital for the poor. As a young man his religious training has been continued first at the Jesuit school, later in the Carmelite order and at the theological study at the University in Salamanca, and finally, it has been completed in the Discalced Carmelite order (although, at that point, mainly through his own efforts). In addition to these points his time in the Carmelite monastery prison in Toledo has doubtlessly contributed significantly to his more specific mystical experience.

At the time of John of the Cross a religious background similar to his was not unusual. Hence, the thriving spiritual religiousness and his personal religious training do not alone explain why he, and not everyone else with a more or less similar religious background, has succeeded in the fulfilment of mystical development. This can only be explained with less easily checkable factors, namely some more specific and unidentifiable aspects of his personal experience and, presumably, some degree of innate disposition. With respect to the latter, such disposition may consist of a relatively low general level of arousal permitting consciousness to grow very deep, extended, and lasting.

On the basis of John of the Cross' works, it is clear that his mystical experience has emerged out of his mystical ideas. The foundation of this complex of ideas are the closely associated conceptions that the human and the divine natures are contraries and separated by an immense distance, but that it is nevertheless possible to liken the soul to God (by stripping it of its human nature) and overcome the distance thereby enabling union of the two. On the basis of these conceptions, John of the Cross reasons that the degree of union of God and the soul is dependent on the soul's condition at any point in time. This implies that the more the soul is liberated from its humanness, the more room there is for God to unite with it (in it), and the more complete the union will be. The process of approximating God mystically is conceived of as a gradual, mystical dying of human nature. It is only natural death that can terminate this process, though, which means that the union of God and the soul is not fulfilled until the eternal union of post-mystical life.

In John of the Cross' understanding, the actual processes resulting in the mystical development of a person are at once purifying and transforming. The soul subjected to these processes is rendered gradually more and more pure and transformed. Somewhat more concretely, the process of purification is conceived of as a gradual emptying of the soul. Initially, the soul is emptied of its desires for and interests in the things of the world whereby it is freed from its attachment to the world. This kind of emptiness produces a very strong desire for God which motivates the person to proceed with the process of approximating Him in spite of the considerable suffering it causes. Later on the soul is emptied of (or drained of) its knowledge of the world which renders the person completely ignorant of and indifferent to worldly matters. This kind of emptiness is even more profitable than the first kind, because it permits the soul to be filled with divine knowledge. More generally, the essence of the process of purification can be described as the elimination of the soul's natural knowledge. The essence of the process of transformation can, on the other hand, be described as the gradual exchange of the soul's natural knowledge with divine knowledge. In this way, the process of transformation actually encompasses that of purification and is thus the more general of the two.

Basically, the means of purification and transformation are the same. The soul is at once purified and transformed through the exertion of mystical love. From a general perspective, any love of God originates in God Himself, inasmuch as the soul's love of God first has to be infused in it by Him. Somewhat more concretely, though, the soul is able to contribute slightly to the total amount of love, although the degree of the soul's contribution to the love is most significant before the actual processes of purification and transformation are initiated. After these processes, the soul's contribution rapidly diminishes until vanishing completely. Although John of the Cross does not make this point explicit, it seems that the soul's contribution to the love of God mainly consists in the elimination of the love of — and interest in — the things of the world, thereby making room for the love of God.

If the processes that first empty and later refill the soul are explained with the theories of consciousness and emotions, it seems to be the continual and growing consciousness of conceptions of mystical love that gradually empties the mind of worldly knowledge or, rather, which reduces the quantity and the significance of this knowledge. Yet, it is the responding emotions of mystical love (which I will suggest *is* that which John of the Cross identifies as divine knowledge) that fill it up with new knowledge or increase the quantity and the significance of this kind of knowledge. The intense consciousness focused on mystical love is initially achieved through meditation (eased by the reduction of sensory stimulation) and later primarily through recurrent mystical states.

At a more general level the developmental process, as it is displayed in the works of John of the Cross, entails two kinds of change yielding each their developmental product, namely the mastery of having mystical states and the mastery of emotions of mystical love. The first kind of mastery permits a person to have conscious states of mystical content in such a quantity that there is complete unawareness of the external world. The second kind of mastery permits the person exclusively to have mystical states dominated with the consciousness of emotions of mystical love.

The development of mastery of having mystical states is obtained through the elaboration and the implementation of a strategy permitting the internalization of attention. At a more specific level, the elaboration and the implementation of a strategy presumably involves an expansion of the net of intersystemic communication (presumably through the generation of new synaptic connections). The internalization of attention is, in turn, profitable for the strengthening of epicentres of mystical love (because it eases the growth of the consciousness of mystical love by eliminating the competition from externally derived epicentres). In John of the Cross' case, the development of this strategy has been aided considerably by the transmitted knowledge of his time that meditation is the way to initiate the process leading to mystical development. This kind of developmental change seems, in more general terms, to entail the application of knowledge of one thing to that of another thing.

The knowledge transferred from one thing to another springs from the fundamental ideas about the relation of the soul and God. The foundation of the mystical ideas of the soul's approach to God is that God and the soul are contraries and therefore cannot be united. To this is added the idea that love causes semblance of lover and beloved wherefore the love of God is the means of uniting with God. The point is, that the love of one thing subtracts in equal proportion from that of other things (this might, in fact, be based on the experience that one cannot simultaneously be conscious of God and some worldly thing combined with the experience that the more that one is conscious of something, the more this occupies one's mind). On the basis of this reasoning one gets the idea that a decrease in the love of the things of the world will allow an increase in the love of God which, in turn, will result in the desired union with God. Hence, the feat is to reduce and eventually eliminate the love of worldly things. This is where the accumulated spiritual knowledge of the 16th century really has been a great help. John of the Cross has known from his predecessors in spiritual life that certain kinds of behaviour combined with the reduction of sensory stimulation would help direct one's love and interests away from the things of the world. To put it differently, John of the Cross' mystical ideas (synthesized and elaborated on the basis of the general ideas of the Christian tradition and the more specifically mystical ideas developed by the Franciscans earlier in the century) have enabled the development of a strategy permitting the internalization of attention which, in turn, has enabled the realization of mystical states of consciousness.

The further enrichment of the ability in having mystical states and the development of mastery of emotions of mystical love is, on the other hand, presumably obtained through the combined processes of acquiring new knowledge (that is to say, more knowledge about the love between God and the soul) and possibly of redescribing this knowledge representationally. It is during the gradually growing and recurrent mystical consciousness of representations of conceptions and emotions of mystical love that new knowledge is acquired. At the neurological level it is due to the activities of the neurons involved in the generation of consciousness that the synaptic connections are strengthened with the storage of representations of the conceptions and emotions of mystical love as the result. Yet, it is supposedly during wakeful states of consciousness that the knowledge is redescribed representationally. More specifically, this probably involves expansion of both the net of intra- and intersystemic communication which, at the neurological level, can be explained with the generation of new synaptic connections.

With the theory of consciousness, the more specific, internal processes leading to the two kinds of behavioural mastery can further be explained as the gradual strengthening of specific groups of neurons at the expense of others. Initially, the intense conscious focus on various ideas related more or less directly to mystical love begin to build up epicentres of the various topics of mystical love. At this point, it seems that, on the one hand, the conceptions of mystical love are relatively varied and, on the other hand, only weak emotions are generated in response to the diverse conceptions. This further means that the synaptic connections modified may be relatively more dispersed than those modified in the later part of the developmental process.

A little further on in the developmental process (when the process classified by John of the Cross is entered) actual mystical states of consciousness begin to be realized at the same time, as consciousness is focused more specifically on the mystical love between God and one's own soul which means that more selected epicentres of mystical love are strengthened. Since consciousness is directed more specifically at the particular love between God and the soul, the responding emotions also begin to grow relatively stronger. This further means that the emotional representations begin to take up a greater part of the total synaptic strength of the groups of neurons forming the epicentres concerned.

The tendencies of the first stage are reinforced in the second stage which means that consciousness still is focused very specifically on the love between God and the soul. The responding emotional representations are therefore also amplified which means that the degree of consciousness of this aspect of mystical love is enhanced continuously. Inasmuch as the emotional represen- tations apparently have a stronger effect on neural structures than the con- ceptual aspect, the former begins to take up a gradually greater part of the total synaptic strength until at some point the two are more or less even. At that point (which probably is well into the second stage), the two kinds of representations of mystical love begin to compete for the dominance of consciousness. Occasionally, the emotional representations manage to overcome the more conceptual representations assigning these to the periphery of consciousness. The latter are still able to take over the dominance of con- sciousness, though, inasmuch as they still occupy a great deal of synaptic strength of the diverse epicentres of mystical love. It is therefore not surprising that the shift from one consciousness to another associated consciousness during a mystical state may involve a shift in the kind of representations dominating consciousness thereby alloting the emotional representations to the periphery.

In the third stage of the process, consciousness is focused exclusively on the emotional representations of mystical love whereby the more conceptual representations are relegated to the extreme periphery of consciousness. Appa- rently, the subject is no longer aware of the more conceptual representations, although they probably still have a certain degree of influence on the actual mystical states of consciousness.

On the basis of John of the Cross' writings, it should furthermore be pos- sible to distinguish some more general features that are characteristic of this kind of mystical experience in a little more detail. It is not possible to describe the very specific contents of each of a whole number of particular mystical states, though, because his works provide no evidence of this. Nor is it possible to detect *the* typical content of all mystical states, inasmuch as this changes in the course of development. That which *can* be distinguished are some few, general features that each are typical of the diverse points in the developmental process. Some of these features are characteristic of mystical states only, whereas others pertain more generally to a delimited part of the developmental process. Moreover, some of these aspects of mystical experience are either partial or ultimate goals of mystical development while others simply are side-effects of the developmental processes.

The cultivation and refinement of mystical states of consciousness are the general goals of the mystical process in this life. More specifically the aims change according to the developmental state of the person, though. Initially the purpose of development is the internalization of attention and the focus of it on various topics of mystical relevance insofar as this is the precondition for the cultivation of the conceptions of mystical love. Somewhat later on, the purpose of development is the facilitation of mystical consciousness of cognitive representations of conceptions of mystical love. This partial end has two advantages, namely that these representations replace other highly undesirable representations and that they in themselves are profitable insofar as they are the means of generating the desired responding emotions of mystical love. The final purpose of mystical development in this life is to permit the realization of mystical consciousness dominated by cognitive representations of emotions of mystical love (generated in response to conceptions of mystical love). The ultimate end of mystical development is not mystical, though, but post-mystical. It is the natural and eternal union of two divine natures (God and the divinized part of the soul).

Mystical development further has some more unintended side-effects of which various kinds of pain are the more significant. I will suggest that the diverse kinds of pain mentioned by John of the Cross can be divided into three kinds. First, there is a physical pain which is felt during the early mystical states of the first stage. I have suggested that this kind of pain is felt simply because consciousness in mystical states grows very deep. The point is that in early mystical states the mystical contents of consciousness are not yet all that powerful which means that an enhanced awareness of any existing pain (that has nothing whatever to do with the mystical state) is permitted. Later on, other contents of consciousness easily override this kind of pain. Second, there is a more psychological pain that derives from the recognizance of one's lowliness and God's remoteness. This kind of pain really seems to be very intense. It is presumably felt more generally throughout the major part of the first two stages in the actual process of mystical development, although probably not in the mystical states during which the distance between God and the soul is reduced. To be specific it actually seems that the two first stages of mystical development are best described as a gradually increasing depression that is temporarily relieved during the mystical states. Towards the end of the second stage this kind of pain reduces rapidly and nearly disappears in the third stage both because the subject at that point is so well developed mystically that he/she, in his/her own view, has acquired more valuable qualities and because God seems less remote as mystical states are more frequent and more enduring. Third, the remainders of the pain resulting from the distance between God and the soul lingers on in the third stage in the form of an intense longing for God and the eternal union, although this pain is similarly relieved during the very frequent mystical states.

In addition to the changing contents of consciousness, mystical development also produces a continuously increasing general estrangement and indifference to worldly matters. The persistent suppression of attention to things and people of the world and the equally persistent cultivation of attention to divine matters simply reduces the relevance and the cognitive value of the former while augmenting that of the latter. It is the gradual detachment from the external world that produces the alienation from it. This estrangement and indifference is thus at once a means and a by-product of mystical development.

I have suggested that John of the Cross' works not only reveal his mystical states and mystical development but additionally his changing conceptualization of these. In agreement with Karmiloff-Smith's theory, it is the repeated redescriptions of the accumulated representations of conceptions and emotions of mystical love that makes this knowledge continuously more and more explicit and accessible to conscious reconsideration. I have suggested that the processes of describing the mystical experience in written form and subsequently interpreting the written give a very strong impetus to the process of representational redescription. Accordingly, the joining of the processes of description and interpretation with that of representational redescription speeds up the general processes resulting in conceptual development significantly.

John of the Cross' *Spiritual Canticle* does, in particular, document his conceptual development because it reveals the products (in the form of conceptual changes) yielded by this aspect of the developmental process. The reason why this work displays the conceptual changes is that he has elaborated on it over a period of several years. Hence he has undertaken quite fundamental changes according to his changing conceptualizations of the content of the work at the various times of reinterpreting it.

I have not analyzed all of the minor changes of the *Canticle* that John of the Cross has carried out at various points in time, although they all give evidence of some degree of conceptual development. I have focused specifically on those changes that document *major* changes in his conceptualization of either his mystical states or, as is more often the case, of his mystical development as they are described by himself in the *Canticle*. In my view, the crucial changes in the *Canticle* can analytically be associated with specific periods during which his conceptual development has bounced forward thus resulting in some major conceptual changes. I have suggested that the evidence in the *Canticle*, documented through his changing interpretations of the work, of these more critical periods of conceptual development should be appointed layers of interpretation.

I have furthermore pointed out that the layers of interpretation tend to relate more or less directly to different levels of describing and conceptualizing the diverse aspects of mystical experience. Thus, it seems that John of the Cross has started out describing mystical states, presumably blending traits from a number of such states, that have been typical of the diverse points in the developmental process. Occasionally, he has shifted to the description of his mystical states in a more general perspective relating general changes in mystical states resulting from mystical development. At some point, he has begun to see his mystical development from a far more general perspective thus classifying the diverse stages of the process and identifying the points marking the shifts between the stages.

The earliest evidence of John of the Cross' conceptual development is his most primitive poetic *Canticle* (that is, the first 30/31 verses of the poem) which exclusively describes the progression of his mystical development at the level of the improvements and regressions from one mystical state to another. This is not yet an interpretational layer, though, as it is the result of representational redescription only. The first layer of interpretation is displayed coincidentally in the original poem and the concrete interpretations of the single verses and, like the earliest poem, documents the progression of mystical development at the level of mystical states, but with the addition of descriptions of more general changes in mystical states resulting from mystical development. The second layer of interpretation is revealed in the first general argument about the content in the poem and demonstrates how John of the Cross has begun to view the progression of mystical development at the far more general level of the stages of development. The third layer of interpretation is displayed in the revised *Canticle* as a whole and similarly describes his mystical development at the general level of the stages, but in a far more systematic and generalized form.

The theory of mystical experience that I have offered on the basis of my analysis of John of the Cross' works, suggests that mystical states and mystical development arise out of an unusual and extreme capitalization on general cognitive resources. The person striving to develop mystically cultivates some abilities excessively and suppresses others as far as possible. More specifically, it is the abilities to intensify the focus of attention and internalize it that are encouraged along with the inhibition of the natural tendency to attend to events and objects in the external environment. Along with the intensification and the nourishment of the attention to internal processes, the focus of attention is gradually directed towards certain ideas (that potentially will generate corresponding emotions) at the expense of others. In this way, the mystic at once attempts to expand focused consciousness and to control the content of it eventually giving rise to mystical states of consciousness. The recurrence of mystical states of consciousness will in itself further permit the expansion of all susbsequent consciousnesses of similar contents. On the basis of this, it is furthermore plain that the quality of mystical consciousness will vary in varying degrees from one culture to another and from one person to another.

However, since the person may need to acquire new knowledge in order to sustain a very deep consciousness of the desired content, then it further-more makes sense that mystical states will change in the course of mystical development. The point is that since it is the total knowledge reserve of something that sustains and constrains the consciousness of that something, then the gradual expansion of this knowledge reserve will inevitable lead to changes in the consciousness focused on that something. Finally, it should be pointed out that, if all mystical states occurring during a reasonably stable developmental period should be focused on exactly the same desirable content, then the knowledge reserve would need to be so limited that it only sustained very similar cognitive representations. Yet, at the same time, this would imply that it would be very hard to direct the focus of consciousness to that something and even more difficult to hold on to that focus. In general, this means that earlier mystical states will not all be dominated by equally desirable contents, while later mystical states will be dominated by a greater variety of desirable contents.

Turning more specifically to the mystical experience typical of the Christian religious tradition, it seems to emerge from the continual and intense focus on the conceptions and the responding emotions of the mystical love between God and the soul of a person. It furthermore seems to be typical of Christian mystical experience, in particular, that the more general experience (brought out during the wakeful states of consciousness) of a mystic during the early stages of mystical development involves considerable psychological pain and apparently has much in common with that of a depression. A fundamental difference is, of course, that the mystic regularly is relieved from the depressed (wakeful) states of consciousness during the mystical states of consciousness. Furthermore, the qualities of the two kinds of experience are only alike with respect to the negative value of the ideas sustaining them. Obviously, the more specific contents cannot, on the other hand, be expected to have anything in common.

Bibliography

A Benedictine of Stanbrook Abbey 1954. *Medieval Mystical Tradition and St. John of the Cross*. London: Burns and Oates.

Allard, T. et al., 1991. 'Reorganization of Somatosensory Area 3b Representations in Adult Owl Monkeys After Digital Syndactyly'. In *Journal of Neurophysiology*, vol. 66, no. 3, 1048-57.

Almond, P.C. 1982. *Mystical Experience and Religious Doctrine*. Berlin: Mouton Publishers.

Alonso, D. 1942. *La poesía de San Juan de la Cruz (desde esta ladera)*. Madrid: Editorial Aguilar.

Andrés, M. 1975. *Los recogidos, nueva visión de la mística española (1500-1700)*. Madrid: Ediciones Iundsción Universitaria Española.

Andrés, M. 1983. *Historia de la teología española I*. Madrid: Biblioteca de Autores Cristianos, 409-711.

Aquinas, St. Thomas 1975. *Summa Contra Gentiles* 1, 2 and 4. C.J. O'Neil, (trans.). Notre Dame: University of Notre Dame Press.

Aquinas, St. Thomas 1982. *Theological Texts and Philosophical Texts*. T. Gilby (ed. and trans.). Durham, N.C.: Labyrinth Press.

Armstrong, A.H. (ed.) 1970: *Cambridge History of Later Greek and Early Medieval Philosophy*. Cambridge: Cambridge University Press.

Augustine, St. 1948. 'Confessions, The Enchiridion, and On Grace and Free Will'. In W.J. Oates (ed.), *Basic writings of St. Augustine*. New York: Random House, 147-82, 658-731, and 733-74.

Barsalou, L.W. 1987. 'The Instability of Graded Structure'. In U. Neisser (ed.), *Concepts and Conceptual Development*. Cambridge: Cambridge University Press.

Barsalou, L.W. 1992. *Cognitive Psychology. An Overview for Cognitive Scientists*. Hillsdale, N.J.: Erlbaum.

Baruzi, J. 1931 (1924). *Jean de la Croix et la problème de l'experience mystique*. Paris: Felix Alcan.

Baruzi, J. 1942. 'Introducción al estudio del lenguaje místico'. In *Boletín de la Academía de Letras*. Buenos Aires, 7-30.

Bates, E.A. and J.L. Elman 1993. 'Connectionism and the Study of Change'. In M.H. Johnson (ed.), *Brain Development and Cognition. A Reader*. Cambridge, Mass.: Blackwell.

Bateson, G. 1958: 'Epilogue'. In *Naven: a Survey of the Problem Suggested by a Composite Picture of a New Guinea Tribe, Drawn from three Points of View*. Stanford: Stanford University Press.

Bateson, G. 1979: *Mind and Nature: a Necessary Unity*. London: Wildwood House.

Björkqvist, K. 1982. 'Ecstasy from a Physiological Point of View'. In N.G. Holm (ed.), *Religious Ecstasy*. Stockholm: Almquist and Wiksell International, 75-86.

Blanco, M.G. 1967. 'La lengua española en la época de Carlos V'. In *Boletín de Seminario de estudios y Literatura y Filología*, vol. II. Valladolid, 45-68.

Boyer, P. 1994. *The Naturalness of Religious Ideas: A Cognitive Theory of Religion*. Berkeley, Cal.: University of California Press.

Boyer, P. 1995. 'Religion and the Bounds of Sense. A Catalogue of the Supernatural'. Draft version.

Boyer, P. 1995. 'Remarks on Intuitive Ontology in Cognitive Development'. Paper presented at the 21st Annual Meeting of the Society for Philosophy and Psychology. Draft version.

Broch, H.B. 1985. 'Crazy Women are Performing in Sombali: A Possession-Trance Ritual on Bonerate'. Indonesia. In *Ethos* 13, 3, 262-82.

Canticum Canticorum 1986. In *Nova Vulgata Bibliorum Sacrorum*. Rome: Libreria Editrice Vaticana, 1109-1122.

Carey, S. and E. Spelke 1994.'Domain-specific Knowledge and Conceptual Change'. In L.A. Hirschfeld and S.A. Gelman (ed.), *Mapping the Mind*. Cambridge: Cambridge University Press.

Changeux, J-P. 1985. *Neuronal Man: The Biology of Mind*. Oxford: Oxford University Press.

Changeux, J-P. and S. Dehaene 1993. 'Neuronal Models of Cognitive Function'. In M.H. Johnson (ed.), *Brain Development and Cognition: A Reader*. Cambridge, Mass.: Blackwell.

Churchland, P. 1988. 'Reductionism, Connectionism and the Plasticity of Human Consciousness'. In *Cultural Dynamics*, vol. 1, 1.

Churchland, P. 1993. 'On the Nature of Theories: A Neurocomputational Perspective'. In R.G. Burton (ed.), *Artificial and Natural Minds*. New York: State University of New York Press.

Clark, A. 1991. *Microcognition: Philosophy, Cognitive Science, and Parallel Distributed Processing*. Cambridge, Mass.: The MIT Press.

Colledge, E. 1984. 'Historical Data'. In Meister Eckehart I, *Classics of Western Spirituality*. London: SPCK, 5-23.

Collins, J.E. 1991. *Mysticism and New Paradigm Psychology*. Savage, MD.: Rowman and Littlefield Publishers.

Covarrubias, Sebastián de 1943 (1611). *Tesoro de la Lengua Castellana o Española*. Martín de Riquer (ed.). Barcelona: S.A. Horta.

Crisógono de Jesús 1929. *San Juan de la Cruz, su obra científica y su obra literaria II*. Madrid: Editorial Mensajero Santa Teresa, 17-34 and 243-310.

Crisógono de Jesús 1975. *Vida y Obra de San Juan de la Cruz*. Madrid: Editorial Mensajero Santa Teresa, 20-355.

Damasio, A.R. 1994. *Descartes' Error: Emotion, Reason and the Human Brain*. New York: G.P. Putnam.

d'Aquili, E.G. and C.D. Laughlin, Jr. 1979. 'The Neurobiology of Myth and Ritual'. In E.G. d'Aquili et al. (eds.), *The Spectrum of Ritual*. New York: Colombia University Press.

Deikman, A.J. 1969. 'Deautomatization of Mystical Experience'. In C.T. Tart (ed.), *Altered States of Consciousness: A Book of Readings*. New York: John Wiley, 23-43.

Det Ny Testamente 1992. In: *Bibelen, Den Hellige Skrifts Kanoniske Bøger*, København.

Dionysius Areopagita 1979. *The Divine Names and The Mystical Theology*, (trans. by C.E. Rolt). London: SPCE.

Eco, U. 1984. *The Role of the Reader*. Bloomington: Indiana University Press.

Edelman, G. 1994. 'The Evolution of Somatic Selection: The Antibody Tale'. In *Genetics*, The Genetics Society of America, 138, 973-81.

Elliott, J.H. 1963. *Imperial Spain*. London: Edward Arnold, 1469-1716.

Ellwood, R.S, Jr. 1980. *Mysticism and religion*. Englewood Cliffs, N.J.: Prentice Hall.

Eulogio de la Virgen Carmen (Pacho) 1968. 'San Juan de la Cruz: Vida y escritos'. In: *Ephemerides Carmeliticae*, 29, 71-87.

Ferguson, M. 1978. 'Karl Pribram's Changing Reality'. In *Human Behaviour*, 7(5), 28-33.

Fernández Leborans, M.J. 1978. *Luz y oscuridad en la mística española*. Madrid: Cupsa Editorial.

Fischer, R. 1978. In A.A. Sugerman et al., (eds.), *Expanding Dimensions of Consciousness*. New York: Springer Publishers.

Fischer, R. 1986. 'Toward a Neuroscience of Self-Experience and States of Self-Awareness and Interpreting Interpretations'. In B.B. Wolman and M. Ullman (eds.), *Handbook of States of Consciousness*, 3-30. New York: Van Nostrand Reinhold.

Foulkes, D. 1985. *Dreaming: A Cognitive-Psychological Analysis*. Hillsdale, New Jersey, Erlbaum.

Foulks, E.F. and F. Schwartz 1982. 'Self and Object: Psychoanalytical Perspectives in Cross-Cultural Fieldwork and Interpretation, A Review Essay'. In *Ethos* 10(3), 254-78.

Galin, D. 1979. 'The Two Modes of Consciousness and the Two Halves of the Brain'. In D. Goleman and R.J. Davidson: *Consciousness: Brain, States of Awareness, and Mysticism*. New York: Harper and Row, 19-23.

Garside, B. 1972. 'Language and the Interpretation of Mystical Experience'. In: *International Journal for Philosophy of Religion* 3, 93-102.

Gaudreau, M.M. 1976. *Mysticism and Image in John of the Cross*. Frankfurt: Peter Lang.

Geels, A. 1982. 'Mystical Experience and the Emergence of Creativity'. In: N.G. Holm (ed.), *Religious Ecstasy*. Stockholm: Almquist and Wiksell International, 27-62.

Geertz, A.W. 1990: 'Mystik, visioner, ekstase, besættelse: En direkte linie?' In: P. Bilde and A.W. Geertz (eds.), *Mystik — den indre vej?* Aarhus: Aarhus University Press, 107-38.

Gellhorn, E. and W.F. Kiely 1972. 'Mystical States of Consciousness: Neurophysiological and Clinical Aspects'. In: *The Journal of Nervous and Mental Disease*, 154, 399-405.

Gelman, S.A., J.D. Coley and G.M. Gottfried 1994: 'Essentialist Beliefs in Children: The Acquisition of Concepts and Theories'. In: L.A. Hirschfeld and S.A. Gelman (ed.), *Mapping the Mind*. Cambridge: Cambridge University Press.

Gilson, E. 1985. *History of Christian Philosophy in the Middle Ages*. London: Shield and Ward.

Gopnik, A. and H.M. Wellman 1994. 'The Theory Theory'. In L.A. Hirschfeld and S.A. Gelman (ed.), *Mapping the Mind*. Cambridge: Cambridge University Press.

Greenfield, S.A. 1995. *Journey to the Centers of the Mind: Toward a Science of Consciousness*. New York: W.H. Freeman.

Greenough, W.T., J.E. Black and C.S. Wallace 1993. 'Experience and Brain Development'. In M.H. Johnson (ed.), *Brain Development and Cognition: A Reader*. Cambridge, Mass. Blackwell.

Guillén, J. 1962. Lenguaje y poesía: Algurios casos españoles. Madrid: Revista de Occidente.

Hardy, A. 1979. *The Spiritual nature of man: A Study of Contemporary Religious Experience.* Oxford: Clarendon Press.

Hardy, R.P. 1976. 'The Hidden God and Juan de la Cruz'. In: *Ephemerides Carmeliticae* 27, 241-62.

Haren, M. 1985. *Medieval Thought: The Western Intellectual Tradition from Antiquity to the 13th Century.* London: Macmillan.

Henry, J.L. 1982. 'Possible Involvement of the Endorphins in Altered States of Consciousness'. In *Ethos* 10(4), 386-94.

Herrera R.A. 1966. 'Conocimiento y metáfora en San Juan de la Cruz'. In: *Revista de espiritualidad*, vol. 25, 587-98.

Highfield, R. 1972. *Spain in the 15th Century.* Essays and extracts by historians of Spain. London: Macmillan.

Hirschfeld, L.A. 1994. 'Is the Acquisition of Social Categories based on Domain-Specific competence or on Knowledge Transfer?' In: L.A. Hirschfeld and S.A. Gelman (ed.), *Mapping the Mind.* Cambridge: Cambridge University Press.

Horn, G. 1993. 'Brain Mechanisms of Memory and Predispositions: Interactive Studies of Cerebral Function and Behaviour'. In: M.H. Johnson (ed.), *Brain Development and Cognition: A Reader.* Cambridge, Mass.: Blackwell.

Hornsby, J. 1986. 'Physicalist Thinking and Conceptions of Behaviour'. In: P. Pettit and M. McDowell (eds.), *Subject, Thought, and Context.* Oxford: Clarendon Press.

Huttenlocher, P.R. 1993. 'Morphometric Study of Human Cerebral Cortex Development'. In M.H. Johnson, (ed.), *Brain Development and Cognition: A Reader.* Cambridge, Mass.: Blackwell.

Icaza, R.M. 1957. *The Stylistic Relationship of Poetry and Prose in the Cántico Espiritual of San Juan de la Cruz.* Washington, D.C.: The Catholic University of America Press.

James, W. 1902. *The Varieties of Religious Experience: A Study in Human Nature.* London: Longmans, Green & Co.

Janowsky, J.S. 1993. 'The Development and Neural Basis of Memory Systems'. In: M.H. Johnson (ed.), *Brain Development and Cognition: A Reader.* Cambridge, Mass.: Blackwell.

Jantzen, G.M. 1989. 'Mysticism and Experience'. In: *Religious Studies.* Cambridge, vol. 25, 3, 295-315.

Jenkins, W.M. et al., 1990 (a): 'Neocortical Representational Dynamics in Adult primates: Implications for Neuropsychology'. In: *Neuropsychologia*, vol. 28, no. 6, 573-84.

Jenkins, W.M. et al., 1990 (b): 'Functional reorganization of Primary Somatosensory Cortex in Adult Owl Monkeys After Behaviourally Controlled Tactile Stimulation'. In: *Journal of Neurophysiology*, vol. 63, 1, 82-103.

Jilek, W.G. 1982. 'Altered States of Consciousness in North American Ceremonials'. In: *Ethos* 10(4), 218-326.

John, E.R. 1979. 'How the Brain Works. A New Theory'. In: D. Goleman and R.J. Davidson (eds.), *Consciousness: Brain, States of Awareness, and Mysticism*. New York: Harper and Row, 14-16.

Johnson, M. 1987. *The Body in the Mind: The Bodily Basis of Meaning, Imagination and Reason*. Chicago: University of Chicago Press.

Johnson, M.H. 1993. 'Constraints on Cortical Plasticity'. In: M.H. Johnson (ed.), *Development and Cognition: A Reader*. Cambridge, Mass.: Blackwell.

Juan de la Cruz, San 1988. *Obras Completas*, Madrid: Editorial de espiritualidad.

Kamiya, J. 1969. 'Operant Control of the EEG Alpha Rythm and Some of Its Reported Effects on Consciousness'. In C.T. Tart (ed.), *Altered States of Consciousness: A Book of Readings*. New York: John Wiley, 507-17.

Karmiloff-Smith, A. 1992. *Beyond Modularity: A Developmental Perspective on Cognitive Science*. Cambridge, Mass.: The MIT Press.

Karmiloff-Smith, A. 1993. 'Self-organization and Cognitive Change'. In: M.H. Johnson (ed.), *Brain Development and Cognition: A Reader*. Cambridge, Mass.: Blackwell.

Karmiloff-Smith, A. and M.H. Johnson 1994. 'A Dynamic Systems Approach to the Development of Cognition and Action by E. Thelen and L.B. Smith'. Review in *Nature*, vol. 372, no. 6501, 53-54.

Katz, S.T. 1978: 'Language, Epistemology, and Mysticism'. In: S.T. Katz (ed.), *Mysticism and Philosophical Analysis*. London: Sheldon Press.

Katz, S.T. 1982. *Models, Modeling and Mystical Training*. In: *Religion* 12. London: Academic Press, 247-75.

Katz, S.T. 1983: 'The Conservative Character of Mystical Experience'. In: S.T. Katz (ed.), *Mysticism and Religious Traditions*. Oxford: Oxford University Press, 3-60.

Keller, C.A. 1978: 'Mystical Literature'. In: S.T. Katz (ed.), *Mysticism and Philosophical Analysis*. London: Sheldon Press.

Knox, S.S. 1981. *Biofeedback of EEG Alpha: Methodological Aspects and Theoretical Considerations*. Reports from the Dept. of Psychology, University of Stockholm, Stockholm.

Kristo, J. 1982. 'The Interpretation of Religious Experience: What do Mystics Intend When They Talk about Their Experiences?' In: *The Journal of Religion* 62, 21-38.

Lakoff, G. 1987. *Women, Fire and Dangerous Things: What Categories Reveal about the Mind*. Chicago: University of Chicago Press.

Lakoff, G. and M. Turner 1989. *More than Cool Reason: A Field Guide to Poetic Metaphor*. Chicago: University of Chicago Press.

Lakoff, G. 1990. 'The Invariance Hypothesis: Is Abstract Reason based on Image-Schemas?' In: *Cognitive Linguistics*, vol. 1, 1. New York: Mouton de Gruyter.

Laughlin, C.D. Jr., John McManus, and E.G. d'Aquili 1979. 'Introduction'. In: E.G. d'Aquili et al. (eds.), *The Spectrum of Ritual*. New York: Colombia University Press.

Lawson, T.E. and R.N. McCauley 1990. *Rethinking Religion: Connecting Cognition and Culture*. Cambridge: Cambridge University Press.

Lawson, E.T. and R.N. McCauley 1993. 'Connecting the Cognitive and the Cultural: Artificial Minds as Methodological Devices in the Study of the Sociocultural'. In:

R.G. Burton (ed.), *Artificial and Natural Minds*. New York: State University of New York Press.

Lawson, E.T. and R.N. McCauley 1993. 'Crisis of Conscience, Riddle of Identity. Making Space for a Cognitive Approach to Religious Phenomena'. In *Journal of the American Academy of Religion*, LXI, 2.

Lévi-Strauss, C. 1950. 'Introduction a l'Oeuvre de Marcel Mauss'. In: *M. Mauss: Antropologie et Sociologie* (I-LII). Paris: Presses Universitaires de France.

Lex, B. 1979. 'The Neurobiology of Ritual Trance'. In: E.G. d'Aquili et al., (eds.), *The Spectrum of Ritual*. New York: Colombia University Press.

Lewis, I.M. 1986. *Religion in Context: Cults and Charisma*. Cambridge: Cambridge University Press.

Lindhardtsen, S. 1977. 'Den mystiske seksualitet: en analyse af "Cántico espiritual" af San Juan de la Cruz (1542-1591)'. *Semiotica*, 22-38.

Llinás, R. and U. Ribary 1992. 'Coherent 40-Hz oscillation characterizes dream state in humans'. In: *Neurobiology*, vol. 90, 2078-2081, March 1993.

Locke, R.G. and E.F. Kelly 1985. 'A Preliminary Model for the Cross-Cultural Analysis of Altered States of Consciousness'. In *Ethos* 13(1).

López-Baralt, Luce 1978. 'San Juan de la Cruz: una nueva concepción del lenguaje poético'. In: *Bulletin of Hispanic studies*, 55, 19-32.

Louth, A. 1981. *The Origins of the Christian Mystical Tradition. From Plato to Denys*. Oxford: Clarendon Press.

Lovett, A.W. 1986. *Early Habsburg Spain 1517-1598*. Oxford: Oxford University Press.

Ludwig, A.M. 1969: 'Altered States of Consciousness'. In C.T. Tart (ed.), *Altered States of Consciousness: A Book of Readings*. New York: John Wiley, 9-22.

Luria, A.R. 1979: 'The Brain's Three Principal Functional Units'. In: D. Goleman and R.J. Davidson, *Consciousness: Brain, States of Awareness, and Mysticism*. New York: Harper and Row, 10-13.

Luther, M. 1983. 'Om den trælbundne vilje'. In: *Luthers skrifter i udvalg*, vol. 5. Aarhus: Aros.

MacKay, A. 1977. *Spain in the Middle Ages, From Frontier to Empire. 1000-1500*. Oxford: Clarendon Press.

Maio, E.A. 1973. *St. John of the Cross: The Imagery of Eros*. Madrid: Editoria Playor S.A..

Mancho Duque, M.J. 1982. *El simbolo de la noche oscura de San Juan de la Cruz, estudio léxico-semantico*. Salamanca: Ediciones Universidad de Salamanca.

Mandler, J. 1992. 'How to Build a Baby II. Conceptual Primitives'. In: *Psychological Review*, vol. 99, no. 4, 587-604.

Marler, P. 1993. 'The Instinct to Learn'. In: M.H. Johnson (ed.), *Brain Development and Cognition: A Reader*. Cambridge, Mass.: Blackwell.

McCauley, R.N. 1987. 'The Role of Theories in a Theory of Concepts'. In: *Concepts and Conceptual Development*, U. Neisser (ed.), Cambridge: Cambridge University Press.

McCauley, R.N. 1995. 'Religious Ritual and Memory Dynamics'. Presentation at the IAHR conference in Mexico.

McGuinn, B. (trans.) 1984 and 1986. Meister Eckehart: 'The Essential Sermons, Commentaries, Treaties and Defense', vol. I and II. In *Classics of Western Spirituality*. London: SPCK.

Meier, E. 1982. *Struktur und Wesen der Negation in den Mystischen Schriften des Johannes vom Kreuz*. Altenberge: Verlag für Christlich-Islamischen Schriften.

Merzenich, M.M. 1990. 'Adaptive Mechanisms in Cortical Networks Underlying Cortical Contributions to Learning and Nondeclarative Memory'. In: *Cold Spring Harbor Symposia on Quantitative Biology*, vol. 4, 873-83.

Monod, J. 1972. *Chance and Necessity: an Essay on the Natural Philosophy of Modern Biology*. New York: Vintage Books.

Moore, P.G. 1973. 'Recent Studies of Mysticism: A Critical Survey'. In: *Religion* 3, 146-56.

Moore, P.G. 1978: 'Mystical Experience, Mystical Doctrine, and Mystical Technique'. In: S.T. Katz (ed.), *Mysticism and Philosophical Analysis*. London: Sheldon Press.

Morin, E. 1974. *Det glemte mønster. Den menneskelige natur*. Viborg: Gyldendal.

Neher, A. 1962. 'A Physiological Explanation of Unusual Behavior in Ceremonies Involving Drums' (151-160). In: *Human Biology*, 34.

Neisser, U. 1987. 'From Direct Perception to Conceptual Structure'. In: U. Neisser (ed.), *Concepts and Conceptual Development*. Cambridge University Press.

Neisser, U. 1993. 'Without Perception, There Is No Knowledge: Implications for Artificial Intelligence'. In: R.G. Burton (ed.), *Artificial and Natural Minds*. State University of New York Press.

Nieto, J.C. 1982. *Místico, poeta, rebelde, santo: En torno a San Juan de la Cruz*. Madrid: Editorial Swan.

Nieto, J.C. 1988. *San Juan de la Cruz, el poeta del amor profano*. Madrid: Editorial Swan.

Orozco, E. 1959. *Poesía y Mística, introducción a la lírica de San Juan de la Cruz*, (159-228). Madrid: Ediciones Guadarama.

Peers, E.A. 1954. *Handbook to the Life and Times of St. Teresa and St. John of the Cross*. Westminster, MD.: Newman.

Penner, H.H. 1983. 'The Mystical Illusion'. In: S.T. Katz (ed.), *Mysticism and Religious Traditions*. Oxford: Oxford University Press, 89-116.

Plotkin, H.C. 1991. 'The Testing of evolutionary Epistemology'. In: *Biology and Philosophy* 6. Kluwer Academic Publishers, 481-97.

Pribram, K.H. 1971. *Languages of the Brain*. Englewood Cliffs, N.J.: Prentice Hall.

Pribram, K.H. and M.M. Gill 1976. *Freud's "Project" Reassessed*.

Pribram, K.H. 1981. *Psychoanalysis and the Natural Sciences: The Brain-Behaviour Connection from Freud to the Present*. Freud Memorial Inaugural Lectures. London: University College London.

Pribram, K.H. 1982. 'Localization and Distribution of Function in the Brain'. In: J. Orbach (ed.), *Neuropsychology after Lashley*. Hillsdale, N.J.: Lawrence Erlbaum Associates, 273-96.

Price, B.B. 1992. *Medieval Thought, An Introduction*. Cambridge, Mass.: Blackwell.

Prince, R. 1968. 'Can the EEG be Used in the Study of Possession States?'. In: R. Prince (ed.), *Trance and Possession States*. Montreal, 121-37.

Prince, R. 1982. 'The Endorphins: A Review for Psychological Anthropologists'. In: *Ethos* 10(4), 300-303.

Prince, R. 1982. 'Shamans and Endorphins: Hypothesis for a Synthesis'. In: *Ethos* 10(4), 395-409.

Rakic, P. 1993. 'Intrinsic and Extrinsic Determinants of Neocortical Parcellation: A Radial Unit Model'. In: Johnson, M.H. (ed.), *Brain Development and Cognition: A Reader*. Cambridge, Mass.: Blackwell.

Rappaport, R.A. 1979. *Ecology, Meaning and Religion*. Richmond, Cal.: North Atlantic Books.

Recanzone, G.R. et al., 1992 (a). 'Progressive Improvement in Discriminative Abilities in adult Owl Monkeys performing a Tactile Frequency Discrimination Task'. In: *Journal of Neurophilosophy*, vol. 67, no. 5, 1015-1028.

Recanzone, G.R. et al., 1992 (b). 'Topographic Reorganization of the Hand Representation in Cortical Area 3b of Owl Monkeys Trained in a Frequency-Discrimination Task'. In: *Journal of Neurophilosophy*, vol. 67, no. 5, 1031-1054.

Reeke, G.N. Jr., et al., 1990. 'Synthetic Neural Modeling of the "Darwin" Series of Recognition Automata'. In: *Proceeding of the IEEE*, vol. 78, no. 9, 1498-1528.

Rose, S. 1979. 'The Human Brain'. In: D. Goleman and R.J. Davidson (eds.), *Consciousness: Brain, States of Awareness, and Mysticism*. New York: Harper and Row, 3-9.

Rossi, I. 1974: 'Theoretical Assumptions and Their Historical Antecedents'. In: I. Rossi (ed.), 'The Unconscious in Culture: the Structuralism of Claude Lévis-Strauss in Perspective'. New York: Dutton.

Rumelhart, D.E. and J.L. McClelland, 1987. 'A Distributed Model of Human Learning and Memory'. In: Rumelhart, McClelland, and the PDP Research Group, Parallel Distributed Processing, *Explorations in the Microstructure of Cognition*, vol. 2, 170-215. Cambridge: MIT Press.

Schipperges, H. 1978. *Hildegard von Bingen*. Otten: Walter-Verlag A.G.

Shannon, C.E. and W. Weaver 1963. *The Mathematical Theory of Communication*. University of Illinois Press.

Smart, N. 1978. 'Understanding Religious Experience'. In: S.T. Katz (ed.), *Mysticism and Philosophical Analysis*. London: Sheldon Press.

Smart, N. 1983. 'The Purification of Consciousness and the Negative Path'. In: S.T. Katz (ed.), *Mysticism and Religious Traditions*. Oxford: Oxford University Press, 117-29.

Smart, N. 1986. 'Interpretation and Mystical Experience'. In: *Concept and Empathy*. Houndmills: Macmillan.

Sperber, D. 1985. 'Anthropology and Psychology: Towards an Epidemiology of Representations'. In: *Man* (N.S.) 20, 273-89.

Sperber, D. and D. Wilson 1988. *Relevance, Communication and Cognition*. Cambridge, Mass.: Harvard University Press.

Sperber, D. 1991. 'The Epidemiology of Beliefs'. In: C. Fraser and G. Ceskell (eds.), *Psychological Studies of Widespread Beliefs*. Oxford: Oxford University Press.

Sperry, R.W. 1982. 'Forebrain Commissurotomy and Conscious Awareness'. In: J. Orbach (ed.), *Neuropsychology after Lashley*. Hillsdale, N.J.: Lawrence Erlbaum Associates, 497-522.

Sullivan, L. 1977. 'Saint Gregory's "Moralia" and Saint John of the Cross'. In: *Ephemerides Carmeliticae* 28, 59-103.

Tart, C.T. 1975. *States of Consciousness*. New York: E.P. Dutton & Co. Inc.

Tart, C.T. 1979. 'The Systems Approach to States of Consciousness'. In: D. Goleman and R.J. Davidson (eds.), *Consciousness: Brain, States of Awareness, and Mysticism*. New York: Harper and Row, 87-88.

Teresa de Jesús, Santa 1988. *Obras Completas*. Madrid: Aguilar.

Thelen, E. and L.B. Smith 1994. *A Dynamic Systems Approach to the Development of Cognition and Action*. Cambridge, Mass.: The MIT Press.

Thelen, E. 1993. 'Self-organization in Developmental Process: Can Systems Approaches Work?' In: M.H. Johnson (ed.): *Brain Development and Cognition: A Reader*. Cambridge, Mass.: Blackwell.

Thompson, C.P. 1985. *El poeta y el místico; un estudio sobre "El Cántico Espiritual" de San Juan de la Cruz*. Madrid: El escorial.

Thomsen, S.U. 1994. In: *Kritik. Tidsskrift for litteratur, forskning, undervisning*, no. 110, København.

Trinkaus, C. 1970. *In Our Image and Likeness*. London: Constable, 3-28.

Trinkaus, C. and H.O. Oberman 1974. *The Pursuit of Holiness in Late Medieval and Rennaissance Religion*. Leiden: E.J. Brill, 93-103 and 367-70.

Turkewitz, G. and P.A. Kenny 1993. 'Limitations on Input as a Basis for Neural Organization and Perceptual Development: a Preliminary Theoretical Statement'. In: M.H. Johnson (ed.), *Brain Development and Cognition: A Reader*, Cambridge, Mass.: Blackwell.

Turner, M. 1987. *Death is the Mother of Beauty*. Chicago: University of Chicago Press.

Turner, V.W. 1985. *On the Edge of the Bush*. Tucson, Az.: The University of Arizona Press.

Underhill, E. 1923. 'A Historical Sketch of European Mysticism From the Beginning of the Christian Era to the Death of Blake'. In: E. Underhill, *Mysticism. A Study in the Nature and Development of Man's Spiritual Consciousness*. London: Methuen, 541-62.

Vandenbroucke, D.F. 1968. 'New Milieu, New Problems'. In: L. Bouyer et al., *A History of Christian Spirituality II, the Spirituality of the Middle Ages*. New York: The Seabury Press, 223-543.

Vilnet, J. 1949. *Bible et mystique chez Saint Jean de la Croix*. Paris: Desclée de Brouwer.

Walker, S.S. 1972. *Ceremonial Spirit Possession in Africa and Afro-America*. Leiden: E.J. Brill.

Wainwright, W.J. 1981. *Mysticism: A Study of Its Nature, Cognitive Value, and Moral Implications*. Madison: University of Wisconsin Press.

Wilhelmsen, E.C. 1980. *Process of Knowledge and Process of Communication*. Ann Arbor, Mich.: University Microfilms International.

Wulff, D.M. 1991. *Psychology of Religion*. New York: John Wiley.

Index